KARAHAN TEPE

"Andrew Collins's new book is a riveting, page-turning account of the incredible discoveries being made right now at Karahan Tepe and their implications for the profound cosmological understanding possessed by its forgotten civilization. It is an extremely valuable addition to the forbidden archaeology bookshelf."

GRAHAM PHILIPS, AUTHOR OF *THE MYSTERY OF DOGGERLAND*

"This book represents the triumphant climax of Andrew Collins's own journey and that of his books. With his usual infectious enthusiasm and sense of wonder, but also incisive argument and research, he traces the great cosmic shamanic purpose and connections between cosmological secrets and an ancient culture that flourished in what is today's Turkey. His findings are truly momentous and incredibly wide-ranging, radically shaking up our understanding of early human civilization. And surely the best part is that archaeologists are effectively playing catch-up with him."

LYNN PICKNETT AND CLIVE PRINCE,
AUTHORS OF *WHEN GOD HAD A WIFE*

"Andrew Collins's *Karahan Tepe* gifts us with a comprehensive introduction to and overview of a truly significant ancient archaeological site dating from the same approximate era and tradition as the renowned Göbekli Tepe sanctuary. These are enhanced for us by a wealth of professional photographic images, careful pursuit of the site's archaic history, informed impressions of the site's possible ancient uses, and the likely symbolism of its enigmatic features and alignments."

LAIRD SCRANTON, AUTHOR OF *CHINA'S COSMOLOGICAL PREHISTORY*,
POINT OF ORIGIN, AND *SACRED SYMBOLS OF THE DOGON*

"*Karahan Tepe* is an awesome journey in understanding the meaning of the features, including the carved art, of this 11,000-year-old temple in southeastern Anatolia, Turkey—the Garden of Eden. Collins's deep exploration of this temple, examining it from every angle, offers repeated verifications and meanings of its features. Central to these features is the creative force of the snake and the psychopomp figure of the vulture on the Milky Way path of the dead to the world of the spirits. Alignment of the sunrise at the winter solstice calls upon it to provide direction to this journey, a feature also found at Göbekli Tepe. The structure and the carved images create a synchronized reflection of the night sky and its asterisms along the Milky Way. Biblical scholars have estimated that the creation of the first man, Adam, and the story of Eve and the Serpent, occurred 6,000 years ago, more recently than Karahan Tepe. I find Collins's journey truly amazing and inspiring.

NICHOLAS E. BRINK, PH.D., AUTHOR OF
THE POWER OF ECSTATIC TRANCE, BALDER'S MAGIC, AND
BEOWULF'S ECSTATIC TRANCE MAGIC

KARAHAN TEPE

CIVILIZATION OF THE ANUNNAKI AND THE COSMIC ORIGINS OF THE SERPENT OF EDEN

ANDREW COLLINS

Bear & Company
Rochester, Vermont

Bear & Company
One Park Street
Rochester, Vermont 05767
www.BearandCompanyBooks.com

Bear & Company is a division of Inner Traditions International

Cataloging-in-Publication Data for this title is available from the Library of Congress

ISBN 978-1-59143-478-8 (print)
ISBN 978-1-59143-479-5 (ebook)

Printed and bound in China by Reliance Printing Co., Ltd.

10 9 8 7 6 5 4 3 2 1

Text design by Priscilla Harris Baker and layout by Debbie Glogover
This book was typeset in Garamond Premier Pro with Gill Sans MT Pro, Futura Std, and
Orpheus used as display typefaces

Image Credits: Nick Burton, figs. 9.4, 16.3, 33.1, 33.2, 34.1; Andrew Collins, figs. 1.1,
1.2, 1.3, 2.1, 2.2, 2.3, 3.1, 3.2, 3.3, 3.4, 3.5, 3.6, 4.1, 4.2, 4.3, 5.1, 5.2, 5.3, 5.4, 6.1, 7.2,
7.3, 8.1, 8.2, 8.3, 8.4, 9.3, 10.1, 11.1, 12.1, 12.3, 13.1, 13.3, 14.1, 14.2, 17.2, 17.3, 21.1,
21.2, 22.1, 26.1, 30.2b, 30.3, 33.5, 33.6, 35.3, 37.1, 37.2, 37.4a and 37.4b, and plates 1–40;
Creative Commons Agreement, fig. 32.1 (CC BY 4.0 by ESO/NASA/JPL-Caltech/M.
Kornmesser/R. Hurt), fig. 23.2 (by Jastrow), fig. 24.4 (by Katolophyromai), fig. 13.2 (CC
BY-SA 3.0 by Klaus-Peter Simon), fig. 32.2 (by NASA, ESA, and the Hubble Heritage Team
(STScI/AURA)), fig. 9.2 (CC BY-SA 3.0 by Wvbailey), fig. 13.4 (CC BY-SA 3.0 by yuber);
Google Earth, figs. 8.5, 13.3, 22.1, 26.1, and 37.2; MLL, fig. 30.2a; Rodney Hale, figs. 2.1,
4.4, 7.1, 7.2, 14.2, 17.1, 18.1, 18.2, 19.1; Russell M. Hossain, figs. 24.2, 30.1; Hugh Newman,
fig. A.1; Stellarium, figs. 8.6, 12.2, 14.3, 15.1, 23.3, and 37.3. All other images are in the
public domain. Original sources of noncopyright images are indicated in the caption. Every
attempt has been made by the author to clarify the ownership of illustrations used in this
book. Any oversights or omissions will be corrected in future editions.

To send correspondence to the author of this book, mail a first-class letter to the author c/o
Inner Traditions • Bear & Company, One Park Street, Rochester, VT 05767, and we will
forward the communication, or contact the author directly at **andrewcollins.com**.

To the memory of John Major Jenkins (1964–2017),

a man ahead of his time

Contents

＊

Part 7
GNOSIS

＊

Part 8
THE ETERNAL RETURN

＊

In Quest of a Supercivilization

HUGH NEWMAN

September 2014. Dust from the dirt track was blasting into the sky behind the vehicle as we feverishly looked over the old map, attempting to locate a site Andrew Collins had first visited 10 years beforehand. We had been on the road for an hour, having earlier visited the 11,600-year-old Pre-Pottery Neolithic site of Göbekli Tepe. However, another site was on our radar, and Andrew had remembered that a standing stone on the side of the road marked the track to the farm where it was located. We took numerous wrong turns and were on the verge of giving up when suddenly we saw the solitary monolith casting a shadow in the distance. We cheered in unison and turned right, continuing through the arid Tektek Mountains with the realization that we were now close to our destination.

We approached a farm, and a sign displayed its name, Keçili. Andrew and I, along with our local guide, exited the vehicle and strolled over to the farmhouse, where the owners greeted us. The members of the family welcomed us in for tea, and very quickly they recognized Andrew from his earlier investigation of the site. We respectfully accepted the invitation, anticipating the upcoming main event we were here to see. Knowing that excavations had not yet taken place, and being on private land, we dutifully asked permission to explore. This chance to visit a megalithic complex that was still mostly buried atop the nearby limestone hill was foremost in our minds. We had found what we were looking for—the site of Karahan Tepe.

As we walked up the hill we could see nothing except stone cairns at its peak, yet, before long, what appeared to be slabs of stone a few feet long were visible, placed in pairs in front of us. These were not simply stones lying on the surface, but rather the tops of unexcavated T-shaped pillars still buried deep in the ground. They were everywhere, and they resembled those present at Göbekli Tepe. We also noticed cup marks carved out of the bedrock, strange etchings, parts of porthole stones, and a remarkable unfinished pillar on the hill's western flank. We were certainly in awe of the possibilities lying before us, even though at the time we had no conscious inkling of what astonishing treasures awaited discovery directly beneath our feet.

The western slope's unfinished T-pillar fascinated me, as a similar "unfinished" monolith is also still in the quarry area of Göbekli Tepe. It was as if these stones were left in place to mark the birthplace of the temple complex. Other important megalithic sites such as Stonehenge, Easter Island, and Aswan in Egypt also still have large unfinished stones left at quarry sites. The example at Karahan Tepe was 18 feet (5.5 meters) in length and displayed toolmarks and cupules, and although this was the most prominent part of the site when we visited there in 2014, within a few years this impression would change dramatically.

I thank Andrew for my initial introduction to Karahan Tepe, and since then we have visited the location on various occasions. We have also become friends with the family, who are today actively involved in maintaining and protecting the site. What I realized pretty quickly is that we were standing on something that might be as important as Göbekli Tepe, yet we had no proof as we could not get our trowels out and start excavating. Andrew pointed out a spot on the northern knoll of the mound, which he felt sure was directed toward another hill to the north, known today as Keçili Tepe. In his opinion it marked the setting of the bright star Deneb in the constellation of Cygnus as viewed from Karahan Tepe.

Andrew's foresight became a reality in 2021, when it became clear that the point where he had made his prediction looked over the newly excavated Structure AD, a huge stone enclosure some 75 feet (23 meters) in length that today dominates the site. His proposed alignment toward the setting of Deneb, it soon became clear, parallels exactly a line of sight between the structure's southern recess and the orientation of the nearby Pillars with its enigmatic porthole window. This was only one of many accurate predictions that Andrew has made relating to these sites.

Our investigations continued one year later, in May 2015, with Keçili Tepe as our main focus. Andrew acquired a full hazmat suit, gloves, a ladder, and other equipment to descend into the "snake pit," with me filming and documenting the investigation (see chapter 12 of this book and plates 26 and 27 also). The pit was a large, bell-shaped hypogeum cut into the level bedrock. Such structures are thought to have been used to capture rainwater. Due to the presence thereabouts of stone tools from the Pre-Pottery Neolithic Age and the site's precise alignment with nearby Karahan Tepe, he considered that this structure, along with various other rock-cut features seen on the hill, could be extremely ancient.

The hypogeum caves and rock-cut areas of Keçili Tepe made no sense at the time, but the hunch that at least some of them were many thousands of years old is today proving to be correct. In May 2023, Ismail Can, one of the family members at Karahan Tepe, informed us that Keçili Tepe was now "out of bounds" to visitors as it had become a site of extreme interest to archaeologists, who suspected that some of its features could be prehistoric, which is exactly what Andrew had predicted almost a decade earlier.[1] We should therefore include this recent revelation among Andrew's list of ideas that have proved correct.

It is a list that should include his hypothesis that the shamanic elite behind the emergence of southeastern Anatolia's T-pillar building culture were descendants of human groups whose origins could be looked for as far east as Siberia and Mongolia, this being based on the gradual migration of microblade technologies that are known to have existed in northern Asia as much as 30,000 years ago. Andrew first explored these ideas in books such as *Göbekli Tepe: Genesis of the Gods* (2014) and *The Cygnus Key* (2018). His observations were, perhaps inevitably, ignored by mainstream archaeology and even ridiculed on occasion. As we shall see, this same hypothesis is now being proposed by Turkish archaeologists who have also traced the origins of Anatolia's Pre-Pottery Neolithic culture back to Siberia and Mongolia during the Upper Paleolithic Age.

Early on, I learned to listen carefully to Andrew's ideas and intuitions, as more often than not they eventually came to fruition. Furthermore, and as Graham Hancock pointed out in the foreword to *Göbekli Tepe: Genesis of the Gods*, as far back as the mid-1990s Andrew predicted something big was going to be found in southeastern Anatolia. It would, he said, provide compelling evidence that this region was the original Garden of Eden of biblical tradition, where mythical beings such as the Watchers and Nephilim in Hebrew legend and the Anunnaki builder gods of Sumerian and Babylonian myth are said to have given humanity the rudiments of civilization.

These ideas were initially featured in Andrew's influential book titled *From The Ashes of Angels*, originally published in 1996. Immediately after its release, Andrew had a sudden eureka moment when seeing for the first time the photographs of newly uncovered T-pillars at the first excavated Pre-Pottery Neolithic site of Nevalı Çori, which is located on a branch of the Euphrates in the northern part of Şanlıurfa province. The existence of these monumental stone pillars, as well as the remarkable sculpted carvings found at the site, confirmed his conviction that this was the location of an extremely high culture responsible for the foundation of human civilization.

Andrew even compared Nevalı Çori's remaining central pillar, which still stood in the middle of the settlement's cult building when discovered, with the monolith featured in the Stanley Kubrick film *2001: A Space Odyssey*; this was how much the site impacted him. As this was happening, the first surveys were being conducted at Göbekli Tepe, situated elsewhere in Şanlıurfa province. This was some 4 years before the site was brought to the notice of the public in 2000. As time went on, Andrew's words were routinely attacked by archaeologists as "pseudoscience," yet later repeated, without due credit, by the same "academics" who had dismissed him years earlier. It's as though they simply "forgot" who came out with these ideas first.

September 2021. Karahan Tepe was now 3 years into its excavation under the guidance of Necmi Karul of Istanbul University. Aerial photos and footage of the site had been published for the first time, and as soon as I saw these I sent them to Andrew, asking him to take a closer look at the site to see if any celestial alignments could be determined. He got back to me almost immediately, noting how the site's Structure AA, which we have since dubbed the Pit Shrine, appeared to target sunset on the summer solstice in around 9000 BCE, the time frame of its construction. Then, just two and a half hours after sunset, the Milky Way would have stood vertical on the horizon where the sun had earlier disappeared from view, offering the possibility that this was the shrine's primary target. It felt like this was the beginning of a new chapter in uncovering the truth about Karahan Tepe.

Since then more discoveries and star movements have been found at Karahan Tepe, but this initial analysis by Andrew inspired our discovery of the Pillars Shrine's winter solstice alignment. Because the summer solstice sunset and the winter solstice sunrise are on approximately the same alignment (but in opposite directions), JJ Ainsworth and I felt that something important might be found at the site on the shortest day of the year. And we were right.

After a series of serendipitous events and challenges, we arrived at Karahan Tepe just in time for sunrise on December 20, 2021, and witnessed a remarkable solar phenomenon in which the rising sun shone through the small porthole window to illuminate the giant stone head carved out of the bedrock on the western wall of the Pillars Shrine. This spectacle lasted for 45 minutes. At the time we didn't fully understand the significance of the discovery. but when writing up our initial report we realized that this extraordinary spectacle had not been witnessed for nearly 10,000 years. We knew this must be the case because photos of the site from December 2020 showed that excavations were still in progress there. The details of this discovery are outlined in the appendix written by JJ and me.

Since excavations began at Karahan Tepe in 2019, it is estimated that a mere 5 percent of the site has so far been exposed. The methodical pace of the excavations, combined with surveys of the area, have revealed that the scale of Karahan Tepe is much larger than previously recognized, covering around 13 hectares (33 acres), which is much bigger even than the site of Göbekli Tepe. New discoveries on the top of the hill (in September 2023) have verified more of Andrew's previous theories on northern alignments to Cygnus, which he first proposed in connection with key enclosures at Göbekli Tepe in his book *The Cygnus Mystery*, published as far back as 2006. Furthermore, a stunning vulture statue has been found placed below a porthole stone in this new enclosure, a remarkable and incredibly meaningful discovery since the vulture is a primary symbol not only of the Pre-Pottery Neolithic world's cult of the dead in Anatolia, but also of the Cygnus constellation itself, a story I will leave Andrew to tell.

Karahan Tepe is proving to be as important as Göbekli Tepe in many different ways, and what you see today is really just the tip of the iceberg. Indeed, this site along with Göbekli Tepe and several other T-pillar sites in the region are now being excavated under the umbrella term of "Taş Tepeler," meaning "stony hills" or "stone hills." As many as 12 or even 13 such sites are now under investigation. Some have yet to be excavated, but what is coming out of the ground at Pre-Pottery Neolithic locations such as Sayburç, Sefer Tepe,

Harbetsuvan, and Ayanlar Höyük, for instance, suggests this culture formed part of something much wider, an organized society with sophisticated stonework, intricate artifacts, and astronomical alignments that I see as the world's first *supercivilization*.

With the predictions and insights Andrew routinely presents in his books about sites such as these, the words you are about to read will ruffle a few feathers in the archaeological and academic worlds, but for the reader and researchers like JJ and me, the text in your hands may well provide more examples of inspired foresight by one of the leading researchers and authors in his field. *Karahan Tepe: Civilization of the Anunnaki and the Cosmic Origins of the Serpent of Eden* will become another classic to be referred to over and over again in the decades to come.

HUGH NEWMAN, AUTHOR OF
GÖBEKLI TEPE AND KARAHAN TEPE:
THE WORLD'S FIRST MEGALITHS

Acknowledgments

First, I wish to thank Richard Ward and Debbie Cartwright for their innovation and inspiration, which helped direct this book's outcome, and Hugh Newman and JJ Ainsworth for their essential contributions to every aspect of making the book possible and for allowing the publication of their classic article on the brilliant discoveries made at Karahan Tepe in December 2021. Thanks also to Neslihan Tokat and Ufuk Bölükbaşı for their friendship and representation in Turkey; Sabahattin Alkan for his recall of Kurdish folk stories; Helena Reznor, Ani Williams, Greg Little, and Lora Little for their continued support and friendship; Nick Burton and Russell M. Hossain for their advice, help, and illustrations; Rodney Hale for overseeing the technical aspects of this project; Maria Louise for her thoughtful insights; Amanda Mariamne Radcliffe for her encouragement on the book's Gnostic elements; and Khanna Omarkhali and Ayşe Karacadağ for their knowledge of Yezidi tradition.

In addition to this, I want to thank Ismail Can and his family as custodians of Karahan Tepe; William F. Romain for his thoughts on Serpent Mound, Ohio; Ran Barkai for his help on Jericho's Neolithic solar alignments; and all the staff at Inner Traditions International for their continued belief in me.

I want to thank all my loyal friends and colleagues for their continued support, including Adora Gonzales, Catja di Lorenzo, Caroline Wise, Michael Staley, Lisa Weaver, Kerry Ann Dar, Yuri Leitch, Paul Weston, Jan Summers, Rob Macbeth, Leela Bunce, Buster Todd, Abbie Todd, and the Todd family, Joan Hale, Yvan Cartwright, Graham Phillips, Renee Goulet, Özgecan Berdibek, Damla Selin Tomru, Fatih Aslan, Chloe Golden, Chrissie Bampton, Elena Amber, Graham Hancock, Loire Cotler, Glen Velez, Giorgio A. Tsoukalos, Erich von Däniken, Rowan Campbell Miller, Eileen Buchanan,

Roma Harding, and Roxanne, along with everyone at Prometheus Studios; and Jason Liggett, Diana Maxwell, and all the staff at Gaia.com. I want to thank everyone I have had the pleasure of meeting on Megalithomania tours to Turkey. Your thoughts and insights regarding the function, construction, and symbolism of Göbekli Tepe and Karahan Tepe have helped me better assess what I have written in this book. Finally, I wish to acknowledge the incredible work being done right now by Necmi Karul and his colleagues from Istanbul University at Karahan Tepe, by Lee Clare and the *Göbekli Tepe* Project at *Göbekli Tepe*, and by Eylem Özdoğan and her team from Istanbul University at the village of Sayburç. Without their invaluable contributions to the subject of Taş Tepeler books such as this could not be written.

The Coming of the Serpent

Out of the darkness emerges a strange sound. It is high-pitched, repetitive, and constant in its intent, never ceasing, just rising and falling as if circling around and around. It is compelling, hypnotic, drawing you like magnetism toward its source. As it seems to get ever closer, its presence is now accompanied by the sight of bonfires illuminating a large valley located beneath the protection of an enormous limestone hill shaped like the body of a woman.

Central among the rings of fire is an amphitheater, elliptical in shape and with a pair of enormous T-shaped pillars standing proud at its center. Many more such pillars are positioned between stone benches in its perimeter wall, which terminates at its western end in huge, rock-cut features—great thrones and towering buttresses shaped into the likeness of abstract human beings. Their presence alone confirms the fact that whatever is happening right now is the product of an extremely advanced culture whose people's minds are united in a single purpose.

On the carved thrones sit important individuals—key shamans, elders, dignitaries—while on the benches sit those making the incessant sounds that are being carried through the nighttime air. Although the setting is mostly in darkness, the fires give away at least some of their features. Each person wears garments of either leather or fur. Dark feathers, stone beads, holed stones, snake teeth, and snake vertebrae are worn on leather cords around necks, hips, and arms. Their bodies are caked in white lime and black soot with geometrical forms drawn in finer paint. If not bald, they bear bizarre Mohican-style haircuts or display a tangled mass of dreadlocked hair. Both men and women are taking part in these highly focused ritualistic actions.

Through the creation of sound they are generating enough magic, enough power, to open and sustain a doorway between this world and the next. To do this, they need to create a constant cacophony of noise made by banging together a mixture of stone tools and singing rocks picked up in the surrounding landscape. All the time, the sound circles around in such a mesmerizing manner that it seems to tear at your very soul. It is intoxicating, exciting, sensual, inducing a distinct feeling of vertigo where the mundane world no longer matters.

The sensation causes you to become possessed, overtaken, ridden even, by an invading spirit, a great serpent that enters inside you. It moves up through your body like a powerful, intelligent force. Falling to the ground, you half slither, half crawl, toward the chosen place of exit from this world. It is a small, rectangular porthole cut into a thin wall of stone.

Every ounce of effort is required for you to reach the porthole and pull yourself through to the other side—a liminal realm where contact with the vistas of space now becomes possible. The true nature of this guiding force is unknowable, since it exists outside the material universe, in the darkness of the night, and yet its influence, its brilliant light, is felt by all who experience it, for not only does it govern the movement of the celestial bodies, but it also controls the destiny of life on Earth. It is the Great Serpent, and its presence is seen every night with the first appearance of the Milky Way.

This is an imaginary scenario born out of our current understanding of what might have been going on at Karahan Tepe, the twenty-first century's most important archaeological discovery. Here, the site's highly sophisticated Pre-Pottery Neolithic community would appear to have been obsessed with the symbol of the snake. As we shall see, this symbol was seen as being in control of the dynamic mechanisms responsible for the turning of the heavens and the rise and fall of life on this planet. These ideas will be reflected in the extraordinary findings of this book, which proposes that the newly excavated structures at Karahan Tepe, situated in the remote Tektek Mountains of southeastern Anatolia, were used not only to sustain a link between this world and the next but also to make contact with the primary creative force behind the very existence of our own Milky Way galaxy.

Compelling evidence is presented to demonstrate that the extraordinary bedrock structures found at Karahan Tepe were aligned to either the rising or the setting of the sun at the time of summer and winter solstices. This was done not only to synchronize with important moments in the solar year, but also, it will be argued, to connect with a cosmic entity, serpentine in nature, seen in terms of a divine source of knowledge and wisdom. Moreover, and as we shall see, what was taking place at Karahan Tepe in the tenth millennium BCE would go on to become mythologized in Hebrew tradition as Adam and Eve's temptation by the Serpent in the Garden of Eden and adopted also by those cultures that would arise thousands of years later on the nearby Harran Plain.

Among them were the Chaldean astrologers of Harran, Sogmatar, and ancient Edessa, modern-day Şanlıurfa. It was their knowledge of the movement of the stars that would go on to inspire the invention of astrology, ideas that were inherited both by the Orphic mystery schools of Greece and Anatolia and by the serpent-worshipping Gnostics, who would come to rival orthodox Christianity during late antiquity. This extraordinary story of discovery will admirably demonstrate that the people of what we know today as the Taş Tepeler—or "stone hills"—culture of ancient Anatolia not only had a truly profound understanding of the cosmos and beyond, but can also be seen as the founders of the world's first post–Ice Age civilization.

PART 1

DISCOVERIES AND REVELATIONS

1

The Great Discovery

September 10, 2023. On every visit I make to Karahan Tepe—currently one of the most exciting archaeological sites in the world—I discover something new. Since first setting eyes on this important Neolithic ceremonial and ritual complex, located deep within the Tektek Mountains of southeastern Turkey, in June 2004, I had imagined what might lie beneath the thick layers of soil and rubble, where the heads of dozens of T-shaped pillars could be seen just poking out above the surface of the ground.

Would Karahan Tepe compare with the extraordinary discoveries made at its sister site Göbekli Tepe, located near the ancient city of Şanlıurfa some 23 miles (37 kilometers) to the west-northwest? Ever since this extraordinary ritual complex, often described as the world's first temple, was first identified as a Pre-Pottery Neolithic site by German archaeologist Professor Klaus Schmidt in 1994, a series of quite extraordinary stone enclosures had been exposed there. Almost all of them were found to contain multiple T-shaped pillars, anthropomorphic in style, with many of them bearing relief carvings of birds, animals, and other creatures of the natural world.

Archaeologists had known about the treasures awaiting discovery at Karahan Tepe since the mid-1990s, although it was not until 2018 that a team under the leadership of Necmi Karul, head of the Prehistory Department at Istanbul University, had properly surveyed the site. In just five excavation seasons, between 2019 and 2023, the team had uncovered a set of stone enclosures unique to world history. Three of them (Structures AA, AB, and AD), located at the base of Karahan Tepe's eastern and northeastern slopes, were found to be either wholly or partly cut out of the hill's limestone bedrock. As we see in chapters 2 and 3, the appearance, symbolism, and proposed function of these extraordinary ritual structures changes much of what we know about the mindset of the Pre-Pottery Neolithic peoples that once inhabited the site as much as 11,000 years ago.

Now, I was back at Karahan Tepe, leading a tour group alongside my colleagues Hugh Newman and JJ Ainsworth, and once again we hoped there would be something new for us to see—perhaps a newly uncovered T-pillar or a carving we hadn't previously noted. Even before we entered the site something incredible had been revealed to us. Apparently, an examination of plant material found at the site has now provided firm evidence that occupation began there around 13,000 years ago, during the Epipaleolithic Age,* this being as much as 1,500 years before the construction of the first stone enclosures there around 9400 BCE.

After listening to an introduction to the newly uncovered stone enclosures by site guardian and archaeological student Ismail Can, the tour group followed him to the top of the hill. Hugh and I lingered, taking photos and making observations. Conscious of having left the group behind, we navigated our way around the southern end of the present excavations and started our ascent toward the top of the hill. This took us past various exposed enclosures, most containing standing T-pillars.

We could never have imagined what would happen next, for on reaching the summit of the hill we were met by a soldier dressed in army fatigues holding an automatic rifle against his chest. He stood guarding a newly exposed stone enclosure visible within a deep, 33-foot-square (10-meter-square) excavation trench. As he saw us approach, he clutched the rifle tighter and kept saying: "No photo. No photo. No photo."

Happy to comply, Hugh and I simply held up our arms as if in surrender, asking only that we might be allowed to make some quick calculations regarding the structure's orientation. Not understanding what we wanted to do, the guard simply repeated his mantra: "No photo. No photo. No photo."

We didn't need photos, for what we could see in front of us was already etched firmly into our minds. It was a massive enclosure, at the northern end of which was what appeared to be a perimeter wall made of stacked rows of dry stones. A limestone porthole, round in shape with a small, circular hole in its middle, had been inserted into this wall. Such porthole stones are a familiar

*The age of the site is now given as 13,000 years on a new signboard at the visitors center.

sight within the enclosures at Göbekli Tepe, although these are generally not round but rectangular slabs stuck upright in the ground with centrally placed holes just large enough for a human head to fit through. These porthole stones are almost always located on the north side of an enclosure, directed, as we shall see, toward the same bright star, one that in ancient cultures worldwide was seen to mark the entrance to the sky world.

Set on either side of the porthole stone were twin stone pillars, originally no doubt T-shaped, although their tops were now missing due to exposure above the surface of the hill for as much as 11,000 years. Wedged between these pillars and lying directly beneath the holed stone was a stone extension acting, seemingly, as an early form of an "altar." Its presence indicated the directionality of the enclosure, which was toward the north. This seemed especially certain in the knowledge that, to the south, the hilltop continued to rise.

As we stood trying to convince the guard of our honesty, I attempted to visually line up the enclosure's altar, twin pillars, and porthole stone with the local landscape. I noted that its axis clearly targeted a nearby hill marked by a cluster of farm buildings. This was located in the north-northeast—an important realization, since it suggested that the enclosure might once have been aligned to a star seen to rise from the summit of this hill. Exactly which star would have to wait until I had a chance to consult Stellarium, the free, open-source planetarium, which can display the night sky during any epoch.

In addition to the twin pillars and porthole stone in its northern wall, the enclosure contained two further pillars in the southernmost part of the excavation trench. Both were on the ground and were heavily fractured. Each one, we subsequently learned, is around 16 feet (4.8 meters) in length, making them as big as any T-pillar found at the site so far. The enclosure's floor was the underlying bedrock, which had been perfectly planed in a manner similar to that seen at various installations at Göbekli Tepe, such as Enclosures C and D, as well as Structure AD on Karahan Tepe's lower level.

The first thing Hugh did after leaving Karahan Tepe that afternoon was sketch what we'd just seen. Realizing, however, the obvious significance of the new enclosure, I knew we needed more information. Why was it important? Why was it under guard?

I reached out to my contacts in Turkey, one of whom provided the answer. Something remarkable had been found there that would apparently "change everything" and make Karahan Tepe even more famous than its sister site Göbekli Tepe. What is more, this incredible discovery would soon be revealed to the world. In the meantime, it was being kept secret, hence the armed guard making sure that no one was able to inspect the enclosure too closely. This, we now realized, was huge in size and spanned more than three excavation trenches, suggesting that it was as much as 75 feet (around 23 meters) across making it equal in size to Structure AD on Karahan Tepe's lower level (see chapter 2).

These extraordinary revelations led Hugh, JJ, and me to make further inquiries about what had been found, especially as it would apparently "change everything" we knew about the site.

Later that evening, as I was readying myself for bed in a hotel room in the heart of Şanlıurfa, our inquiries paid off. I received a communication from a reliable source telling me precisely what had been found. Realizing its significance, I knew I had to message Hugh and JJ, suggesting they come to my room immediately, despite the late hour.

A knock on the door sounded their arrival just a few minutes later. Both were eager to learn more, and after settling down I told them what I knew. Two quite extraordinary statues had been found. One was of an extremely tall, male figure, which, being as much as 11,000 years old, now constituted the oldest full-size, naturalistic representation of the human form ever discovered. It had been unearthed only a few weeks earlier in a horizontal position within the enclosure. Next to it excavators had unearthed the statue of a vulture, which was still standing in its original position.

Clearly, there was a relationship between the two statues, the male human figure and the vulture, since they had been found next to each other. Vultures, I knew, had played a significant role in Anatolian religion during the Neolithic Age. They were important symbols of the transmigration of the soul to and from the realm of the dead—what is known, respectively, as excarnation and incarnation. Vultures were seen as psychopomps, an ancient Greek term meaning "soul carriers" or "soul accompaniers."

SKY BURIAL

The belief in excarnation was linked intrinsically with the manner in which human cadavers were taken to elevated positions away from the community and vultures allowed to come down and consume their flesh until all that remained were those bones too big to be carried away. Known as "sky burial," it is a process still practiced today by some Tibetan Buddhist communities on the Tibetan Plateau (just Google "Tibet" and "sky burial," and some very gruesome images will appear).

Sky burial is considered to be a clean and effective way of disposing of human bodies, and in the past it was accompanied by religious beliefs and practices that helped determine the ultimate fate of the human soul. The late Professor Klaus Schmidt thought that sky burials had taken place at Göbekli Tepe,[1] just as they are known to have occurred at the Ceramic Neolithic site of Çatal Höyük in southern-central Anatolia, circa 7500–5000 BCE.[2] We can therefore presume that sky burials also took place at Karahan Tepe, making the presence of a vulture statue in the new enclosure no doubt important to the community's own beliefs concerning the destination of the soul in death.

Following the completion of our tour of Turkey, which in the next week would take us to the extreme northeastern part of the country, Hugh, JJ, and I returned to Şanlıurfa and visited Karahan Tepe on two further occasions. Thereafter, we flew back to the United Kingdom, where we waited for further news of the incredible discoveries made in the newly uncovered enclosure.

Life returned to normal, with other more pressing matters occupying our minds. Indeed, we almost forgot about the whole matter. This all changed on September 30, 2023, one week after our return from Turkey. A Google alert notified me of the online publication of a news story containing the words "Karahan Tepe." It had been posted the previous day by the Turkish news agency Hurriyet and was based on information released by Turkey's Ministry of Culture and Tourism.[3] Clicking the link, I saw for the first time photo images of the two statues. Both were even more spectacular than I could have imagined. They showed, for instance, that the giant human sculpture was in fact in a seated position and had originally been placed upright within a stone bench to the east of the two T-pillars set into the perimeter wall (see fig. 1.1). The vulture, on the other hand, was held upright by a curved extension to the stone altar located beneath the porthole stone. I could also see that one, or possibly even two, stone platters had been found in situ on the

Fig. 1.1. First view of the new enclosure on Karahan Tepe's northern summit. Illustration by Andrew Collins.

altar, with another, larger example having been found on the floor next to it (see plate 1).

A HUMAN GIANT

The human statue was enormous even in a seated position, at 7 feet, 5 inches (2.3 meters) in height. It was found in three main pieces. These were reattached and the whole thing replaced in its original position. The statue's head was extremely long and wide with prominent jaws, a long pointed beard, piercing eyes complete with eyeballs, and hair swept back behind the ears and a possible shaved area above the ears in a unique style resembling a 1980s-style mullet! I had never seen anything quite like this before at any of the Pre-Pottery Neolithic sites in the region.

In addition to this, the statue—fashioned from local limestone—had arms in high relief. These wrapped around the figure's body and ended in hands that emphasized the figure's three-dimensional penis, which does not appear to have been circumcised. This, I subsequently learned, had been found separate from the statue and only reattached afterward (I say this as some early photos of the statue show the figure without his manhood!).

In many ways the statue could be classed as, quite literally, a human giant (see fig. 1.2), begging the question of why it was so large. Did it represent a living individual of great size, or was it simply symbolic of a divine ancestor who had to be shown much bigger than his living descendants?

The vulture statue was around 22 inches (59 centimeters) in height and, like the human statue, made of limestone. Its wings were folded and it faced into the enclosure. Being almost a caricature in appearance, there seemed little doubt as to its identification. With its bald head and hooked beak it was definitely a vulture, something that the archaeologists must also have concluded themselves (see fig. 1.3, p. 10). Its presence meant that it had to reflect the importance of the soul's journey into the afterlife, with the fact that it was found facing into the enclosure perhaps signifying its return from the realm of the dead.

How exactly these extraordinary statues, as well as the new enclosure itself, fitted into our current understanding of the highly sophisticated society known to have existed at Karahan Tepe around 11,000 years ago was something I wanted to start investigating immediately.

Fig. 1.2. The giant statue found in the new enclosure at Karahan Tepe.
Illustration by Andrew Collins. (See also color plate 1.)

My findings are presented in the final chapter of this book, the original manuscript of which I had submitted to the publisher several months before our visits to Karahan Tepe in September 2023. As the reader will see, the book provides a comprehensive overview of all that has been discovered about the accomplishments of southeastern Anatolia's Taş Tepeler culture, a term explained in chapter 7. We see also how the achievements, and even the failings, of its prime movers were preserved in Hebrew myth, as well as within the rich mythologies that would eventually develop on the Mesopotamian plain in what is today southern Iraq. Only in the final chapter will we come to realize what the giant human statue found at Karahan Tepe almost certainly represents.

First, however, we look at the incredible rock-cut structures discovered there by Necmi Karul and his team between 2019 and 2021. An understanding

Fig. 1.3. The vulture statue found within the new enclosure at Karahan Tepe.
Photo by Andrew Collins.

of their layout, design, and suspected function will demonstrate the impact Taş Tepeler likely had on the development of cosmological beliefs and practices that would eventually emerge as the basis of religious and mystical doctrines at the root of Greek Orphism, Gnostic Christianity, and even Hindu and Buddhist yogic and tantric practices involving the importance of the kundalini snake.

2

Karahan Tepe— The Bedrock Enclosures

Three interconnected, subsurface structures were revealed at Karahan Tepe during excavations that took place between 2019 and 2021. Each was found beneath the thick layers of soil and rubble covering the hill's eastern and northeastern slopes. These have been designated Structures AA, AB, and AD. A fourth rock-cut enclosure, circular in shape, much smaller in size, and dubbed Structure AC, lies immediately to the east of Structure AA.

STRUCTURE AD (THE GREAT ELLIPSE)

The three interconnected structures are carved either in part or entirely out of the limestone bedrock. The largest, Structure AD—popularly called "the Great Ellipse"—is elliptical in appearance with a maximum length of 75 feet (23 meters) and a width of approximately 65 feet (20 meters). The northern, eastern, and southern sections of its perimeter wall are made up of drystone walling with a thickness of around 5 feet (1.5 meters). Built into this wall were originally a series of 18 T-pillars, between which were stone benches similar to those found at other Pre-Pottery Neolithic cult centers such as Nevalı Çori and Göbekli Tepe (see fig. 2.1 for an overhead plan of Structure AD, and plates 2 and 3, which show what it looks like today). At least one of the bench tops remaining in situ is clearly the stem of an old T-pillar as it displays carved decoration on its front narrow edge (see fig. 2.1 on the next page).

A number of limestone statues, as well as large platters and bowls carved from a variety of stone materials, were found on or around these benches.[1]

11

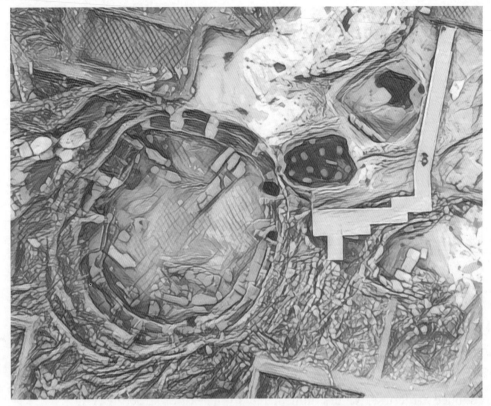

Fig. 2.1. Overhead plan of Karahan Tepe's structures AD (the Great Ellipse),
AB (the Pillars Shrine), and AA (the Pit Shrine).
Illustration by Andrew Collins and Rodney Hale.

These appear to have been deliberately left in place when the structure was decommissioned and afterward buried beneath countless tons of soil and rubble, an act perhaps seen as "killing" or "putting to rest" the enclosure's active spirit.[2]

At the center of Structure AD, two enormous T-pillars would have stood within holes cut into the bedrock. Today these pillars are in multiple fragments, although their original positions can still be determined (see plate 4). Whether or not they were deliberately broken or were the subject of intense environmental erosion before the abandonment of the enclosure is unclear.

Piecing together the various fragments of these twin pillars indicates they were slightly smaller than an unfinished example still attached to the bedrock on the hill's western-facing slope. This example is approximately 18 feet (5.5 meters) in length. The carved decoration on the western central pillar shows two vertical lines in high relief that curve outward just beneath the T-shaped head. It is difficult to know exactly what this shows, although it could signify the hems of a draped garment.

Whether or not the two central pillars, as well as those within the structure's walls, acted as roof supports is debatable. If the enclosure did have a wooden roof as archaeologists strongly suspect then the chances are it only partially covered its interior or it was present only on a temporary or seasonal basis.

THRONES AND BUTTRESSES

The western half of Structure AD is unique. Three enormous carved stone benches have been cut directly out of the hill's bedrock (see plate 5). Each one looks like a rock throne, and on these one might imagine community elders sitting during important rituals and ceremonies. Separating the stone thrones, which have an additional curb or step at their base, are three (originally perhaps four) towering buttresses, each one cut entirely out of the hill's eastern slope to a maximum height from ground level of 14 feet (4.3 meters).[3] They acted as solid rock variations of the anthropomorphic T-pillars with horizontal extensions at their terminations, although these have long since disappeared due to the buttresses being exposed above the surface of the soil and rubble covering the hillside. From what we can see, they constituted four out of eighteen of the original T-pillars featured in the design of the enclosure, the rest having been removed from the bedrock before their placement within the structure's retaining wall.

Confirmation that these buttresses were seen as anthropomorphic in nature is the fact that two of them, the most southerly of the four, display carved relief showing leopard skin loincloths below their presumed waistlines, these appearing on their front narrow edges. Archaeologists working at the site suggest the carvings are actually leopards, although the carvings closely resemble the style and position of fox pelt loincloths seen on the two central pillars in Göbekli Tepe's Enclosure D (Pillars 18 and 31). Such a realization suggests that Karahan Tepe's occupants wore leopard skin pelts as items of adornment. (A similar leopard pelt loincloth can be seen on the front narrow edge of the T-pillar stem being used as a bench seat on the northern side of the enclosure.)

Reliefs of animals adorn the sides of the rock buttresses, just like those seen on free standing T-pillars. On the south side of the most southerly example, for instance, is what appears to be a quadruped. It stands upright, its legs facing toward the hill slope (and thus toward the person sitting on the throne next to it). Other animals adorn the southern side of the buttress next to it, although their identification is difficult to determine due to being almost entirely eroded away.

Various deep pits cut into the bedrock are seen in the floor of the enclosure, one of which is close to the benches on its north-northwestern side. The function of these pits is unknown, although the fact that they can also be seen in major enclosures at Göbekli Tepe and also at Sayburç (see chapters 6 and 30) shows they played an important role in the activities taking place in these structures as much as 11,000 years ago.

STRUCTURE AB (THE PILLARS SHRINE)

Even more spectacular rock architecture is present at Karahan Tepe within what is unquestionably its most enigmatic rock-cut installation. This is Structure AB, popularly known as the Pillars Shrine. This is situated immediately to the north-northwest of Structure AD, to which it is linked via a 27.5 inch (70 centimeter) rectangular porthole window cut out of a thin wall of rock deliberately left in situ for this purpose (see fig. 2.2 and also plate 6). On the other side of this window are five crudely carved steps leading down to the structure's stone floor.

Carved entirely out of the hillside, the Pillars Shrine is trapezoidal in shape with rounded corners. In size it is 23 feet (7 meters) in length with a maximum width of 20 feet (6 meters), its southern end being narrower than its northern end. Its limestone walls rise to a height of 7.6 feet (2.3 meters), beyond which is the artificially leveled rock surface.

Filling the interior of Structure AB are 11 standing pillars, 10 of which are fashioned directly out of the bedrock (see plates 7 and 8). Four of them form a line oriented roughly north-south, close to the shrine's western wall. Each one is approximately 5.25 feet to 5.6 feet (1.6 to 1.7 meters)[4] in height with slightly wider heads as terminations, giving them a distinct phallic appearance.

The other six rock-hewn pillars are smaller in size. They vary in height between 3.25 to 4.6 feet (1 to 1.4 meters) and are between 12 to 20 inches (30 to 50 centimeters) in diameter.[5] Five are positioned roughly north-south in a noticeable zigzag pattern, while the sixth example is located slightly back from

Fig. 2.2. The porthole window in the stone wall between
Karahan Tepe's Structure AD and the adjoining Structure AB (the Pillars Shrine).
Photo by Andrew Collins. (See also color plate 6.)

the others, close to the structure's southeastern corner. Some of the smaller pillars also have slightly larger heads, while the most northerly example has what appears to be a tethering hole two thirds of the way up its southern side. This could have been used to attach a rope or cord, although for what purpose is unknown.

The zigzag-like arrangement of these smaller pillars could imply a navigational route for the supplicant entering the shrine via the porthole stone. Having said this, these smaller pillars have to be viewed in association with the four larger examples on the western side.

An intimate relationship must have existed between all ten pillars, a point to remember as we now explore the shrine's eleventh pillar. Unlike Structure AB's other pillars, this one was not cut out of the bedrock. Instead it was carved into shape before being placed upright in a rectangular slot cut into the shrine's stone floor. It is around the same height as the tallest of the rock-cut columns. Significantly, it is crescent-shaped with a slightly wider area around its upper termination, offering the impression of a striking snake facing roughly toward anyone entering through the porthole window. This suspicion is additionally indicated by a linear indentation on the stone's western side corresponding to the position of its "mouth." It is my suspicion that this standing slab acted in the capacity of a *genius loci*, the "spirit of the place," in much the same way that in both Hindu and Buddhist tradition snake spirits or *nagas* are considered to guard sacred places and hidden treasure.

THE GIANT STONE HEAD

The importance of snake symbolism in the Pillars Shrine is further indicated by the presence on the shrine's western wall of something quite extraordinary. Carved once again out of the bedrock about 7 feet (2.1 meters) off the ground and in the central area of the rock face is a giant human head on the end of a long vertical neck. The head is enormous, being as much as three times that of a normal human being (see fig. 2.3 and plates 9 and 10). On the underside of the neck are a series of parallel striations perpendicular to its angle of projection. These surely are there to emphasize the head's serpentine nature.

The head itself faces slightly toward the structure's entrance porthole (its true orientation is just south of east), giving the impression that it is turning to look at anyone entering the room. It has a flat top and actually looks like it is

Fig. 2.3. The stone head emerging out of the west wall of
Karahan Tepe's Structure AB. Photo by Andrew Collins.
(See also color plates 9 and 10.)

wearing a medieval knight's helmet complete with nose guard. This, however, is simply an illusion, since its flat top probably marks the lower limit of a framed roof that almost certainly enclosed the shrine. This seems possible since horizontal ledges at the same height as the top of the head can be seen at the top of the shrine's walls on its eastern and western sides, indicating that they once supported crossbeams presumably made of wood.

The stone head's mouth is carved in high relief and is elliptical in shape, offering the impression that it is talking to you. Once again, this is unlikely to be without purpose.

So what exactly does this stone head represent? Did it feature in some ritual practice involving a person entering the shrine and having to not only navigate the phallic pillars and acknowledge the curved, snake-like slab stand-ing at its northern end but also commune with the serpentine human head itself? Answers can perhaps be gleaned by looking at the third and final inter-connected structure uncovered during the first years of excavation at the site— a place known today as the Pit Shrine.

3

Structure AA–The Pit Shrine

On the north side of the Pillars Shrine cut into the level bedrock at Karahan Tepe is a deep winding groove that connects with the southeastern edge of a third and final subsurface feature known as Structure AA, popularly called the Pit Shrine (see plates 11 and 12). Trapezoidal in shape with rounded corners, it is approximately 28 feet (8.5 meters) in length, 23 feet (7 meters) across, and just over 3.5 feet (1.1 meters) in depth, making it much shallower than the two previously described installations.

Within the structure's western wall is a curved bench around 12 feet (3.6 meters) in length. On its front vertical edge is an extremely long snake incised using a method known as the scraping technique (see fig. 3.1). Its head, which displays two incised eyes and is itself trapezoidal in shape, is turned upward almost like a directional marker toward the sky above. The whole thing faces northward, and immediately beyond it is a standing fox in incised relief;

Fig. 3.1. Incised snake (left) and carved relief of a fox (right) on the front edge of the long curving bench in Structure AA (the Pit Shrine). Photo by Andrew Collins.

this is also facing northward. The fact that both the snake and the fox form part of the same register suggests a relationship between the two creatures, a matter looked at in detail later in this book.

Cut into the level floor at the room's northern end is an irregularly shaped pit with rounded corners. This descends into the bedrock for a depth of around 7.5 feet (2.3 meters). At ground level on its western side is a carved recess large enough for a person to crawl inside.

Steps carved into the shrine's eastern wall allow access to the room. Interestingly, the position of these steps corresponds very roughly to the end of the aforementioned winding groove. In fact, close to the other end of this groove four similarly carved steps lead down into the northeastern corner of the Pillars Shrine. This suggests a connection between the two structures, almost as if when you have finished in one, the curved groove guides you to the entrance of the other.

Necmi Karul writes that those entering the Pillars Shrine likely crawled through the porthole stone from Structure AD (the Great Ellipse) using the carved steps.[1] They would then have exited the room via steps in its northeastern corner, meaning that the supplicant would have followed the deep winding groove before entering the Pit Shrine for whatever was to take place there. Karul suggests this clear direction of movement shows a relationship between the Great Ellipse and the Pillars Shrine, implying that any ritualistic experience undertaken by a supplicant would have begun in the former and continued through into the latter structure.

These proposed actions would no doubt have constituted steps one and two of an experiential journey, a shift into an otherworldly state or realm, with the third and final part taking place in the Pit Shrine. Why this course should have been from south to north and culminated in a room with an enormous pit cut into its floor can only be guessed at today. Who, for instance, would have sat on the Pit Shrine's long bench, part of which lies directly above the deep hole carved into the floor? Could this pit have been used to contain live animals, snakes perhaps, or did supplicants lie down within its carved recess to enter into an altered state of consciousness? What we can say is that there appears to be no obvious means of descending into the pit, meaning that access to its interior must have been via a rope or a ladder.

The fact that the winding nature of the deeply cut groove linking the Pillars Shrine with the Pit Shrine resembles a moving snake is also unlikely to be with-

Fig. 3.2. The long, deeply carved groove in the level bedrock running between Karahan Tepe's Structure AB (the Pillars Shrine) and Structure AA (the Pit Shrine). Note the porthole dividing this structure with Structure AD (the Great Ellipse) in the background. Photo by Andrew Collins. (See also color plate 6.)

out meaning. Karul describes it as a "serpentine channel."[2] It can almost be imagined that the spirit of the snake guided the supplicant from one structure to the next (see fig. 3.2). Suggestions that the function of the curved groove was to carry liquid into the Pillars Shrine is indeed possible. What this would imply is that on occasions the room's interior was filled with water for some special purpose, arguably to symbolize the primordial waters of birth and/or creation.

INSIDE THE SNAKE'S HEAD

If the winding groove is indeed indicative of serpentine movement, then its relationship to the Pillars Shrine could suggest the two features are related. If so, was it more than simply a directional marker from one structure to the next? The fact that any experiential journey would begin with the supplicant moving from the Great Ellipse into the Pillars Shrine via the porthole window could suggest Structure AB was seen as a three-dimensional representation of a snake's head, its curving body implied by the deep groove next to it.

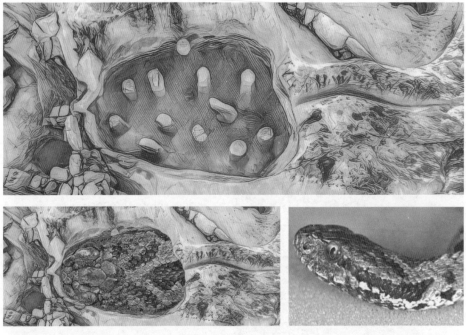

Fig. 3.3. Overhead view of Structure AB, above, and below, the shrine with
the head of the Anatolian meadow viper (*Vipera anatolica*) overlaid.
Illustration by Andrew Collins.

One species of snake indigenous to the Tektek Mountains is the highly
venomous Anatolian meadow viper (*Vipera anatolica*). Synchronizing the
head of this species with the overhead profile of the Pillars Shrine shows a
close match (see fig. 3.3). In observing this match we can see that the serpentine groove cut into the bedrock on its northern side seems to indicate
the actual neck of the snake, which is defined by the level bedrock on the
shrine's northern side. This eventually curves around the Pit Shrine's eastern
perimeter where it is then lost.

The quite dramatic realization that the Pillars Shrine is a three-dimensional
representation of a snakehead offers some interesting speculation. It means that
anyone entering the structure via the porthole window would have been entering the creature's mouth, wherein would lie its teeth, that is, the ten bedrock
pillars. The curved eleventh pillar, resembling a striking snake, might have
formed the creature's tongue, with the giant head emerging from the western
wall acting as some kind of snake genius during the supplicant's unfathomable
ritualistic journey.

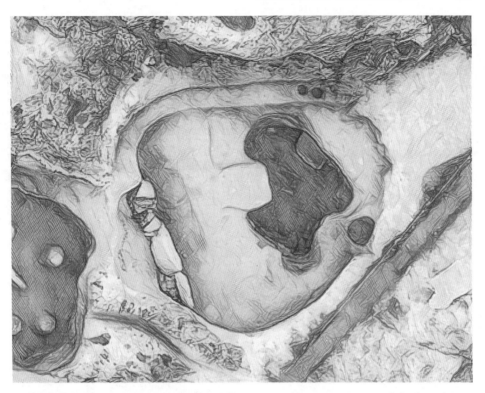

Fig. 3.4. Overhead image showing the serpent-like appearance of the bench inside Karahan Tepe's Structure AA (the Pit Shrine). Illustration by Andrew Collins.

The inordinate amount of snake symbolism in both the Pillars Shrine and the Pit Shrine tells us just how important snakes must have been to the Karahan community. Indeed, if we look more closely at the Pit Shrine, even more snake symbolism presents itself. Cut into the level surface of its long curved bench are two large boreholes positioned one in front of the other. These holes are 8 inches (20 centimeters) in diameter and 4 inches (10 centimeters) deep.[3] From above they combine with the curved shape of the bench to imply yet another snake, the holes representing their eyes, an observation that once noted becomes difficult to ignore (see fig. 3.4).

The fact that the "eye" holes at the northern end of the bench correspond with the position of two crude steps leading out of the shrine at its northwestern corner suggests that the bench, along with the incised snake and fox reliefs immediately beneath it, are all directed toward this point. So it looks as if the supplicant entered the structure via the stone steps at the northern end of the deeply carved groove and afterward exited the room via its northwestern corner, a course that would have taken them onto the hill's northern slope. It cannot be coincidence that this area of the bedrock also marks the start of the winding neck of the snake whose head is the Pillars Shrine. What this implies is that the creature is manifesting out of the northwest, perhaps indicating the importance of this direction to the site's serpentine symbolism.

We can take the matter further by proposing that the Pit Shrine is itself a representation of a snake's head. From above this certainly seems possible, although in comparison to the overall shape of the Pillars Shrine it is somewhat squatter. How might this surmise be tested? The incised snake on the front

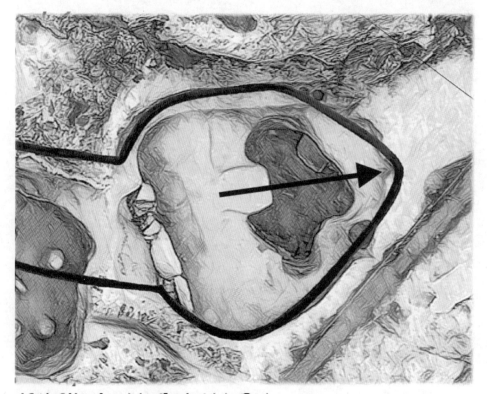

Fig. 3.5. Overhead image of Structure AA, top, with the head of the snake incised on the front of the shrine's bench overlaid. On the bottom we see the outline of the snake's head for comparison. Illustration by Andrew Collins.

edge of the bench has a squat head, trapezoidal in appearance, so perhaps this helped define the shape of the enclosure, or vice versa. To find out whether this is correct, I overlaid an outline of the incised head on an overhead image of the Pit Shrine. The match is more or less perfect (see fig. 3.5).

RITUALISTIC DIRECTIONALITY

Whether or not this exercise is meaningful remains to be seen. What it does do is raise the possibility that both the Pillars Shrine and the Pit Shrine represent snake heads, one—the former—facing toward the south-southwest, and the other facing out toward the west-northwestern horizon.

Thus, the experiential journey imagined as having taken place inside these three interconnected enclosures would appear to have begun in the Great Ellipse. It then continued into the mouth of the snake, represented by the Pillars Shrine, and culminated in the Pit Shrine, which is arguably yet another snakehead in design. Thereafter the celebrant would have emerged onto the level bedrock either via the steps at the end of the bench or via the steps cut into its northeastern wall. Karul proposes this same basic journey:

> Str. AB [the Pillars Shrine] is reached by passing through Str. AD [the Great Ellipse]; there is also a connection from Str. AB to Str. AA [the Pit Shrine]. Nonetheless, the main entry is via Str. AD. Therefore, we could assume Str. AD to be the actual place of activities that took place in this structure. The present evidence strongly suggests a ceremonial process, entering the building from one end and exiting at the other end, having to parade in [the] presence of the human head featuring a phallic symbolism.[4]

This ritualistic directionality also makes sense of another observation made by Karul. The three interconnected structures uncovered at Karahan Tepe's lower level are all on the hill's eastern or northeastern slopes. No cult structures have so far been found on the hill's western or southern sides. This has led Karul to surmise that the site's southern plain "must be the living area of the dwellers of the settlement."[5]

This same south-to-north directionality is found also in connection with special buildings at other Pre-Pottery Neolithic sites in the region, such as Göbekli Tepe, Çayönü, Hallan Çemi, and Aşıklı Höyük, as well as at Nevalı Çori, where the settlement's sole cult building was found to be aligned perfectly northeast. It is present also at later Pottery Neolithic (or Ceramic Neolithic) sites such as Çatal Höyük in southern-central Anatolia, where there is a specific directionality in the use of rooms. The north and east would always seem to be associated with death and rebirth,[6] while the south was reserved for domestic usage. Indeed, British archaeologist Ian Hodder, who led excavations at Çatal Höyük between 1993 and the mid-2010s, has written that the northern part of a building would be set aside for decoration and burial, thus connecting it with the spirit realm, leaving its southern side for hearths, ovens, human debris; indeed, everything that was deemed "dirty" or mundane.[7]

THE STRUCTURES AS LIVING ENTITIES

How the community at Karahan Tepe viewed the three interconnected, rock-cut structures can perhaps be seen in the fact that at the end of their useful life they were deliberately buried beneath layers of rock, soil, and debris, a process that Karul suggests is evidence of a systematic decommissioning process. In his words:

> *The burial of buildings is somewhat comparable to that of human burials, signifying the strength of the meaning attached to the building.* . . . Considering the labor and time required for the construction of such structures, they must have held great meaning for Neolithic societies.[8] (Original author's emphasis.)

The structures thus seem to have been treated as living entities inhabited in the same way that, in many cultures, a person's physical body is seen to be animated by a nonphysical force or spirit. As such, these enclosures had to be treated with due respect even after they had completed their useful life. They were therefore ritually "killed" and afterward "buried" in a manner befitting a human being.

ADDITIONAL ENCLOSURES

Beyond these three enigmatic structures—the Great Ellipse, the Pillars Shrine, and the Pit Shrine—other enclosures have also been discovered. Aside from the

Fig. 3.6. Karahan Tepe's Structure AC, partly covered over for protection.
Photo by Andrew Collins.

extraordinary new enclosure exposed on the top of the hill that was introduced in chapter 1, we have Structure AC, a more basic feature, round in shape, cut out of the sloping bedrock a little way to the east of the Pit Shrine. It was found buried beneath tons of rubble, perhaps as part of a decommissioning process similar to the shrines already described (see fig. 3.6). At its southern end is a rock-cut bench that was clearly meant for those inside to gaze out toward the northern and northeastern horizon.

On the southern side of the three interconnected structures are several more enclosures built into the hillside. These appear similar in design to features at Göbekli Tepe that are thought to date to the Early Pre-Pottery Neolithic B period (thus circa 8800–8000 BCE). Each contains pairs of T-pillars ranging in height from 4.5 feet to approximately 10 feet (1.4 meters to 3 meters). Some of the pillars display anthropomorphic features, including articulated arms terminating in hands with fingers that curl around on to their front narrow edges. Above these hands are parallel vertical lines signifying garment hems and basic, V-shaped "neckties," similar to those seen on T-pillars at other early Neolithic sites in the region.

Curiously, the number of fingers shown on pillars at Karahan Tepe can vary. For instance, one fair-sized T-pillar in Structure AH, located at the extreme southern end of the current excavations, has eight digits. Why it would have eight fingers is unclear. Did this number have symbolic meaning to the local community, or was it purely a case of idiosyncratic workmanship on the part of the stone carver? There are no clear answers at present (see plate 13).

The side of the T-pillar showing eight fingers in Structure AH is also quite curious. It shows the figure's articulated arm and shoulder in high relief, although they have been executed to suggest that the shoulder is a bird head, almost certainly that of a vulture. With the vulture statue unearthed in the new enclosure on top of the hill, it becomes clear that, like the leopard and the snake, this particular species of bird was an important totem at the site.

To date, just 5 percent of Karahan Tepe's prehistoric settlement has been excavated, meaning that dozens, or even hundreds, of stone enclosures still await discovery beneath its deep layers of soil and rubble. Uncovering these will be crucial in helping us better understand not only what was going on there as much as 11,500 years ago, but also perhaps who its builders might have been.

Necmi Karul and his excavation team have their work cut out at Karahan Tepe for many years to come. Indeed, it might even take multiple generations of archaeological exploration to fully expose what is there, and that's not taking into account the many other T-pillar sites in the same region that are also now under investigation, one of which has been crucial in uncovering knowledge of this quite extraordinary prehistoric society that thrived as much as 11,500 years ago. This is Göbekli Tepe, and it will be necessary to factor in the discoveries made there across the past three decades to better understand the genesis of Anatolia's Pre-Pottery Neolithic revolution, and through it the emergence of Karahan Tepe.

4

It Began with Göbekli Tepe

Göbekli Tepe, located within Asiatic Turkey's Şanlıurfa province, is one of the most important archaeological sites in the world. Situated on top of an exposed mountain ridge 2,490 feet (760 meters) above sea level at the southern reaches of the Anti-Taurus mountain range, it is a vast complex of stone enclosures built approximately 9600–8000 BCE.

Some of its most important structures, which also just happen to be its oldest, are composed of elliptical rings of T-shaped pillars, many as much as 6.5 feet (2 meters) to 10 feet (3 meters) in height. Between these are usually stone benches on which participants in ceremonies and rituals would presumably have sat.

Göbekli Tepe's T-pillars are placed like spokes of a wheel to face two much larger T-shaped monoliths positioned side by side at the center of the enclosures (see fig. 4.1). Many display relief carvings and even three-dimensional sculptures of strange creatures of the prehistoric world. Among them are representations of mammals (boars, foxes, bovines, sheep, goats, and large felines), birds (vultures, waders, and at least one flightless species), insects (ants, arachnids, and scorpions), as well as numerous depictions of snakes, some with triangular heads, others with more rounded heads.

Additionally, some of the stones display anthropomorphic features on their stems, including articulated arms that begin with stylized shoulder sockets. These end in hands with long spindly fingers that curl around onto the stone's front narrow edges. Above these hands are, occasionally, twin vertical lines signifying the hems of hanging garments, perhaps an open robe or cloak of some kind. Above these are V-shaped necklaces, at the base of which are sometimes carved glyphs that arguably signify emblems of office or affiliations to a particular clan

Fig. 4.1. Göbekli Tepe's Enclosure C, showing the remains of its
two central T-Pillars. Photo by Andrew Collins.

or tribal alliance. These, like many of the other features seen on these stones, are also present on the T-pillars at Karahan Tepe.

One of the monoliths at Göbekli Tepe—Pillar 18 in Enclosure 18—sports a wide belt festooned with curious glyphs. These consist of what appear to be abstract crescent moons and also a symbol like the letter *H* on its side. The same glyphs occur on pillars elsewhere in the enclosures, which constitute the southeastern depression of the tepe—or occupational mound—which occupies an area measuring around 24.7 acres (10 hectares).

HILL OF THE NAVEL

The word *tepe* in Turkish means "hill," while *göbek*, the root behind *göbekli*, means "navel," implying, visually at least, that the mound looks like a pregnant belly. Göbekli Tepe's name is usually interpreted as meaning "hill (*tepe*) of the navel (*göbek*)," a reference not only to its belly-like appearance, but also to the fact that, to indigenous Kurdish peoples of the region, the site has always been seen as a place of great sanctity.

Fig. 4.2. Göbekli Tepe's Enclosure D's twin central monoliths (from left to right, Pillars 31 and 18). Photo by Andrew Collins.

Both Pillar 18 and its neighbor Pillar 31, which stand side by side at the center of Enclosure D (see fig. 4.2), display carved fox pelt loincloths seen hanging from the wide belts that encircle their stems. The two monoliths constitute the largest (and the oldest) pillars so far discovered at the site, being as much as 18.5 feet (5.5 meters) in height and an estimated 11 U.S. tons (15 metric tonnes) apiece in weight. Both were placed upright in rectangular slots located within rock-cut pedestals sculpted out of the structure's level stone floor.

Carved Human Forms

Almost certainly, the T-shaped terminations of the standing pillars at Göbekli Tepe, Karahan Tepe, and several other similar sites across the Şanlıurfa region (see chapter 6) were meant to represent human heads, their rear extensions being either elongated craniums and/or long dreads tied into a bun, while the protruding extensions at the front probably signified pronounced brow ridges and heavy jawlines.* Who these carved human figures represent is open

---

*Interestingly, some pillars found in 2021 at a village named Sayburç, just west of Şanlıurfa, only have extensions at their rear and not at their front, indicating that they could indeed represent elongated heads (personal observation by the author in December 2022).

to debate. Perhaps they expressed the presence, and continuing influence, of great ancestors, most notably the spiritual founders behind the emergence of the advanced culture responsible for the creation of these enigmatic stone monuments.

Technological Sophistication

The stone structures found at Göbekli Tepe make it clear that its faceless founders, who thrived during an age of human development known to archaeologists as the Pre-Pottery Neolithic (9600–6500 BCE), must have been immensely sophisticated. (See fig. 4.3 for a full breakdown of the prehistoric periods of Anatolia featured in this book.) This is evidenced, for instance, in the fact that the oldest structure uncovered so far, Enclosure D, also happens to be the most impressive.

Geological age	Archaeological period	Dates	Some primary sites mentioned in text
Pleistocene	Upper Paleolithic	43,000–9600 BCE	
	Epipalaeolithic	12,000–9600 BCE	Hallan Çemi, Kortek Tepe, Guzir Höyük
Holocene	Pre-Pottery Neolithic A	9600–8800 BCE	Göbekli Tepe, Karahan Tepe, Çayönü, Helwan
	Pre-Pottery Neolithic B	8800–6500 BCE	Nevalı Çori, Aşıklı Höyük, Jericho
	Pottery Neolithic Age	6500–5500 BCE	Çatal Höyük
	Halaf culture	6500–5500 BCE	Tell Brak, Tell Arpachiyah, Tell Halaf
	Ubaid culture	5500–3800 BCE	Uruk (Erech), Eridu I
	Copper Age (Uruk)	4000–2900 BCE	Uruk, Ebla,
	Sumerian civilization	2900–2000 BCE	Uruk, Lagash, Ur, Eridu
	Old Babylonian period	1894–1595 BCE	
	Kassite period	1595–1155 BCE	

Fig. 4.3. Breakdown of dates featured in this book, from the Paleolithic Age to the foundation of the earliest city-states of Mesopotamia.

Built circa 9745–9314 BCE,[1] Enclosure D is approximately 65 feet (20 meters) in size, elliptical in shape, with 12 carved T-pillars set into its perimeter wall that have stone benches placed between them (again, a feature we now also find within the structures being uncovered at Karahan Tepe). The existence of this enclosure tells us that the advanced engineering capability available to the earliest inhabitants of Göbekli Tepe must have extended back long before its epoch of construction.

Some archaeologists suggest that earlier, more basic structures, will eventually be found beneath the site's immense layer cake of human occupation. Since less than 5 percent of the site has been excavated to date, this might well prove to be correct.

In addition to the immense sophistication displayed in the building construction at Göbekli Tepe, there exists compelling evidence of precision geometry. At least four installations—B, C, D, and H—incorporate a 4:3 ratio in their overall design (see fig. 8.1, p. 63).[2] From the age of Pythagoras in the sixth century BCE onward, such whole number ratios have been associated with the creation of musical intervals, which refers to the combination of two different notes to produce a perfect pitch. The fact that such proportions defined the shape of enclosures at Göbekli Tepe suggests they were built with acoustic considerations in mind, a matter examined in chapter 7. In other words, the builders purposely enhanced the installations' acoustic properties to maximize the human experience during ritual performances.

COSMIC HARMONY

Beyond this is the extraordinary realization that the cross axis of all the main enclosures at Göbekli Tepe (based on the mean orientation of their two central monoliths) could well have been astronomical in nature. Each installation faces north-northwest toward the setting of Deneb (see fig. 4.4), the brightest star in the constellation of Cygnus, the celestial bird.[3] Why? The answer seems to be because Deneb highlights the northern entrance to the Milky Way's Dark Rift, otherwise known as the Great Rift or Cygnus Rift. This is a series of interconnected "dark clouds" formed by dust and debris directly in line with the galactic plane (or galactic equator). It is for this reason that the Dark Rift has long been seen as a path along which souls reach the afterlife, with the best example of this being among the Maya of Central America, for whom it was Xibalba Be, the Road to Xibalba, with Xibalba being the name given to the underworld.[4]

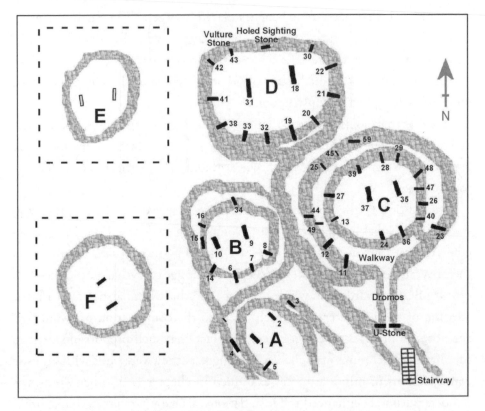

Fig. 4.4. Plan of Göbekli Tepe's main enclosures.
Diagram by Rodney Hale.

As the present author discusses elsewhere,[5] this apparent interest in the Milky Way implies that the peoples of Göbekli Tepe adhered to cosmological beliefs regarding the destiny of the soul that were once widespread not only among the Indigenous peoples of the Americas, but also among many cultures of the Eurasian continent.[6]

In contrast, rectilinear structures built at Göbekli Tepe during its later stages—circa 8800–8000 BCE, a time frame corresponding to the early part of what is known as the Pre-Pottery Neolithic B period—appear to have been oriented toward the first appearance of the sun at important turning points in the calendar year. Enclosure F, for instance, is aligned to the midsummer solstice sunrise, while the Lion Pillars Building is aligned east-west.[7] This means it targets the rising of the sun at the time of the equinoxes, with these being the 2 days in the year when day and night are of equal length.[8] Why, then, should there have been this switch from stellar alignments to solar orientations at Göbekli Tepe?

The answer to this question is that by around 8500–8000 BCE, prehistoric peoples in both Anatolia and the Near East were transforming from a hunter-gatherer existence into more sedentary lifestyles. No longer would their main source of sustenance be wild game caught during hunting expeditions. Instead meat would be procured through the domestication of animals such as sheep, goat, and wild cattle, along with the cultivation of cereal crops, including wheat and barley. This allowed the production of beer and food products, which could sustain entire communities. Evidence of this is the presence of large stone vats found in many of the younger, cell-like structures at Göbekli Tepe, which were used for beer fermentation.[9] Similar stone bowls have been found at Karahan Tepe, and these too were likely used to brew or contain beer.

Growing cereals, as well as legumes and flax, required adherence to specific growing seasons determined by the annual cycle of the sun. Aligning special buildings to the first appearance of the solar orb therefore became a higher priority. This was especially so in the knowledge that stars appearing where the sun rose or set at the equinoxes or solstices could be used to signal important stages in the agricultural calendar.

As the centuries rolled by, the structures built at Göbekli Tepe grew gradually smaller and more basic in design. Benches were still incorporated into their interior architecture, while pairs of T-pillars, now greatly reduced in size, would be inserted into walls or placed at one end. These square or rectangular structures, often positioned side by side to form an ever expanding urban environment, would be built on level ground created when older enclosures were deliberately buried beneath huge volumes of stone chippings, accumulated rubble, and human refuse. This created multiple levels of activity that ended up as enormous occupational mounds (Turkish *höyük* or *tepe* and Arabic *tell*). The one at Göbekli Tepe probably rose to a height of around 50 feet (approximately 15 meters), this being the overall height between the stone floors of various bedrock enclosures and the foundations of the uppermost, cell-like structures.

In 2021 Göbekli Tepe was formally recognized as a UNESCO World Heritage Site for its outstanding value as "one of the first manifestations of human-made monumental architecture" anywhere in the world.[10] This sealed its position not only as one of the most important archaeological sites in the world, but also as the world's first temple complex. It was in the fall of this same year, 2021, that the incredible new discoveries being made at Karahan Tepe were revealed to the world during a high profile press conference held at Şanlıurfa.[11] What this did was confirm once and for all that Göbekli Tepe was not a one-off, an anomaly in time, created by a lone group of overimaginative hunter-gatherers at the end of the last ice age. Göbekli Tepe and Karahan Tepe formed part of a highly sophisticated culture that had thrived in the region as much as 11,500 years ago. This is something I had been saying in connection with southeastern Anatolia's Pre-Pottery Neolithic culture since the publication of my book *From the Ashes of Angels* published in 1996, and in various other books since first visiting these incredible sites back in 2004.* It is a story that I again now need to tell.

---

*Göbekli Tepe would go on to feature in various of my books, including *The Cygnus Mystery* (2006), *Göbekli Tepe: Genesis of the Gods* (2014), *The Cygnus Key* (2018), and *Denisovan Origins*, co-authored with Gregory L. Little and published in 2020. A Turkish language edition of *The Cygnus Mystery* was published in Turkey in 2012 under the title *Kuğu Takımyıldızı'nın Gizemi: Yaşamın Kozmostaki Kökenlerinin Kadim Sırrı Çözülüyor.*

5

Hill of the Dark Lord

It was in June 2004, while exploring the so-called Astronomical Tower located amid the sprawling ruins of the seventh-century CE Paradise Mosque at Harran—the ancient city of the Chaldean astrologers located some 25 miles (40 kilometers) southeast of Şanlıurfa—that I first learned about Karahan Tepe.

Some entrepreneurial children seemed intent on selling me a secondhand copy of a guidebook on the city's ancient past.[1] After purchasing it, I flicked through its pages and noticed it contained a photo of a unique T-shaped pillar. Alongside this picture was a brief description of what had been found at the site in question, which was named Karahan Tepe.[2] This included the conical lower half of an anthropomorphic statue along with an incised limestone fragment showing three incised animals, a rabbit, a gazelle, and an unidentified quadruped.[3]

It was, however, the photo of the T-pillar that captivated me. Lying on its side, the stone showed on its front narrow edge in high relief a ball-headed snake with a long curling body. A measuring rod in front of the pillar implied it was around 6.5 feet (2 meters) in length.[4] The top of a second carved stone, seemingly another T-pillar, lay immediately behind it.

Karahan Tepe's T-pillar bore no obvious anthropomorphic features like those found previously at Göbekli Tepe and another site in the north of Şanlıurfa province named Nevalı Çori, although there was certainly something unique about the manner in which its snake had been carved (see fig. 5.1). With these thoughts in mind, I became determined to return to the area in an attempt to find Karahan Tepe.

At the time I was participating in a cultural festival being held at Diyarbakır, the administrative center of southeastern Turkey, following the publication in

Fig. 5.1. The first T-pillar to be found at Karahan Tepe. Note the round-headed snake on its front narrow edge, this forming the first clue as to the site's clear serpentine influence. Illustration by Andrew Collins.

2002 of the Turkish language edition of my book *From the Ashes of Angels*. The mayor of Diyarbakır had welcomed me personally on arrival in the city and by way of a thank you for all the work I had done showing that the region was almost certainly the cradle of Western civilization I was given a driver and interpreter so that I could visit some of the early Neolithic sites featured in my books. This included, of course, Göbekli Tepe, which I had inspected for the first time earlier that day.

My chance came to visit Karahan Tepe just a couple of days later, although the problem was that no one we encountered in the Tektek Mountains, close to the border with Syria, seemed to know where the site was located. Finally, after almost giving up, a man in Arabic dress working in a plowed field directed us toward a secluded farmhouse on a remote road southeast of the village of Kargalı. On arrival, a small boy emerged from the one-story building and pointed, almost without conversation, to a bare limestone hill about a third of a mile (half a kilometer) to the south. This, apparently, was Karahan Tepe.

As I approached our destination across the plowed fields, I noticed prehistoric stone tools scattered about. Their number increased exponentially the closer we got to the hill until finally they were everywhere, something I had previously noted as I had navigated the rugged terrain on my approach to Göbekli Tepe (back then there were no obvious roads to the site).

On reaching the base of Karahan Tepe's northern and eastern slopes I counted the exposed tops of as many as 30 T-pillars, their heads just about visible above ground level (see plate 14). They seemed to be scattered across an extremely wide area, showing the sheer size of the site. A few had pits dug around their heads and stems, these being dug mostly by local men looking for buried treasure.

I came across one fallen fragment of a T-shaped pillar in the valley to the east of the main hill. As I slid my hand beneath the stone to see whether it might bear any carved relief on its underside, our driver, a proud Kurd with epic moustache wearing a starched white shirt, black waistcoat, and baggy black shalvar trousers, stepped forward and turned over the heavy weight.

Doing so revealed that directly where my hand had been was a large blue scorpion, which I must have almost touched! The thought took me aback, as I realized I could have been stung and even killed by this impressive, albeit highly dangerous creature (see fig. 5.2).

On the many occasions I have been back to Karahan Tepe, I have never seen another scorpion, making this incident not only difficult to forget but also, as we shall see as this book proceeds, a curious and powerful portent regarding the importance of the scorpion in the iconography, symbolism, and suspected beliefs of the region's Pre-Pottery Neolithic culture.

Fig. 5.2. The actual blue scorpion the author encountered beneath
a fragment of T-pillar at Karahan Tepe in June 2004.
Photo by Andrew Collins.

Also at the site I noted various right-angled fragments of porthole stones just lying around. These once acted as doorframes into now lost enclosures (see plate 19 and 20), although whether they stood upright in dry stone walls or were placed overhead within sturdy wooden roofs remains a matter of debate. More complete porthole stones had already been found at Göbekli Tepe. One, for instance, can still be seen on the floor of Enclosure B. The bizarre thing about these scattered stone fragments all around Karahan Tepe was their age. Each piece was as much as 11,000 years old, and yet they were little different in style and appearance to the stone mullions found within the window frames of medieval buildings in Europe. One could quite easily be mistaken for the other.

In addition to these discoveries, an 18-foot-long (5.5-meter) unfinished T-pillar with its base still attached to the bedrock could be seen on Karahan Tepe's western slope (see plate 21), while at the hill's northern end, on an exposed rocky outcrop I refer to as the northern knoll, were dozens of carved cupules or cup marks. Each was around 5 to 8 inches (12.7 to 20 centimeters) in diameter and as much as 4 inches (10 centimeters) deep (see fig. 5.3).

Fig. 5.3. Cupules or cup marks on exposed bedrock on the top of Karahan Tepe's northern knoll. Photo by Andrew Collins.

Fig. 5.4. Two large cupules seen at the northern summit of Karahan Tepe.
Their resemblance to eyes is undeniable. (Ruler in inches.)
Photo by Andrew Collins.

Similar carved stone cupules are present at other Pre-Pottery Neolithic sites in the region including Göbekli Tepe, Hamzan Tepe,[5] and the recently discovered settlement site of Ayanlar Höyük northwest of Şanlıurfa.[6] Some at Karahan Tepe are quite large, being around 12 inches (30 centimeters) in diameter. They are placed side by side in pairs, giving the impression of rounded eyes staring out at you from within the bedrock (see fig. 5.4).

As we inspected the exposed T-pillars on the eastern side of Karahan Tepe, a tall, slim man wearing Arabic dress complete with headscarf approached us. It soon became clear he was the owner of the farm. As he entered into a heated debate with my driver and interpreter, I realized that something was wrong. He was not happy with us being there. However, all three men just crouched down, passed around cigarettes, and quickly sorted things out.

Apparently, the farmer, whose name was Mehmet Can, was the appointed guardian of Karahan Tepe. He had been told not to allow anyone on the site, under threat of severe punishment. When, however, it was explained that I was a serious student of archaeology and was there under the protectorate of the mayor of Diyarbakır, everything seemed to be okay.

Today, the sons of that same farmer are guardians of the farm. Indeed, the little boy who greeted our party back in 2004 is today an archaeological student involved in the excavations taking place at the site. His name is Ismail Can, and across the years I have come to know him, his father, and the entire family. Indeed, in 2015 I presented the household with a brand-new aluminum ladder, which is now used in the excavations. The reason that ladder was needed in the first place is explained in chapter 10.

THE NAMING OF KARAHAN TEPE

This, then, was my first introduction to Karahan Tepe. The site itself had been discovered 10 years earlier, in 1994, by archaeologist Bahattin Çelik.[7] As an expert in the region's Pre-Pottery Neolithic culture, he easily recognized the site's immense importance, having rightly concluded that somewhere beneath the hill's eastern and northern slopes was an enormous settlement comparable in size and importance to that of Göbekli Tepe. A cursory survey of the site was undertaken in 1995, and notice of its existence was publicly recorded in 1997.

Instead of using the hill's traditional name (which is discussed in chapter 10) in his official reports, Çelik chose to give it a new name. This was Karahan, using the components *kara* (black or dark) and *han* (sultan or lord), both of which were taken from nearby villages—Kara Ali to the west and Ulu Han to the east. The purpose of this change in name was, it seems, to help thwart treasure hunters from learning too quickly the whereabouts of this new archaeological farm. It didn't really work, as on various occasions local men arrived at the farm intent on removing artifacts. On one occasion they even called at the farmhouse and asked the Can family to help them carry away a heavy item to their vehicle! Thankfully, the family refused to take part in this illegal activity.

In 2000, Çelik had initiated the digging of test pits around a few of the exposed T-pillars at Karahan Tepe (which, rather amusingly, can be translated as the "Hill [*tepe*] of the Dark Lord [*kara han*]"! He wanted to see whether any of them might display carved imagery similar to that seen at Nevalı Çori and Göbekli Tepe.[8] Then in 2011, as part of the Sanlıurfa City Cultural Inventory, Çelik organized the digging of further test pits at the site.[9]

Thereafter Çelik, like me, visited Karahan Tepe on many occasions looking for further clues regarding the area's Pre-Pottery Neolithic community. His connection with the site continued through to 2018, when an archaeological team from Istanbul University under the directorship of Necmi Karul arrived to conduct a full-scale survey in advance of excavations that would begin the following year, 2019. As we have seen, these excavations have uncovered a whole host of quite remarkable stone structures.

The fruits of my own investigations at Karahan Tepe between 2004 and 2018 have been published in various articles and news bulletins, and these remain available online.[10] I did sense that one day the site would reveal secrets just as important as Göbekli Tepe, and in 2014 I had started to refer to Karahan Tepe as Göbekli Tepe's "sister site,"[11] something now adopted by journalists and researchers worldwide.[12]

With the realization of the importance of these new discoveries being made at Göbekli Tepe, Karahan Tepe, and other similar early Neolithic sites in the Şanlıurfa region, the Turkish Ministry of Culture and Tourism decided that it needed to better define the nature and achievements of this advanced prehistoric culture that had first appeared in southeastern Anatolia around 10,000 BCE. Henceforth it would be called Taş Tepeler, meaning "stone hills," a title that will need some introduction.

6

The Birth of Taş Tepeler

During a press conference held at the Şanlıurfa Archaeological Museum on September 23, 2021, to mark the opening of its new Karahantepe and Neolithic Human Exhibition, Turkey's minister of culture and tourism, Mehmet Nuri Ersoy, spoke about Karahan Tepe's place in the emerging landscape of southeastern Anatolia. On behalf of the ministry, as well as the Turkey Tourism Promotion and Development Agency, he announced the establishment of what he called "Taş Tepeler" (pronounced "tash-tepah-lar"), a project that "aims to reveal the land where the change in human history took place and a great transformation from hunter-gatherer way of living to agriculture [occurred]."[1]

As Ersoy made clear, "The Şanlıurfa region is home to the first examples of organised labour and specialisation in the history of civilization."[2] He added that in the near future excavations would be conducted at all 12 of the locations involved in this project, which, of course, included Karahan Tepe and Göbekli Tepe.

"It is believed that the finds from these excavations will make considerable and far-reaching contributions to our knowledge of humanity in prehistoric times, including their daily lives and rituals," he told the packed audience of journalists, archaeologists, dignitaries, and officials who had gathered for the launch of the Taş Tepeler Project.[3] This, he said, referred to "the beginning of the transformation of shelters into houses 12,000 years ago, and in which villages emerged, stratified society formed, and the ability to carry out basic trade developed."[4]

Taş Tepeler translates into English as "stone hills," or "stony hill country." The term relates to the manner in which this advanced culture built monuments of stone, in particular enclosures containing T-pillars. For the most part these megalithic, or "great stone," structures would come to be preserved within *tepes*, huge artificial hills seen scattered about the landscape of southeastern Anatolia.

All of these occupational mounds contain a layer cake of human activity spanning the course of many thousands of years. Some go back to the early Neolithic Age, although most of them are much younger and contain the remains of settlements that thrived during the Bronze Age and later Iron Age. Most of them have yet to be properly excavated. Those found within Şanlıurfa province, which is a vast region embracing nearly 7,200 square miles (8,600 square kilometers) and spanning a distance of approximately 130 miles (210 kilometers), have been found to contain evidence of the all-important T-pillar building culture, hence its new title of Taş Tepeler, meaning the megalithic builders of the *tepe*-hills.

THE ŞANLIURFA NEOLITHIC RESEARCH PROJECT

Minister Ersoy concluded his address to the assembled audience by proclaiming that, "In the coming days, excavations will begin in the mounds of Ayanlar, Yoğunburç, Harbetsuvan, Kurttepesi and Taşlıtepe settlements, as part of the first phase of the Şanlıurfa Neolithic Research Project which will take place between 2021–2024. Geomagnetic measurements and ground-penetrating radar measurements," he said, "have already been carried out in some of these areas. These measurements will continue in parallel with the excavations."[5]

Of the Taş Tepeler sites scheduled for excavation, one of the most exciting is Ayanlar Höyük, a huge settlement preserved within an enormous occupational mound some 12.5 miles (20 kilometers) west-northwest of downtown Şanlıurfa (see plate 22). It covers an area of 34.5 acres (14 hectares),[6] bigger even than Göbekli Tepe and Karahan Tepe, which are 24.7 acres (100 hectares) and 27 acres (11 hectares) in size, respectively.[7] Like these other two complexes, Ayanlar Höyük is thought to have been a major ceremonial center.[8]

Another site of immense potential value to our understanding of Taş Tepeler is located beneath the village of Sayburç, which lies to the south of Ayanlar Höyük. In 2021 it was realized that under one of its houses are the rock-cut foundations of an elliptical enclosure, on the north wall of which are extraordinary carvings in high relief. They include an animated human figure holding what appears to be a snake or a rattle with a large bovine advancing toward him (see plate 23) and a standing male figure holding his phallus with large felines approaching him on either side (see plate 24). The style of both the felines and the bull match those seen in carved relief on T-pillars found at Göbekli Tepe that are thought to belong to the Pre-Pottery Neolithic A period, circa 9600–8800 BCE. An archaeological team led by Eylem Özdoğan from Istanbul University is now exploring Sayburç to uncover its many secrets.[9] (See chapter 30 for a fuller review of the incredible discoveries being made right now at Sayburç.)

The Turkey Tourism Promotion and Development Agency is today using the term Taş Tepeler to signify the first appearance of the material culture responsible for the T-pillar sites (see fig. 6.1 for a map of the known Taş Tepeler sites). Their construction is now seen as having begun as early as 12,000 years ago, a time frame corresponding to the later part of the 1,200-year cold spell or mini ice age known as the Younger Dryas. This ceased quite abruptly around 9600 BCE.

Not only does 9600 BCE mark the end of a geological age known as the Pleistocene and the commencement of the current epoch known as the Holocene, but it also marks humanity's transition from the Paleolithic (or

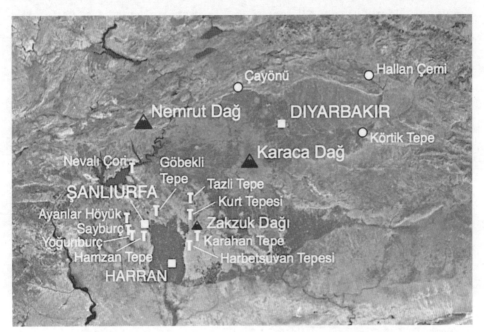

Fig. 6.1. Map showing Taş Tepeler sites featured in this book.
Each is denoted by a letter *T*. Other Epipaleolithic and Pre-Pottery Neolithic sites featured in this book are shown as circles.

"Old Stone") Age into the Neolithic (or "New Stone") Age. It also just happens to be the generally accepted date for the foundation of Göbekli Tepe, when, almost overnight, extraordinarily sophisticated stone enclosures started to be built there.

Everything about the meeting at the Şanlıurfa Archaeological Museum in September 2021, with its announcement about the formation of the Şanlıurfa Neolithic Research Project, spoke of the seriousness now being afforded the highly advanced and clearly innovative culture that came to occupy the region during the final stages of the Younger Dryas.

SIBERIAN ORIGINS

The ethnic and geographical origins of the Taş Tepeler cultural tradition are now the bigger questions, and this is something I have attempted to tackle in books such as *The Cygnus Key* (2018) and *Denisovan Origins* (2020), the latter co-authored with Gregory L. Little.[10] Both provide compelling evidence that although Indigenous Anatolian peoples might have been responsible for creating the Taş Tepeler sites, they were in fact descendants of human groups that came originally from the Russian steppe, their migrational journey having begun as far east as Siberia and Mongolia as much as 30,000–40,000 years ago.

This remote and extremely cold region was the birthplace of various new technologies during the Initial Upper Paleolithic, circa 40,000–45,000 years ago. These technologies were then transmitted westward by a series of human groups who were forced southward across the Caucasus Mountains into Anatolia at the height of the Younger Dryas event some 12,500–12,000 years ago.

What this did was introduce into Anatolia some of the Epipaleolithic (or terminal Upper Paleolithic) cultural traditions of the Russian steppe at a time coincident with the first appearance of a number of important early Pre-Pottery Neolithic sites on the Upper Tigris River, bordered by Diyarbakır in the west and Lake Van in the east.

Some of these archaeological sites, which date back to the Epipaleolithic Age, circa 10,000 BCE, have been found to contain features similar to those seen at later Taş Tepeler settlements including Göbekli Tepe, Ayanlar Höyük, Karahan Tepe, and nearby Sefer Tepe. They include the presence of beautifully carved stone vessels, which were probably manufactured at Kortik Tepe, an early Pre-Pottery Neolithic site located southwest of Batman in

Diyarbakır province. It would seem to have been a center for the production of decorated stone vessels, many of which are on display today in Diyarbakır's Archaeological Museum.

Another similarly aged site in the Upper Tigris basin is Boncuklu Tarla, located in the Dargeçit district of Mardin province, which has revealed levels of occupation dating from the Late Epipalaeolithic Age to the Late Pre-Pottery Neolithic B period (thus circa 10,000 BCE to approximately 6600 BCE). During excavations carried out there in 2012 under the auspices of the Mardin Museum and then later in 2017 by Ergül Kodaş of the University of Mardin, cult structures were exposed that are thought to be older than Göbekli Tepe.[11]

Within the interior of one of these enclosures at Boncuklu Tarla are the remains of two rectangular pillars made of stacked rocks, while in another a circular porthole stone is placed upright in its retaining wall. Such discoveries have led to comparisons with the more sophisticated stone enclosures containing T-pillars at Taş Tepeler sites found further west in Şanlıurfa province. Did the founders of Taş Tepeler really come from sites located as far east as Lake Van, whose own origins would appear to be linked with Epipaleolithic cultures that thrived far to the north on the Russian steppe?

A PAPER TRAIL OF TOOLS

Among the incoming technologies carried into eastern and southeastern Anatolia by Epipaleolithic groups living on the Russian steppe was the manufacture of multifaceted stone tools known as microblades. These are created by prizing long slivers of raw material from a prepared core using a specialized process known as pressure flaking. Its presence among Upper Paleolithic human societies becomes a signature marker that can be recorded moving gradually westward, almost like a paper trail, from its point of origin in the Altai Mountains of Siberia and farther east in Mongolia all the way along the entire length of the Russian steppe into eastern Europe and southwestern Asia. For this reason, we know that what was going on in eastern Anatolia around 12,000 years ago was the culmination of a migrational journey that had begun as much as 30,000–40,000 years ago at Upper Paleolithic sites in northern Mongolia, such as those currently under investigation at Tolbor, just south of the huge inland sea known today as Lake Baikal.

THE SIBERIA-GÖBEKLI TEPE HYPOTHESIS

As far-fetched as these theories might at first seem, some Turkish archaeologists are today looking at these same ideas regarding the ethnic and geographical origins of Anatolia's Pre-Pottery Neolithic culture. At an important archaeological congress held at Istanbul in June 2022, Semih Güneri, a retired professor from the Caucasian and Central Asian Archaeology Research Center of Dokuz Eylül University, and his colleague, Professor Ekaterine Lipnina, presented what they are calling the Siberia-Göbeklitepe hypothesis.[12] This proposes that the prime movers behind the emergence of Göbekli Tepe's advanced culture were the descendants of human groups who had begun their migrational journey in Siberia as much as 30,000 years ago.

"The relationship of Göbeklitepe high culture with the carriers of Siberian microblade stone tool technology is no longer a secret,"[13] Güneri told the assembled audience, meaning that the origins of Anatolia's Taş Tepeler culture can be traced back to key Upper Paleolithic sites in Siberia, as well as in northern Mongolia, south of Lake Baikal, as much as 30,000 years ago.

Paleogenetics can also now help back up these theories, Güneri stated, pointing out that: "The results of the genetic analyzes of Iraq's Zagros region confirm the traces of the Siberian/North Asian indigenous people, who arrived at Zagros via the Central Asian mountainous corridor and met with the Göbeklitepe culture via Northern Iraq."[14] For him, "The upper paleolithic migrations between Siberia and the Near East is a process that has been confirmed by material culture documents."[15]

What Güneri is implying is that a clearly recognizable migration of microblade tool technologies from Siberia and Mongolia westward into southwestern Asia took place between approximately 30,000 years ago and 12,000 years ago, the latter date corresponding with the emergence of Taş Tepeler in southeastern Anatolia.

On the matter of how exactly these technologies were transmitted to Anatolia across a distance of some 4,350 miles (7,000 kilometers), Güneri is more cautious, stating only that, "It is not clear whether this technology is transmitted directly to long distances by people speaking the Turkish language at the earliest, or it travels this long-distance through using way stations."[16]

In *Göbekli Tepe: Genesis of the Gods* (2014), I proposed that the migration of these stone tool technologies from the Russian steppe down into Anatolia was achieved via a series of carrier cultures of extraordinary capability. They were able to cover vast distances trading both exotic raw materials and also finished blade products between different human populations from the Ural Mountains in the east all the way across to the Carpathian Mountains of eastern Europe in the west.[17]

Evidence for the southward spread of these microblade technologies during the Younger Dryas period has been confirmed as far south as the Caucasus Mountains in what is today Georgia.[18] From there this same tool-making process entered Anatolia, most probably via the Armenian Highlands, with its influence spreading to some of the earliest Pre-Pottery Neolithic sites to emerge on the Upper Tigris River.*

Güneri and his colleagues believe that this precision-tool-making process that began its journey as early as 30,000 years ago entered Anatolia via the Zagros Mountains to the east of the country, this being slightly different from my own proposal that they entered Anatolia from the north via the Caucasus Mountains. Neither theory is likely to be incorrect, for migrations into the country would have come in waves, some entering Anatolia from the east with others coming down from the north.†

FROM ANATOLIA TO EGYPT VIA THE LEVANT

This is not to say that other influences might not have been involved in the emergence of Anatolia's Taş Tepeler culture. In *The Cygnus Key* (2018) I show that trading in stone tool technologies between Anatolia in the north and sites like Helwan in what is northern Egypt today will have brought the Upper Paleolithic cultures of the Levant, most obviously the Natufians and Harifians, into contact with the forerunners of the Taş Tepeler culture. This means that

---

*It should be pointed out that on more than one occasion Klaus Schmidt, the discoverer of Göbekli Tepe, hinted that in his opinion those responsible for the creation of what we now see in terms of the Taş Tepeler Project were linked with the Epipaleolithic cultural tradition north of the Black Sea, most obviously that which thrived in Crimea. He also compared the hunting activities of southeastern Anatolia's Pre-Pottery Neolithic culture with those of the Swiderian cultural tradition of eastern Europe. For the full story, see Collins 2014a, 166, 219–20.

†Güneri and his colleagues' breakthrough paper on their findings regarding the Siberian origins of Göbekli Tepe's Pre-Pottery Neolithic culture was published in August 2022 (see Güneri, Avcı, and Bayburt 2022).

the Indigenous peoples of the Levant might themselves have contributed to the emergence of monumental architecture at Pre-Pottery Neolithic sites in southeastern Anatolia.[19] The appearance of monumental architecture at similarly aged sites in the Levant—like Jericho in the Palestinian West Bank and Beidha in southern Jordan—is undoubtedly related to what was going on in the northern part of what archaeologists refer to as the Fertile Crescent, in other words southeastern Anatolia, where animal husbandry and cereal cultivation are known to have begun as much as 10,500 years ago, and arguably even earlier (a matter explored in chapter 35).[20]

At Jericho, for instance, an incoming Pre-Pottery Neolithic community transformed an existing Natufian settlement into a massive 10-acre (4-hectare) town complex, which dates to circa 8500 7000 BCE. The entire occupational mound there known today as Tell es-Sultan was enclosed within a stone wall 10 feet (3 meters) thick and 13 feet (4 meters) high that is nearly half a mile (800 meters) in length. Beyond this a gigantic ditch was cut into the limestone bedrock that is 9 feet (2.75 meters) deep and 27 feet (8 meters) wide. This, too, extended for roughly half a mile, prompting one British archaeologist to describe it as "a considerable feat in the absence of metal tools."[21] Jericho's inhabitants also constructed an enormous stone tower 33 feet (10 meters) in diameter and 28 feet (8.5 meters) high, accessed through a west-facing doorway that connected with an internal stone staircase of 22 steps.

The reason for mentioning Neolithic Jericho's engineering achievements is that they bear similarities to the manner in which the rock-cut enclosures, particularly Structure AD (the Great Ellipse), were carved out of the bedrock at Karahan Tepe, suggesting communication between the two regions. As we see in chapter 22 and in the appendix, the fact that both Jericho and Karahan Tepe would seem to have employed the use of astronomical alignments toward the sun at the time of the summer solstice only strengthens the connection between the two regions.

These then are the most up-to-date theories regarding the origins of the Taş Tepeler culture responsible for the construction of Anatolia's unique Pre-Pottery Neolithic complexes. So how then does Karahan Tepe fit into this emerging picture? Were its builders truly descendants of Upper Paleolithic peoples who had come all the way from Siberia or Mongolia? How old was the site really, and how long had it been functional before closing up shop to await its rediscovery in the modern era?

DATING KARAHAN TEPE

Bahattin Çelik, in a paper from 2014 summarizing what was known about the various T-pillar sites discovered in the Şanlıurfa region, wrote that based on the size of the pillars and the type of tools found at Karahan Tepe the settlement there was arguably the same age as the Layer II activity at Göbekli Tepe, these being located above the much older Layer III structures constructed on the bedrock as early as 9600 BCE. (Layer I there simply refers to surface finds from more recent periods of history.) Thus, in his opinion, Karahan Tepe "should be dated as late PPNA and early PPNB,"[22] a time frame corresponding to circa 9100–8800 BCE. From the large quantities of stone tools found at the site, it seems clear the settlement continued to thrive through to the middle of the Pre-Pottery Neolithic B period; thus, circa 8000 BCE. It is possible there was later activity there since Necmi Karul's team found fragments of pottery in the fill used to deliberately bury both Structure AB (the Pillars Shrine) and Structure AA (the Pit Shrine).[23]

According to our current knowledge, the earliest pottery in the region dates to circa 7500–7000 BCE, so this must in turn define Karahan Tepe's earliest possible time of abandonment. Prior to the discovery of these pottery sherds, Çelik spoke of Karahan Tepe as a "single period settlement only—that is to say, in the Pre-Pottery Neolithic period."[24] This then is why so much human debris from the Neolithic Age, and only from the Neolithic Age, lay strewn about the surface of the site when first discovered in the mid-1990s.

Everything about Karahan Tepe so far, from its rock-cut architecture to its T-pillars and carved statues (plates 15 and 16) and exquisite stone bowls and platters (plates 17 and 18), suggests that it flourished during the later stages of the Pre-Pottery Neolithic A phase of the Taş Tepeler culture, thus circa 9100–8800 BCE, a fact confirmed by Karul in an important paper on Karahan Tepe published in 2021.[25]

Having made this statement in one news interview Karul said that Karahan Tepe *could* have been built circa 9400–9200 BCE, a little earlier than the time frame offered by both him and Çelik in published reports.[26] Karul, of course, has the advantage of seeing firsthand everything being found during excavations there. In the same news story, however, Karul goes on to admit that the settlement could be much *younger* than we think or, alternately, it could be much *older* than has been assumed.[27]

So until a full range of radiocarbon dates for the site is released into the public domain, we will assume that its extraordinary rock-cut architecture was created toward the end of the tenth millennium BCE, an important point to remember as we now move forward to determine what might have been going on there at this time.

PART 2

SOUND AND RITUAL

7

The Mysteries of the Great Ellipse

Gazing down at the overhead images of Karahan Tepe's Structure AD that were released into the public domain when news of the excavations there was first made known in the fall of 2021, I could not help but notice that it was almost perfectly elliptical in shape, the reason why I started referring to it as the Great Ellipse. The whole design of the enclosure with its carved buttresses and thrones, its stone benches, its multiple T-shaped pillars, and its thick retaining wall all seemed specifically placed to enhance its geometric design.

Several years earlier I had determined that similar geometrical principles had gone into the design of almost all the larger enclosures at Göbekli Tepe. Working alongside British chartered engineer Rodney Hale, I was able to determine that at least four of its key installations—Enclosures B, C, D, and H— bore the form of an ellipse with a 4:3 whole number ratio; in other words, if the structure's long axis constituted four units of measurement, then its cross axis, perpendicular to the long axis, constituted three units of the same measure (see fig. 7.1). These findings were detailed in my book *The Cygnus Key*, published in 2018.[1]

Similar whole number ratios also appear to be behind the measurements of a Layer II structure at Göbekli Tepe known as the Lion Pillars Building, built circa 8500 BCE,[2] this being rectangular in design and oriented precisely east-west. Having looked at its overall dimensions, I determined that its length constituted four units of measure while its width was almost precisely three units of measure. Why then might the builders of Göbekli Tepe have wanted to incorporate whole number ratios into the design of their stone enclosures?

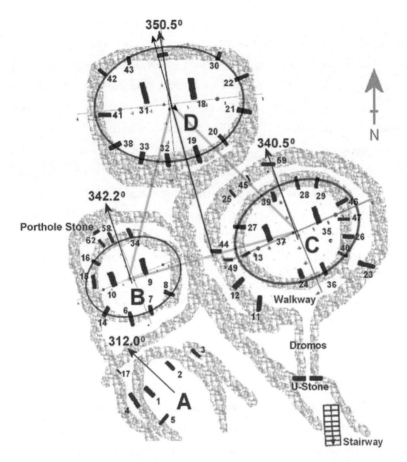

Fig. 7.1. Plan of Göbekli Tepe's main enclosures showing the apparently deliberate 4:3 whole number ratio in their design. The equilateral triangle linking the centers of Enclosures B, C, and D was determined by Israeli archaeologists Gil Haklay and Avi Gopher (see Haklay and Gopher 2020). Diagram by Rodney Hale.

Other than perhaps a need for harmonious symmetry or aesthetic beauty, the presence of whole number ratios in the creation of such structures, whether elliptical or rectilinear in shape, could very well relate to the enhancement of their inherent acoustic properties. This would be for the purposes of better carrying the human voice during ritualistic or ceremonial activities taking place inside them. Such ratios are critical in creating harmonious musical intervals. These are the combining of two separate but proportionally related notes to produce a pitch-perfect harmony. Pythagoras explored this concept and created harmonious sounds by combining whole number ratios in the lengths of strung cords or the weights of striking hammers that would afterward become important in the design of musical instruments as well as the construction of buildings used for public performances. A ratio of 4:3 was particularly favored as this produced what is known as the perfect fourth, a medieval term describing the combination of a fourth, fifth, and octave in the musical scale to produce a unified sound or musical interval that is considered "perfect."

Not only does a 4:3 ratio appear in connection with the design of elliptical enclosures at Göbekli Tepe, but it can also be traced in the construction of megalithic monuments in southern Britain, most notably the 5,700-year-old Neolithic long barrow at West Kennet in southwestern England. The work of acoustics expert Steve Marshall has adequately shown that the appearance of a 4:3 ratio in the dimensions of side chambers within the monument generated specific sound frequencies.[3]

Hale himself found a 4:3 ratio in the dimensions of the House of the Auroch Skulls, a cult building uncovered during the 1990s at the 11,000-year-old Pre-Pottery Neolithic site of Jerf el-Ahmar in northern Syria. Another communal building, rectangular in shape, found within the Neolithic ruins of Tell es-Sultan (ancient Jericho) in the Palestinian West Bank was also found to have a near-perfect 4:3 ratio incorporated into its design.[4]

Whether or not whole number ratios such as 4:3 were routinely used to enhance the acoustic properties of ancient building structures is unclear. What we do know, however, is that a 4:3 ratio is still recommended today in the design of buildings to enhance acoustic capabilities.[5]

With this knowledge there seems good reason to suspect that whole number ratios were indeed used in the construction of enclosures at Göbekli Tepe to maximize the sound quality available in buildings where ritual or ceremonial performances were to take place. Studies conducted at the site have also determined that key structures such as Enclosures C and D were specifically designed to enhance the creation of sound.[6]

With all this in mind, I wondered whether the layout of Karahan Tepe's Structure AD might itself reveal the presence of whole number ratios in its construction. Measurements were taken, and after determining these in terms of whole number units, a certain realization became clear. The enclosure's long axis, which is aligned approximately east-west, could be divided into six units, with the structure's roughly north-south cross axis being around five units of the same measure.

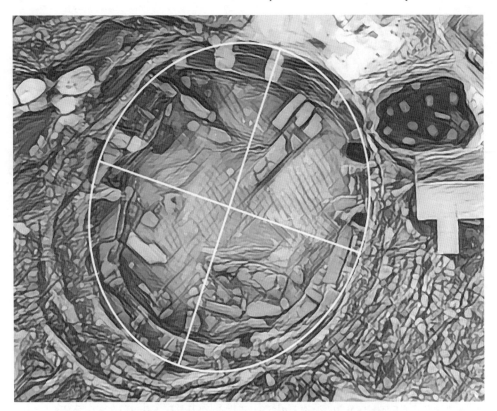

Fig. 7.2. Plan of Karahan Tepe's Structure AD (the Great Ellipse)
showing the 32:27 whole number ratio in its design.
Diagram by Andrew Collins and Rodney Hale.

In musical terms 6:5 corresponds to what is known as a minor third, which in Pythagorean tuning corresponds with a whole number ratio of 32:27. On learning this I tried to apply this much older ratio to the dimensions of Karahan Tepe's Great Ellipse and found it to be an even better match than a 6:5 ratio (see fig. 7.2).

Minor third intervals are known to have featured in the tuning of ancient Chinese zhong bells, which have been found extensively, usually in sets, within tombs across the country. Studies by Chinese musicologists have found that in almost every case, individual bells, which are made of bronze and can be anything between 2,000 and 3,600 years old, have exactly the same property: they display two tones, a major third and a minor third (a major third uses a 5:4 whole number ratio). The bells, which are clapperless and were struck using a type of mallet, were even determined to have marks on the side so that percussionists would know where to strike them to produce the two tones, making it clear they are really two bells in one.[7] The melodies produced by zhong bells were used both for ritual purposes and for entertainment.

The reason for stating these facts regarding Chinese zhong bells is to show the importance a minor third is known to have played in ancient ritual practices. Having said this, it seems doubtful that those taking part in rituals and ceremonies inside Karahan Tepe's Great Ellipse at the height of its use would have possessed similar bells. More likely, the creation of sound there would have involved chanting, singing, intoning, and pronouncements, all of which might have been maximized by the building's elliptical design.

This does not mean that instruments were not used at Karahan Tepe, even though to date none have been found. Quite likely, the inhabitants would have used rocks and stones holding what is known as sonorous or lithophonic properties in that they "sing" when struck. Hitting such stones in unison, or perhaps in specific sequences, would have created a mesmerizing wall of sound guaranteed to affect human consciousness, especially if the ritual was conducted under firelight at night.

On the bare, rocky hills surrounding Karahan Tepe are calcareous metamorphic rocks that when struck do indeed emit a high-pitched sound, making them perfect for use as lithophones. A good example of this type of rock being used at the site is a large, multifaceted stone block presently lying just beyond the eastern edge of the Great Ellipse (see fig. 7.3). When tapped it produces a perfect ringing noise.

Can we thus imagine celebrants inside the Great Ellipse sitting either on the stone benches or on the carved thrones at its western end using natural lithophones picked up in the local landscape to produce a wall of sound during rituals and ceremonies? Was this sound enhanced through the incorporation into the building's design of measurements featuring a whole number ratio of 32:27, synonymous with the Pythagorean minor third?

Sound produced in this manner would have been carried around the enclosure to create not only a swirling cacophony of noise but also quite possibly a standing wave in line with the enclosure's long axis. The reflective qualities of an ellipse mean that sound created at one end can be reflected by the structure's curved perimeter to then recombine at its opposite end and vice versa. What this means is that anyone standing in the center of the enclosure is going to be bombarded with identical sounds coming at them from two different directions at the same time.

Fig. 7.3. Large stone block on the east side of Karahan Tepe's
Structure AD (the Great Ellipse) that when struck emits a ringing sound.
Photo by Andrew Collins.

Sound bombardment on this level would surely have helped induce an altered state of consciousness in any supplicant chosen to take part in a ritual journey involving all three interconnected structures. What might have happened when this took place is something discussed in due course. More important is to examine what impact a 32:27 whole number ratio incorporated into the design of the Great Ellipse might have had on its relationship with the site's other bedrock structures.

8

Aligning with the Stars

During the fall of 2021 I examined the newly released overhead plan of Karahan Tepe's Great Ellipse (Structure AD) and attempted to determine the directional orientation of its cross axis. This was found to be approximately 10 degrees east of north or, alternately, 10 degrees west of south. At its southern termination, this axis line perfectly targets the central area of a rectangular recess, vertical in appearance, located between two pillars, while at its northern end it exactly bisects a long stone bench clearly being used as an altar (see fig. 8.1). This is made up of a horizontal T-shaped pillar in secondary use. Carved onto its front narrow edge is a leopard skin pelt seen below the waistline of the individual represented by the stone, adding weight to the importance of the leopard to the inhabitants of the site.

In the middle of the aforementioned recess is a small niche where an important carved statue was found placed upside down. This can be seen today in the Şanlıurfa Archaeological Museum (see fig. 8.2 on page 64 and plate 25).

The enclosure's long axis—perpendicular, of course, to its cross axis—is oriented 10 degrees north of west in one direction and 10 degrees south of east in the other direction. At its western end it targets the most central of the rock-cut buttresses cut into the slopes of the hill, while its eastern termination corresponds with a break in the structure's perimeter wall (see fig. 8.3, p. 65). This break, marked by a hole in the ground, is where archaeologists suspect there was an entrance into the installation. Since the western termination of the structure's long axis faces the inclined slope of the hill it seems clear that its true orientation was in the opposite direction toward the hills located a short distance to the east of the site; the two being divided by a wide valley basin now thought to contain a number of currently unexcavated stone enclosures.

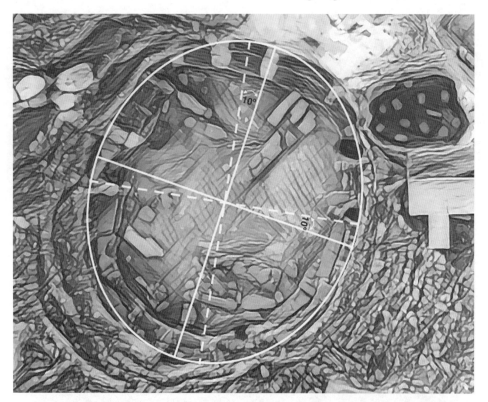

Fig. 8.1. Overhead image of Karahan Tepe's Structure AD (the Great Ellipse) showing its 32:27 elliptical shape and cross axes with the cardinal directions marked as broken lines. This indicates that the structure's axis is 10 degrees east of north or, alternately, 10 degrees west of south. Illustration by Andrew Collins.

This exercise in defining the cross axis and long axis of Structure AD will become of major importance in our understanding of the Great Ellipse's suspected function at the height of its use. That said, certain problems arise from these findings. For instance, the former positions of the twin pillars at the center of the installation, as defined by the slots in the ground in which they once stood, do not seem to correspond with the structure's tight elliptical geometry. In their standing positions they would have been around 4.5 degrees askew of the ellipse's cross axis. Although, as we see in chapter 22, it is a matter that can be resolved when we come to explore the significance of the site's solar alignments.

Further confirmation, however, of the orientation of the enclosure's two axes comes from the fact that the neighboring Pillars Shrine (Structure AB) is aligned perfectly toward the center of the southern recess where the Great Ellipse's cross axis ends (see fig. 8.4, p. 65). This line of orientation

Fig. 8.2. The recess located at the southern end of Structure AD's proposed cross axis. Note the recess in its rear wall where an important carved statue was found during excavations. This is on display today in the Şanlıurfa Archaeological Museum (see inset). Photo by Andrew Collins.

Fig. 8.3. The buttresses and thrones cut into the bedrock at the western end of Karahan Tepe's Structure AD. Photo by Andrew Collins.

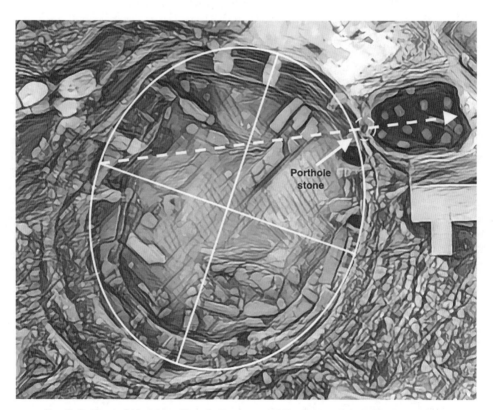

Porthole stone

Fig. 8.4. Plan of Karahan Tepe's Structure AD showing the alignment from the start of its cross axis in its southern recess through the center of Structure AB (the Pillars Shrine). Illustration by Andrew Collins.

enters the Pillars Shrine via its rectangular porthole window, and once inside the room runs centrally through it parallel with the four tall phallic pillars on its western side. In addition to this, the line targets the centrally positioned curved pillar that stands right in front of the room's northern wall.

Since I had already determined that this crescent-shaped slab likely represented the shrine's *genius loci*, or guardian spirit, then this alignment from the southern end of the Great Ellipse's cross axis through the Pillars Shrine was quite obviously purposeful. What I also find of interest is that this line, having passed centrally through the Pillars Shrine, if continued, coincides with the path of the deep, serpent-like groove cut into the bedrock located between this structure and the neighboring Pit Shrine (Structure AA). All this helps validate not only the importance of Structure AD's elliptical design incorporating a 32:27 whole number ratio, but also the fact that its primary axis is indeed 10 degrees east of north, with its cross axis 10 degrees south of east.

My next step was to determine the angle of this suspected line of orientation running from the central area of the niche at the southern end of the Great Ellipse through the porthole into the Pillars Shine and beyond to the deep curving groove linking this structure with the neighboring Pit Shrine (Structure AA). This turned out to be approximately 20 degrees west of north or, alternately, 20 degrees east of south; in other words, 340 degrees azimuth in one direction and 160 degrees azimuth in the other. This was some 30 degrees different from the already determined cross axis of the Great Ellipse, which is around 10 degrees *east* of north.

So did this line of projection passing through the Pillars Shrine possess some special meaning to those who created these bedrock structures? The answer would appear to be yes, for if the line is continued out into the local landscape for a distance of around three quarters of a mile (just over 1 kilometer) it hits the summit of a hill known today as Keçili Tepe, with Keçili being the name of the farm on which both this hill and Karahan Tepe are located.

As early as 2014, when standing on Karahan Tepe's bare, exposed northern knoll, located immediately above the current excavations, I had noted the presence toward the north-northwest of Keçili Tepe (see plate 26). With these thoughts in mind, I had asked Rodney Hale to check the angles between the two hills to establish whether these might relate to an astronomical alignment or some kind. What he found is that the basic angles between Karahan

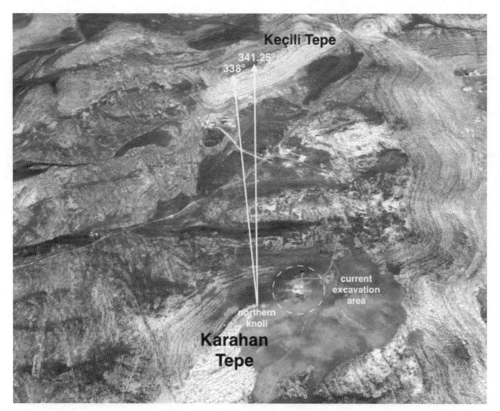

Fig. 8.5. The line of orientation between Karahan Tepe's northern knoll and nearby Keçili Tepe, showing maximum and minimum angles based on the position of the summit. Underlay image by Google Earth.

Tepe's northern knoll and the flattened summit of Keçili Tepe spanned an azimuth range between 338 degrees and 341.25 degrees (see fig. 8.5).

Hale further established that during the proposed epoch of construction at Karahan Tepe, the star Deneb in the constellation of Cygnus would have been seen to set into the summit of Keçili Tepe as viewed from Karahan's northern knoll (see fig. 8.6).

What this astronomical alignment makes clear is that Karahan Tepe's northern knoll, with its surface covered in rock-cut cupules, must itself have been important to the local community, particularly as it is located immediately above and behind the three main rock-cut enclosures uncovered during recent excavations. What is more, when standing on Karahan Tepe's northern knoll, the eye is automatically drawn north toward Keçili Tepe, the view to the south being obscured by the hill summit. This makes it certain that if the

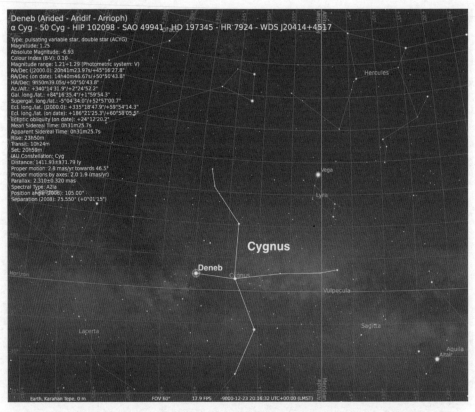

Fig. 8.6. View of the setting of the Cygnus star Deneb (α Cygni) as seen from the latitude of Karahan Tepe for a date of 9000 BCE. It would have extinguished as it reached an azimuth of around 340–341 degrees. This is the same approximate angle of the alignment between the southern recess in Structure AD and the directional orientation of Structure AB. This image was made using the Stellarium free open-source planetarium.

inhabitants of Karahan Tepe were focusing their attention on any area of the night sky then it was toward the stars and constellations circling the northern celestial pole. One such constellation was Cygnus, which would have set into the summit of Keçili Tepe only to reappear again on the north-northeastern horizon just a few hours later.

So why might an alignment toward the setting of the star Deneb have been important to the peoples of Karahan Tepe? As we see next, the answer would appear to lie not so much with the star itself but in what it marked.

9

The Place of Emergence

My research into the function of the stone enclosures at Göbekli Tepe across a period of almost two decades had determined that each of its larger installations was directed north-northwestward during the time frame of its construction. More than this, the larger installations targeted the setting of the star Deneb (α Cygni), the brightest star in the constellation of Cygnus. These ideas were proposed originally in my book *The Cygnus Mystery*, published in 2006,[1] and refined in subsequent books.[2]

Despite claims from detractors insisting that the enclosures could not have been oriented north-northwest toward Cygnus since they must have been pointing south-southeast toward the constellation of Orion[3] or, if not, toward the star Sirius[4]—claims examined and found to be completely untenable*—an independent study into potential astronomical alignments at Göbekli Tepe conducted in 2015 by two Italian mathematicians, Alessandro De Lorenzis and Vincenzo Orofino of the University of Salento in Lecce, found that the axial orientation of Enclosures B, C, and D did indeed suggest that the star Deneb was their directional target. In their opinion, "These orientations [of the enclosures at Göbekli Tepe toward the setting of Deneb] and the relative dating proposed by Collins [and Hale] . . . have been verified."[5]

With regard to the theory that the same enclosures were aligned to the rising of Sirius during the epoch of their construction, see Magli 2019. He proposes that the mean azimuths of the twin pillars in Enclosures B, C, and D targeted Sirius as it reappeared in the night skies at the latitude of Göbekli Tepe after

---

*See Collins 2014a, 78–80, for problems with the main enclosures at Göbekli Tepe being aligned to the belt stars of Orion. They simply do not match with any degree of accuracy.

being missing due to precession for around 4,500 years. However, Magli is incorrect in this respect. In 9600 BCE when the earliest enclosures were being built Sirius did not even rise above the horizon as can clearly be seen by a cursory examination of the skies during this epoch as offered by the free, open-source planetarium Stellarium. It was only many hundreds of years later that the star began to rise enough to make a brief, shallow arc across the southern sky. At such times it would have been barely visible due to the effects of atmospheric absorption and aerosol pollution making it an unlikely stellar target for the region's Taş Tepeler culture to orientate their enclosures toward. (For more on this topic see Collins 2014a, 80; Collins and Hale 2014; and Collins and Hale 2015.)

THE MILKY WAY'S DARK RIFT

Why then might the stars of Cygnus—Deneb in particular—have been so important to southeastern Anatolia's Taş Tepeler culture? The simple answer is that in astronomical terms they mark the northern entrance to what is known as the Dark Rift, also known as the Great Rift or Cygnus Rift. This is a region of dust and debris precisely in line with the galactic plane, the visible outer rim of our own Milky Way galaxy (see fig. 9.1). Its presence causes the Milky Way to look as if it has split into two separate streams, something that begins in the vicinity of the star Deneb. The Dark Rift then continues to divide the Milky Way all the way down to where the ecliptic—the path of the sun as it makes its annual course through the 12 houses of the zodiac—crosses the Milky Way in the vicinity of the constellations of Sagittarius, Ophiuchus, and Scorpius (the zodiacal constellation of Scorpio). It is directly above this last constellation that the eastern branch of the Milky Way peters out leaving its western arm to connect with the Milky Way as it enters the southern hemisphere.

The Milky Way has long been seen by Indigenous cultures worldwide as a road, river, or cosmic waterway used by souls of the departed to reach the sky world.[6] Where the Milky Way bifurcates in the region of the Cygnus constellation was generally seen as a portal or entrance to a realm that was outside of the visible universe and guarded by a sky figure. In Native American tradition, this sky figure formed part of a popular death journey known today as the Path of Souls.

According to the reports of a number of ethnographers who recorded the accounts of as many as 30 to 40 different tribal nations from the eighteenth century onward, the soul or spirit either of a deceased person or that of a sha-

Fig. 9.1. The Milky Way's Dark Rift from its northern opening at the top marked by the Cygnus star Deneb to its southern termination at the bottom in the region of the stars of Sagittarius, Ophiuchus, and Scorpius (from Trouvelot 1882, plate xiii).

man or initiate would be expected to make a leap of faith into the night sky shortly before sunrise on the morning of the winter solstice (December 21 in the current calendar). Its target was the stellar object M42 (Messier 42), otherwise known as the Orion Nebula, located in the "sword" hanging down from the three stars making up the "belt" of Orion. This sky portal, or *ogee* as it was called in Native American tradition, enabled the soul access to the Milky Way. From there it would journey onward, reaching the point where the Milky Way split into two separate streams in the vicinity of the star Deneb. As a sky figure the stars of Cygnus were most commonly identified as an anthropomorphic bird or birdman that went under the name of Brain Smasher.*

On encountering Brain Smasher, the soul was judged on whether or not it was worthy enough to enter the sky world proper. If it was, then it would be allowed to pass through another ogee into the afterlife, and if it was not then it would either be forced to reincarnate or it would be hurled downward into the jaws of an underworld monster known as Water Panther or Winged Dragon, identified with the stars of Scorpius.[7]

Work carried out by mound builders expert Gregory L. Little at a large number of mound complexes across the United States, dating from the Adena period (500 BCE–100 CE) through to the Mississippian era, found that they almost always featured alignments toward not only the sun at the time of the midwinter solstice, but also toward the constellation of Orion and the Cygnus star Deneb. Little believes that the employment of these recurring stellar targets formed part of a systematic pattern of construction crucial for ceremonies and rituals involving the transmigration of the soul from this world to the next.[8]

A similar sky journey existed in Central America, where, as previously noted, the Maya identified the Milky Way's Dark Rift as Xibalba Be, the Road to Xibalba, with Xibalba being the name of the underworld.[9] Its presence is associated with iconography and mythological references to a world tree of the Maya identified by Linda Schele and her colleagues in the book *Maya Cosmos* (1993) as the Milky Way and known as Wakah-Chan (Raised Up Sky) or Sak Be (The White Road). They speculate that the tree represents the starry stream from the stars of Scorpius, identified with a scorpion shown at the tree's base, all the way up to the vicinity of the North Star marked by the presence of a bird in the tree's upper branches known as Seven Macaw.[10]

---

*The suspected reason why the sky figure identified with the star Deneb was known as Brain Smasher is because he was seen to break open the head of the deceased to release the spirit for its final entry into the afterlife. Just like in prehistoric Anatolia (as we shall see), many Native American tribes imagined the soul or spirit of a disincarnate individual as a human skull, the manner in which it is artistically depicted on a great number of funerary items attached to the Southeast Ceremonial Complex (S.E.C.C.). This is the name given to the loose system of religious beliefs, iconography, artifacts, ceremonies, and mythology attached to the Mississippian period of North American Indigenous history circa 800 CE to 1600 CE.

The same World Tree is shown in carved art at two major temples at the Mayan city of Palenque in southern Mexico. One is the Temple of the Foliated Cross, which Mayan experts have determined is oriented northwest toward to the setting of the star Deneb.[11] The temple's dedication makes it clear that Deneb is being used as a horizonal marker since it is representative of the northern opening of the Milky Way's Dark Rift. Moreover, the dedication also makes clear that this alignment is specific to the Mayan Feast of the Holy Cross (Day of the Cross), which among the K'iche' (Spanish: Quiché) Maya of the Guatemalan highlands marked the beginning of the maize planting season, a moment in the agricultural calendar signaled by the return to the night skies of the Dark Rift.[12] Cygnus, it should be pointed out, is known in Christian sky lore as the Northern Cross, an appellation that may well have been meaningful to the Maya well before the arrival of the first Spanish missionaries in the first quarter of the sixteenth century.

It was not just in the Americas that the stars of Cygnus formed the point of entry to the sky world. In ancient Egypt, for instance, the Pyramid Texts found on the walls of Old Kingdom pyramids from around 2350 BCE onward make it clear that after being released from its trials and tribulations in the *duat*-underworld, the soul of the pharaoh, in its role as the god Osiris, rose up to the stars of Orion, which as a sky figure named Sah or Sahu greeted him as his brother.

From there the soul gained access to the Milky Way, referred to as the Winding Waterway, after which it would continue its journey to the northern part of the sky. There the deceased, still in his guise as the god Osiris, would be greeted by his mother, the sky goddess Nut, who would welcome her son back into her womb. Although often seen as representing the sky as a whole, the goddess Nut was personified as the Milky Way with the stars of Cygnus signifying the goddess's womb, where the pharaoh was reborn and allowed to enter the afterlife.*

Very clearly the death journey of the ancient Egyptians matched those of the Native American peoples, and seemingly also that of the Maya, so there seems every reason to suspect that beliefs in which the Milky Way's Dark Rift was considered a road or river to the sky world, with the star Deneb marking

---

*For more information on these topics, along with all primary reference sources, see my books *The Cygnus Mystery* (2004), *Göbekli Tepe: Genesis of the Gods* (2014a), *The Cygnus Key* (2018), as well as *Path of Souls* (2014b) by Gregory L. Little, with contributions by myself.

the point of entry to the sky world, were once universal. If correct then the fact that they existed on the American continent as well as in ancient Egypt suggests that they probably predated the submergence some 11,600–11,000 years ago of the Bering land bridge linking Alaska to the Russian Far East. If so, then the chances are that similar beliefs in a sky world reached via the Milky Way's Dark Rift and the Cygnus star Deneb would have been known to the Pre-Pottery Neolithic peoples of southeastern Anatolia.

So alignments at places like Göbekli Tepe and Karahan Tepe toward the northern opening of the Milky Way's Dark Rift would almost certainly have involved beliefs and practices that had the express purpose of enabling the soul, either that of a deceased person or that of the shaman, to enter a perceived sky world accessed via the star Deneb. (Shamans would have entered deathlike states in order to make these journeys out of the body.) From the point of view of the shaman or initiate the purpose behind such activities would, we can only assume, have been to gain otherworldly knowledge, gain the support of spirits to heal the living, accompany souls to and from the hereafter, and deal with the supernatural forces—cosmic tricksters—seen as having the power to bring about chaos and destruction in the physical world.[13]

Finding an alignment at Karahan Tepe toward the northern opening of the Milky Way's Dark Rift should thus not be seen as unique, especially since similar alignments at Göbekli Tepe would appear to have determined the primary axis of its key enclosures. What seems more important is that at Karahan Tepe this alignment not only shows a relationship between the hill's northern knoll and the nearby Keçili Tepe, but it also connects Karahan Tepe's Great Ellipse with the directional axis of the nearby Pillars Shrine.

Can the relationship between Karahan Tepe and Keçili Tepe, and the former's proposed astronomical alignment toward the northern opening of the Milky Way's Dark Rift, help us to better understand the purpose of the remarkable bedrock features seen inside the Pillars Shrine? As already noted, its phallic-looking stone columns are arguably representative of the teeth of a snake whose head is the room itself. In this manner, their presence symbolized the supplicant's entry into the mouth of a serpent whose tongue was perhaps the eleventh removable pillar and whose spirit or genius was the giant head emerging from the west wall. That the shrine was aligned toward the Milky Way's Dark Rift must clearly have formed part of this cosmological process.

KEÇILI TEPE AS A SIPAPU

Should this be the case, then Keçili Tepe to the north of Karahan Tepe might well have been seen as a place where human souls either emerged into or departed from this world. Similar ideas are found, for instance, among the Native American tribal nations of the southwestern United States. The Zuni, Hopi, and Navajo (Diné) all possess creation myths regarding a sacred location, usually seen in terms of a hole, depression, or cave out of which the first humans emerged from the Lower World, in other words the underworld existing beneath our feet. Such sites are often hills envisaged as the womb or body of a primeval Great Mother.

The most well-known example of a *sipapu*, the name given to these Earth portals, is a flat-topped hill with a concave depression within its summit situated in the Little Colorado Gorge where the Little Colorado River meets the Colorado River in the Marble Canyon area of the Grand Canyon.[14] Other noted sipapu are thought to exist within the Navajo territories of the San Luis Valley in Colorado as well as in an area south of Sedona, Arizona, a location sacred to both the Hopi and the Zuni peoples of the region.*

The importance of sipapu—a Hopi word meaning "spirit hole"—is reflected in the layout and design of *kiva*. These are ritual huts built by ancestral Pueblo peoples, some of which are still used today by modern Pueblo communities of the American Southwest. The kivas in the Mesa Verde National Park, for example, are prime examples of this tradition. In each of them is a small circular hole in the floor symbolizing the sipapu, the place of emergence of the first humans into this world (see fig. 9.2, p. 76).[15] These holes also acted as places of contact with the spirit realms and the ancestral beings thought to inhabit them.

The reason for this diversion into Native American tradition is to show that spirit entrances in the form of holes, whether natural or manufactured, acted as boundaries between the physical world and a liminal realm beyond. This, I believe, is present at Karahan Tepe with the porthole window dividing the Great Ellipse from the Pillars Shrine (as well as the example seen in the northern wall of the new enclosure discovered on the summit of the

---

*In the case of Sedona the site of the sipapu sacred to the Zuni was a natural pyramid hill situated in an area known as Turkey Creek, a little way south of the town. Its location was revealed to me by the late Zuni elder Clifford Mahooty (1944–2022), whose family would regularly visit Sedona to make offerings to the ancestors.

Fig. 9.2. Native American kiva hut with sipapu. The larger hole is a fire hearth.
Photo by Wvbailey.

Fig. 9.3. Porthole
stone within the
perimeter wall
of Göbekli Tepe's
Enclosure D.
Photo by
Andrew Collins.

hill). They are also present in various key installations at Göbekli Tepe (see fig. 9.3), including Enclosures B, C, D, and H, and in every instance there they conform to the installation's axial orientation toward the setting of the star Deneb.[16]

In European tradition such entrances were known as soul holes or, in German, *seelenloch*, with their earliest manifestation outside of Anatolia's Pre-Pottery Neolithic culture coming from megalithic monuments known as dolmens. Consisting most often of four upright stone slabs supporting a large horizontal "table" stone, they are found across the Eurasian continent from Ireland in the west to South Korea and China in the east. Usually they are either Neolithic or Bronze Age in date, although in some places, like in India, they were still being built during the Iron Age (circa 1500 BCE–200 BCE).

Very often the entrance facades of dolmens have a circular hole that was probably intended to allow the spirit of those interred within its stone chamber to make the journey between the land of the living and the spirit realm beyond, and vice versa.*

The porthole stones at Göbekli Tepe along with the porthole windows at Karahan Tepe are simply variations of the circular or sometimes rectangular holes seen within the facades of megalithic dolmens. Usually such holes are only just large enough for a human head to fit through, and this was deliberate since, for the Neolithic peoples of Anatolia and the Near East, as with Native American funerary beliefs and iconography, the spirit of a person was thought to reside in a person's head or skull.[17] Any soul hole or porthole therefore only needed to be the size and shape of a human head because it was only the soul of the individual that needed to pass through them.

RITUAL OF THE SNAKE

Contradicting this belief ideology, however, is the fact that the porthole connecting Karahan Tepe's Great Ellipse with the Pillars Shrine is rectangular in shape and large enough for a living person to crawl through. Clearly, the creators of these enclosures must have deliberately designed the porthole in question to allow the shaman or initiate to pass between this world and a perceived

---

*False doors built in ancient Egyptian tombs were used for similar purposes—enabling the *ka* or spirit double of the internee to move freely from the tomb into the outside world and back again.

liminal realm seen as existing *inside* the Pillar Shrine. If so, then how might this have related to the structure's rock-cut columns, along with its curved stone slab, and the giant human head seen emerging out of its west wall?

The only way we can answer these questions is to go back to the time frame of construction of these bedrock enclosures and try to imagine what might have been taking place inside them. Would members of the local community have gathered in the Great Ellipse for the express purpose of attaining and holding open a consciousness link between this world and the next? Did these individuals enhance their ceremonial or ritualistic actions through the creation of a continuous wall of sound using "singing stones" picked up perhaps in the local landscape? Would this cacophony of noise have been established and sustained by the structure's finely tuned acoustic qualities?

If this is correct, are we to imagine a scenario whereby a chosen supplicant was able to achieve an altered state of consciousness both through the buildup of sound and perhaps through the ingestion of psychoactive substances? Although no evidence for the use of hallucinogens has so far come to light at Karahan Tepe, the fact that fragments of large stone platters were found on some of the benches inside the Great Ellipse could suggest they were used to hold sacraments (similar stone platters were found on and around the altar in the new enclosure uncovered on the summit of the hill). These could have taken the form of psychoactive plants or fungi.*

As to what might have happened next, we can only but speculate. The presence, however, of snake symbolism in every part of the Karahan Tepe complex could imply that the supplicant came to believe they were gradually being possessed, ridden, eaten, or overshadowed by the spirit of a snake, an animal that although perhaps dangerous in real life would work with the individual to ensure the success of the ritual.

The idea of being possessed by a snake, or indeed any animal, is something that might seem abhorrent to modern society. However, this is not the case in certain parts of the world, even today. At Wat Bang Phra, in Nakhon Pathom, Thailand, for instance, during the annual Wai Khru ceremony, men become possessed by snakes after receiving the sacred Sak Yant tattoo, which often depicts a snake or snakes alongside ancient Khmer script (see fig. 9.4).

---

*In *The Cygnus Mystery* (2006, ch. 18) I propose that the heads of the carved snakes found both at Nevalı Çori and at Göbekli Tepe bear the distinct appearance of psychoactive mushrooms, perhaps indicating their use by shamans and initiates to enter altered states of consciousness.

Fig. 9.4. Sacred tattoo known as the Sak Yant available to men prior to the start of the annual Wai Khru ceremony at Wat Bang Phra, Nakhon Pathom, Thailand. Illustration by Nick Burton.

By receiving this tattoo, the men become endowed with great strength and guile. Ritual activity then continues throughout the day and culminates with some of the participants slithering along the ground believing they have taken the form of snakes. Adding further to the serpentine connection is the fact that the tattoos are often created using a mixture of snake venom, herbs, and cigarette ash.[18]

Among voodoo practitioners in Haiti, Damballa, a *loa* or spirit in the form of a snake, can possess those taking part in rituals. Individuals can writhe around the ground in the firm belief that Damballa has taken over their body.[19]

It thus becomes possible that at the height of rituals taking place in Karahan Tepe's Great Ellipse, supplicants were possessed by the spirit of a snake, causing them to quite literally crawl through the porthole into the Pillars Shrine. As far-fetched as this scenario might seem, climbing through that small, rectangular window would not have been easy, and thus any such movement could very easily have been interpreted as the person adopting the guise of a snake.

Once inside the Pillars Shrine, amid the rock-sculpted pillars, the chances are that the supplicant would have been confronted by complete darkness due to the fact that the shrine almost certainly had a roof. Thereafter, I suspect, the supplicant would have been required to navigate the rock-cut pillars in a certain order, meditating perhaps on each one as if gradually ascending toward some kind of expanded reality.

The purpose of such ritual activity would perhaps have been to be absorbed, taken over, or eaten even by the snake represented by the room. This would have been to achieve communion with the creature's spirit or genius either via the giant head and/or through contact with the crescent-like slab slotted into the bedrock floor. The celestial alignment toward the stars of Cygnus and the northern entrance to the Milky Way's Dark Rift featuring the Great Ellipse, Pillars Shrine, and nearby Keçili Tepe would, I suspect, have helped animate any supernatural power or spirit presence thought to be manifesting inside this strange place.

There is something very precise in the way the Pillars Shrine was constructed, and in my opinion its uniquely carved features suggest that whatever was going on there went far beyond achieving a state of oneness with great ancestors or communicating with a perceived snake genius. Something more profound was taking place there, of this I am sure. For the moment, however, I want to turn my attention toward the site's second hill, Keçili Tepe, to better understand how it might fit into the emerging picture of what we suspect was going on at Karahan Tepe at the height of its use.

PART 3

STARS AND SNAKES

10

Mad Englishmen

"These men, they think you are crazy," were the words of our Turkish guide Yusuf, translating what the four local men sitting next to him had just said. The date was September 11, 2015, and I was once again at Karahan Tepe, the purpose of the visit being to better understand the site's northern hill, Keçili Tepe. I had first clambered over its bare limestone slopes and investigated its hypogeum-like caves earlier that year, but at the time I had been ill-equipped to fully explore what lay within their dark interiors.

My traveling companion, the mysteries researcher and writer Hugh Newman, and I sat on long cushions decorated with Anatolian kilim designs positioned around the walls of the room. The only other features of note were an old TV on a low wooden table and a bashed-up metal teapot sitting on the concrete floor before us. This provided a constant flow of black tea, sweetened with granulated sugar from a glass bowl. Through the constant haze of cigarette smoke our hosts could not help but smile at the antics of these mad Englishmen.

"They say these caves have snakes," Yusuf continued, conveying the men's thoughts on the matter.

Snakes? There really were snakes up there in the caves?

"Yes, and they don't know why you want to go there," he said, the men openly perplexed at our reasons for wanting to go inside such filthy and, seemingly, quite dangerous places.

I have to admit the idea did trouble me. There was a very real danger of encountering poisonous snakes in the hypogeum-like caves found scattered about the sparse, sun-scorched landscape of the Tektek Mountains. Yet I simply had to do it. When I'd explored previously unrecorded caves at Giza in Egypt in 2008, great discoveries had been made.[1] Exploring caves was just something I did.

Slightly worrying, however, was the fact that a couple of weeks earlier I had experienced a strange dream-vision regarding the caves on Keçili Tepe. Before knowing anything about them, I had found myself in a circular pit surrounded by a bed of snakes. It was like something out of an Indiana Jones movie!

The cave in question was a curious beehive-shaped structure I had first noted on the hill's southern slope earlier that year. Following the dream I had started referring to it as the Snake Pit in anticipation of what indeed might lurk inside its perilous interior. Now I was being told there were real snakes in those caves, a daunting thought indeed!

The following day Hugh and I returned to Karahan Tepe fully equipped to begin our explorations of Keçili Tepe. In the blazing hot sun and in the company of Yusuf and one of the youths from the farm, we climbed the hill's bleached limestone slopes in search of its caves.

Weighing heavy on my shoulders was a brand new, 10-foot (3-meter) metal ladder. This I'd purchased earlier that day from a hardware store on the outskirts of Şanlıurfa. Being made of aluminum it was supposed to be light in weight, but ascending Keçili Tepe with it slung over my shoulder was no easy thing.

A few minutes later Yusuf offered to carry the ladder, having seen me struggling to tackle some of the more difficult rock faces. I reluctantly agreed, although it was not really his job to carry our equipment. Shortly afterward, we came within sight of our first port of call. It was a long, narrow cave entrance filled almost entirely with loose sand and rubble.

Taking off my grass hat and desert jacket, I slipped on a white one-piece protective coverall, as well as kneepads, a breathing mask, and all-purpose industrial gloves, aware that no bare skin should be exposed for what I was about to do.

Hugh, Yusuf, and the young farmhand watched as I crawled through the slim opening, which was clogged with decades of harsh mountain vegetation. This particular site, I knew, was important for a number of reasons. First, its entrance faced out toward Karahan Tepe, situated some two-thirds of a mile (1 kilometer) away on the other side of the shallow plain dividing the two hills.

Pondering Keçili Tepe's importance in relation to its better-known neighbor had led me to look more closely at its name. As previously made clear, Bahattin Çelik had given Karahan Tepe its name because he hoped this would help thwart local men from going to the site and removing archaeological finds.

The owners of the farm, the Can family, however, tell me that Karahan Tepe's *real* name is Keçili Tepe, or just Keçili, the same name as the farm. In contrast, and please try not to get too confused here, the hill we know today as Keçili Tepe—the one being climbed on that day—is actually called Mağaraları Tepe, which means "hill [*tepe*] with caves [*mağaraları*]," an allusion, of course, to the fact that it contains three notable caves—two on its western slopes and one on its eastern side. The hill's Arab name, apparently, is Rucum el-mağāra, which also records the presence of caves there since *mağāra* means "cave" both in Ottoman Turkish and in Arabic.

WHAT'S IN A NAME?

In Turkish *keçili* means "goat," which would make Keçili Tepe the "hill of the goat." Since goats and sheep are reared on the farm this makes good sense. The owners, however, insist that the root of the name is not Turkish but Kurdish, deriving from the root *keç* (pronounced "ketch," as in "ketchup"). Translated into English this means "bald," a reference, the farm's owners say, to Karahan Tepe's bare limestone summit. This is possible, although there is another interpretation of the word root *keç*. In the Northern Kurdish language of Kurmanji, still spoken extensively in southeastern Anatolia, *keç* means "woman," "daughter," "maiden," "girl," and even "queen."[2]

Fig. 10.1. The vulva-shaped recess cut into the rock face
on Karahan Tepe's eastern side. Photo by Andrew Collins.

As a place name *keçili* would thus refer to the abode of a notable woman, meaning that the hill was seen as feminine in nature. This is an interesting prospect, especially since on Karahan Tepe's eastern slope, a little way to the south of the current excavations, is an oval-shaped opening carved into the rock face. This shallow recess penetrates the bedrock for no more than 4 feet (1.2 meters) and is just large enough for a child to fit inside. The most important aspect of this carved feature, which could very easily date back to the Neolithic Age, is that it bears the distinct appearance of a vulva (see fig. 10.1).

GODDESS OF THE LANDSCAPE

Attributing a female gender to landmarks—hills in particular—is found throughout the ancient world. In Ireland, for instance, a hill range near Killarney in County Kerry is known as the Paps of Anu, the "breasts of the goddess Anu," while a hill range on the Greek island of Mykonos is referred to as the "breasts" of the goddess Aphrodite. More significantly, a group of hills on the Isle of Lewis, off the northwest coast of Scotland, bear the name Cailleach na Mointeach, meaning the "Old Woman of the Moors," or, alternately, the "Sleeping Beauty."

Cailleach is the name given to the goddess who rules the dark half of the year in Scottish folk tradition. At the time of the major lunar standstill, which occurs every 18.61 years, the full moon when viewed from the nearby Callanish stone circle is seen to roll over the "breasts" of the Sleeping Beauty. All these examples relate to hills or hill ranges that are thought to resemble women lying on their backs—women who are seen as embodiments of a primeval mother of life.[3]

Could both Karahan Tepe and what we today call Keçili Tepe have been seen as physical personifications of an earth mother, highlighted by the vulva-like feature in the former and the hypogeum-like caves in the latter? Did these signify entrances into a womb-like realm existing inside the Earth? That Göbekli Tepe in Turkish means the "hill [*tepe*] of the navel [*göbek*]," while in Kurdish its name is Girê Navoke, meaning "hill [*girê*] of the swollen belly [*navoke*]," is supportive of these ideas.

A second Kurdish name for Göbekli Tepe is Girê Mirazan, meaning "hill [*girê*] of wishes [*mirazan*]." It is a reference to the fact that since time immemorial local Kurdish people have climbed to the top of the hill, and in the vicinity of a notable mulberry tree, would sacrifice a sheep in the hope that a woman would be granted a child. Thus in folk tradition this Pre-Pottery Neolithic mound, over 11,500 years old, has always been associated with human fertility. This is an important realization as it helps us to better understand why both Karahan Tepe and Keçili Tepe might also have been connected in the past with human reproduction and fertility.[4]

ENTERING A SECOND LIFE

As we saw in chapter 9 Keçili Tepe appears to have acted as a backsight when seen from nearby Karahan Tepe, marking the setting each night of the northern opening of the Milky Way's Dark Rift and the Cygnus star Deneb. It would have been through this sky portal that the souls of the deceased, as well as those of shamans and initiates, were thought to gain access to the hereafter. Entering this unseen realm, identified directly with the Milky Way, would have been seen as entering a second life or afterlife, some understanding of which has come down to us from Bronze Age texts found during archaeological excavations in central Anatolia.[5]

Great preparation was required for a person to be reborn in the next world. The body of the deceased had to be appropriately disposed of with the correct funerary rites so that it did not linger on the earth plane as a ghost. If everything was done correctly, the soul could then return from whence it had come in the first place. As for shamans, this process would have been conducted during so-called death trances achieved through the attainment of ecstatic states.

Were the caves on Keçili Tepe really symbolic points of entry and exit for spirits going between this world and the next? Was it by this means that new spirits were seen to enter this world, while those of shamans were able to experience a second life via these symbolic womb chambers before returning to their material life in the physical world? Is this something that was truly practiced by Karahan Tepe's Taş Tepeler community? The answer, as we see next, is both enigmatic and intriguing at the same time.

11

Descending into Snake Holes

With thoughts of entering the body of some primordial snake that day on Keçili Tepe in September 2015, I got down on my hands and knees, squeezed through the narrow gap between the bottom edge of the cave roof and the accumulated layers of sand and debris, and went in search of answers.

Having successfully navigated the entrance area, I quickly found myself inside a long straight chamber that stretched away toward the north-northwest. With the walls and ceiling of the cave never more than a few inches away, I continued with caution. Foolishly, I shone a flashlight on the ceiling and saw that it was crawling with big black spiders. That venomous creatures inhabited the area was not in doubt, as I recalled the big blue scorpion I had encountered in the valley below Karahan Tepe just over a decade beforehand.

Some distance into the cave the main corridor came to an abrupt end. To the right was a keyhole shaped opening around 3.5 feet (1 meter) in height and much less in width. Such distinctive cave profiles are caused by the heavy action of water passing through fissures and cracks in the limestone rock across tens if not hundreds of thousands of years. This made it clear that the cave must have been present for a very long time and had probably been open to the elements when the area supported a Pre-Pottery Neolithic community. No ancient culture was going to ignore such places, whether they were used simply for domestic purposes or they were seen as entrances to the underworld.

Inside the side chamber I was able to access an even deeper level of the cave system. Beginning to advance in this direction I became aware of a constant buzzing sound coming out of the darkness. Listening carefully, I realized its source was a swarm of large insects, hornets most probably. Very clearly there was a hive there, and making me think this was the fact that I had encountered a similar hive in one of the hypogeum-like caves on the hill's western face earlier that year. Whatever was in there was not, I imagined, going to take too kindly to my intrusion.

Without panicking I withdrew slowly and assuredly before coming to a halt a few yards back from where I had been. I wanted to make sure I was not being stupid in backing away. I again approached the side chamber, but once again I heard the same buzzing sounds, so under the circumstances I made the only sensible decision: get the hell out of there!

As I emerged into the bright sunlight covered in muck and dirt, Hugh Newman was there to record the moment on camera. My own video footage inside the cave, although not of good quality, did reveal something of potential importance. The slim opening between the cave mouth and main corridor bore the distinct likeness of a vulva. In shape it was a vertical ellipse extremely suggestive of an entrance into a symbolic womb chamber (see fig. 11.1), just like the carved opening seen on the eastern slopes of nearby Karahan Tepe.

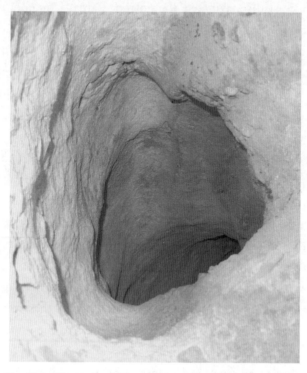

Fig. 11.1. The vulva-like opening within the cave on the eastern side of Keçili Tepe. Photo by Andrew Collins.

For the shaman or initiate, crawling through this hole would undoubtedly have seemed like entering the birth canal of a primordial cave mother or the gullet of a giant snake in readiness for a journey into the next life. The additional fact that the cave entrance faced out toward Karahan Tepe made it even more likely that this natural opening into the belly of an imagined landscape goddess would not have gone unnoticed by those who had come to occupy the area during the Neolithic Age. The lack, however, of any obvious evidence of a human presence inside the cave meant that this conclusion would have to remain a matter of speculation, for the time being at least. If I really wanted to find evidence that the Pre-Pottery Neolithic peoples of Karahan Tepe had seen Keçili Tepe as important to their cosmological beliefs and practices, I would have to continue the search elsewhere.

THE SNAKE PIT

So we moved on to the next site—the ominous Snake Pit, a strange beehive-shaped structure carved out of the limestone bedrock using primitive tools. I had certainly not encountered any snakes in the first cave, but what about this one? Would the warning given by the owners of the farm as well as my own dream-vision prove correct? Did these caves really contain live snakes?

An infrared measuring device told me that the drop from the opening to the base of the structure was 9 feet (2.76 meters). I prayed this figure was correct as I extended the full length of the ladder into the darkness. Yet it easily made contact with the loose pile of rocks that had accumulated at the bottom of this artificial structure. Still dressed in the white all-purpose coveralls, I began my descent into the Snake Pit, watching carefully for any sudden movement below.

Reaching the bottom, I looked around with the flashlight but, thankfully, I was alone. No snakes anywhere, just bones of animals that had presumably fallen through the circular hole and had died of starvation. Even though I was alone, in the living sense at least, I had no intention of staying around any longer than I had to, so I set about recording every detail I could about the structure.

The cave was perfectly round, like a beehive, with a base diameter of approximately 14 feet (4 meters). The drop from the circular opening to the bedrock below the accumulated rock debris was the same—about 14 feet (4 meters).

The walls were perfectly chamfered, the toolmarks still plainly visible. A lot of time and effort had gone into the construction of this structure. But who carved it, and for what purpose?

Beehive caves are usually explained as either water cisterns for collecting rainwater or storage silos for holding grain. Both explanations were plausible for the examples at Keçili Tepe (two others—one of which is covered by a large block of stone with a circular hole cut into it—are also present on the hill's southeastern slopes), but a third possibility also came to mind. Structures like this might well have been used for ritual purposes, most obviously initiation rites of some kind, or even for the observation of stars crossing overhead. The fact that this cave was two-thirds of the way up a steep, rocky hill slope that rises some 150 feet (47 meters) above the surrounding plain and is around a quarter of a mile (450 meters) from the farmhouse, did seem to lessen the likelihood of it being created for practical purposes alone.

After staring for far too long at the carefully chamfered walls and the skulls and bones scattered about the rock-covered floor, I decided to return to the surface (see plate 27). Nothing I had seen could tell me who was responsible for creating this structure. The truth is that it could have been carved at any point in the past 11,500 years. There was nothing there that was going to help me determine whether or not Keçili Tepe had been important to Karahan Tepe's Taş Tepeler community.

ROCK-CUT ALCOVE

On exiting the Snake Pit, I noticed that immediately behind it, to the north-northwest, was a symmetrically carved recess in the rock face. It was rectilinear in shape, around 6.5 feet (2 meters) in height, some 5 feet (1.5 meters) in width, with a depth of around 20 inches (0.5 meters). It almost seemed like an alcove, and so its presence just 10 paces back from the Snake Pit seemed important. Almost certainly the two structures were the product of the same highly accomplished, stone-carving society.

I then realized something significant. If a person stood within the rectangular-shaped recess with their back against the wall they would stare out across the valley directly toward Karahan Tepe. The alignment was perfect.

Since I knew that following the abandonment of Karahan Tepe by the Pre-Pottery Neolithic peoples around 8000 BCE the entire site was abandoned, this strongly suggested that there was indeed some link between these rock-cut structures on Keçili Tepe and the carved stone monuments on Karahan Tepe. Even if this was the case, there was simply nothing concrete to prove the connection. I would have to continue my search elsewhere on Keçili Tepe to find out what it might have meant to the Neolithic peoples of the area.

12

Half Moons and Rock Temples

On Keçili Tepe's western slope are two hypogeum-style caves located on a level platform just below the hill's summit. Each one has carved entrances and areas within them that have clearly been enhanced to give their interiors a more rectilinear shape (see plate 28). They also possess side chambers that seem to have been carved with a specific purpose in mind. Here and there are alcoves and recesses that are also artificial, adding weight to the conclusion that these caves once served some special purpose. This might have been to contain burials, although there is little evidence present to suggest this was the case. On the other hand, these apparent hypogeums (rock-cut chambers), which seem like crude versions of the famous example at Ħal Saflieni on the island of Malta (which is conventionally thought to be around 6,000 years old), could very easily have been used for ritual purposes, their presence symbolic of descending into the body of Earth itself.

When I had first inspected these caves earlier that year, I found nothing that might tell me who had created them. They could have been carved out from preexisting natural caves, although equally they could only date back a few thousand years. The fact, however, that the hill's true name is Mağaraları Tepe, meaning the "hill with caves," does seem to confirm the importance of the caves to the location. All I can add is that the owners of the farm still use these two hypogeums as places of refuge for their animals during the winter months. That's why their interiors smell quite bad and why the walls and ceilings are covered in thick soot from hundreds if not thousands of years of illumination through the use of oil lamps and torches.

Outside, on the slopes below the caves, I did notice a few scattered pot-sherds. These ranged in age from Roman times through to the Islamic period. I also noted several small flakes of flint and chert, their presence the result of stone knapping at the location. None of the fragments showed any recognizable style in their manufacture, and the knowledge that farmhands still use local stone and even ancient flint tools to make blades for basic sickles meant that the examples on the hillside could be from any age.

Having already seen all that I needed to see inside the caves, I left Hugh Newman to explore their interiors as I climbed on to the summit of Keçili Tepe. Once there I found myself on a long, rocky ridge that stretched away toward the north-northeast. The young farmhand did not, however, pause to inspect the breathtaking views on offer from this elevated vantage point. Instead, he had something he wanted to show me.

Reaching the extreme northern limits of the hill's summit, he came to a halt just before the ground started to drop away to a lower level. Gesturing silently with his hands, he pointed out on the level surface a cleared area of bedrock some 13 feet (4 meters) in size. It was bordered at its northern end by a crescent-shaped arc of large stone blocks deeply embedded in the earth. Most were between 1.5 and 2.5 feet (0.5 to 0.75 meters) in size. A second row of similarly sized stones lay immediately behind the first. Bordering the crescent's southern end was an east-west running line of smaller blocks half embedded in the soil, giving the whole enclosure the distinct appearance of a half moon (see fig. 12.1).

As I inspected this clearly artificial feature I saw that just beyond the end of its northeastern edge was a perfectly rectilinear stone stuck upright in the hard gravel soil covering the bedrock. It belonged to a half-buried third cres-cent of stones and bore some resemblance to the head of a T-pillar, like those seen emerging from the topsoil on the slopes of nearby Karahan Tepe.

The curious half-moon-shaped stone setting at the northern edge of Keçili Tepe resembles a "round-planned building" investigated by Bahattin Çelik at a Pre-Pottery Neolithic settlement site named Başaran-Herzo Tepesi, just 12.5 miles (20 kilometers) west-northwest of Karahan Tepe.[1] At around 16.5 feet (5 meters) in diameter, it is almost the same size as the stone structure on Keçili Tepe.

If not created as a lookout during some more recent age, then Keçili Tepe's half-moon feature could very easily be Neolithic in age. Its elevated position at the northern end of the hill's summit makes you look in one direction, and one

Fig. 12.1. The half-moon-shaped structure on the summit of Keçili Tepe.
Photo by Andrew Collins.

direction only, and this is toward the north. Indeed, this would be a perfect vantage point to watch the stars turn about the northern celestial pole, which at the latitude of Karahan Tepe is at an altitude each night of 37 degrees. Some of those stars would only just kiss the horizon on what is known as their lower transit of the north-south meridian line before rising back up into the sky.

Is it possible that Karahan Tepe's Taş Tepeler community used prominent stars crossing the meridian on either their upper or their lower transit for timekeeping purposes? In the tenth millennium BCE the night sky looked a lot different from what it does today, although a quick check with Stellarium shows that the best candidate by far for this role would have been the bright star Arcturus (α Boötis), the brightest star in the constellation of Boötes, the celestial herdsman.

As seen from this elevated position on Keçili Tepe, Arcturus would have hung immediately above the summit of Zakzuk (or Zagzuk) Dağı,[2] an extremely prominent hill 1.7 miles (2.8 kilometers) and 4 degrees east of north of where I stood and 2.5 miles (4 kilometers) due north of Karahan Tepe. On the summit of Zakzuk Dağı, which means the "mountain of the [legendary] zakzuk bird," are a rock-cut rectilinear fortress (Turkish *kalesi*) and cave church, both dating to the

Abgarid dynasty of Anatolian history (circa 134 BCE to 242 CE). (See plate 29.) The hill also contains cave tombs that date from a similar age, although both these and the rock church—which has Syriac script carved deeply into its soot-stained walls—could very easily have begun their lives as natural caves.

The fact that in the tenth millennium BCE the bright star Arcturus would have been seen hanging directly above Zakzuk Dağı as viewed from Karahan Tepe would not have gone unnoticed by its Taş Tepeler community. Almost certainly this prominent hill, being the highest spot in the region, would have been utilized in some capacity. (During an inspection of Zakzuk Dağı in December 2022 the present author noted the presence on its slopes of blade-tool fragments that were at least 9,000 years old.)[3]

The importance to the Karahan Tepe community of Zakzuk Dağı will have been emphasized by the fact that as Arcturus was crossing the meridian on its lower transit immediately above the hill's summit, the Cygnus star Deneb was just 11 minutes away from crossing the meridian on its *upper* transit; this

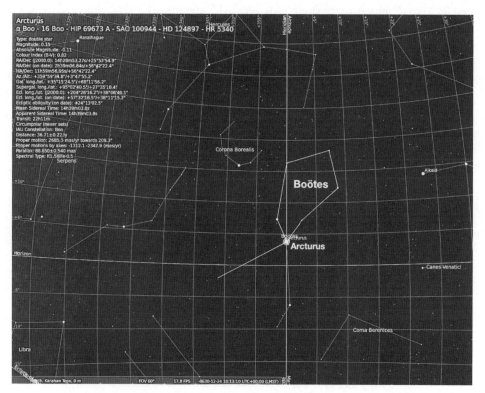

Fig. 12.2. View of the star Arcturus (α Boötis) just above the northern horizon as seen from the latitude of Karahan Tepe in 8630 BCE. This image was made using the Stellarium free open-source planetarium.

being for a date of 9000 BCE. Due to the effects of precession (the slow wobble of Earth's axis across a cycle of approximately 25,800 years), the time between the synchronization of these two stars as they crossed the meridian would have decreased to just 6 minutes by 8800 BCE, just 3 minutes by 8700 BCE, and zero minutes by 8630 BCE (see fig. 12.2 on the previous page).

THE ROCK TEMPLE

Looking up from examining the half-moon-shaped stone setting, I saw the young farmhand waiting for me to catch up. He stood at a slightly lower level a little to the north of my position and seemed to be indicating toward a sunken pit full of rock debris, but it was what lay in front of him that now drew *my* attention.

Reaching the site necessitated climbing down a gentle slope, and as I approached the spot and spied what lay before me I became excited. It was a large sunken area, rectilinear in shape, that had been cut out of the level bedrock to a depth of perhaps 1.6 feet (0.5 meters). In size the feature was approximately 34.5 feet (10.5 meters) in length and 24.5 feet (7.5 meters) in width, meaning that it went close to displaying a 4:3 ratio in its dimensions (see fig. 12.3 and plate 30). This structure had vertically cut walls on its northern,

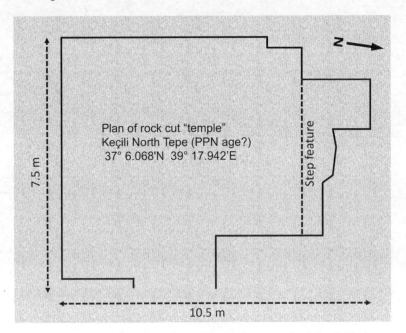

Fig. 12.3. The Rock Temple at the northern end of Keçili Tepe.
Diagram by Andrew Collins.

southern, and western sides, while at its eastern edge the ground sloped away gently, suggesting a direction of entry.

Immediately beyond the western limits of the Rock Temple, as I quickly dubbed it, was a rock outcrop aligned northwest-southeast made up of two enormous natural blocks of stone that towered above head height. Their presence would have blocked any view toward the west, just as Karahan Tepe blocked any sight of the western horizon from the interiors of the three interconnected bedrock structures.

On the northern edge of the cutaway area of the Rock Temple was a low step or curb running from east to west along the width of the structure, perhaps determining its primary direction of orientation. Did the Rock Temple look toward the north, or, alternately, did it look eastward, the direction of the rising sun at the time of the equinoxes? Maybe the answer was both.

The one thing I knew as Hugh, who had now caught up, and I inspected this unique bedrock feature was that to date no paper featuring Karahan Tepe had mentioned any of these archaeological features on Keçili Tepe, whether this be the natural cave, the two hypogeums, the beehive-shaped "snake" pit, the cutaway recess immediately behind it, the half-moon-shaped stone setting on the hill's summit, or the bedrock structure just described. From what I knew they had all been dismissed by the few archeologists who had climbed the hill to investigate them as the result of human activity there during Roman times. None were considered to date back to the Pre-Pottery Neolithic Age.*

Such opinions could very easily apply to some of the rock-cut features on Keçili Tepe (as well as on Zakzuk Dağı, where there is also an assortment of very similar bedrock features). Others, however, could very easily be monuments of the Pre-Pottery Neolithic Age. I still, however, needed something more to prove this surmise was indeed correct. And then I found what I was looking for. On returning to the half-moon-shaped stone feature, I spotted, lying next to it on an exposed rock surface, a finely worked stone tool. Some 1.2 inches (3 centimeters) square and made of a pale brown-gray chert, it is what archaeologists refer to as a prismatic blade segment. This specific type of stone tool technology, which involved the blades being prized from carefully

---

*Further exploration of Keçili Tepe by Necmi Karul and his team in 2023 has indicated that its rock-cut features are indeed of archaeological interest, with the suggestion being that the hypogeum caves were perhaps used as Christian chapels during late antiquity. Until a proper survey of the site can take place, access to the hill is no longer permitted.

prepared cores using a specialized process known as pressure flaking, dates from the Mid to Late Pre-Pottery Neolithic B period, meaning it had to be at least 9,000 years old.[4]

It seemed unlikely that this stone tool had been brought to this spot in comparatively recent times. Indeed, on the way up the hill while carrying the aluminum ladder, I had noticed another similar, but slightly less well-made, example of a prismatic blade. So the example seen next to the half-moon-shaped stone setting on Keçili Tepe could easily have been there since the Neolithic Age.*

If correct, and we find that some of the rock-cut structures on Keçili Tepe were indeed used at this time, then I see no reason why the settlement's inhabitants might not have considered both this hill and Karahan Tepe to the south as symbolic womb chambers belonging to a primordial earth mother. In other words, the Karahan community could very easily have viewed these caves as points of contact with otherworldly realms linked directly with the perceived location of the afterlife. This, as we saw in chapter 9, corresponded in celestial terms with the Cygnus star Deneb and the northern opening of the Milky Way's Dark Rift, which in the early Neolithic Age would have synchronized each night with Keçili Tepe as viewed from Karahan Tepe.

EVIDENCE OF REAL SNAKES

Before leaving Keçili Tepe the young farmhand had one more thing to show me. He took me to a sunken pit immediately to the north of the Rock Temple. This, I later learned, marks the site of a robbed-out grave from the Roman period. Looking into it, all I could see was a circular hollow filled with rock debris.

I asked the youth what I was looking at, and, understanding my words, he made a slithering movement with his hand implying this was a place of snakes. As if to prove his point he bent down and picked up a slewed snakeskin, which he handed to me. This was something I had not expected. So the men at the farm had been correct. Snakes really do inhabit Keçili Tepe. I could genuinely have encountered one inside any of the hill's pits or caves. It was a chilling

---

*I revisited Keçili Tepe's half-moon feature and Rock Temple in December 2022 and noted the presence of further examples of prismatic blade segments in the same vicinity. This confirmed to my own satisfaction that the hill must have been frequented during the Mid to Late Pre-Pottery Neolithic B period.

thought, and one that instantly made me recall my own premonition regarding the snakes seen in the beehive-shaped pit I had explored earlier. Left in my mind now was the question of whether or not snakes really had been important to those who perhaps used the caves to conduct their rituals and ceremonies. It was a matter I would return to many times in the months and years that followed.

One conclusion I did come to following this visit to Keçili Tepe in September 2015 was that much of the local belief about the caves of Keçili Tepe being the abode of snakes is simply the product of local folklore. There really are snakes on that hill, although not enough to warrant the stern warnings Hugh and I had been given the previous day.

It was my suspicion that the hill's connection with snakes was age-old and related to the manner in which the creature had become a major totem among the Pre-Pottery Neolithic peoples of southeastern Anatolia. I suspected also that any primordial earth deity associated both with Karahan Tepe and with Keçili Tepe would have borne serpentine qualities—snakes being symbols of the underworld in many parts of the ancient world. Were these hills seen as the "womb" of a primeval Snake Mother that shamans and initiates had to enter in order to experience the afterlife? Was this supernatural form connected with the sky world and, in particular, the Milky Way's Dark Rift? Who was this Snake Mother, and how might the Neolithic and later Bronze Age inhabitants of Anatolia have seen her? It is these questions we explore next, starting with the tale of the Shahmaran.

13

Realm of the Snake Mother

Folktales told throughout Anatolia speak of a half woman, half snake known as the Shahmaran (Turkish: Şahmeran). She was a mother of snakes who lived in an underworld cave realm. Her story is famous throughout Turkey and beyond into Syria and Iran. It speaks of how, one day, a woodcutter named Cemshab (Turkish: Cemşab) fell down a deep well and, being unable to get back out, was left there to die. Then, however, he saw a scorpion and so decided to follow where it was going. The creature led Cemshab through passages and corridors until eventually they arrived at a secret cave that was the home of the Shahmaran. Soon Cemshab and the Shahmaran fell in love, despite the fact that although she had the head, arms, and upper torso of a beautiful woman, she had the body of a snake.

The two lived together in the Shahmaran's cave world. Cemshab knew that he could never leave her realm, since if he did there was every chance he would reveal where he had been and cause her to be killed. So Cemshab accepted his new life, although very gradually he became homesick. He missed his family and friends and wanted to be with them once more. Realizing this, the Shahmaran eventually allowed her mortal lover to return to the upper world. She told him, however, that he was never to reveal the whereabouts of the entrance into her domain. What is more, he was never to show anyone his back, which, through contact with her own body, now bore the scales of a serpent.

So Cemshab returned to his family and friends, and never did he reveal where he had been or show anyone his back. For a while life went on as usual, but shortly after this the ruler of the country, the sultan, fell seriously ill. As he lay on what he thought would be his deathbed, his vizier told him there was a cure for his malady. He had to eat of the body of the fabled Shahmaran.

Secretly, however, the vizier had other motives behind revealing this information. He wanted to eat of her himself since he knew that in doing so he would gain her otherworldly wisdom.

Knowing that anyone who had ever come in contact with the Shahmaran would have developed the scales of a snake on their back, the vizier told the king to order that every man take a public bath. This, he felt sure, would expose the Shahmaran's rumored lover. When it came to Cemshab's turn to enter the bath he took off his clothes and the vizier could see that the skin on his back was covered in snake scales, showing that *he* was the Shahmaran's lover.

So Cemshab was detained, but at first he refused to reveal the entrance to the Shahmaran's abode. Finally, under torture, he gave away his secret and agreed to lead the king's vizier and some soldiers to the Shahmaran's lair deep underground. On their arrival the snake woman knew her fate. She had known this outcome was inevitable after allowing her mortal lover to return to the upper world. So this is what she told the vizier: "Whoever eats of my body will be cured of their malady. Whoever eats of my snake scales will gain wisdom, and whoever eats of my head will die instantly."

So after the king's soldiers had killed the Shahmaran, the vizier immediately consumed her snake scales (some accounts talk about them being made into a broth), while Cemshab accepted his own fate for revealing the whereabouts of his lover and so ate of her head, expecting to die immediately. The sultan was able to eat of the Shahmaran's body and so fully recovered from his malady. But there was a twist in this tale, for instead of the vizier gaining infinite wisdom through eating of the snake woman's scales, he died instantly, while Cemshab, having eaten of her head, remained alive.

The Shahmaran's plan had worked. Through eating her head Cemshab had gained her otherworldly wisdom, while the evil vizier who had eaten her scales was poisoned. Heartbroken, however, at what he had done and the loss of his lover, Cemshab left the country and forever wandered from one mountain to the next searching for solace and redemption, and there the story ends.

This, then, is the basic legend of the Shahmaran, the Anatolian mother of snakes, and how falling in love with Cemshab caused not only her dismemberment, but also the manner in which her snake wisdom was passed on to humankind. Variations of these stories are told to this day throughout Anatolia, with images of the Shahmaran either painted on glass or beaten into copper plates, a familiar sight in stores all over southern, eastern, and southeastern Turkey (see fig. 13.1). Invariably, the Shahmaran is shown with a human head, the body of a snake, and six short legs ending in snake heads, her serpentine tail also ending in a snake's head, making seven in total. At other times she is shown more simply as a snake with the arms, head, and upper body of a beautiful woman.

Despite the fact that many scholars believe the story of the Shahmaran entered Turkey from neighboring Persia (modern-day Iran) as recently as the sixteenth century CE (her name coming from the Persian *shāh*, meaning "king," and *mārān*, meaning "snakes." Even if this is correct the Shahmaran's role as Snake Mother reignited the ancestral memory of a more localized snake goddess—one venerated across eastern and southern Anatolia prior to the arrival of Christianity and Islam during the first millennium CE. How the legend of the Shahmaran relates to what might have been going on at Karahan Tepe will at first seem difficult to understand, yet within her story are kernels of information that can be shown to throw considerable light on the importance of the snake as a deity in prehistoric Anatolia.

Fig. 13.1. Traditional representation of the Anatolian Snake Mother known as the Shahmaran, the "king of snakes." Illustration by Andrew Collins.

Fig. 13.2. The goddess Išhara at the Hittite site of Yazilikaya (Relief #50), an open-air sanctuary dated to around 1250 BCE situated on high ground near the civilization's capital Hattusa in central Turkey. Photo by Klaus-Peter Simon.

There are two female figures in southeastern Anatolia who might be linked with the roots of the Shahmaran legend, the first of whom is Eve (Arabic: Ḥawwā), the wife of Adam, the First Man, who features both in the Hebrew Bible and also in the Holy Koran. I shall have much to say about her in chapter 36. The other snake-related woman once important to the inhabitants of Anatolia was the goddess Išhara, whose principal symbols were the serpent and scorpion (see fig. 13.2), both of which feature in the legend of the Shahmaran.[1] As we saw, the Shahmaran was half human, half snake, while the creature that permitted Cemshab entry into her otherworldly domain was the scorpion (Turkish: *akrep*).

IŠHARA, DAUGHTER OF ENLIL

As daughter of the sky god Enlil and the goddess Abandu, Išhara was seen among the peoples of northern Syria as mother of the Sebitti or Sebittu, meaning "the seven," the "group of seven," and even the "seven gods."[2] These were seven warlike gods, sons of the god Enmesharra, who carried bows and arrows and were personified in the sky as seven individual stars, a link perhaps to the Shahmaran's seven snake heads.

Having originated among the West Semitic-speaking peoples of Ebla in northern Syria as early as 2400 BCE, the cult of Išhara quickly spread throughout the Near East.[3] The Hittites of Anatolia, the Hurrians of southeast Anatolia, as well as the Neo-Sumerians, the Babylonians, and particularly the Assyrians all adopted her as a celestial deity, whose principal secular role was to preside over the binding of oaths. The goddess's name was invoked on documents, and if anyone broke an oath they could expect to suffer the "illness of Išhara," this being a crippling malady that afflicted the stomach region.[4]

Išhara was venerated by both Semitic and non-Semitic peoples alike and would come to be seen as a goddess of love and sexuality, her attributes gradually merging with those of the more popular Akkadian goddess Ishtar, who was seen as "Queen of Heaven."

MOTHER OF THE GODS

In some astrological texts the goddess was known as "Išhara Tiamat," or Išhara of the Ocean,"[5] an indication that she was seen as the natural successor of Tiamat, a female serpent-dragon of Mesopotamian mythology who was the personification of the saltwater oceans surrounding the known world. Tiamat was said to have mated with Absu, the god of all freshwater sources, to create the first gods, making her mother of the gods. According to the Babylonian creation myth titled the *Enūma Eliš* (meaning "when on high"), Tiamat was eventually slain by the god Marduk, her body being split into two to form heaven and earth.

Išhara herself was known also as Ama, "mother,"[6] clearly showing that her role was more than simply a goddess presiding over carnal desires and legal issues. She was a snake mother par excellence, the same role played by the Shahmaran in eastern, southern, and southeastern Anatolia. According to Old Assyrian texts dating to circa 2000–1700 BCE, Išhara's main cult center was located in the ancient kingdom of Kizzuwatna in southern-central Anatolia, this being close to the gulf of Iskenderun.[7] These same texts speak of a temple of Išhara existing on "Išhara Mount,"[8] a mountain in the Taurus mountain range near the towns of Neriša and Tarša—modern-day Tarsus[9]—some 12.5 miles (20 kilometers) from the Mediterranean coast.

What seems important here is that the city of Tarsus celebrates the story of the Shahmaran in the belief that this is where her story was played out. Indeed, the cave entrance into the Snake Mother's underworld domain is pointed out to visitors even to this day. Similar claims regarding the entrance to the Shahmaran's underworld domain are attached to the city of Adana, which lies some 25 miles (40 kilometers) to the east-northeast of Tarsus. So a connection between the perpetuation of myths relating to the Shahmaran and the presence in the same region of cult centers of the goddess Išhara seems beyond coincidence, the two being the memory of a primeval mother goddess associated both with snakes and with scorpions.

Among the Hittites, Išhara bore the title "lady of the mountains and rivers of the Hatti kingdom [the pre-Hittite peoples of Bronze Age Anatolia]."[10] In this manner she was a primeval earth mother associated with the ancestral realms of the later Hittites.[11] Confirmation of this comes from ancient Mesopotamian texts that speak of her as one of the "Ancient gods," or "Underground gods,"[12] showing that, like the Shahmaran of Anatolian folklore, Išhara was seen as an underworld snake deity.

So could Išhara have had anything to do with the beliefs and practices associated with Karahan Tepe's Taş Tepeler settlement? We should recall here that the hill's true name is Keçili, which, as we saw in chapter 10, derives from the Kurdish root *keç* meaning "woman," "daughter," "maiden," "girl," and even "queen."[13] It therefore seems likely that this place-name hides within it the memory of a primeval female deity who across the millennia would eventually come to be identified both with Išhara and with the legendary Shahmaran.

INTO THE KHABUR TRIANGLE

Išhara's closest recorded cult center to the Tektek Mountains was in the Upper Khabur basin,[14] located around 93 miles (150 kilometers) east-southeast of Karahan Tepe in what is northern Syria today. In this region, known to archaeologists as the Khabur Triangle, a number of important Neolithic and later Chalcolithic (or Copper) Age settlements have been found. They include Tell Brak and Tell Halaf, the last of which became the type-site for the Pottery Neolithic culture of this name (see fig. 13.3, p. 106).

The importance of the Halaf culture was first recognized through the excavations of the celebrated German lawyer, explorer, and archaeologist Max von Oppenheim (1860–1946). He formerly identified their unique style of painted pottery ware, which dates to circa 6500–5000 BCE (see fig. 13.4, p. 106).

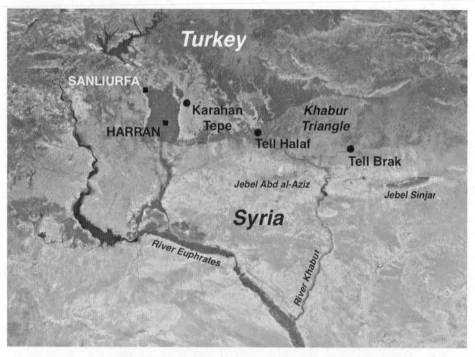

Fig. 13.3. Map showing key Neolithic sites in Syria's Khabur Triangle.
Image by Google Earth and Andrew Collins.

Fig. 13.4. An example of the Halaf culture's painted ceramic ware.
Photo by yuber.

Tell Halaf is just 45 miles (72 kilometers) east-southeast of Karahan Tepe, meaning there is every chance that after the site was abandoned around 8000 BCE, its community might have gone on to inspire the emergence of the Halaf culture. Indeed, there is little question that the blade tool industry discovered in connection with Halafian sites in the Khabur Triangle can be seen as a natural progression of that present among the Pre-Pottery Neolithic peoples of southeastern Anatolia.*[15]

It should be noted also that Max von Oppenheim explored the Tektek Mountains, recording any ancient sites he came across. Ismail Can, one of the sons of the owner of Keçili farm, strongly suspects that the German archaeologist arrived there looking for archaeological remains. Unfortunately, however, Ismail has been unable to find any pictorial evidence of von Oppenheim's visit to the locality. Von Oppenheim did, however, record details about Zakzuk Dağı, the prominent hill located just 2.5 miles (4 kilometers) north of Karahan Tepe (see chapter 12),[16] which had almost certainly been a place of interest to the Pre-Pottery Neolithic peoples of the area.

SUMERIAN TRADITIONS

In addition to being associated with the Bronze Age cult of the goddess Išhara, there are indications that the Khabur Triangle is connected with mythological stories from Sumerian tradition that speak of a "river of the netherworld" known as Hubur (also ḪUBUR or Hu-bur). This could well be the Khabur River, which defines the boundaries of the region. The realm of Hubur was said to be the domain of a primordial dragon, monster, or serpent named Ummu-Hubur, who is thought to have been a form of Tiamat, the primordial serpent-dragon and mother of the gods killed by the god Marduk. As we have seen, her cult appears to have been linked with that of Išhara, who in some astrological texts is referred to as "Išhara Tiamat," generally translated as "Išhara of the ocean."[17]

Within the *Enūma Eliš*, Hubur is referred to as "mother sea Hubur, who fashions all things," a reference once again to Tiamat in her role both as the personification of the primeval waters of the oceans and as the creator of the

---

*See, for instance, blade tools found at sites such as Umm Qseir in the Upper Khabur basin, many of which are made of obsidian from sites in eastern Anatolia.

two major rivers of the region—the Tigris and Euphrates. These are said to have been formed from the tears that poured from Tiamat's eyes when her body was dismembered.[18] The connection with the Khabur Triangle is in the fact that the Khabur River is the largest perennial tributary of the Euphrates River, confirming its association with Tiamat.

Such beliefs may have strengthened the importance of the goddess Išhara in the minds of the Bronze Age peoples who came to inhabit the Khabur basin. It should also be noted that Tiamat, who is described as the "snake of darkness," almost certainly helped influence the development of myths relating not only to the Shahmaran, who was herself dismembered, but also the dragon snake of Hittite folktales named Illuyanka.[19]

THE COMING OF THE ANUNNAKI

In Sumerian mythology, the souls of the dead were said to have crossed a desert to pass over the Hubur. Having done this they could reach the mountain of Kur (also known as Kharsag), where the builder gods known as the Anunna or Anunnaki tended a "civilized settlement both architecturally and politically."[20] This is the first mention of the infamous Anunnaki, the "gods of heaven [*An*] and earth [*ki*]" of Sumero-Akkadian and later Babylonian tradition, who would appear to have had an earthly origin—one associated with the place of the ancestors and the destination of dead souls.

There seems every reason to suspect that, even before the rise of the Sumerian city-states down on the Mesopotamian plain in what is today the country of Iraq, the cult of Tiamat thrived in the Khabur Triangle and that she was indeed a personification of "mother sea Hubur, who fashions all things." Furthermore, there seems every reason to suspect that the cult of Išhara took over from that of Tiamat-Hubur in the same region, the two deities clearly having similar attributes and affiliations.

In addition to this, it seems possible that the root of the concept of the otherworldly mountain known as Kur or Kharsag, which lay beyond—that is, north of the "river of the netherworld"—reflects a memory of the Pre-Pottery Neolithic world of Taş Tepeler in southeastern Anatolia, one that was almost certainly preserved and perpetuated by the Halaf culture that rose to dominance in the Khabur Triangle as early as 6500 BCE. It also seems likely that the cult of Išhara, in her role as Snake Mother, flourished in the same region from a very early date indeed having taken over from that of both Tiamat and Ummu-Hubur.

With their clear associations with the symbol of a snake, the earliest manifestations of Tiamat, Išhara, and the Shahmaran very likely arose among the region's Taş Tepeler culture. For them, it would seem, she was not only the personification of a primordial Snake Mother, but also an ancestral goddess with prominent hills representing her body and caves symbolizing her womb and vulva. If this is correct (and it should be pointed out that in some folktales the Shahmaran is considered male), how does any of this relate to what we know about the activities that might have taken place at Karahan Tepe during its heyday?

My thoughts kept going back to the incised snake with the elongated body seen in Karahan Tepe's Pit Shrine (Structure AA). Was the deep hole cut into its leveled floor envisaged as a womb chamber, its carved recess the place where a supplicant might undergo some kind of experiential journey involving a primordial Snake Mother? If so, then what would the destination of such a shamanic journey have been? Was it simply a deep part of the subconscious, or was the purpose of such ritual processes to project your mind or soul into the darkness of space toward a celestial counterpart of the primordial Snake Mother of the type explored within these pages?

One clue, I suspected, was the carved relief of a fox immediately in front of the long, incised serpent on the front edge of the Pit Shrine's carved stone bench. Both creatures, the serpent and the fox, faced north, but toward what? As we see next, a much closer examination of this curious structure will provide major clues regarding its suspected function as a shamanic launchpad into a sky world where the celestial counterparts of the snake and fox await our arrival.

PART 4

THE SUN
AND THE SERPENT

14

Celestial Synchronization

Karahan Tepe's Structure AA, what we call the Pit Shrine, is a peculiar sight. As previously indicated, it is trapezoidal in shape with a sunken floor just 3.5 feet (1.1 meters) below the level bedrock. Along its western wall is a long, slightly curved bench carved out of the bedrock. Stretched out along almost the entire length of its front edge is an incised serpent, its head toward the north. Immediately beyond it is the carved relief of a standing fox that also faces north. Since the shrine contains no other carved imagery there is presumably a connection between these two creatures.

By far the most curious aspect of the room, which like the Pillars Shrine next to it was probably carved to resemble the likeness of a snake's head, is why an enormous, irregularly shaped pit was cut into its floor. The pit drops to a depth of around 7.5 feet (2.3 meters) and, like the structure itself, is roughly trapezoidal in shape. At ground level on the western side of the pit is a hollowed-out recess just large enough for someone to crawl inside (see plate 31). That this action might have involved assuming a fetal position raises the question of whether the carving out of this deep pit was a deliberate attempt by those who constructed the shrine to create an artificial womb chamber. If so, then was it seen to exist within the body of a primordial earth mother whose principal totem was the snake, an ultimate symbol of transformation through its ability to slew its skin and regenerate?

One other peculiar feature of the structure is that on the south side of its sunken pit, at the same height as the level bedrock, is a rectilinear lip that has the unlikely appearance of a Stone Age diving board (see fig. 14.1).

What was this for? Did someone stand there to look down into the pit's hollowed-out alcove positioned directly beneath it, or could it have served a

Fig. 14.1. The lip overlooking the sunken hole seen in Karahan Tepe's Structure AA (the Pit Shrine). Photo by Andrew Collins.

higher purpose? Archaeologists at the site suggest that it could be the blank for another carved head like the one seen in the neighboring Pillars Shrine, a theory I find difficult to comprehend. The same archaeologists also suspect that since Structure AA is so irregular in appearance it might have been left unfinished, something I also find difficult to accept. To me it is perfect in its design. What function it had in the rituals that took place there is, however, the much greater challenge to understand.

When I first saw images of Karahan Tepe's Pit Shrine during the fall of 2021, it was its unique orientation that captured my attention, for this seemed greatly at variance with both the Great Ellipse (Structure AD) and the Pillars Shrine (Structure AB). They, as explained in chapter 7, appear to be locked into an alignment based on the presence of an ellipse displaying a 32:27 whole number ratio. This alignment exactly bisects the Pillars Shrine's long axis, hits the curved serpentine slab of stone at its northern end, and then very roughly follows the course of the deep, snake-like groove that connects the structure with the nearby Pit Shrine.

What also seemed clear was that the alignment linking Karahan Tepe with Keçili Tepe and through this the northern opening of the Milky Way's Dark Rift coincided with the directional axis of the Pillars Shrine, which is approximately 20 degrees west of north. This alignment, as we have seen, would have targeted the setting of the Cygnus star Deneb as it sank down into the summit of Keçili Tepe.

In contrast, the orientation of the Pit Shrine seemed entirely different. Its directional axis clearly took advantage of the hill's northern slope, giving it a west-northwesterly directionality with uninterrupted views of the western, northern, and eastern horizon. Neither the Great Ellipse nor the Pillars Shrine possess a similar visual perspective, since, for them, the entire western horizon is blocked by the hill.

ALIGNED TO THE SUN

I had my suspicions immediately regarding what the Pit Shrine's unique orientation could imply. Since it was oriented west-northwest, there was every chance it targeted the setting of the sun at the time of the summer solstice. This is the most northerly point the sun reaches on its yearly course before beginning its journey southward toward the winter solstice at which it achieves its most southerly rising and setting position.

The term solstice is derived from the Latin words *sol* meaning "sun" and *sistere* meaning "to stand still." It is a reference to the fact that when the sun reaches its most northerly and southerly rising and setting positions it appears to remain there across a two- to three-day period. The solstices also mark the longest and shortest days of the year, which, in the northern hemisphere, occur, respectively, on the summer solstice in June and winter solstice in December. In the southern hemisphere it is the opposite way around, with the summer solstice occurring in December and the winter solstice taking place in June.

Of course, my suspicions regarding the suspected orientation of the Pit Shrine would require considerable investigation before they could be either validated or dismissed. To this end, I asked Rodney Hale to examine all available overhead images of Karahan Tepe's three interconnected structures to determine as best as possible the Pit Shrine's orientation. After some back and forth between us, we were finally in agreement that the structure's primary directional axis is 302 degrees azimuth (+/– 0.5 of a degree); that is, 32 degrees

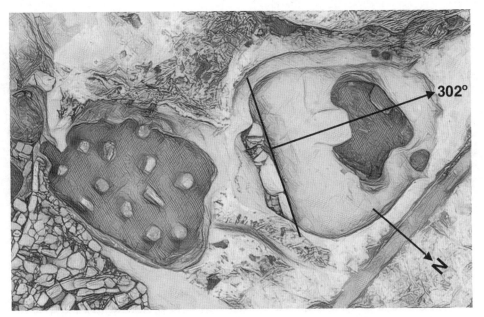

Fig. 14.2. Plan of Karahan Tepe's Structure AA showing its alignment
toward the setting sun at the time of the summer solstice in 9000 BCE.
Illustration by Andrew Collins and Rodney Hale.

north of west (see fig. 14.2). Significantly, this orientation lines up very well
with the lip feature overlooking the deep pit and, to a lesser degree, with the
position of the carved recess cut into its side wall.

Hale and I then checked the position of the solstitial sun from the latitude
of Karahan Tepe during the epoch of its construction. This showed that at
the time of the summer solstice the sun set at an azimuth of approximately
302 degrees (see fig. 14.3).[1] So we can be fairly sure that the directional axis of
the Pit Shrine did indeed line up with the setting sun on the day of the summer solstice.

What is more, since the stone floor of the structure is only 3.5 feet
(1.1 meters) below the level surface of the bedrock, it means that anyone standing on the lip feature at the time of its construction would have been able to
view the sun setting directly in front of them on this day. So not only was this
lip a means of looking down into the pit, but it also enabled the observer to
look at the sun as it set on the day of the summer solstice, a solar spectacle that
perhaps formed part of some more complex ceremony or ritual involving all
three of the interconnected bedrock structures.

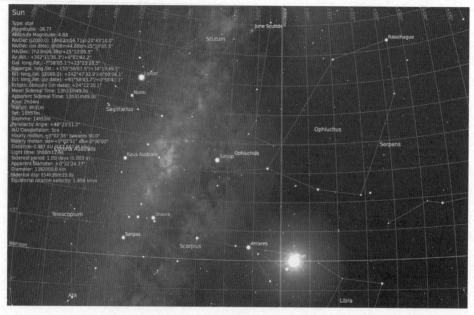

Fig. 14.3. View of the sun setting at the time of the summer solstice
as seen from the latitude of Karahan Tepe in 9000 BCE.
This image was made using the Stellarium free open-source planetarium.

The implications of this discovery are immense, for it suggests that Karahan Tepe's Pit Shrine is perhaps the oldest solar observatory in the world. Having said this, it should be noted that I had previously recorded similar solar alignments in connection with Layer II structures at Göbekli Tepe. The site's Lion Pillars Building, for instance, being oriented east-west, targets the rising of the sun at the time of the spring and fall equinoxes, while Enclosure F would seem to have been aligned to the rising sun at the time of the summer solstice.[2] These particular buildings, however, are slightly younger than Karahan Tepe's Pit Shrine, which was probably constructed during the Late Pre-Pottery Neolithic A period, circa 9100–8800 BCE. The Layer II structures at Göbekli Tepe were built during the Early to Mid Pre-Pottery Neolithic B period and thus date from circa 8800–7600 BCE.

Having established these facts, I could not fully confirm the Pit Shrine's solstitial alignment until I had a chance to inspect the excavations firsthand. This I was finally able to do across a period of 3 days in September 2022 and then again on two occasions in December that year. From my onsite calculations and observations I was able to determine that from the interior of the Pit

Shrine at the time of its construction the sun would indeed have been seen to set down on the west-northwesterly horizon perfectly in line with the structure's directional orientation at the time of the summer solstice (see plate 32 to see how the setting sun can be viewed from Structure AA).

Yet questions remained. Why, for instance, had a deep pit been cut into the floor of the shrine? Why did this have a hollowed-out recess on its western side? Had this really acted as a womb chamber within the body of a primordial Snake Mother represented by Karahan Tepe itself? Did the shrine's orientation toward the setting sun at the time of the summer solstice form part of a calendrical rite that either began or culminated on this day? The answers to these questions, as we see in the coming chapters, elevate what might have been going on at Karahan Tepe to a whole new level.

15

The Scorpionic Gateway

The free planetarium software program Stellarium had given me a glimpse of what the skies might have looked like from the latitude of Karahan Tepe at the time of the summer solstice during the epoch of its construction. It is easy to just click the computer keyboard and watch as the sun slowly sets into the west-northwesterly horizon, perfectly in line with the orientation of the site's enigmatic Pit Shrine (Structure AA).

Such observations taking place at Karahan Tepe during the Pre-Pottery Neolithic Age would have been well before the emergence across the region of wide-scale agriculture, so the Pit Shrine's alignment toward the summer solstice sunset must, I concluded, have formed part of some much earlier tradition. But what could this have been, and did it only involve the sun, or was there something more to the Pit Shrine's solstitial alignment?

With these thoughts in mind, I continued to click the keyboard to see what would happen after the sun had sunk below the horizon at the time of the summer solstice during the epoch in question. Very quickly, twilight gave way to a darkened sky filled with stars, planets, and the outlines of various constellations.

What I saw next was staggering in its implications and would make me reconsider everything I felt I knew about what the builders of Karahan Tepe were attempting to achieve during their rituals there. I say this because approximately two and a half hours after sunset at the time of the summer solstice, a person standing on the lip feature inside the Pit Shrine would have beheld a wondrous sight.

Exactly where the sun had earlier set on the west-northwesterly horizon, the Milky Way would have been seen standing vertically upward with the stars

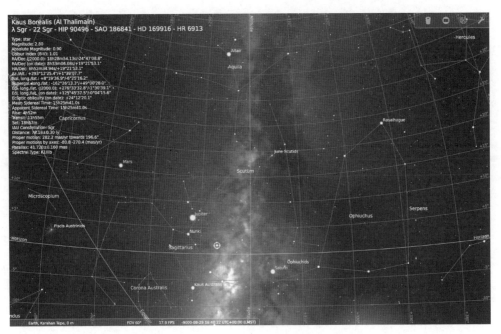

Fig. 15.1. View of the Milky Way rising vertically into the sky two and a half hours after sunset, as seen from the latitude of Karahan Tepe at the time of the summer solstice in 9000 BCE. Note the constellations of Sagittarius and Ophiuchus standing on the horizon with the southern termination of the Milky Way's Dark Rift showcased between them. This image was made using the Stellarium free open-source planetarium.

of Sagittarius to its west and those of Ophiuchus, the serpent bearer or snake charmer, to its east. Both asterisms would have been seen directly above the horizon before gradually setting as the evening progressed. It was almost as if, as sky figures, they were seen to guard not just the Milky Way, but more importantly the southern termination of the Dark Rift, which, being imme-diately above the horizon, would have appeared like a starry portal ready to accept spirits of the living and the dead onto the Milky Way (see fig. 15.1). Perhaps the setting of the sun at the time of the summer solstice acted as a time marker for this process to begin as well as a directional marker indicating in which direction a person standing in the Pit Shrine should face to commence their journey to the celestial realms.

What we can also say is that as all this was taking place the Milky Way would have stretched from the horizon all the way up to the Cygnus star Deneb and the northern opening of the Dark Rift, which at the time would have been crossing the meridian on its upper transit at an altitude of 75 degrees. This was just 15 degrees short of zenith—that is, directly overhead.

At this same time, the bright star Arcturus in the constellation of Boötes would have been crossing the meridian on its lower transit immediately above the peak of Zakzuk Dağı located 2.5 miles (4 kilometers) due north of Karahan Tepe. As we saw in chapter 12, the presence on this prominent local hill of rock-cut structures that probably started as natural caves tends to indicate that it was of special interest to the area's Taş Tepeler community. This seems especially so with the knowledge that from its summit you can see right across to Şanlıurfa in the west-northwest and with it Göbekli Tepe perched high up on the southern reaches of the Anti-Taurus range.*

ENTERING STARRY PORTALS

The implied orientation of the Pit Shrine toward the southern termination of the Milky Way's Dark Rift at the time of the summer solstice is of incredible importance to what might have been going at Karahan Tepe. In their seminal work on the development of beliefs and practices relating to world ages, cosmic axes, and the concept of precessional time, titled *Hamlet's Mill* (1969), Italian-American philosopher and historian of science Giorgio de Santillana and German anthropologist Hertha von Dechend had much to say about such alignments.

Drawing on star lore and mythological traditions from such diverse places as North and South America, Polynesia, Egypt, and Mesopotamia, Santillana and Dechend gathered together compelling evidence to suggest that there once existed a collective understanding regarding the soul's journey to the afterlife via the Milky Way. This, they proposed, was accessed via two sky "gates" corresponding to where the ecliptic, the sun's annual path through the zodiacal constellations, crosses this starry stream marking the outer rim of our own Milky Way galaxy. One of these sky gates was located in the vicinity of Scorpius, Sagittarius, and Ophiuchus with the other on the opposite side of the sky close to the constellations of Gemini, Taurus, Orion, and the cluster of seven stars known as the Pleiades. Both sky gates became accessible to the land of the liv-

---

*Also visible from Zakzuk Dağı is Karaca Dağ, an extinct volcano situated 45 miles (72 kilometers) to the northeast. As we see in chapter 35, Karaca Dağ has its own part to play in this story.

ing when they lined up with the local horizon at the time of the summer and winter solstice.[1]

More crucially, Santillana and Dechend identified the goddess Išhara as the guardian of the sky gate marked by the stars of Scorpius, comparing her role with that of similar scorpion goddesses, such as the one revered among the Sumo and Mosquito tribes of Honduras and Nicaragua.[2] In this respect they cited the words of American anthropologist Hartley Burr Alexander from 1920, which in their original form read:

> The Mother Scorpion of this myth is regarded by the Mosquito as dwelling at the end of the Milky Way, where she receives the souls of the dead; and from her, represented as a mother with many breasts, at which children take suck, come the souls of the new-born—a belief which points to a notion of reincarnation.[3]

Although Alexander does not state that the Mother Scorpion was herself the Scorpius constellation, the fact that she resides "at the end of the Milky Way, where she receives the souls of the dead," makes it clear this was almost certainly the case. His words, however, prompted Santillana and Dechend to write that the Mother Scorpion's role, "also fits the Scorpion-goddess Selket-Serqet of ancient Egypt and the Ishara tam.tim of the Babylonians. Ishara of the sea, goddess of the constellation Scorpius, was also called 'Lady of the Rivers' [that is, the Milky Way]."[4]

It seems clear, therefore, that Išhara, like other scorpion deities around the world, was originally a guardian of the Milky Way's Scorpionic gateway—that is, the southern termination of the Dark Rift—in which role she was seen as "Lady of the Rivers." There she received the souls of the dead, and those of shamans and initiates, and, we must assume, was seen to give birth to new souls entering this world (see fig. 15.2).

Išhara's association with the stars of Scorpius, the celestial scorpion, goes back to the beginning of Sumerian times where she is identified in Sumero-Akkadian and later Babylonian astronomy as the celestial scorpion ^{mul}GIR.TAB (a Sumerian word meaning something like "sharp weapon" or "sharp sting," a reference to the creature's stinger).[5] It also seems clear that the "star of Išhara" mentioned in some Mesopotamian texts is a reference to Scorpius's red giant star Antares (α Scorpii),[6] no doubt the reason why,

Fig. 15.2. The constellation of Scorpius (the zodiac sign of Scorpio)
by Johann Bayer from his star atlas titled *Uranometria* published in 1603.

during an important Hittite festival known as Hissuwa, the goddess wore a red dress.[7]

The goddess's original form was not, however, a scorpion but, as we have seen, a snake, a totemic form of the Scorpius constellation from very earliest times.[8] This was the case, for instance, among the Hebrews, whose ancestral roots can be traced back to the earliest West Semitic populations of northern Mesopotamia (southeastern Anatolia) and Syria. In addition to identifying Scorpius as Akrabh (*'aqribh*), the Scorpion, the Hebrews associated this particular constellation's influence with one of the 12 tribes of Israel. This was the Tribe of Dan, whose founder is described in the book of Genesis as "a serpent by the way."[9] The tribe's banner shows "a crowned Snake or Basilisk," which is considered to be a representation of the Scorpius constellation.[10]

Then we have the story of the Shahmaran. In this tale, it is a scorpion that leads Cemshab to find the Snake Mother's otherworldly domain, an allusion not only to the Shahmaran's identity as a primeval snake deity, but also to the fact that one of her forms was that of the scorpion. This seems certain with the knowledge that the stories of the Shahmaran flourish today in the same regions that the cult of Išhara once prospered. This can be seen not just in southern Anatolia in cities like Tarsus and Adana but also within the Khabur Triangle of northern Syria. In this region, cultural art featuring the Shahmaran is still produced. For instance, in the Al-Hasakah district of northern Syria, close to Tell Halaf, the type-site of the Halaf culture, there exists to this day a thriving local industry producing representations of the Shahmaran.[11] Both Tell Halaf and Al-Hasakah are within the Khabur Triangle, where major cult centers of the goddess Išhara existed during the Bronze Age.[12]

Thus it seems extremely likely that Scorpius's identification as a celestial snake both in Anatolia and in the Near East as a whole is extremely ancient indeed. The fact that its stars were identified as a snake or scorpion personified as a female deity venerated in these same regions is especially important, telling us that the constellation of Scorpius in its role as guardian of the sky gate located at the southern termination of the Milky Way's Dark Rift could well have been of primary importance to Anatolia's Taş Tepeler population.

If this is correct, then it seems likely that the builders of the three interconnected bedrock structures at Karahan Tepe saw the stars of the three main constellations associated with this sky gate—namely Sagittarius, Scorpius, and Ophiuchus—as celestial reflections of whatever shamanic activities were taking place there.

It is important to remember also that the Great Ellipse (Structure AD) and the Pillars Shrine (Structure AB) appear to have been aligned to the *northern* opening of the Milky Way's Dark Rift, marked, as we have seen, by the Cygnus star Deneb. What this implies is that *all three* interconnected bedrock structures at Karahan Tepe were aligned either toward the northern entrance of the Dark Rift or toward its southern termination, once again suggesting a special interest in this area of the night sky. Even though by the time the Milky Way appeared on the horizon on the night of the summer solstice the stars of Scorpius would have set alongside the sun, both the constellations of Sagittarius and Ophiuchus *would* have been clearly visible on either side of the starry stream.

THE THIRTEENTH SIGN

Both Scorpius and Sagittarius are, of course, signs of the zodiac, meaning that they are located on the ecliptic, the circular path along which the sun is seen to move across the course of a year. The constellation of Ophiuchus, a name that means "serpent bearer," is also located on the ecliptic, although it is *not* classified as an official zodiacal constellation. This appellation is reserved only for the 12 more familiar signs, which are each allotted 30 degrees of the 360-degree circle of the ecliptic no matter what area of sky they occupy. What this does is create 12 houses of the zodiac, each of which is allotted a time period or "house" of 30.43 days. It should be noted, however, that the actual time the sun spends passing through each zodiacal constellation varies considerably based on the constellation's size as well as the manner it is positioned on the ecliptic.

Despite Ophiuchus not being classed as one of the signs of the zodiac, the sun passes through this constellation for a period of 18 days, something that occurs in the Gregorian calendar between November 29 and December 17 each year. In contrast the sun spends just 6 or 7 days in the constellation of Scorpius (November 23–28 in the modern calendar), a staggering fact that has led some astrological writers to draw attention to the role Ophiuchus must play in astrology.

The possibility of a lost thirteenth sign of the zodiac has appealed to a number of western astrological writers (see, for instance, James Vogh's intriguing book *Arachne Rising: The Thirteenth Sign*, published in 1977).[13] So I find no reason why we cannot give Ophiuchus this title. As we see next, the sun's association with this constellation is crucial in understanding the timing, purpose, and symbolism of any rituals that might have taken place at Karahan Tepe at the height of its occupation.

16

The Cosmic Snake Charmer

Located partially on the ecliptic and partially on the Milky Way, Ophiuchus takes its name from the Greek ὀφιοῦχος (*ophioûkhos*), meaning the "serpent bearer" or "serpent holder." Among the Romans, Ophiuchus was known as Serpentarius, the "serpent handler," from Latin *serpēns*, meaning "serpent" or "snake," and *serpentis*, a genitive singular form of *serpēns*. The snake in question is formed from the stars of a separate constellation known as Serpens. These are seen on either side of Ophiuchus, with those on its western side being known as Serpens Cauda, the

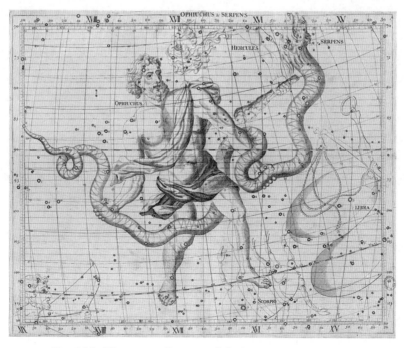

Fig. 16.1. The constellations of Ophiuchus and Serpens
by John Flamsteed (1646–1719) from his *Atlas Coelestis*, published in 1729.

125

"Serpent Tail," and those on its eastern side—which look far more snakelike in appearance—being known as Serpens Caput, the "Serpent Head." (See fig. 16.1.)

Very little sky lore is attached to the stars of Serpens (although see chapter 27 on the role it plays in Ophite Gnostic tradition).[1] This seems reserved almost exclusively for Ophiuchus, since both constellations were at one time seen as a single asterism.[2] During the classical age the stars of Ophiuchus were identified with the Greek god Asclepius, a great healer and medical practitioner who used magic herbs to cure the sick and even raise the dead. His primary totem was the snake, a universal symbol of magic and medicine. According to legend, Hades was unhappy that Asclepius had brought the giant huntsman, Orion, back to life and so asked his brother Zeus to intervene. He crushed Asclepius with his thunderbolt but afterward brought him back to life and placed him in the sky as the constellation of Ophiuchus.[3]

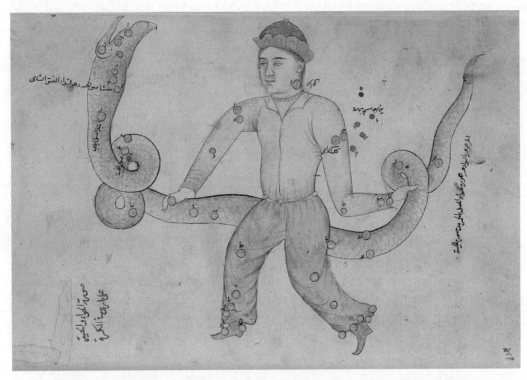

Fig. 16.2. Constellation of Al Hawwā, the "snake charmer," the Arabic and Persian form of Ophiuchus. From the *Suwar al-kawākib*, written by the astronomer 'Abd al-Rahman ibn 'Umar al-Sufi, also known as Azophi (903–986 CE), and published originally in 964 CE. The illustration is from an edition that appeared in Samarkand (present-day Uzbekistan) in 820 AH (1417 CE), the copy in question being rebound around circa 1730 CE and held by the Library of Congress.

Fig. 16.3. Two representations of the sky figures known as the Sitting Gods in
ancient Mesopotamian literature (after Black and Green 1992, fig. 137).
The example on the right perhaps incorporates not only the stars of Ophiuchus
and Serpens, but also some from the neighboring constellation of Scorpius,
hence the arm ending in a scorpion.
Illustration by Nick Burton.

In medieval Arabic and Persian astronomy, Ophiuchus is depicted as a
strong, male figure clutching a serpent made up of the stars of Serpens (see
fig. 16.2).[4] Here he is known as Al Hawwā, the "snake charmer," while in
Turkish sky lore Ophiuchus becomes Yilange (modern Turkish: Yılan-cı),
which translates as "a person who belongs to the snake tribe," from *yılan*,
meaning "snake."[4]

In Babylonian astronomy, Ophiuchus was perhaps a lost constellation
known, confusingly, as the "Sitting Gods" ([mul]DINGIR.TUŠ.A-MEŠ).[6] As a
sky figure, the Sitting Gods constellation was shown in art as a human figure
with his legs ending in two separate snakes (see fig. 16.3). Sometimes the figure is shown grasping the neck of a serpent, similar to some representations of
Ophiuchus.

THE RISE OF THE ANUNNAKI

The Sitting Gods constellation was the dualistic personification of a primeval deity or *genius loci* of the E-Kur (the "house [E-] of Kur"), with *kur* being an Akkadian and later Babylonian word meaning "mountain" and/or "netherworld," implying a "house of the mountain."[7] As a geographical location it was thought to exist in the extreme north, northeast, or east of the Mesopotamian plain, where it was identified with a mythical mountain named Kharsag (Sumerian: ḪAR.SAG̃). On this was the primeval occupational mound (tepe) known as Du-ku, where lived the Anunnaki gods of Sumero-Akkadian and later Babylonian and Assyrian mythology. From there they provided humanity with the gift of "Sheep and Grain,"[8] a clear reference to the invention and spread of animal husbandry and cultivated wheat during the Pre-Pottery Neolithic Age (a subject we look at more closely in chapter 35).

In his 2012 book *Göbekli Tepe: A Stone Age Sanctuary in South-Eastern Anatolia*, Professor Klaus Schmidt (1953–2014), the discoverer of Göbekli Tepe, wrote that the Du-ku mound of Sumerian tradition might well be based on a lingering memory among the Indigenous populations of southeastern Anatolia regarding the importance of Göbekli Tepe. "Is it possible," he asked, "that behind Göbekli Tepe there hides Mount Du-ku, and are the anthropomorphous pillars of Göbekli Tepe—suddenly surprisingly real—the ancient Anuna Gods?"[9]

If this is correct and the Du-ku mound *is* indeed a memory of either Göbekli Tepe or one of the other Taş Tepeler tepes in the Şanlıurfa region, then the fact that the Sitting Gods constellation was also said to have emerged from the Du-ku mound, the home of the Anunnaki, suggests that serpent veneration took place there. If this, too, is correct, it might well reflect the memory of some kind of interest in the stars of Ophiuchus, in particular any legends associating not only the constellation, but also this entire area of the sky, with snakes. What this also suggests is that the Anunnaki of the "Sheep and Grain" story are a memory of the prime movers behind the emergence of Taş Tepeler, a matter we return to in chapter 37.

FROM SNAKE SHAMANISM TO ASCLEPIEIA

Every legend regarding Ophiuchus and his relationship to the stars of Serpens centers around acts of snake charming, snake bearing, and, through the god

Asclepius, snake medicine, snake magic, and even dream incubation. All of these ritualized practices were once associated with Asclepieia—that is, temples and sanctuaries dedicated to the god.

The cult of Asclepius embraced many distinct aspects of snake veneration and snake worship, including the use of plant medicines. These would no doubt have included the employment of psychoactive substances by priests and initiates to achieve altered states of consciousness and, through them, acts of transformation and rebirth in the second life. Interestingly, Asclepius was seen as a chthonic god associated with caves inhabited by snakes, bringing him closer to other primeval snake deities such as Išhara and, of course, the Shahmaran, both of whom were connected with underworld environments.

THE SNAKE CHARMERS

So does Ophiuchus's associations with snake handling and snake charming, along with his identification as the Sitting Gods of Mesopotamian astronomy and the god Asclepius of Greek tradition, indicate that he is simply the celestial personification of a snake priest or snake shaman? Dutch Orientalist and mathematician Jacob Golius (1596–1667) wrote that Ophiuchus was a member of the Psylli or Psylle, a legendary Berber tribe that inhabited Cyrenaïca, a former large territory in Libya, North Africa.[10] They were known for their ability to control snakes and cure the bites of poisonous serpents.[11] Ophiuchus's association with the Psylli is confirmed with the knowledge that he is named as "le Psylle" in a French translation of a work by the Persian astronomer ʿAbd al-Rahman ibn ʿUmar al-Sufi.[12]

Little is known about the Psylli other than the fact that they had an incredible, almost magical, control of snakes.[13] They are often compared with the Marsi, hereditary healers, magicians, and snake charmers from the Abruzzo region of Italy. To this day they acknowledge the power of Angitia (pronounced "an-jit-sia"), an ancient Italian snake goddess whose name comes from the Latin *anguis*, meaning "serpent." The Marsi, who are descended from an Iron Age tribe of the same name, are able to handle, hold, and perform tricks with poisonous snakes that will never bite them. Every year on May 1, dozens of Marsi gather in the village of Cocullo to show off their extraordinary snake-handling skills and pay their respects to Angitia, whom they acknowledge as the tribe's ancestress.

THE SNAKE CHARMERS OF THE YEZIDI

There are many other snake-charming peoples across the ancient world. In Anatolia and the Near East, for instance, hereditary snake handlers were once common among the Yezidi (also written Yazidi), the much-persecuted ethnic group of Kurdish ethnicity who hold the serpent as sacred. Their snake charmers were once widespread throughout the various territories they inhabited. These stretched from Şanlıurfa province in the west to Armenia and Georgia in the north, the Sinjar and Khabur regions of northern Syria in the south, and Iraq and Iran in the east. Yezidi snake charmers claimed descent from a legendary holy man named Sheikh Mand, who was said to have had power over serpents.[14]

British cultural anthropologist, Orientalist, and novelist Ethel Stefana Drower (1879–1972), respectfully known as Mrs. Drower, met a Yezidi snake charmer and his daughter Jehera, meaning "Snake-Poison," when visiting the village of Bashiqa in northern Iraq during the 1930s. This is how she recalled the encounter:

> The *shaikh* and his little daughter now entered our courtyard. Large serpents, one brown and one black, were draped about the necks of the man and child, their tails falling behind like fur boas worn years ago by European women. The *shaikh* unwound the big black snake from Jahera's neck, and it slithered along in the sparse grass looking very evil indeed. It was some five or six feet in length and its body two inches or more in thickness. He caught it again, returned it to the child and then displayed his own. I disbursed an offering and then the *shaikh* and the ugly little girl posed for their photographs, holding the snakes' flat heads close to their lips."[15] (Original author's emphasis.)

One of the photos of the sheikh and his daughter, complete with snakes draped around their necks, appears as fig. 16.4 in this book. As I wrote in *From the Ashes of Angels* (1996), the Yezidi retain core elements of an arcane religion with its roots in beliefs and practices that thrived in eastern Anatolia during the Neolithic Age.[16]

Perhaps inevitably, one of the key sacred symbols of the Yezidi is the snake, which is displayed standing upright in bas relief on the sides of doorways leading into religious sanctuaries as well as the tombs of important sheikhs (see fig. 16.5, and plates 33 and 34).[17] How the snake, which is always shown as black in color, became so important to the Yezidi is lost today. Its obvious importance

Fig. 16.4. Photograph taken during the 1930s by Mrs. E. S. Drower showing a Yezidi snake charmer and his daughter she encountered in the village of Bashiqa in northern Iraq.

Fig. 16.5. The standing black snake seen at the side of entrances into Yezidi religious shrines, cemeteries, and some major tombs. The example shown is from the entrance doorway into the shrine of Sheikh Adi at Lalish in northern Iraq. From Ussher, 1865, 409.

to the religion, however, hints at the symbol's immense antiquity, as well as its indirect association with snake charming and even snake shamanism.

REFLECTIONS IN THE STARS

The plethora of snake symbolism on display at Karahan Tepe makes it clear that its Pre-Pottery Neolithic community venerated the creature in a manner comparable to that of the Psylli of Libya, the Marsi of Italy, and, more importantly, the Yezidi of southwestern Asia. If this is correct, then did its shamans and initiates see their own connection with snakes reflected in the stars? Might they have been responsible for first attributing serpentine qualities to the stars of Ophiuchus and nearby Scorpius? Were these two asterisms originally conceived as celestial counterparts of the Pre-Pottery Neolithic people's own beliefs and practices involving snake handling, snake charming, and, most important of all, snake shamanism?

Ophiuchus's identification with chthonic deities such as Asclepius and Scorpius's association with the snake and scorpion goddess Išhara suggest a real connection between physical cave environments, serpentine imagery, and the southern termination of the Milky Way's Dark Rift, the Scorpionic gateway as we might call it. If this is correct, then it becomes possible that the hypogeum-like caves on the slopes of Keçili Tepe, and perhaps even Karahan Tepe's Pit Shrine, were seen as symbolic points of contact with this sky portal, which enabled supplicants to access the Milky Way in its role as a road or river to the sky world.

We can only assume that rituals featuring this area of the sky were timed to coincide with the summer solstice, which provides us with both the longest day of the year as well as the shortest night. Just two and a half hours after sunset on this day the southern termination of the Milky Way's Dark Rift would have appeared exactly where the sun along with the stars of Scorpius had earlier disappeared below the horizon. I strongly suspect that at this time the supplicant would have descended into the pit and crawled into the recess so that part of their consciousness could be projected out through the Scorpionic gateway to reach the Milky Way's Dark Rift. Once there, communication would presumably have taken place with sky figures personified by the stars of Scorpius, Ophiuchus, and, of course, Serpens, the snake being wrestled by Ophiuchus.

I am deliberately leaving out the other main constellation in the vicinity of the Scorpionic gateway, which is Sagittarius. This, as we see next, has its own role in this imagined scenario played out by Karahan Tepe's Pre-Pottery Neolithic inhabitants. For that, however, we must now go to Göbekli Tepe, where we find what is arguably the greatest pictorial key to unlocking the cosmological world of southeastern Anatolia's Taş Tepeler culture. I speak here of the ever-enigmatic Pillar 43.

PART 5

THE SKY MAP

17

Pillar 43–Part One

The Vulture and the Scorpion

One of the most familiar T-pillars at Göbekli Tepe is Enclosure D's Pillar 43, popularly known as the Vulture Stone. It sits in the northwestern section of the installation's perimeter wall immediately to the west of the structure's porthole stone, which is located exactly in line with the building's north-northwest to south-southeast cross axis. This, in turn, once targeted the setting of the Cygnus star Deneb and with it the northern opening of the Milky Way's Dark Rift. (For more on this topic see chapter 9 of this current book, as well as my 2014 book *Göbekli Tepe: Genesis of the Gods*[1] and my 2018 book *The Cygnus Key*[2]).

Behind Enclosure D is an enormous wall of stone chippings, rock debris, and human refuse making up the central area of the tepe or occupational mound. As I stood on the walkway between Enclosure C and Enclosure D at Göbekli Tepe in 2012, Klaus Schmidt spoke to me of a rocky knoll he felt sure would be found at the center of this solid mass of rubble. This, and the fact that some western archaeologists now believe that the smaller cell-like structures of the site's Layer II phase constitute a collection of domestic houses focused around a few communal structures on the bedrock below, has led some researchers to dismiss any possible orientation of the main enclosures toward Cygnus and the Milky Way's Dark Rift.

Against this argument is the fact that the tepe is built entirely of imported rock debris and to date no rocky knoll has been confirmed to exist beneath the mound's central area. Indeed, the topography of the surrounding landscape gives no indication whatsoever that there is a rise in the bedrock at this point. Furthermore, assertions that the wall of rubble beyond enclosures Enclosures B,

C, and D would have prevented anyone from ever seeing the stars of the northern night sky is a nonstarter since it is clear that when these structures were built there was no occupational mound; this built up very gradually over the course of approximately 1,500 years, an extremely long time indeed.

DECIPHERING PILLAR 43

Turning now to the relief art on Pillar 43, we can plainly see that it has two distinct registers—one on its overly large T-shaped head and the other on its broad stem. (There are two relief carvings also on the front narrow edge of its head, one being a predator, arguably a panther-leopard, with the other being a large insect.)

The central feature on the pillar's T-shaped head is a huge vulture with its wings partially open to give them the distinct appearance of the letter *W*. Its legs are articulated toward the front, showing that the creature has anthropomorphic characteristics. In other words it is most likely a psychopomp, in the form of a vulture deemed to have humanlike qualities.

Fig. 17.1. Pillar 43 in Göbekli Tepe's Enclosure D (left) with the constellations of Cygnus and Scorpius as they appeared in the night sky circa 9500 BCE.
Image by Rodney Hale.

As far back as 2010, Professor Vachagan Vahradyan of the Russian-Armenian (Slavonic) University proposed that the central vulture on Göbekli Tepe's Pillar 43 represented the Cygnus constellation in its role as a celestial bird. He noted that it resembled the shape of the constellation as it appeared in the skies around 12,000 years ago and not as it does today (the proper motion of certain of its stars having altered its shape across time).[3]

Vahradyan had another reason to conclude that the vulture on Pillar 43 might well signify the constellation of Cygnus. This was because in Armenia, which not only borders Anatolia in the northeastern part of the country but also once extended into southeastern Anatolia, the stars of Cygnus are identified as Angegh or Angel (Armenian *anggh*), a celestial vulture or winged griffon identified also as a "birdlike angel god."[4]

At the same time that Vahradyan was focusing his attention on Pillar 43's vulture relief, archaeoastronomer Juan Antonio Belmonte was examining another of its carved images. This was a scorpion seen on the stone's wide stem. It reaches up with its claws toward the pillar's T-shaped head.

Belmonte realized there was every chance that Pillar 43's scorpion represented the constellation of Scorpius. In the knowledge that the Sumerians recognized a scorpion among the same group of stars as early as 3000 BCE, Belmonte argued that the example seen on Göbekli Tepe's Pillar 43 was a prototype form of the zodiacal constellation.[5] Remember that in both Sumerian and later Babylonian astronomy the celestial scorpion known as ^{mul}GIR.TAB was identified with the goddess Išhara,[6] while the "star of Išhara" was almost certainly Scorpius's bright star Antares, which appears red to the human eye.[7] (It is also important to note that the Maya of Central America would also appear to have identified the stars of Scorpius as a celestial scorpion.)

So with Pillar 43's central vulture and upraised scorpion identified as, respectively, the constellations of Cygnus and Scorpius, was it possible that more of its carved imagery might represent stars and asterisms located in the same region of sky?

THE HEADLESS MAN

Another prominent figure on the stem of the pillar is a headless man seen riding on the back of a large bird, arguably another vulture. In the prehistoric art of Anatolia a headless figure generally represents the body of a deceased person or shaman whose soul or spirit, symbolized by a disembodied head or skull, has already departed to begin its journey to the afterlife.

If the headless person on the stem of Pillar 43 does represent a person who is "dead," whether this be in actuality or on a temporary basis, then the bird on which he sits, seemingly another vulture, acts as the vehicle by which the shaman is able to reach the hereafter. As we saw in chapter 1, vultures feature heavily in beliefs and practices associated with "sky burials," this being the deliberate manner these huge birds are encouraged to completely deflesh human cadavers left out in charnel areas for this purpose.

That sky burials took place in Anatolia during the Neolithic period does not seem in doubt since it is shown taking place in an important mural uncovered during the early 1960s at the Ceramic Neolithic site of Çatal Höyük in southern-central Anatolia. It shows two wooden towers tended by human figures, perhaps priests or keepers of the dead (see fig. 17.2). Ladders or walkways lead up to the summits of the towers, on the top of one of which we see vultures attacking a human figure represented by a headless matchstick person. Almost certainly, this shows excarnation in process—in other words, vultures devouring a cadaver.

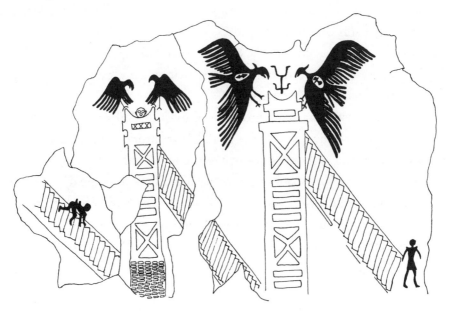

Fig. 17.2. Wall fresco uncovered at Çatal Höyük showing what appear to be two excarnation towers, one with vultures attacking a headless corpse (right) and the other (left) with vultures taking a human head under their wing. Illustration by Andrew Collins.

On top of the second tower we see two vultures with their wings almost wrapped around a naively drawn human head that has two round eyes to emphasize what is being represented. Abstract human heads or skulls shown in Neolithic art almost certainly represent the soul or spirit of a person that has departed the physical body.

The manner in which drawn or carved human skulls and even plain circles were used in Anatolia during Neolithic times to represent the human soul was made clear in 1974 by Turkish statesman and Neolithic rock art specialist Muvaffak Uyanik (1905–1975). In his important study titled *Petroglyphs of South-Eastern Anatolia* he wrote:

> In the Mesolithic age [i.e., during the epoch of the region's Taş Tepeler culture], it was realized that man had a soul, apart from his body and, as it was accepted that the soul inhabited the head, only the skull of the human body was buried. We also know that the human soul was *symbolized as a circle* and that this symbol was later used, in a traditional manner, on tomb-stones without inscriptions.[8] (Current author's emphasis.)

Thus, what we see in the mural from Çatal Höyük are vultures protecting the soul of a person who is in the process of being released from their physical body. It might even be said that the huge birds are taking the soul "under their wing," an interesting term in itself, and one that, whatever its origin, is appropriate to the situation being described.

The likely reason that the birds are taking the soul under their wing is because they are not physical vultures at all but anthropomorphized spirit birds that will protect the soul on its journey to the hereafter.

This then is most probably why we see a headless individual on the back of a second vulture on Göbekli Tepe's Pillar 43. The bird is helping the soul of the individual to journey from this world to the next. It is acting in the role of psychopomp, a "soul carrier" or "soul accompanier." The full meaning, however, of the carved relief only really becomes clear once we ask the most obvious question: Where is the individual's head?

The clear answer to this question is found when a vertical line from the headless man shown on the pillar's stem is drawn upward to the large vulture on the pillar's T-shaped head, which is also to be seen as a psychopomp. On the bird's left wing (its right one as we look at it) is a large filled-in circle, which has drawn the interest of those who have attempted to decipher Pillar 43's carved imagery. To some it is the sun, leading to speculation that the vulture symbolizes the zodiacal constellation of Sagittarius,[9] the whole design being a snapshot of the moment when fragments of a comet rained down on Earth, devastating large parts of the northern hemisphere.[10]

As compelling as such ideas might seem they ignore the more obvious solution that the filled-in circle signifies the missing head of the headless individual shown directly beneath it on the pillar's stem. This is an opinion that I am sure Neolithic rock art specialist Muvaffak Uyanik, were he alive today, would have concurred with, seeing that the same symbol is found repeatedly in a funerary context elsewhere in southeastern Anatolia, where it is quite clearly an abstract representation of the human soul.

The location of the plain circle on Pillar 43 also helps confirm it represents a human soul. We can see that it is being supported, cared for even, by the vulture almost as if it is under its protection. This, of course, is exactly the same theme that we see in the wall mural from Çatal Höyük—a human head being taken into the care of vultures in readiness for its journey into the afterlife.

Voyage of the Soul

The fact that the Pre-Pottery Neolithic peoples of southeastern Anatolia might have seen the stars of the Cygnus constellation in terms of a celestial vulture also makes sense of the solution described above, since in its role as a psychopomp the constellation's function was to guide and protect human souls wishing to enter the sky world. This, as we have seen, was reached via one or the other of two sky gates situated where the ecliptic, the sun's annual path, crosses the Milky Way on opposite sides of the sky—one being in the vicinity of Scorpius, Sagittarius, and Ophiuchus and the other in the vicinity of Gemini, Taurus, Orion, and the Pleiades star cluster.

The identification of the central vulture on Pillar 43 as a sky figure made up of stars from the Cygnus constellation can thus be seen as confirmation that its carved imagery reflects the soul's journey to the sky world. This is symbolized both by the headless figure riding the vulture shown on the pillar's stem and by the plain circle seen directly above the vulture's left wing, which shows the individual's ascended soul. If so, then very clearly the true entrance into the hereafter was considered to have been located somewhere in the vicinity of the northern opening to the Milky Way's Dark Rift, just like it is in

Native American and Mayan traditions. Where exactly that entrance might be found we'll explore in due course. For the moment, however, we should go on to explore further elements of Pillar 43's carved imagery.

MORE SKY FIGURES

On the T-pillar's carved stem is, as already noted, a headless man on the back of what appears to be a vulture, along with an upraised scorpion, its claws reaching up toward the horizontal division defining the start of the stone's T-shaped head. This has a mesmerizing array of relief carvings, including a juvenile bird with a hooked beak that is almost certainly a young vulture. There is also a wading bird of some kind, to the right of which is the head and neck of another bird. Below this is a triangular head that could be that of a snake. To its side are two glyphs with the appearance of a letter *H* turned 90 degrees. The same H glyph appears on several of the T-pillars at the site, being shown both upright and transposed 90 degrees. I argue elsewhere that the *H* glyph is probably a symbol of the mirrorlike relationship between this world and the next.[11]

Between the wader bird and the head of the large central vulture on the upper part of the head of the pillar are a line of squares. Above and below these squares are a series of double chevrons pointing, respectively, upward and downward, those on the top roughly mirroring those underneath. Above this curious feature, which stretches across almost the entire width of the head, are three carved rectangles, each with a loop connected to its upper edge. To the right side of each loop is shown a single creature, which from left to right are a wading bird, a large feline (probably a leopard), and, finally, a frog or toad, which is seen close to the right-hand edge of the register.

The Man Bag Myth

Let's tackle the rectangles with loops first. You will see it written in various places that these devices signify "man bags" like those seen in the hands of shaman-kings rising out of the clutches of an underworld monster in Olmec art or those held in the hands of winged genii seen in relief frescoes at Assyrian royal palaces in northern Iraq. There is a problem with this explanation, however. Although the symbolism might *seem* the same in all these cases, the use of such containers varies from culture to culture. For instance, those shown in Olmec art are almost certainly containers for magic herbs used by shamans and kings to achieve altered states of consciousness, while the man bags seen in the hands of Assyrian winged genii are in fact buckets containing sacred oils that are being used to anoint a stylized Tree of Life shown in front of the figures in question. This ritualistic act was accomplished through the use of the pinecone shown in the winged genii's other hand.

What is more, the "man bags" seen on Pillar 43 are not man bags at all. The loops imagined as "handles" are all offset to the left of the rectangles, meaning they have to represent something else. As my colleague Rodney Hale has proposed, the rectangles are almost certainly highly abstract representations of built structures, with the loops being either domed roofs or adjoining pens. The fact that each "man bag" is associated with a different creature tends to suggest they signify different influences, perhaps relating to celestial houses like the three divisions of the sky recorded in Babylonian astronomy.

Celestial Bridges

With this solution in mind, what might we make of the line of interlinked squares with mirrored V-shaped devices emerging from their upper and lower surfaces? Is it possible that this device is either a wooden trackway or perhaps a series of stepping stones across a river? Wooden trackways are known to have existed in Britain by around 4000 BCE,[12] with at least two examples from Ireland dating to the Mesolithic Age. One, found within the ancient Lullymore Bog, part of the Bog of Allen, in Co. Kildare, was a pine trackway constructed using transversely laid and radially split pine logs of some considerable size. It measured 5.9 feet (1.8 meters) in width, although its purpose, or exactly where it came from or led to remains unclear. Radiocarbon testing of timber from the trackway provided dates going back as early as the last quarter of the seventh millennium BCE.[13] Some bridges across rivers and streams constructed from large megalithic blocks also probably date back to the prehistoric age. A perfect example is the stone bridge spanning Stainforth Beck at Stainforth in the English county of Yorkshire (see fig. 17.3). If the line of squares on Pillar 43's head can be seen as a stepping stone bridge, then the V-shaped patterns above and below the line of squares probably signify rushing water passing between the large blocks.

Whether or not the Pre-Pottery Neolithic peoples of southeastern Anatolia were building wooden trackways and/or stepping stone bridges of the type suggested remains to be seen. Wood rots and decays too quickly for it to be

Fig. 17.3. Stepping stone bridge over the Stainforth Beck at Stainforth in Yorkshire, England. Does a similar stepping stone bridge appear as a line of squares on Göbekli Tepe's Pillar 43? Photo by Andrew Collins.

preserved across such an extended period of time, while stepping stone bridges can quite easily be destroyed. The fact, however, that Anatolia's Taş Tepeler culture was clearly immensely sophisticated—as is demonstrated by the design and construction of key enclosures at places like Göbekli Tepe and Karahan Tepe—means its population probably had the technological capability to build permanent walkways and bridges across running water.

With this knowledge, the question then becomes what does the walkway or bridge on Pillar 43 actually represent? If the rest of the T-pillar's imagery can truly be seen as abstract representations of celestial objects then perhaps we should look for a feature in the night sky interpreted in terms of a flowing river or stream. Most obviously, this would be the Milky Way, for in the sky lore of many ancient cultures and Indigenous peoples this stream of stars arching across the night sky was seen as a celestial river.

In China, for instance, an old folk story tells of how, once a year, all the magpies in the world fly up into the sky and create a bridge across the Milky Way in its role as a celestial river. This act allows two lovers, Zhi Nü, the Weaver Princess, and Jian Niu, the Ox Driver, to meet together. These two individuals are represented, respectively, by the bright star Vega (α Lyrae) in the constellation of Lyra, the celestial lyre, and the star Altair (α Aquilae) in Aquila, the celestial eagle, which are located opposite each other on either side of the Milky Way.

The stars of Cygnus, Deneb in particular, mark the position of the bridge.[14] These three stars—Vega, Aquila, and Deneb—known in Western astronomy as the Summer Triangle, are celebrated to this day during a major cultural festival in China honoring the story of the Weaver Princess and the Ox Driver.*

Another bridge associated with the Milky Way is that of Bifrost, the bridge that led from Midgard, or Middle Earth, to Asgard, the realm of the gods. It was said that only the gods could cross this bridge, which was guarded by the god Heimdall.

Thus, the series of interlinked squares and chevrons shown on Pillar 43's head are probably meant to signify a bridge across the Milky Way. If so, then it adds weight to the idea that not only the large vulture and scorpion, but also the "man bag"-like structures, the line of squares and chevrons, as well as many, if not all, of the other figures it shows are astronomical in nature. This is something we should remember as we now go on to examine the rest of the stone's fascinating carved imagery.

---

*In my book *The Cygnus Mystery* (2006) I go into some detail regarding the precessional information contained within the myth of the Weaver Princess and the Ox Driver (see Collins 2006, 198–202).

18

Pillar 43–Part Two

The Hole in the Sky

Fully aware of the celestial implications of Göbekli Tepe's Pillar 43, engineer Rodney Hale used a suitable sky program to synchronize its carved imagery with the night skies during the epoch of 9600 BCE. The fixed markers would be the pillar's central vulture relief on the T-shaped head, representing the area of sky occupied by the Cygnus constellation, along with the scorpion on the broad stem signifying the constellation of Scorpius. The results of this simple exercise were truly amazing and extremely far-reaching in their implications.

As can be seen in figure 18.1, the central vulture overlaid on the Cygnus constellation is seen about to set on the north-northwestern horizon, symbolized by the divide between the pillar's head and stem. At the same time, the upraised scorpion occupying the position of the stars of Scorpius is seen immediately below the horizon, where it has just set.

More incredible is the fact that the plain circle on the wing of the great vulture is seen to correspond with the northern celestial pole. I realize that we have already identified this filled circle as the soul or spirit of the headless figure seen directly beneath it on the stem, but it now seems this plain disk has an additional function in that it marks what in the shamanic traditions of North Asia is known as the "hole in the sky." This is the name given to an imagined entrance into the sky world corresponding to the northern celestial pole, the pivot or turning point of the heavens signified by the presence of what is known as the Pole Star or, alternately, the North Star.[1]

Due to the effects of precession, the slow wobble of Earth's axis across a cycle of approximately 25,800 years, the celestial pole moves in a tight circle

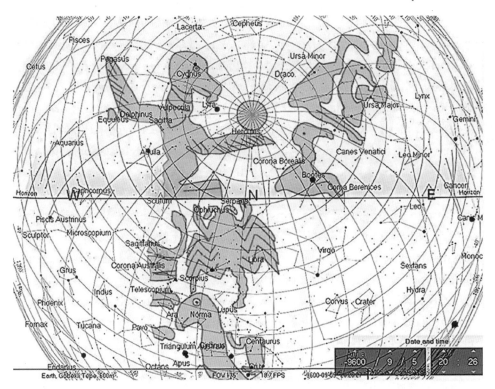

Fig. 18.1. The different components of Pillar 43 overlaid upon the night sky
as seen from the location of Göbekli Tepe for the epoch 9600 BCE.
Image by Rodney Hale.

around what is known as the ecliptic pole. For the past 2,000 years the honor
of Pole Star has gone to Polaris (α Ursae Minoris) located in the constellation
of Ursa Minor. During the age of Göbekli Tepe and Karahan Tepe the celestial pole was crossing through the constellation of Hercules (Greek Heracles),
although no bright star was close enough to be classed as Pole Star.

For this you would have to go back approximately 15,000 years when Vega
in the constellation of Lyra was the closest bright star to the celestial pole.[2]
Prior to this, and for a period of approximately 4,500 years, the northern
celestial pole had been crossing through the Milky Way, initially within the
constellation of Cepheus circa 18,500–16,000 BCE and then after that in the
constellation of Cygnus circa 16,000–14,000 BCE. Indeed, during its passage
through Cygnus, three separate stars came close enough to the celestial pole to
be considered as pole stars. These were Deneb (α Cygni), Sadr (γ Cygni), and
Rukh (δ Cygni).

It was during its time in Cygnus that the celestial pole would have coincided with the northern opening of the Milky Way's Dark Rift. Thus, at this time the northern limits of the Dark Rift, known to astronomers as the Northern Coalsack, would have been seen as the true entrance to the sky world, the true Hole in the Sky, a role it appears to have retained even after the celestial pole passed out of the Milky Way on its way toward the star Vega. Indeed, with the presence of alignments toward the Cygnus star Deneb at both Göbekli Tepe and Karahan Tepe, it seems clear that even at this time the star remained important in the soul's journey to the afterlife.

Despite no bright star marking the celestial pole when Göbekli Tepe was constructed around 9600 BCE, it seems clear from Enclosure D's Pillar 43 that Cygnus in its role as the celestial vulture was acknowledged as still guarding the entrance to the sky world, both in its capacity as the northern opening of the Milky Way's Dark Rift and as the now quite separate celestial pole. If this was the case, then something else of immense value can now be determined with respect to the T-pillar's carved relief.

FINDING THE MERIDIAN LINE

An invisible line running vertically from the circle on the wing of the vulture down to the neck of the headless figure riding on the back of a vulture seen on the stem of the T-pillar corresponds precisely to the meridian, the imagined north-south line that divides the sky into two halves. One half, its eastern side, is where stars rise into the sky, while the other half, its western side, is where they are seen to set down into the horizon. The meridian itself marks the highest and lowest a star reaches on its nightly course, this being known as its upper and lower transit respectively.

So when looking at Pillar 43 we can see that the left-hand side of both the head and stem could well represent a star or asterism's descent from the meridian down to the local horizon, while everything shown on the stone's right-hand side could well show stars and asterisms rising upward toward their culmination on the meridian. So with the horizontal division between the head and stem of the pillar representing the local horizon, a near-perfect cross, marking at its center the meeting of the meridian and local horizon, can be drawn by adding a line from the plain circle on the vulture's wing down to the headless figure riding on the second vulture at the base of the stem (see fig. 18.2).

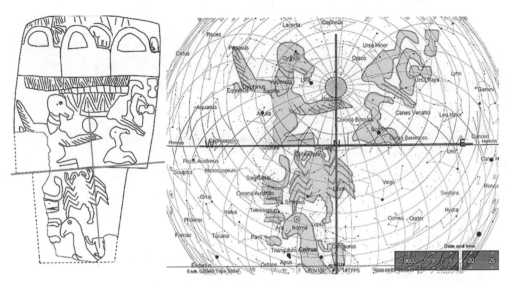

Fig. 18.2. Göbekli Tepe's Pillar 43 (left) with the meridian and local horizon marked.
Note how the meridian line links the ball on the large vulture's left wing with the
headless figure's apparent head on the stone's stem.
Images by Rodney Hale.

Thus, although highly abstract and somewhat naive in design, Pillar 43 can be seen as a sky map of the northern night sky as viewed from the perspective of Göbekli Tepe during the epoch of the enclosure's construction, with the scorpion and any other carved relief on its broad stem showing celestial objects that have already set below the local horizon.

Since the only remaining unidentified features on the stem of Pillar 43 are on its right side, they likely depict either stars or constellations rising upward into the night sky. Having said this, the wader bird and two H-shaped glyphs have so far proved difficult to identify. The juvenile vulture beneath them, however, could simply be Cygnus as the celestial vulture being reborn, like a phoenix rising from the ashes. Its position on the right side of the head corresponds almost precisely to where the main vulture situated on the left-hand side of the panel is seen about to set beneath the horizon; the two display a near-perfect symmetry.

The imagery seen in carved relief on Pillar 43 could thus exist on multiple levels. Some sky figures are stars and constellations that are setting down into the horizon (Cygnus as the main vulture), while some (such as the juvenile vulture) could signify the same stars (that is, Cygnus) rising back up into the sky.

Those on the stem (Scorpius and others we'll come to shortly) appear to show stars and asterisms that have already set beneath the horizon, and are thus in the underworld. What this implies is that the headless figure riding the vulture is emblematic of the soul's journey through this chthonic realm. Being headless the man is technically "dead," his body having been denuded by vultures (symbolically at least). His erection, however, tells us that he is likely a shaman in an induced state of trance.

Pillar 43 is thus an instructional tool to help those wishing to learn the nature of the sky world and all it contains for the purpose of achieving access to the afterlife, either on a temporary or more permanent basis. Admittedly, we can't interpret every symbol or glyph on Pillar 43 (and this includes the feline and insect seen in relief on the front narrow edge of its head), although I feel the work initiated by Rodney Hale is the right way forward in any attempt to try and understand the stone's carved imagery and what it might signify.

There is, however, now much more on offer if we are able to accept this particular interpretation of Pillar 43's carved relief. For we must not lose sight of the new discoveries being made right now at Göbekli Tepe's sister site of Karahan Tepe and, in particular, the alignment of the Pit Shrine (Structure AA) toward the setting sun at the time of the summer solstice and its apparent focus toward the southern termination of the Milky Way's Dark Rift (the Scorpionic gateway). An examination of the carved imagery seen in association with Pillar 43's scorpion, which seems clearly representative of the constellation of Scorpius, will finally help reveal the true identity of the serpentine sky figure toward which the Pit Shrine was directed during the epoch of its construction.

19

Pillar 43–Part Three

The Fox and the Snake

The upraised scorpion and headless figure seen riding on the back of a vulture on the stem of Göbekli Tepe's Pillar 43 is not its only carved imagery. Immediately to the left (or west) of the scorpion, which archaeoastronomer Juan Antonio Belmonte has identified as the constellation of Scorpius, are two more figures—well, half figures at least, since parts of their bodies remain obscured by Enclosure D's intact perimeter wall. We don't know their full form, although from what we can see there is clearly an upraised fox, similar in style to several other foxes carved in relief on stones at Göbekli Tepe, as well as the head and neck of an upturned snake. Positioned above the fox, this serpent reaches toward the feet of the central vulture on the pillar's T-shaped head.

If the scorpion can be seen as the constellation of Scorpius, identified by the Sumerians and later Babylonians as the celestial scorpion ^{mul}GIR.TAB, then surely the pictographs next to it—the fox and snake—must also signify stars or asterisms in the same area of sky. And sure enough, when the skies of 9600 BCE are synchronized with the carved figures on the stem of Pillar 43 with Scorpius as the scorpion, Cygnus as the main vulture, and the circle on its wing as the northern celestial pole, the fox and snake do indeed correspond with specific stars of known constellations (see fig. 19.1 on the next page).

Although we should perhaps look only for approximate correspondences, it appears that the head of the fox marks key stars in the constellation of Sagittarius, including Kaus Medius (δ Sagittarii) and Kaus Australis (ε Sagittarii), while the snake corresponds not only to the position of Kaus

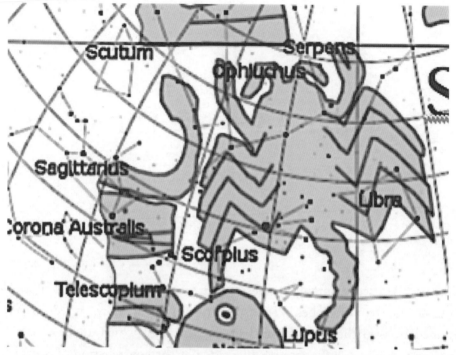

Fig. 19.1. The fox and snake on Göbekli Tepe's Pillar 43
superimposed on the night sky of 9600 BCE.
Image by Rodney Hale.

Medius, but also to other key stars in Sagittarius such as Theta Sagittarii (θ Sagittarii) and Lambda Sagittarii (λ Sagittarii), also known as Kaus Borealis. What is more, the raised head of the snake reaches the foot of Ophiuchus, the serpent bearer or snake charmer who, as we saw in chapter 15, constitutes the lost thirteenth sign of the zodiac. Since in Mesopotamian, Greek, and Arab tradition Ophiuchus has snake charming and snake handling attributes and holds in his hands the body of Serpens, the snake, it implies that the serpent reaching up toward the vulture on Pillar 43 existed in the vicinity of the southern termination of the Milky Way's Dark Rift and, of course, the stars of Scorpius. If so, then it was toward this very same serpentine influence that Karahan Tepe's Pit Shrine would appear to have been directed as darkness fell on the night of the summer solstice. What is more, it was this same snake that would appear to have been incised onto the front of the long bench carved into the west wall of the enclosure, the one shown alongside the relief of a fox.

We should perhaps recall also that the goddess Išhara, who in celestial terms was personified in the night sky as the stars of Scorpius, Antares in particular, was herself seen both as a scorpion *and as a snake*. As we saw in chapter 15, Scorpius's association with the symbol of a snake appears to be very ancient indeed since we are told that the Tribe of Dan's banner was "a crowned Snake or Basilisk," while its founder was "a serpent by the way," both statements being references to Scorpius's role as a celestial serpent.[1]

So if this primordial sky snake was located in the same region of sky as the later Greek constellations of Ophiuchus, Serpens, and Scorpius, then what about the fox shown both on Pillar 43 and on the bench in Karahan Tepe's Pit Shrine? Could its existence be found in either Mesopotamian or Near Eastern sky myths?

In Babylonian astronomy, a sky figure called "the Fox" was associated with a star in the constellation [mul]mar.GiD.da, the Wagon, corresponding to our Ursa Major.[2] This, however, seems too far away from Sagittarius to have any direct relevance to this debate. The planet Mars was also identified as a celestial fox in Mesopotamian tradition, while the stars of Canis Major, a constellation of the southern skies identified as a dog in Greek astronomy, was seen as a bow and arrow in Babylonian sky lore.

None of this appeared to have any connection with the sky fox I was looking for. Further investigations, however, revealed that in a Greco-Egyptian pseudoastronomical handbook dating from around 150 BCE and attributed jointly to Petosiris, a priest of Thoth, and a mythical king named Nechepso, a constellation known as the Fox is listed as one of the three asterisms or decans belonging to the house of Scorpius, meaning it must have been somewhere in its vicinity.[3] This constellation of the Fox is found also in the same list of "Decani" recorded in a fourth-century CE astronomical text written by prose writer Julius Firmicus Maternus.[4] Here it is said to be located north of Scorpius *in the vicinity of Ophiuchus*.[5] This would place it next to Sagittarius, right where it is shown on Rodney Hale's synchronization between the skies of 9600 BCE and the carved relief on Göbekli Tepe's Pillar 43. The primary sources of these astronomical texts are unclear, although they were almost certainly influenced by Chaldean astrological works, which, as we see in chapter 24, almost always had their origins in the city of Harran right in the heart of Taş Tepeler country.

AMERICAN FOX

Perhaps worth mentioning is that the Maricopa and Pima people of Arizona, in the United States, recognize a fox constellation among the stars of Sagittarius.[6] According to naturalist and author Dorcas S. Miller in her important work *Stars of the First People* (1997), "Fox, Coyote's brother, intent upon some prank, ran along the Milky Way toward the south and fell off, where he may be seen as six stars (in Sagittarius?) arranged like the seven stars that represent Coyote [that is, the Big Dipper]."[7]*

What I find interesting here is that, like the Maya of Central America, the Maricopa and Pima also recognize a scorpion among the stars of Scorpius, an extraordinary discovery if it could be established that these traditions were not contaminated by incoming European pioneers bringing with them their own interpretation of Greek and Roman sky lore.[8] If so then the presence among the Indigenous peoples of Arizona of a sky figure identified as a fox and composed of stars belonging to Sagittarius could suggest these ideas formed part of a universal interpretation of the night skies formulated, most probably on the Eurasian continent, during the Upper Paleolithic Age, circa 45,000–9600 BCE.[†]

With this potential new understanding of the fox, snake, and scorpion found on Göbekli Tepe's Pillar 43, as well as the snake and fox carvings seen on the bench of the Pit Shrine, can we go on to reveal the true identity of this great snake of the sky that would appear to have been so important to the Karahan community? It is this pressing question we address next.

---

*Also perhaps worth mentioning is the fact that the Inca of Peru recognized the presence of a celestial fox in connection with the Milky Way's Dark Rift (see Jenkins 1998, 55).

†That some Native American tribal peoples recognized sky figures that almost exactly match those found on the Eurasian continent does not seem in question. See, for instance, the work of Elio Antonello (2013) on the shared sky lore concerning the constellation of Ursa Major found both on the Eurasian continent and in North America. See also the work of Alistair Coombs (2017) on the Upper Paleolithic origins of stories found worldwide concerning the Pleiades, as well as the current author's work on the Paleolithic origins of the Cygnus constellation as a bird associated with the human soul (see Collins 2018, ch. 39).

PART 6

THE COSMOS

20

The Milky Way Serpent

After due thought, there seems just one answer as to the identity of the celestial serpent that southeastern Anatolia's Taş Tepeler culture recognized as existing somewhere in the vicinity of the southern termination of the Milky Way's Dark Rift. It has to be none other than the Milky Way itself, which, since it forms the visible edge of our own local galaxy, is seen to encircle our planet. Wherever you are in the world you will see this starry stream at some point during the night, occasionally even wrapping itself around the horizon like some glowing snake of light. This was how many ancient cultures envisaged the Milky Way—as a world-encircling serpent biting its own tail, a symbol familiar to us from Greco-Egyptian art and literature as the Ouroboros snake (see fig. 20.1).

The existence of this Earth-encircling snake is found, for instance, in Norse mythology, where it becomes Jörmungandr, the Midgard Serpent or World Serpent, known additionally as the Weltum-spanner, or "Stretcher-round-the-world."[1] It was thought to surround not only Midgard, or Middle Earth, but also the World Tree, Yggdrasil, which, as the polar axis of Earth, was connected with the underworld or below world via its roots and with the sky world via its uppermost branches. (See fig. 20.2 for an artistic impression of the Norse concept of the three interconnecting worlds with the Midgard Serpent surrounding Middle Earth).

Fig. 20.1. Ouroboros snake from a fifteenth-century copy of a lost early medieval tract attributed to Neoplatonist, sophist, and Greek bishop Synesius of Cyrene (d. circa 413 CE). Source: Fol. 279 of the *Codex Parisinus graecus* 2327.

Fig. 20.2. Illustration titled "Yggdrasil, The Mundane Tree" by Danish engraver Oluf Olufsen Bagge (1780–1836). It shows the World Tree, Yggdrasil, with the Midgard Serpent encircling Middle Earth (from Percy, 1847, opp. title page).

THE YEZIDI SERPENT

In eastern Anatolia, Kurdish peoples belonging to the Yezidi religion who once thrived in the vicinity of Lake Van also recognized the existence of a great snake that encircled the world. It was forever attempting to bite its own tail, and if and when this happened the world would collapse.[2] The Yezidi serpent's circular motion around the axis mundi, or axis of Earth, matches the manner in which the Midgard Serpent encircles the world tree Yggdrasil of Norse tradition. Interestingly, Kurdish peoples of the Caucasus belonging to the Brukan tribe speak of a mythical dragon serpent named Ziya.[3] Ziya in the Kurdish Kurmanji language means "illuminator" or "divine light," implying perhaps that it too was originally an expression of the Milky Way in its role as a world-encircling snake.

Whether or not the world-encircling serpent of the Yezidi can be equated with the black snake revered by them and shown in high relief standing upright next to the entrances to shrines, cemeteries, and major tombs remains unclear. When asked what this serpent means they say simply that when Noah's Ark was floating in the water following the Great Flood it sprang a leak. The snake stepped forward and offered to plug the hole, thus saving every person and animal on the Ark. It is therefore for this reason that Yezidis revere the snake today. This folk story, however, is extremely unlikely to explain the great importance of the black snake in Yezidi tradition. In my opinion this derives from now forgotten traditions concerning the existence of the world-encircling serpent recognized by the Yezidi of Lake Van prior to their expulsion from the region around a century ago.

Both the Norse concept of the Midgard Serpent and the Yezidi world-encircling snake have parallels with the Akkadian name for the Milky Way, which is *Hid tsirra* (Assyrian *Nahru tsiri*), the "river (*hid*)-of-the-snake (*tsir*)." This probably explains why in the Hebrew Bible the Milky Way is referred to as the "Crooked Serpent," while in Jewish lore it is called *Nahar di Nur*, the "river [*nahar*] of (night) light [*nur*]".[4]

In Greek myth, Oceanus (or Okeanos), a Titan god personified as the Earth-encircling river of the same name, played the same role. It is not known whether Oceanus was ever identified with the Milky Way although he certainly had a serpentine form.[5]

In the *Enūma Eliš*, the Babylonian creation myth, the Milky Way is formed from the severed tail of Tiamat, the dragon serpent, who was slain and dismembered by the god Marduk. According to the story, Marduk defeated Tiamat in combat by shooting her with an arrow. Her body split in two, creating heaven and earth, and from her eyes flowed the waters that became the Tigris and Euphrates rivers.[6] Once again we see a relationship between the Milky Way and a great serpent, while Tiamat, like Oceanus, was a personification of the saltwater seas that were seen to encircle the known world.

KASSITE KUDURRU STONES

Kudurru are round-topped boundary stones dating from the Kassite dynasty of the Babylonian civilization (circa 1595–1155 BCE). They served as records of grants of land made by a king to a favored landowner. Each one bears pictographic representations of stars, planets, and asterisms important to Babylonian astronomy. One of the most prominent symbols they show is a long snake, which either arches over the top of the stone or is seen rising up its side (see fig. 33.6, p. 283).

In the well-known Babylonian astronomical compendium titled MUL.APIN (dating from the early seventh century BCE and meaning "the plough star"), the serpent shown on Kassite kudurru stones is identified with the southern constellation of Hydra, the Water Snake. It seems clear, however, that originally this snake signified the Milky Way, an identification that has been acknowledged by various commentators on the MUL.APIN.[7]

Other cultures have also identified the Milky Way with a cosmic snake. The Aztecs of central Mexico, for instance, identified the god Mixcoatl— "Cloud Serpent"[8] or "sky snake"[9]—with the Milky Way, while in the Vedic astronomy of northern India the Milky Way is known as Nāgavīthī,[10] meaning the "Path [*vīthī*] of the Snake [*nāga*]."

HINDU MYTHOLOGY

Hindu mythology records that the Milky Way is personified as Kshira Sagara, the "Ocean of Milk," which surrounds the mythical continent Krauncha.[11] Curled up within this ocean lies Sheshanāga ("the snake Shesha," also known as Adishesha, the "first Shesha"), who bears the title Nāgaraya, "King of the Snakes." As a snake demigod, Sheshanāga is considered either to float through space or, alternately, to float on the ocean, his writhing body becoming a bed

Fig. 20.3. Vishnu and Lakshmi on Sheshanāga. From the lotus petals, Brahmā
appears. Watercolor ca. 1870 by an unknown artist, V & A Museum, London.

on which the god Vishnu reclines (fig. 20.3). It is said that from Vishnu's
navel grows a lotus plant and when its petals open, Lord Brahmā, the creator
of the world, appears.

In Vedic art Sheshanāga is usually depicted with a hood ending in seven
heads, although he can also be shown with five heads or even a thousand heads.
His hood supports the earth, and whenever Sheshanāga moves his head an
earthquake occurs. Once again we have in this story a mythical snake associated
with both a continent-encircling ocean and, seemingly, the Milky Way.

THE NORTH AMERICAN GREAT SERPENT

In North America various Indigenous Nations recognize the Milky Way as not
only the Path of Souls, the road or river along which the dead can reach the
afterlife, but also as a world-encircling serpent.[12] These ideas are most common
among the different groups of Algonquin-speaking peoples of the Great Lakes
region known collectively as the Anishinaabe (plural: Anishinaabeg). They
identify the Milky Way as Jivekana, the Serpent's Path.[13]

American astronomer Herman E. Bender of the Hanwakan Center for Prehistoric Astronomy, Cosmology and Cultural Landscape Studies in Fond du Lac, Wisconsin, has undertaken an important study of how Native American peoples of the past and present perceived the Milky Way. During his research he has recorded a number of earthen mounds, pictographs, and examples of rock art showing open-mouthed snakes, either outstretched or curled into a circle and biting their own tails. These, he suspects, represent either the Milky Way in the form of a serpent, or, in some cases, a celestial bridge that crosses over the Milky Way (see fig. 20.4).[14]

Then we have Serpent Mound in Adams County, Ohio, a mound effigy 1,300 feet (396 meters) long thought to have been constructed by the Adena culture around 300 BCE (see figs. 20.5 and 20.6). It is aligned via the directionality of its head toward the sun as it sets at the time of the summer solstice and has been identified by Bender as the Milky Way in its role as a

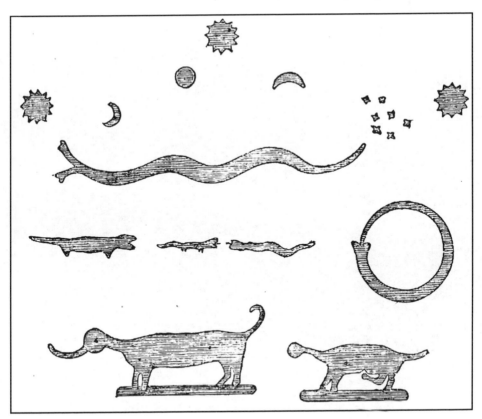

Fig. 20.4. A snake biting its own tail with another stretched out with open mouth from the rock art recorded in Wilson's Cave, Indiana, by archaeologist William Pidgeon (1800–1880). (See Pidgeon 1858, 223, Cut W.)

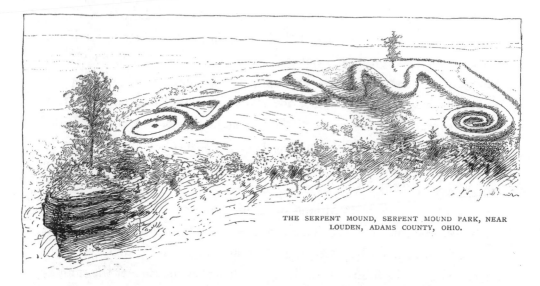

THE SERPENT MOUND, SERPENT MOUND PARK, NEAR
LOUDEN, ADAMS COUNTY, OHIO.

Fig. 20.5. Serpent Mound earthwork, Adams County, Ohio
(from Putnam 1890, 871).

Fig. 20.6. Serpent Mound earthwork showing its location on a prominent rocky
outcrop directed toward sunset at the time of the summer solstice during the
epoch of its construction around 2,300 years ago (from Putnam 1890, 872).

snake.[15] The effigy's open mouth surrounds an oval mound that, as we see in the following chapter, could well represent the egg of creation.

In the knowledge that the Milky Way appears to have been associated with a celestial serpent in various parts of the world, there seems no reason why the Pre-Pottery Neolithic peoples of southeastern Anatolia might not have identified this starry stream as a great snake that encircled the known world. If this is the case, then it raises the question of how the builders of the three, interconnected bedrock structures at Karahan Tepe might have responded to this great serpent's presence in the night sky and how it might have related to the stars of Sagittarius, Ophiuchus, and Scorpius toward which the Pit Shrine was directed at the time of the summer solstice. It is these matters we examine next as we now go in search of the suspected head of the Milky Way serpent.

21

Riding the Snake

Various ancient cultures appear to have identified the Milky Way as a great snake that encircled the world. It was probably for this reason that primeval deities such as Oceanus, Tiamat and Jörmungandr were all imagined as great serpents associated with the saltwater seas and oceans that surrounded the known world.

The question then becomes: Can we go on to identify the Milky Way serpent's head—a head that has been seen to bite or follow its own tail as it revolves constantly about the celestial pole in its role as the axis of the world? The answer to this important question is that this head was almost certainly what astronomers refer to as the Galactic Bulge, this being an extremely bright area of stars (relatively speaking), elliptical in shape and formed by a dense area of luminous interstellar clouds and tightly packed star clusters marking the center of the Milky Way galaxy.

The Galactic Bulge is situated just beyond the two arms forming the southern termination of the Milky Way's Dark Rift in between the constellations of Sagittarius, Ophiuchus, and Scorpius. This, of course, was the location of the sky gate, the Scorpionic gateway, that various ancient cultures would appear to have identified as a point of access onto the Milky Way.

What this implies is that the open jaws of the Milky Way serpent was in some cases identified with the Dark Rift itself (see fig. 21.1 for a reconstruction of how the Galactic Bulge might have looked as a snake's head). This means that souls wishing to access the sky world would first have to enter the mouth of the celestial serpent to reach their destination.

The Maya of Central America, for instance, perceived the southern termination of the Dark Rift as the open jaws of a snake or reptile,[1] while the cluster of seven stars making up the Pleiades was identified with the rattle of a rattlesnake,

Fig. 21.1. Artist's impression of how the ancients might have conceived the
Galactic Bulge as the head of the Milky Way serpent.
Image by Andrew Collins.

hence the name given by the Maya to the asterism, which is Tz'ab ek, meaning "the rattle of the rattlesnake's tail."[2] The Cherokee Nation of the southern
United States also identify the Pleiades as the end of the tail of a celestial rattlesnake and actually allude to the fact that the snake itself is the Milky Way.[3]

American astronomer Herman E. Bender describes the Galactic Bulge as
being like a great light bulb that "before the invention of electric lighting . . .
was said to be so bright it could cast shadows."[4] With such luminosity there
seems no way that the Taş Tepeler inhabitants of Karahan Tepe would have
ignored such a prominent feature of the night sky, making sense of why the
Pit Shrine (Structure AA) was directed toward the southern termination of
the Milky Way's Dark Rift at the time of the summer solstice, and even why
it was shaped like the head of the incised snake seen on the front of the stone
bench inside the Pit Shrine. Very clearly this long winding form was itself a
representation of the Milky Way in its role as the great celestial serpent, which
if correct leads to the perhaps obvious conclusion that inside this shrine rituals
took place whereby the supplicant sought communication with this serpentine
entity by symbolically entering inside its mouth.

TALKING TO THE HEAD

If the Pillars Shrine (Structure AB) was itself sculpted to resemble the three-dimensional head of a snake, then it too could have been an expression of the Galactic Bulge in its capacity as the head of the Milky Way serpent. If so, then how might we consider the actions of the shaman or initiate crawling through the porthole window into the structure's presumably darkened interior? What function would this have served? The answer is that by entering the shrine, the supplicant was perhaps seen to be "eaten" and thus consumed within the snake's body, which, as we have seen, extends away as undulations in the level bedrock toward the direction of the Pit Shrine (Structure AA), which is itself shaped like a snake's head

Communications with the spirit of the Milky Way serpent at Karahan Tepe is also suggested by the ominous presence on the west wall of the Pillars Shrine of the oversized human head. The supplicant would no doubt have come face to face with this serpentine form after their proposed perambulation of the shrine's bedrock pillars. The fact that this supernatural creature has a human head and not that of a snake is important as this tells us that it represents an anthropomorphized form of the cosmic serpent. As its active spirit, the head is able to transmit knowledge and wisdom to those in its presence.

The head's open mouth, as has previously been noted, is a carved ellipse that offers the observer the distinct impression that it is talking to you. Its presence is mesmerizing, and, when you are sitting in front of the head, it becomes difficult not to conclude that it is trying to communicate with you personally. So how might the shamans or initiates at Karahan Tepe have gone about seeking communion with the Milky Way serpent, and for what ultimate reason would these communications have taken place?

As we have seen, during the Neolithic Age the soul of an individual, whether it be that of a deceased person or that of a shaman or initiate, was considered to inhabit their head or skull. It was for this reason that human craniums were put aside for spirit communication. This can be seen from archaeological discoveries made at the Pre-Pottery Neolithic site of Jericho (modern Tell es-Sultan) in the Palestinian West Bank. Intact skulls unearthed there were kept aside and decorated with plaster to be used as points of contact with ancestral spirits, most obviously their former owners.

Fig. 21.2. Carved statue from Nevalı Çori, showing a prominent human head beneath the claws of a large bird, probably those of a vulture.
Photo by Andrew Collins.

Skulls modified for special usage have also been found at Göbekli Tepe,[5] as have various statues and carved reliefs showing heads in the claws of vultures and predators such as panther-leopards. These creatures either constitute psychopomps—that is, soul carriers—or they are symbolic of the shaman's totemic form during altered states of consciousness. Similar carved heads have been found at Nevalı Çori (fig. 21.2) and also at Karahan Tepe, demonstrating the importance of the soul being seen as seated in the head or skull.

If, therefore, the Milky Way was, as I suspect, envisaged by the Pre-Pottery Neolithic inhabitants of Karahan Tepe as a world-encircling serpent, then any communications with its imagined spirit would have been directed toward its head, in other words, the Galactic Bulge. If so, then this makes sense of why both the Pillars Shrine and the Pit Shrine bear the resemblance of snake's heads, and also why the giant human head on the former's western wall is itself serpentine in nature.

One might also recall at this point the story of the Shahmaran. By eating of the Snake Mother's head, her mortal lover, Cemshab, was able to attain her serpent wisdom. This part of the story might almost be seen as a slightly confused metaphor for the way that a shaman or initiate during the age of Taş Tepeler was able to gain wisdom and knowledge from a perceived cosmic serpent through entering the mouth of its earthly counterpart.

The purpose of such interactions with the head of the Milky Way serpent would, I suspect, have related to the attainment of otherworldly wisdom and knowledge via oracular pronouncements delivered when the supplicant was being overtaken by its active spirit. To better understand how the Karahan community might have communicated with the Milky Way serpent we need to look more closely at the ritualistic activities of Indigenous societies in other parts of the world.

SPIRIT LANGUAGES

Among the Indigenous peoples of the Amazonian rainforest, the most common creature encountered by shamans, initiates, and experiencers when using the hallucinogen ayahuasca is the snake,[6] which will be seen to wrap itself around trees, climb doorframes, and attempt one-to-one communication with the person. In Amazonian lore it is believed that these perceived spirit intelligences have their own verbal language or languages, known as *icaros*. Their oral delivery to the experiencer usually includes strange sounds and tunes, which can only be properly interpreted by presiding shamans known as ayahuasceros.[7]

As outlined in chapter 9, spirit possession can take place during such communications with spirits, and very often these spirits can take on the form of snakes. It will be recalled that in Haiti, for instance, followers of the loa in the form of a snake named Dambala believe they can be "ridden" by his spirit. It is a willing act of possession that results in devotees writhing on the ground in the full belief that the loa has taken them over, the purpose of which is to confirm the spirit's presence and convey messages to waiting attendants.[8]

The cult of Damballa relates to a form of voodoo known as the Petwo rite, which was introduced to Haiti by slaves coming from the Mayombe region of the African Congo.[9] Petwo rituals performed in the African homeland would involve priests falling into trances and allowing spirits to speak through them. Participants would communicate in a spirit language that included lots of clicks, whistles, and unusual noises, as well as hand gestures. At such times, the priests were said to become Mvuza, the "jabberer."[10] Only they and the spirits properly understood this unique language, which had the purpose of conveying otherworldly information to waiting attendants.[11]

Elements of the Mvuza's spirit language were carried by Mayombe slaves to Haiti, where they evolved into Lagaj, a secret language used by Creole-speaking Haitians. To this day Lagaj contains many strange words uttered originally by the Mayombe priests of the African Congo. Only voodoo practitioners belonging to Haitian secret societies are able to communicate with each other using the Lagaj spirit language.[12]

SPEAKING WITH A FORKED TONGUE

How might any of this relate to what we suspect was going on at Karahan Tepe at the height of its use? Some idea can be gained from an unlikely source—the age-old expression "talking [or speaking] with a forked tongue," which in recent centuries has come to refer to anyone who lies to or verbally deceives another person. The term is considered to have "a serpentine origin,"[13] and to have derived from the way that, in the Hebrew Bible, the Serpent deceives or beguiles Eve in the Garden of Eden (a matter examined in chapters 35 and 36). It should be pointed out, however, that all snakes have forked tongues, their two prongs being known as tines. These are used to give the creature a better sense of smell.

In Christian Gospel churches, and even among the beliefs of the Catholic Church, those achieving a state of possession are very often said to be "speaking in tongues," in other words, languages that the person had no conscious knowledge of beforehand. So if the Galactic Bulge was indeed the head of a celestial serpent, then the close proximity of the stars of Scorpius—identified itself as a serpent in certain Near Eastern traditions—could suggest they were seen as the forked tongue of the celestial snake. If so, then, as the term "speaking with a forked tongue" implies, this could have become a symbol of the manner in which the celestial serpent imparted messages through the supplicant to waiting attendants, a process that can be likened to the role played by the ayahuasceros of Amazonian shamanism. If correct, then Scorpius more than any other constellation probably acted not only as the active spirit of the Milky Way serpent, but also as its chosen point of contact in the night sky. But what about the Galactic Bulge itself? Did this symbolize more than simply the head of the celestial serpent?

SERPENT MOUND AND THE EGG OF CREATION

As previously noted (see chapter 20), in North America Herman Bender has tentatively identified rock art pictographs and even mound effigies in the form of elongated snakes with open mouths as representative of the Milky Way in its role as a cosmic serpent.[14] We should also recall at this point Serpent Mound in Adam's Country, Ohio, constructed by the region's Adena culture as early as 300 BCE. It has an open mouth at its western termination that is aligned toward the setting sun at the time of the summer solstice. In its mouth is a large oval mound that when seen from above bears the distinct appearance of an egg. What does this mound represent?

American archaeoastronomer William F. Romain proposes that as Serpent Mound's head and oval mound faced the sun setting at the time of the summer solstice, the effigy's head-to-tail alignment would have targeted the bright star Antares in the constellation of Scorpius, which at the time would have been almost due south. As a consequence, he says, the entire earthwork might thus have been seen as a terrestrial equivalent of this asterism in its role as the Great Serpent of Native American tradition.[15] If Romain is correct, then since the Scorpius constellation lies immediately in front of the Galactic Bulge, then it is conceivable that the "egg" held in the mouth of Serpent Mound signifies the bright, central region of this bulge, with the mound's north-south alignment indicating that it represents the serpent's active spirit coming forth from the Scorpius constellation.

I put the matter to Romain, asking him what he personally thought Serpent Mound's oval mound might signify. His answer was twofold. Firstly, he suggests that since the effigy's head is aligned toward the setting sun at the time of the summer solstice, the oval mound—which reflects the same align-ment—possibly represents the sun itself. Secondly, he thinks it possible that the oval shape of the mound was seen as a sky portal, an ogee, through which the deceased were able to gain access to the land of the dead, this being an extension of the Native American concept of the Paths of Souls death journey explored in chapter 9.

Since the southern termination of the Milky Way's Dark Rift, in its role as the Scorpionic gateway, did indeed allow the dead to enter the afterlife in certain shamanic-based religious traditions, there is every reason to suspect that it too was used to reach the sky world via an entry seen to be linked with its

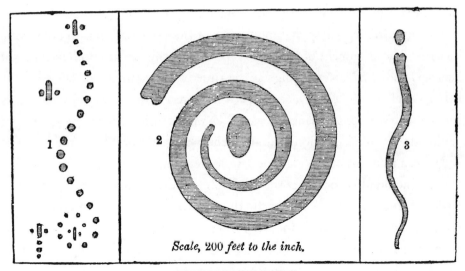

SERPENTINE EFFIGIES.

Fig. 21.3. Serpent mound effigies recorded in the mid-nineteenth century on the Mississippi River close to the junction with Turkey River by archaeologist William Pidgeon (see Pidgeon 1858, 113, Cut H). Note their inclusion of egg-like mounds that Pidgeon identified as tortoises based on the cosmogonic beliefs of local Indigenous peoples he encountered in the region (see Pidgeon 1858, 116).

northern opening located in the area of the Cygnus star Deneb. Indeed, this is implied by the relief imagery seen on Göbekli Tepe's Pillar 43, which shows the headless man on the back of a vulture heading past Scorpius, signified by the scorpion carving, toward the central vulture representing Cygnus in its guise as the celestial vulture. Since the Scorpionic gateway coincides reasonably well with the Galactic Bulge, it makes sense that Serpent Mound's oval mound is an abstract representation not only of this sky gate, or ogee, onto the Milky Way, but also of the bulge itself. What all this suggests is that the Adena culture that created Serpent Mound some 2,300 years ago might have seen this area of sky as a place of cosmic creation, the reason it was represented by an egg-shaped mound, something that Romain admits is "an interesting idea."[16] If so then it could explain why other serpent effigy mounds that formerly existed in the United States are also recorded as having very similar oval-shaped mounds (see fig. 21.3).

Although Ohio's Serpent Mound is on the opposite side of the world to Karahan Tepe in southeastern Anatolia and is separated in age by as much as

9,000 years, the fact is that we could be looking at a common strata of cosmological thinking regarding the importance of the Galactic Bulge to prehistoric societies. The alignment of Karahan Tepe's Pit Shrine toward both the stars of Scorpius and the Galactic Bulge at the time of the summer solstice can thus help to explain why the structure has a large recess in the western side of its sunken pit. Was this a symbolic womb chamber inside which the supplicant could adopt a fetal position and align their consciousness with the Galactic Bulge seen in terms of the place of cosmic creation?

We should also not forget the giant human head in Karahan Tepe's Pillars Shrine (Structure AB). Was it really thought to be able to communicate messages to those who came before it? As we see next, this oversized serpentine head has its own quite remarkable role to play in Karahan Tepe's synchronization with the stars during the epoch of its creation.

22

The Shining Serpent

Ancient mysteries researcher and writer Hugh Newman, whom we have met already in this book, has been visiting Karahan Tepe since 2014. Following the announcement in September 2021 that an archaeological team under the directorship of Necmi Karul of Istanbul University was making extraordinary new discoveries there, Hugh and his partner, the ancient-mysteries researcher JJ Ainsworth, made the decision to visit Karahan Tepe at the earliest convenience. That opportunity came in December 2021, existing commitments having prevented them from going any earlier.

Since December is the time of the winter solstice, Hugh and JJ decided it was a good idea to be at Karahan Tepe at this time. This seemed especially important in the knowledge that I had already announced my own discovery of a summer solstice alignment in connection with the site's Pit Shrine (Structure AA).[1] Aware that it appeared to target the solstitial sun at the time of its construction, Hugh and JJ wondered whether anything similar might occur there at the winter solstice.

Hugh had already made a cursory visit to Karahan Tepe on December 19, but wanted to go back the following day with JJ to further explore the site for future books, articles, and videos (Hugh and JJ run the popular YouTube channels Megalithomania and Megalithic Maiden). It had come to their attention, however, that archaeologists from the University of Istanbul, along with various officials from Şanlıurfa, would be arriving there the next morning to cover over the excavations to preserve them during the winter months. So the only opportunity to see the site before this happened would be first thing, before they arrived. They could then spend a couple of hours getting all they needed before returning to the hotel in time for a late breakfast.

That was the plan at least, and so, on December 20, Hugh and JJ made the 50-minute drive out to Karahan Tepe in the predawn light and managed to arrive there just before sunrise. (Their full account of this incredible journey appears as an appendix. See also Hugh's foreword at the front of this book.) Hugh and JJ climbed the hill and arrived at the Pillars Shrine, where they immediately noticed and photographed a small shaft of sunlight that had appeared on the left-hand side of the giant human head on the west wall of the Pillars Shrine. Looking more closely, JJ realized that this light was entering the structure via the porthole window cut out of the thin wall of bedrock that forms the partition between this room and the Great Ellipse. Both then watched, mesmerized, as the incoming sunlight created an upright golden dagger that slowly illuminated the lower half of the face.

Hugh and JJ watched this breathtaking spectacle play out for around 45 minutes, recording it using video and time-lapse photography, before the angle of the sun became too acute for it to cast any further light onto the head. Some minutes later, however, the sun was high enough for it to pour sunlight down into the shrine via its open roof, something that would have been impossible if, as we suspect, the structure had been roofed.

SOLSTITIAL ALIGNMENTS

What Hugh and JJ had managed to witness and record at Karahan Tepe on that morning was a clear solar alignment predating all other known examples by as much as 6,000 years. For example, at Newgrange in Ireland's Boyne Valley, the sun enters this 5,200-year-old passage grave shortly after sunrise on the winter solstice via a small light box above its entrance. It then casts its light along a long, straight corridor toward the heart of the monument. On reaching the structure's womb-like central chamber, the golden sunlight illuminates carved symbols on its rear wall.

After 50 years of observation in modern times, it is now generally accepted by archaeologists and prehistorians that Newgrange's solstitial alignment does not happen by accident. This and so many other megalithic structures across Europe are now thought to have been aligned purposely toward either sunrise or sunset at the time of the solstices and equinoxes (see the appendix for various examples). With this knowledge it now seems clear that the Neolithic builders of Newgrange must have possessed an advanced understanding of the movement of the sun across the course of a year. This enabled them to design architectural monuments—in this case an enormous passage grave—that were able to capture this extraordinary solar spectacle, presumably for some kind of religious reason.

The remarkable solar phenomenon witnessed by Hugh and JJ at Karahan Tepe now confirms that knowledge of how to align key moments to the turning points of the solar year would appear to have been available to southeastern Anatolia's Taş Tepeler population many thousands of years before the construction of Newgrange, or indeed any other megalithic monument in western Europe. This includes Stonehenge on Salisbury Plain in southern England, famous for its alignments toward the rising sun at the time of the summer solstice and the setting sun at the time of the winter solstice. Indeed, Stonehenge, like Newgrange, exemplifies the view that the ancients felt the need to align their monuments toward the sun and the moon at key moments in their respective cycles, something they saw as synchronizing their own world with its heavenly counterpart, recalling the old axiom of "As above, so below."

The idea, however, that the Pre-Pottery Neolithic peoples of southeastern Anatolia aligned *their* monuments toward turning points of the sun's yearly cycle was, of course, something already known to us. I myself had discovered that Karahan Tepe's Pit Shrine was aligned to the setting sun at the time of the summer solstice. I had also previously determined that two Layer II structures at Göbekli Tepe—Enclosure F and the Lion Pillars Building—were directed toward sunrise on, respectively, the summer solstice and the equinoxes (see chapter 14). What is more, in 2008 Professor Ran Barkai, a paleoarchaeologist at Tel Aviv University, and his co-author Roy Liran, published the results of a study into a potential solar alignment involving the stone tower at Jericho (Tell es-Sultan) in the Palestinian West Bank. They found that an open window at the top of the structure targeted the setting sun at the time of the summer solstice in circa 8300 BCE.[2]

A similar solstitial alignment was recently identified by the author at the newly discovered Pre-Pottery Neolithic A site of Ayanlar Höyük, northwest of Şanlıurfa. As seen from the central area of the currently unexcavated tepe, the sun, on the day of the winter solstice, sets down perfectly into a notch on the horizon made by two distant hills, a spectacle that cannot have gone unnoticed by the settlement's Taş Tepeler inhabitants. This discovery was made during a visit to the village on December 21, 2022.

What's so important about Hugh and JJ's discovery is its quite spectacular nature, showing that the builders of Karahan Tepe very deliberately designed the Pillars Shrine and the porthole between it and the neighboring Great Ellipse (Structure AD) to incorporate this extremely specific alignment.

CHECKING THE FACTS FROM EVERY ANGLE

On returning to the United Kingdom, Hugh and JJ reached out to Rodney Hale and me to see whether we could validate their discovery. If what they'd witnessed at Karahan Tepe on December 20, 2021, was correct, then it meant that the site's three interconnected, rock-cut structures were aligned not only to the northern opening of the Milky Way's Dark Rift, marked by the Cygnus star Deneb, but also toward both the summer *and* winter solstices.

What seemed important to establish from the outset was whether slight changes in the obliquity or tilt of the ecliptic (which defines the angle between the ecliptic pole and the celestial pole) could have prevented the sun from entering the Pillars Shrine during the epoch of its construction. Hale thus set about checking the present angle of obliquity against that of the site's suspected date of construction. What he found is that the change in tilt from then till now is less than a degree, meaning that in the tenth millennium BCE the rising and setting positions of the sun would not have been vastly different to what they are today (see fig. 22.1).

What is more, there is every chance that because the sun rose a degree or so further south than it does today, it would have been at a slightly lower angle as it came into line with the Pillars Shrine's porthole window. This would have meant even more sunlight being cast onto the giant stone head, making this annual spectacle even more impressive than what we see today.

Interestingly, and as Hugh and JJ point out in the appendix, the Great Ellipse's eastern central pillar is positioned so that it would have shut out the initial sunlight entering the Pillar's Shrine via the porthole window at the time of the winter solstice. This means that when it did finally reach the giant stone head, the effect would have been even more dramatic. If this is correct, then it was clearly a deliberate act built into the design of the enclosure—one that would explain why the Great Ellipse's central pillars do not align properly with the enclosure's main axis. (See plate 37 to see how the light crosses the head at the time of the winter solstice.)

Fig. 22.1. The sun's shifting angle as it casts its rays through the porthole window onto the serpentine head within Karahan Tepe's Structure AB (the Pillars Shrine) at the time of the winter solstice. Image by Google Earth and Andrew Collins.

Perhaps relevant to this debate is the fact that Hale was able to determine that once in the 18.61-year lunar standstill cycle, the full moon would have been low enough to cast its light through the Pillars Shrine's porthole window onto the giant stone head. This synchronization with the moon would, however, occur not at the time of the winter solstice, but close to the time of the summer solstice.[3] In other words, the movement of the moon as well as that of the sun might have played a role in the design of the Pillars Shrine.

A ONE-TIME CHANCE OF DISCOVERY

After it became clear that Hugh and JJ had, on December 20, 2021, discovered a genuine alignment at Karahan Tepe, I came to realize that if they had *not* been there to witness this unique solar spectacle when they did, the chances are it would never have been found. The Turkish archaeological team working at the site might not have considered the possibility of such an alignment, and simply examining a survey map of the site would not have led to its discovery either. This is because the sun has to climb to an altitude of 4 degrees before it begins casting its light through the porthole and onto the stone head, something that no one could have predicted beforehand unless they had at their disposal a three-dimensional reconstruction of the Pillars Shrine, complete with an exact understanding of its directional orientation and relationship to the local topography.

What is more, there might never have been a chance in the future to find this alignment. The Turkish Ministry of Culture and Tourism intends to enclose the Karahan Tepe excavations with a permanent roof and walkway even more elaborate than the one now in place at Göbekli Tepe. When this happens, the chances are it will block direct sunlight from reaching the Pillars Shrine, meaning that the site's winter solstice alignment will be lost forever. Thankfully, however, circumstances allowed Hugh and JJ to be at Karahan Tepe at dawn on December 20, 2021, and because of this they were rewarded with this once-in-a-lifetime discovery.

REIMAGINING KARAHAN TEPE

The greater issue for me now was how these incredible revelations concerning Karahan Tepe's function fitted in with what I had already determined about the Pit Shrine's own solstitial alignment. This, of course, was toward the set-ting sun at the time of the summer solstice, coupled with the appearance at the same spot, two and a half hours later, of the southern termination of the Milky Way's Dark Rift. This alignment had helped me understand what might have been going on at Karahan Tepe at the height of its use and in what order any ritual activity might have taken place there.

As previously indicated, ritual activities at the site would probably have begun with a communal ceremony inside the Great Ellipse. After that, and as Necmi Karul proposes, proceedings would then have shifted to the Pillars Shrine before culminating in the Pit Shrine. There, arguably in its sunken pit, the mind or consciousness of the supplicant would, on the night of the summer solstice, have made contact with the active spirit of the Milky Way serpent.

Now I had to contemplate the likelihood that something else of major importance was going on inside the Pillars Shrine at the time of the *winter solstice*. What is more, if the room was indeed a three-dimensional representa-tion of the head of a celestial serpent, then the penetration of sunlight into its interior shortly after dawn on the winter solstice was perhaps seen as the sun bringing alive its active spirit, seen in terms of the giant stone head on the shrine's west wall. This would have been in contrast to the opposite end of the year when, at sunset on the day of the summer solstice, light would have been cast into the Pit Shrine, illuminating any proceedings taking place there. In this knowledge can we envisage communications with the world-encircling ser-pent taking place within the Pit Shrine during the night of the summer solstice with similar activities taking place inside the Pillars Shrine, six months later, at the time of the winter solstice?

Such scenarios are certainly conceivable, although the greater puzzle to solve was why, at the time of the winter solstice, sunlight cast into the Pillars Shrine illuminated the great head—*and only the head*. How was it able to com-municate with those who entered the shrine, and for what ultimate purpose? It is these questions we address next as we attempt to understand the exact nature of oracular communications with perceived supernatural intelligences seen to take the form of a snake.

23

Oracular Communication

The giant stone head emerging out of the west wall of Karahan Tepe's Pillars Shrine is, I suspect, a physical representation of the Milky Way serpent's active spirit. If this is correct, then the stone head would presumably have been a focal point for anyone wishing to communicate with this perceived intelligence in the form either of a snake genius or of an anthropomorphic being with serpentine qualities. The fact that the carved head's oval-shaped mouth offers the impression that it is communicating with the observer is an eerie experience—one that can be compared to the way that the eyes in some paintings seem to follow you around, almost as if they contain the spirit of the individual they depict!

All this could support the hypothesis put forward in this book that the head's function was, and in many ways still is, oracular in nature. In other words, the Milky Way serpent was seen as being able to deliver prophetic messages directly into the mind of a chosen supplicant or, alternately, its sheer presence was enough to trigger a sense of communion with its supernatural counterpart. Under the right circumstances this would presumably have led to the Pillars Shrine's snake genius overshadowing them so that they might convey messages directly to waiting attendants.

THE ORACLE OF DELPHI

A direct historical comparison with what might have been happening at Karahan Tepe is, I believe, the oracular communications recorded as having taken place in preclassical and classical times at Delphi in Greece. Female priestesses called Pythia (Greek: Πύθια, "púthiā") acted in the role of the "Oracle," or

Fig. 23.1. "The Oracle of Delphi Entranced," lithograph by German artist and book illustrator Heinrich Leutemann (1824–1905).

prophetess, delivering divine messages to attendant priests. These communications were thought to come from Apollo in his role as god of prophecy.

The location of the Oracle site at Delphi was beneath a temple of Apollo where the Pythia would sit on a tripod seat immediately above a fissure or chasm in the bedrock floor (see fig. 23.1). Rising vapors or gases said to be from the rotting corpse of a monstrous female serpent (see below) would cause the prophetess (or pythoness) to become intoxicated in such a way that the god would be able to enter them and speak through the priestess's vocal cords. So important and so powerful were the pronouncements of the Pythia that the fates of kings, nations, and even the gods themselves would rest on her words.

In the *Homeric Hymn to Apollo*, the term Pythia is said to derive from Pytho, Delphi's original name.[1] It means "to rot" (from the Greek verb πύθειν, "púthein") and is a reference to the putid stench left behind by the decomposing body of Python, the monstrous snake slain by Apollo, an act carried out when the god was trying to find an appropriate place to establish a temple in his name.[2]

In some ancient accounts the monstrous snake had been set up at the location by Gaia (the Earth) to guard over the future site of the Oracle. This suggests that Python was in fact the location's original *genius loci*, or "spirit of the place," and that her slaying by Apollo hides a far deeper story regarding the site's role as a place of prophecy and divination (for more on this matter, see chapter 33).

Can we imagine similar prophetic announcements being made by chosen supplicants, shamans both male and female, entering Karahan Tepe's three interconnected bedrock structures at the time of the solstices and connecting with the Milky Way serpent? I find it extremely interesting that the entire legend surrounding the Delphic Oracle has recently been interpreted as a star myth featuring all the constellations we have already associated with the southern termination of the Milky Way's Dark Rift. In this scenario, Sagittarius is the god Apollo who uses a bow and arrow to kill Python (in the same way that the god Marduk kills the dragon serpent Tiamat in Babylonian mythology). Scorpius is the monstrous snake Python, while Ophiuchus is the tripod on which the Pythia would sit to become intoxicated by the vapors of the decomposing body of the monstrous serpent.

In this manner Scorpius, as the monstrous serpent Pythia, thus becomes the source of the cosmic serpent's divine wisdom, a point eloquently argued by the author of this far-reaching hypothesis, the mythologist and writer David Warner Mathisen, who writes:

> The ancient myths tell us that the vapors arising from the body of the Python, deep beneath the Oracle, were responsible in part for the trance-state into which the priestess of Delphi (who was known by the title of the Pythia for this reason) would enter when receiving the messages from the Infinite Realm. We can see that the smoky column of the Milky Way itself ascends through the 'body' of the serpent (Scorpio, with which constellation the Python is associated) and upwards past the 'tripod' of Ophiuchus.[3]

If Mathisen is correct in his interpretation of the legend of the Delphic Oracle, then it becomes clear that the monstrous serpent Python is simply a memory of how the active spirit of the Milky Way serpent was able to possess those who attuned to its rotting corpse. Of possible importance here is the fact that Mathisen draws attention to a highly relevant remark made by mythologist Peter Kingsley in his book titled *In the Dark Place of Wisdom* (1999). Here Kingsley writes:

> Alongside the intimacy of Apollo's links with the underworld, there's another aspect of him that also has been pushed into the dark. That's his connection with snakes. In ritual and in art snakes were sacred to him. Even in the case of the myth about the snake he fought and killed at Delphi, he didn't destroy it just to get it out of the way. On the contrary, its body was buried at the centre of his shrine. He killed it so he could absorb, appropriate, the prophetic powers that the snake represents.[4]

So Apollo was himself associated with snakes, meaning that they were an integral part of his cult, especially in connection with how the Pythia at Delphi achieved oracular communication with the god. Snakes would undoubtedly have been involved in this process, both through their association with the site and through their connections with the god Apollo (see fig. 23.2).

Fig. 23.2. Image from a Greek bell krater dating to circa 330 BCE showing the Pythia or Oracle of Delphi sitting atop her tripod with snakes on her forehead and shoulders. The snakes show how Apollo was expected to enter the priestess during trance states. From a vase formerly part of the Hope Collection. Photo by Jastrow.

Kingsley goes on to point out that at a dream incubation shrine dedicated to Apollo in Rome, visiting pilgrims would report that the god had appeared to them in the form of a snake. "This," Kingsley writes, "could seem unusual until you notice how normal it was for Greeks to describe him [that is, Apollo] as assuming the form of a snake."[5]

And as Kingsley goes on to say, these same cult rituals involving prophetic communications with the god Apollo in the form of a snake were passed on to his son Asclepius when his own cult rose to prominence. This included the use of incubation chambers to cultivate dreams in which the god of medicine would feature.[6] Asclepius's arrival would be followed, Kingsley says, "by hissing snakes, to people who approached him; or he'd come in the form of a snake. The hissing, *syrigmos*, was the sound of his presence."[7] (Original emphasis.)

It is important to recall here that the Greeks identified the constellation of Ophiuchus, located close to the Galactic Bulge, with Asclepius, most obviously because of his close affiliation with snakes.

GAZING TOWARD GALACTIC CENTER

Shamanistic activities to communicate with the Milky Way serpent would, I feel sure, have taken place in the rock-cut structures at Karahan Tepe around the time of the solstices. In this manner, the Karahan community would have been attempting to align itself both with the turning of the heavens and also with the celestial influences associated with prominent stars or asterisms, in particular those marking the northern and southern termination of the Milky Way's Dark Rift.

So was there more to the Karahan community's apparent interest in the stars? Did its subsurface, rock-cut structures connect still further with the night sky to ensure an even deeper sense of communion with the world-encircling serpent? The answer would appear to be a definite *yes*.

THE RISING OF THE MILKY WAY SERPENT

Having looked already at the night skies for the latitude of Karahan Tepe at the time of the summer solstice, I now turned my attention to how they might have looked at the time of the winter solstice. This was something that Hugh Newman had asked me to do after his and JJ Ainsworth's extraordinary discovery of the Pillars Shrine's winter solstice alignment. He wondered what might have been going on in the skies immediately prior to first light.

Using the open source sky program Stellarium to examine the predawn sky in the direction where the sun would ultimately rise at the time of the winter solstice, I saw nothing unusual. I then examined the movement of the celestial bodies across the entire night. What I found absolutely blew my mind.

Following the setting of the sun on the night of the winter solstice, the Milky Way would have been seen rising horizontally on the eastern horizon. As this took place, the Galactic Bulge would have been due east, almost exactly in the line of sight of anyone sitting on the stone thrones carved out of the bedrock on the western side of the Great Ellipse.

Such a magnificent spectacle in the clear winter skies above the remote Tektek Mountains would not have gone unnoticed by Karahan's Pre-Pottery Neolithic community. For those seated on the Great Ellipse's stone thrones, it would have seemed as though the Great Serpent was reaffirming its connection with the community. As this spectacle unfolded, the stars of Scorpius would have been positioned vertically upright rising very quickly to 10 degrees south of east (see fig. 23.3), the precise directional orientation of the enclosure's main axis.

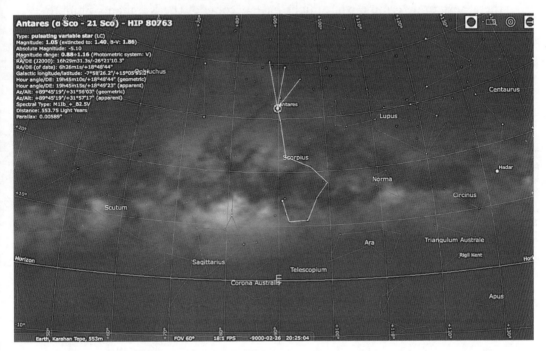

Fig. 23.3. View of the Galactic Bulge rising in the east from the latitude of Karahan Tepe in 9000 BCE. Image made using the Stellarium free open-source planetarium.

Perhaps related to this discovery is the fact that Hugh Newman and I were able to determine that the giant stone head in the Pillars Shrine is itself oriented immediately south of east, matching very well the orientation of the neighboring Great Ellipse. What is more, there is an east-west running channel cut in the bedrock on the eastern side of the Pillars Shrine that allows the stone head to remain fully visible as you move away from the structure. The head's placement, along with its orientation, thus seems deliberate and might well have been designed to allow it to gaze out toward the Galactic Bulge in its role as the head of the Milky Way serpent, along with the stars of Scorpius representing the serpent's active spirit.

In this manner the Pillars Shrine's giant stone head was able to lock into these powerful celestial influences, which, due to their movement through the heavens, would have been seen as integral to the rhythmic cycles of life on Earth. Indeed, it becomes distinctly possible that through a deep understanding of these cosmic forces and their effects on the world, Karahan Tepe's Taş Tepeler community helped inspire the widespread dissemination of what we know today as astrology, something that would go on to flower just 22 miles (35 kilometers) away at Harran, the celebrated city of the Chaldeans. We go there next to determine what might have become of the Karahan community's beliefs and practices surrounding the cyclic nature of the world-encircling serpent.

Plate I. The new enclosure uncovered at Karahan Tepe during the summer of 2023, showing the giant human statue and, on its left, the damaged porthole stone.

All photographs in this color insert are by Andrew Collins or part of his personal collection.

Plates 2 and 3. Karahan Tepe's Structure AD (the Great Ellipse) as seen today. Plate 2 (top) shows the enclosure if looking toward the east, while plate 3 shows the enclosure if looking toward the west.

Plate 4. The fragmented T-pillars located at the center of Karahan Tepe's Structure AD. The two benches on the left are made up of T-pillars in secondary use. The one on the left shows a leopard pelt loincloth in relief.

Plate 5. View of the rock-cut buttresses and thrones at the western end of Karahan Tepe's Structure AD. Note the enclosure's southern recess on the left-hand side.

Plate 6. The curved serpentine groove on the north side of Karahan Tepe's Structure AB (the Pillars Shrine) with the porthole stone visible at its southern end. Beyond this, in Structure AD, is its southern recess, highlighting the approximate north-northwesterly/south-southeasterly alignment between all three features.

Plates 7 and 8. Two views of Karahan Tepe's Structure AB showing its remarkable rock-cut pillars. Plate 7 (top) shows the shrine if looking toward the southwest, while plate 8 shows it looking toward the east.

Plates 9 and 10.
Two views of the giant rock-cut stone head on the western wall of Karahan Tepe's Structure AB.

Plates 11 and 12. Two views of Karahan Tepe's structure AA (the Pit Shrine). Plate 11 (top) looks toward the west, while plate 12 looks toward the east.

Plate 13. The T-pillar in Karahan Tepe's Structure AH showing the remaining central T-pillar. On its stem is the relief of a human arm with its shoulder socket deliberately carved into the head of a vulture.

Plate 14. The author measuring an unexcavated T-pillar at Karahan Tepe in 2014. (Ruler in inches.)

Plate 15. Carved statue found during excavations at Karahan Tepe and on display today at the Şanlıurfa Archaeological Museum. We see this statue as a predator, arguably a panther leopard, riding on the back of a human figure.

Plate 16. Carved statue found during excavations at Karahan Tepe and on display today at the Şanlıurfa Archaeological Museum. It has an elongated head with archaic features, a pronounced occipital bun, and a tight bun of dreadlocks. It also has holes in the ears for earrings or ear plugs.

Plates 17 and 18. Stone platters found during excavations at Karahan Tepe and on display today at the Şanlıurfa Archaeological Museum.

Plates 19 and 20. Two fragments of 11,000-year-old porthole stones seen at Karahan Tepe prior to excavations beginning in 2019. (Ruler in inches.)

Plate 21. Hugh Newman examines the unfinished T-shaped pillar still attached to the bedrock seen on the western side of Karahan Tepe.

Plate 22. Fragment of an 11,000-year-old porthole stone seen in a cemetery at Ayanlar Höyük, the site of a major unexcavated Taş Tepeler site northwest of Şanlıurfa. Among the many items being found in local fields are additional carved fragments as well as pieces of stone platters (see inset), like those found during excavations at Karahan Tepe.

Plate 23. Animated human figure on the north wall of the bedrock enclosure at Sayburç holding what appears to be a snake or a rattle with a large bovine advancing toward him. Is the figure bull leaping?

Plate 24. Three-dimensional carved relief of a standing male figure holding his phallus with felines on either side, as seen on the north wall of the 11,000-year-old bedrock enclosure at Sayburç, just west of Şanlıurfa.

Plate 25. Carved statue found upside down within the niche inside Karahan Tepe's Structure AD's southern recess. The "wings" on the top of the human head are in fact the claws of a predator, most likely a panther leopard. The statue can be seen in the Şanlıurfa Archaeological Museum.

Plate 26. Keçili Tepe as seen from Karahan Tepe's northern knoll.

Plate 27. The author emerging from the beehive structure known as the Snake Pit found on the southern slopes of Keçili Tepe. Note Karahan Tepe in the background at the top of the picture.

Plate 28. Interior of one of the two hypogeum caves on the western slopes of Keçili Tepe.

Plate 29. Syrian cave church at the southern base of Zakzuk Dağı, the prominent hill lying due north of Karahan Tepe.

Plate 30. The bedrock structure known as the Rock Temple at the northern end of Keçili Tepe. Is it simply a quarry or something more?

Plate 31. The recess (right) at the base of the pit inside Karahan Tepe's Structure AA (the Pit Shrine).

Plate 32. The setting sun illuminating Karahan Tepe's Structure AA. Although this shows the sun setting on September 16, 2022, not on the summer solstice, it does demonstrate how the sun is able to reach the enclosure at this time of day.

Plates 33 and 34. Two examples of the black snake from the Yezidi sanctuary at the abandoned village of Mağaraköy in the İdil district of Şırnak province, southeastern Anatolia. Plate 33 (top) shows the entrance into the walled sanctuary, while plate 34 shows the curling black snake on the side of a major tomb.

Plate 35. Incised snake seen on the front edge of the stone bench within Karahan Tepe's Structure AA.

Plate 36. Carved relief of a fox at the northern end of the stone bench within Karahan Tepe's Structure AA, its head indicated with an arrow.

Plate 37. Sequence of images showing the sun hitting the carved stone head in Karahan Tepe's Structure AB shortly after sunrise on the winter solstice in 2022.

Plate 38. The Astronomical Tower amid the ruins of the seventh-century Paradise Mosque at Harran.

Plate 39. Monument dedicated to the seven luminous divine emanations of the Yezidi religion within the community's open-air sanctuary at Mağaraköy in southeastern Anatolia.

Plate 40. Karahan Tepe following the start of excavations in 2019.

24

The Star Worshippers
of Harran

Synchronizing monumental architecture with the sun, moon, and stars at places like Karahan Tepe was surely the first step toward the emergence of what we know today as astrology. This is the belief, held since ancient times, that the timing, position, and relationship of what are described as the "Seven Stars"—that is, the sun, the moon, and the five observable planets as they progress through the 12 houses of the zodiac each year—help determine the fate and destiny of the world and everything in it, including, of course, humanity itself.

Could Karahan Tepe have been one of the foundation places of astrology, which went on to flourish in its greatest form at places like the ancient cities of Harran and Edessa (modern-day Şanlıurfa) and nearby Sogmatar (also known as Sumatar Harabesi), the legendary site of the seven planetary temples of the Chaldeans?

The inhabitants of Harran were known by various names: Harranians, after the name of the city, Chaldeans—that is, the peoples of Chaldea (Greek: Χαλδία, Khaldia), the ancient name for southeastern and eastern Anatolia—and Sabians, this last name deriving from the word *saba*, possibly meaning "star rising."[1] As a provincial capital of first the Assyrians and later the Neo-Assyrians and Neo-Babylonians, Harran's chief deity was the moon god Sin. The term Chaldean came to be applied to the inhabitants of Harran and Edessa, since these had become their chief places of residence. The Chaldeans were renowned for their advanced knowledge of the stars and their impact on the world, leading eventually to the term "Chaldean" being used to describe anyone in the Near East with a profound understanding of astronomy or astrology. Following the Arab invasion of Anatolia in the seventh century CE, the Chaldean inhabitants of Harran and the surrounding area were pressured into converting to Islam, although their knowledge of the stars continued. The magnificent Paradise Mosque was built in the heart of the city, probably on the site of the temple of Sin. This became the centerpiece of a celebrated Islamic university where the ancient wisdom of the Chaldeans continued to be taught to students.

After this time, the influence of the Chaldeans was split between Harran and key cities in the Near East such as Aleppo in Syria and Baghdad in Iraq, paving the way for the sudden emergence of the Islamic sciences. They included the study of astronomy, trigonometry, algebra, mathematics, geometry, and wisdom literature. The Chaldeans were responsible also for the invention of the first astrolabes, circular astronomical devices that were used to measure the movement of the sun and moon, predict eclipses, calculate geographical coordinates, and determine the position of stars (see fig. 24.1).[2] By the tenth century,

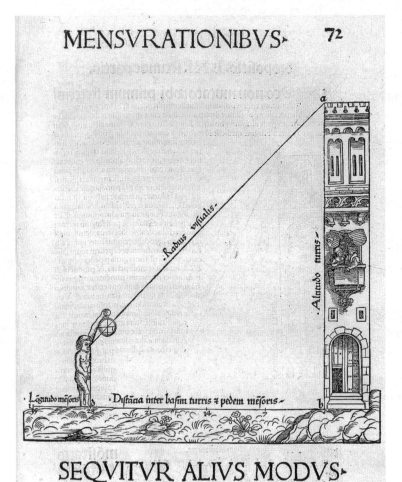

Fig. 24.1. Man using an astrolabe to measure the height of a building, as perceived by German polymath Johannes Stöffler (1452-1531). (From Stöffler, [1512] 1524.)

Fig. 24.2. The famous tenth-century CE astrolabe maker
Al-ʻIjliyyah bint al-ʻIjliyy, otherwise known as Mariam al-Astrulabi,
who lived in Aleppo, Syria.
Illustration by Russell M. Hossain.

astrolabes were being manufactured at Aleppo under the direction of remarkable individuals such as Al-ʻIjliyyah bint al-ʻIjliyy, otherwise known as Mariam
al-Astrulabi (see fig. 24.2), and her father al-ʻIjliyy.*

---

*Al-ʻIjliyyah bint al-ʻIjliyy, otherwise known as Mariam al-Astrulabi, features as a character in
the Netflix series *Vikings: Valhalla* (season 2, 2023), where her advanced knowledge and manufacture of astrolabes is duly acknowledged.

In 1259 or 1260 the city of Harran was captured peacefully by the Mongols but by 1271 had been almost entirely destroyed, forcing its mainly Muslim population to seek new homes not only in places like Aleppo or Baghdad, but also in nearby Şanlıurfa, which did not suffer the same fate.

THE FALLEN TOWER

All that remained standing at Harran following its destruction was its medieval castle, extended sections of the city wall, and parts of the Paradise Mosque. This included a beautiful archway leading into its central courtyard (sayn) and the mosque's tall, square-based tower (minaret), its summit now fractured either through a lightning strike or through some wanton act of vandalism (see plate 38). This ominous structure—long rumored to be the inspiration behind the Tower card of the tarot pack—was introduced to me as the "Astronomical Tower" when I first visited Harran in 2004. This was the name offered by the same children who had presented me with the local guidebook that alerted me to the existence of Karahan Tepe. The Paradise Mosque's minaret would presumably have functioned not only as a place to call worshippers to prayer, but

Fig. 24.3. Medieval Arabian Astrologers (from Macrobius [1483] 1513).

also where Chaldean astronomers, perhaps using astrolabes, repaired to track the movement of the stars (see fig. 24.3).

How exactly Harran became the go-to center of learning for astronomy, mathematics, science, and astrology is unclear. Presumably it was the culmination of an interest in these subjects by its Chaldean inhabitants across an extended period of time. What we can say is that the oldest known occupational mound in the Harran area is the 10,000-year-old Tell Idris, the "mound of Idris."[3] Idris is the Arabic name both for the antediluvian patriarch Enoch and for Hermes, the founder of the wisdom doctrine espoused in the *Corpus Hermeticum*—the books of Hermes—that, although written in Egypt, probably achieved its final form at Harran.

After Tell Idris was abandoned some 8,000 years ago, the focus of attention switched to Harran itself, where a large occupational mound rose up to support the burgeoning local population. This mound, or tepe, is located immediately south of the Paradise Mosque, and fieldwork by archaeologists has indicated that it dates back to the Pottery Neolithic Age, circa 6500–4500 BCE.[4]

CHALDEAN KNOWLEDGE AND WISDOM

When Tell Idris was up and running, Karahan Tepe, situated just 22 miles (35 kilometers) away toward the northeast, was finally being abandoned after nearly 1,500 years of constant usage as a ceremonial and ritual complex. That members of its society went on to live in places like Tell Idris seems inevitable, meaning the possible transfer of astronomical knowledge from one site to another. Is this how the Chaldean descendants of southeastern Anatolia's Taş Tepeler world gained their own intricate knowledge of the stars? Did they inherit their systems of astronomy and astrology from their Neolithic forebears? I think the answer is always going to be *yes*.

As already made clear, Chaldean belief centered around the influence of the Seven Stars, or seven planets, as they make their passage through the 12 zodiacal houses. The Chaldeans believed that the Seven Stars along with the 12 signs of the zodiac were the work of a luminous being seen as the "primal cause" behind all manifestation both in the celestial realms and in the mundane world.[5] His name was Shamal, which is Arabic and means either "north" or "left," as in when I face east toward the rising sun, north is on my left-hand side.[6]

As a deity, Shamal was not only eternal, but also the oldest and greatest of the gods. He was the chief of the jinn and demons, showing the immense antiquity of his cult as it obviously included a reverence of supernatural beings that had long since been condemned as devils and demons by religious authorities.[7] Shamal was seen also as a visible manifestation of the heavenly realm.[8] In this role he was the source of eternal light and power, something that was seen to emerge out of the primeval darkness.[9] Through this manifestation, the cosmic emanations came into being,[10] these including the Seven Stars (or seven planets) and the 12 signs of the zodiac, which together demonstrate Shamal's influence on the world.[11]

NERGAL—LORD OF THE UNDERWORLD

Tamara M. Green, professor in the Department of Classical and Oriental Studies at Hunter College, part of City University of New York, has written that Shamal can be equated with Nergal, the Babylonian god of death, pestilence, and plague, who was also Lord of the Underworld.[12] Nergal was connected with the area of sky occupied by the constellations of Sagittarius and Scorpius, over which he had rulership. In Babylonian astronomy, the strange centaur-like creature named ᵐᵘˡPabilsaĝ, who is shown releasing an arrow from a bow, was not only the prototype for our Sagittarius but was also associated with the underworld through his syncretism with Nergal.[13]

In the Babylonian astronomical compendium known as the MUL.APPIN, Nergal commands the panther-griffin ᵐᵘˡUD.KA.DUH.A, which means "constellation [*MUL*] of the storm demon with the gaping mouth."[14] This was made up of key stars of Cygnus, along with others from the neighboring constellations of Cepheus and Lacerta.[15]

Nergal as Sagittarius and also as the commander of the panther-griffin ᵐᵘˡUD.KA.DUH.A tells us that his domain was the Milky Way's Dark Rift, from its northern opening in the vicinity of the Cygnus star Deneb all the way down to its southern termination in the region of Sagittarius, Ophiuchus, and Scorpius. Indeed, it was probably because of Nergal's guardianship of the Scorpionic gateway that he became the guide of souls wishing to reach the afterlife, something reflected in the belief among Harranians that as the Primal Cause, Shamal was responsible for the birth of human souls and their reception in the afterlife.[16]

Fig. 24.4. Relief sculpture of the first or second century CE from Hatra in northern Iraq showing the god Nergal (identified at the site with the Arabic god Zqyqa) surrounded by scorpions, snakes, and a three-headed, Cerberus-like dog. Photo by Katolophyromai.

Nergal's guardianship of the Scorpionic gateway led to him being connected with totems associated with the constellation of Scorpius. As a carved relief from Hatra in Iraq shows, these included snakes and scorpions, as well as a hound with three heads synonymous with the three-headed dog Cerberus of Greek myth (see fig. 24.4). It is clear that these underworld creatures must all have been seen as guardians of the Scorpionic gateway. Moreover, Nergal's three-headed dog might well be linked with the fox constellation that in Greco-Egyptian and later Roman astrological texts was considered one of the three *decani* of Scorpius.

Could Shamal in his guise as Nergal have been identified with the Galactic Bulge, which, as already indicated, corresponds with the central region of our own Milky Way galaxy? As we have seen, *shamal* means "north," indicating his control over the turning of the heavens about the celestial pole, marked in any age by the Pole Star, also known as the North Star. Thus a direct connection between Shamal and the Milky Way serpent seems unlikely. That said, it is clear that, through his associations with the god Nergal, Shamal was originally more than just a personification of the north as a direction. This tells us that he likely also had command over the Scorpionic gateway and might thus have been seen as the animating force behind the Milky Way serpent—in particular, the Galactic Bulge's role as the serpent's head.

THE CULT OF ORPHEUS

Like the peoples of Harran, the Karahan community appear to have synchronized their world with a cosmic source seen as responsible for controlling the cyclic movement of the heavens and through this the passage of time. The astronomer shamans at Karahan Tepe, however, seem to have gone further, identifying this cosmic force with the Milky Way and seeing it in terms of a celestial serpent able to impart knowledge and wisdom through direct communication. An understanding of the existence and influence of the Milky Way serpent as a sentient being is something that, as we see in the coming chapters, would reemerge much later among the beliefs and practices of various religious sects that thrived in Asia Minor (modern-day Anatolia) during Greek and Roman times. Among those that would appear to have recognized the importance of the Great Serpent were the Greek mystery schools associated with the teachings of Orpheus, a legendary musician, poet, prophet, and son of Apollo.

Although Orpheus was said to have been born in Thrace, a region of eastern Europe embracing what are today parts of Bulgaria, Greece, and European Turkey, the basis of his teachings were derived from what are described as the Orphic hymns, which first began circulating in the Hellenic world during the fifth century BCE.[17]

During the early centuries of the Christian era religious teachings derived from the Orphic hymns began experiencing a huge revival of interest, particularly in Upper Mesopotamia (modern southeastern Anatolia and northern Syria).[18] As I show elsewhere, the roots of Orphism have strong links with Anatolia's cult of Bacchus or Dionysus and before that, most likely, its Pre-Pottery Neolithic communities in the central and southeastern part of the country.[19]

The Maenads, the ferocious female worshippers of the god Bacchus, would adorn themselves in leopard skin garments during festivals, allegedly tearing apart anyone who got in their way. One unfortunate victim of this frenzied activity was, we are told, Orpheus, who was killed by the Maenads. Zeus, however, brought him back to life and placed him in the sky as the constellation of Cygnus, his famous lyre being placed next to him as the stars of the constellation of Lyra, the celestial lyre.

At a very early date the panther leopard, like the vulture, became a sky figure identified with the stars of Cygnus. From this dual combination emerged the panther-griffin ^{mul}UD.KA.DUH.A of Babylonian astronomy. It was no doubt why the Armenian constellation Angegh (Armenian *anggh*), identified with the stars of Cygnus, is classified both as a vulture and as a winged griffon described as a "birdlike angel god" (see chapter 17).

In the earliest Mesopotamian mythology the panther griffin took the form of a "mythical giant bird" or thunderbird known in Akkadian as Zû or Anzû (Sumerian: Imdugud), and this too is suspected as having existed as a sky figure associated with the stars of Cygnus prior to it being phased out in favor of the Babylonian ^{mul}UD.KA.DUH.A.[20] Interestingly enough the Anzû takes its name from the root zû, which relates both to the vulture and to stormy winds.[21] In mythology the Anzû was transformed from a storm bird or thunderbird into a vulture-feline or eagle-feline hybrid (originally probably a panther and then later a lion). Interestingly, the geo-mythical environment surrounding the stories of the Anzû is linked by archaeologist Daniel Weiss with a "mountain in the north-eastern reaches of the Sumerian world, in the region of present-day Turkey where the Tigris and Euphrates originate."[22] It was there that the Anzû was defeated in combat by Ninurta (also known as Ninĝirsu), an early Sumerian god worshipped at Lagash, one of Iraq's most ancient cities.

In the northeastern part of Turkey are the Armenian Highlands, as well as Lake Van and the Ararat plain, which lies beneath the ominous presence of Mount Ararat, close to the border with Armenia and Iran. It would be in this region that I would place the absolute origins of the Epipaleolithic peoples who would eventually establish the earliest Pre-Pottery Neolithic settlements on the

Upper Tigris River before moving westward to inspire the creation of the Taş Tepeler culture sometime between 10,000 BCE and 9600 BCE.

What all this tells us is that the vulture and the panther-leopard, two of the most common creatures represented in Taş Tepeler carved art, both formed sky figures made up of the stars of Cygnus, with extra stars added from the neighboring constellations of Cepheus and Lacerta. Both creatures acted as psychopomps during the prehistoric age, aiding the human spirit to travel from the land of the living to the realm of the dead and, where necessary, back again.

For the Taş Tepeler community at Karahan Tepe the sky world was entered via the northern opening of the Milky Way's Dark Rift. This they accessed either directly when Deneb either rose or set or, alternately, when its southern termination coincided with the local horizon at the time of the solstices or equinoxes. It is for this reason, I feel sure, that various clearly anthropomorphic T-pillars at Karahan Tepe, including the rock-cut buttresses at the western end of the Great Ellipse (Structure AD), appear to show individuals wearing leopard pelt loincloths. Are we seeing in these pillars the earliest ever manifestation of what would become the Maenads of the cults of Bacchus-Dionysus and, of course, that of Orpheus, the son of Apollo? Once again, I am certain the answer is yes.

The cosmogony espoused by the Orphic teachings, which, as we shall see, included knowledge of the Great Serpent's role in cosmic creation, would be embraced by certain Gnostic sects that flourished in the early centuries of the Christian era across Asia Minor and the Near East. Collectively, their practitioners would come to be known as Ophites, a term deriving from the Greek ὄφις [ophis], "snake" or "serpent," and meaning "followers of the snake."

To understand the role played both by Orphism and by the Ophite Gnostics in reenergizing age-old beliefs and practices that almost certainly had their beginnings among the Taş Tepeler sites of southeastern Anatolia, we must start by turning our attention to what is arguably one of the most enigmatic artifacts of late antiquity. I speak of what is known today as the Orphic alabaster bowl. Its curious backstory and unique appearance, along with its stark symbolism can, I believe, throw considerable light on how the inhabitants of Karahan Tepe envisioned their own relationship with the Great Serpent.

PART 7

GNOSIS

I am in the serpent and the serpent is within me.
DEBBIE CARTWRIGHT, 2023, ON THE ROLE OF
THE SNAKE SHAMANS AT KARAHAN TEPE

25

The Mystery of the Alabaster Bowl

Very few artifacts directly associated with Ophite Gnostic rites exist today. Those that do provide us with a clear insight into what these heretic Christians believed, what took place during their mystical rites, and how these ritual practices can be linked with the shamanic activities now thought to have taken place at Taş Tepeler sites like Karahan Tepe shortly after the end of the last ice age. One such relic is a much-discussed alabaster bowl considered by scholars to have belonged to a mystery school that, although nominally Gnostic Christian, adhered to much older Orphic teachings.[1]

The item in question was first made available for study in the 1920s when it was in the custodianship of numismatist and art dealer Jacob Hirsch of Geneva, Switzerland, having previously formed part of a private collection in Leipzig, Germany.[2] Hirsch subsequently moved to Paris and eventually New York before his death in 1955, after which time the location of the bowl was lost.[3] Its authenticity, however, does not seem in doubt as it was subjected to a microscopic analysis by German classical archaeologist Richard Delbrueck and Dutch archaeologist Carl Wilhelm Vollgraff, who, in a paper published in 1934, concluded that the bowl showed no signs of forgery.[4]

According to the German philologist, philosopher, and physicist Hans Leisegang (1890–1951), who made an extensive study of the bowl's symbolism in a landmark paper published in 1939 and titled "Das Mysterium der Schlange" ("The Mystery of the Serpent"),[5] its original owner claimed it had been purchased by his grandfather "somewhere in the Mediterranean region," 87 years before Leisegang first saw photos of the artifact in 1929.[6] This provides us with a date in the region of 1842.

The bowl, which is fashioned out of a single piece of pale white alabaster, faded with age to a yellow-gray, appears to have come either from inner Asia Minor (central Anatolia) or from Syria.[7] Datewise, it is considered to have been carved somewhere between the third and sixth centuries CE,[8] although stylistically there are grounds to suggest it is no later than the third century CE.[9] The first scholar to make a study of the bowl was German classical philologist and teacher Hans Lamer (1873–1939), who in 1931 wrote that he had never seen anything quite like it, characterizing it as "absolutely unique."[10]

The bowl was carved freehand using a knife, explaining its very slightly irregular shape.[11] In size it is 8.6 inches (22 centimeters) in diameter, 3 inches (8 centimeters) in height, and just over 2.2 inches (5.5 centimeters) in depth.[12] Within the bowl's concave interior are 16 naked human figures carved side by side in a radial fashion, their heads toward the edges and their feet toward the center (see fig. 25.1, p. 200). There are seven men and nine women (made up of four older men, three younger men, and nine young women).*

At the feet of the figures is a raised hemispherical device, egg-like in appearance and generally identified as an *umbo* (a raised center like the boss of a shield)[13] or as an *omphalos* (see fig. 25.2 on the next page for a cross section of the bowl).[14] This is a Greek word meaning "navel" and was used in classical times to describe large, egg-shaped stones that marked assumed geographical centers of the known world (the best-known example is the one that stood at the temple of Apollo at Delphi in Greece). Omphali were symbols of first creation, which was considered to have begun from a single point outward in all directions. The presence of an umbo on the vessel identifies it as a *phiale*,[15] a shallow bowl usually made of ceramic or metal with a central protrusion used in the Greek and Roman worlds to offer ritual libations.

---

*The order of the naked figures is not male-female, male-female, etc. Instead males (m) and females (f) are ordered as follows: m-f-f-m-f-m-m-f-m-f-f-m-f-m-f-f (see Leisegang [1955] 1978, 196).

Fig. 25.1. Orphic alabaster bowl main interior
(from Leisegang 1939 as well as [1955] 1978, fig. 1).

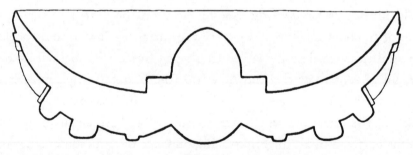

Fig. 25.2. Cross-section of the alabaster bowl highlighting the prominence of its
egg-shaped umbo or omphalos (from Delbrueck and Vollgraff 1934, fig. 2).

THE MYSTERY OF THE COILED SERPENT

Curled up on the bowl's umbo is a winged serpent or dragon with scales, ears, and a mouth full of sharp teeth (see fig. 25.3). It rests its head on the

Fig. 25.3 a and b. *Left*: close-up of the naked figures on the bowl's interior (from Delbrueck and Vollgraff 1934, fig. 4). *Right*: close-up of the winged dragon on the alabaster bowl (from Delbrueck and Vollgraff 1934, fig. 3).

omphalos allowing one of its eyes to gaze out at the naked figures who look toward its position. This has led to the figures being described as "worshippers of the Dragon-god in lowly nudity praying to him in congregation."[16] At the base of the umbo is a "double wreath of rays"[17] that flow beneath the naked figures. This radial device has been interpreted as the "flaming light of the sun."[18] A careful count of these tongues of fire or rays of light shows there are 32 in all, exactly double the number of human figures seen within the bowl's interior.

On the underside of the bowl are two concentric rings radiating out from a central hub that corresponds to the position of the umbo and winged dragon within its concave interior (see fig. 25.4a). Carved around the vertical edge of the bowl are 24 columned arcades, with four more hidden behind four additional figures, meaning there are 28 in total.* These extra figures are also naked with each holding a seashell trumpet to their mouth.[19] It has been proposed that they either

---

*Differences of opinion exist regarding just how many columns are shown on the rim of the alabaster bowl. Lamer (1931, 654) speaks of four arcades, each with 7 columns, making 28 in total. Delbrueck and Vollgraff (1934, 130) say there are 28 columns visible with four others hidden behind the figures, making 32 in total. Leisegang ([1955] 1978, 197) says there are 28 arches of which four are hidden behind the figures. Lozanova-Stantcheva (2016, 94) says there are 24 columns with four hidden behind the figures. I have cited the figure offered by Lamer and also Leisegang as a simple count of columns and arches, which strongly indicates there are 28 of each.

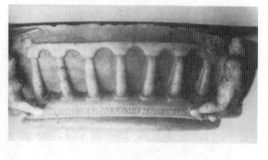

Fig. 25.4a and b. *Left*: Radial lines and central bulge as seen on the underside of the alabaster bowl (from Leisegang [1955] 1978, fig. IIa). *Right*: One of the erotes or representations of the four winds seen on the sides of the alabaster bowl (from Delbrueck and Vollgraff 1934, fig. 5).

represent the four winds,[20] or they are *erotes*,[21] winged gods associated in Greek classical tradition with love and sexuality (see fig. 25.4b).

There is an inscription around the rim of the bowl in four parts, each one being a line from an Orphic hymn, making it clear that those who commissioned the fashioning of this vessel saw the Orphic teachings as important to their own religious beliefs and practices. What is more, the choice of lines used is suggestive of an invocation to a cosmic deity personified as the winged dragon seen on the umbo at the center of the bowl's interior.[22]

The 16 naked figures carved radially around the umbo all make different hand gestures as if supplicating the winged dragon.[23] Some of the women have one hand raised with the other touching their breasts. Others have one hand on their chests and the other touching their pudenda, while still others have one hand on their pudenda and the other on their stomach. Some of the men raise one hand in the air with the other touching their chests.

Hans Leisegang proposed that the 16 figures are *mystai*, initiates of the Orphic mystery school, whose nakedness shows they have entered into an ecstatic state and are now experiencing what he refers to as "supercelestial space,"[24] a kind of supernal realm existing in the primordial darkness beyond the material universe.

As with many of the secret rites associated with Greek mystery cults, nudity was a prerequisite for participation in Orphic rites,[25] with the Greek comic playwright Aristophanes (died 386 BCE), in his work *Clouds*, parodying an Orphic initiation when he says: "Here it is customary that they enter naked."[26] What is more, and as Leisegang points out, "It should further be considered that contact with sacred serpents seems to call for nakedness, and on the alabaster bowl the Aeon [also known as Phanes—see below] is manifested to the mystai as a serpent."[27] He continues:

> The figures on our bowl represent a community of mystery worshipers who have risen to the supercelestial realm at the climax of their cult rite. Here the godhead appears to them in the form of the great serpent, whom they salute in the attitude of servants of the god, the women expecting to conceive by the god, the men praying for them. We would seem to be dealing with a mystery [where] the mystai drew a snake between their thighs in order to consummate a mystical union with the god."[28]

So what does this Gnostic serpent represent, and what is the "supercelestial realm" thought to exist in the primordial darkness beyond the physical universe? More important, how is the rite being performed by the mystai related to what was going on at Karahan Tepe thousands of years earlier? Are the two related in some manner?

Leisegang linked the bowl's symbolism with a stone relief 28.5 inches (72 centimeters) in height and 10.5 inches (26.5 centimeters) wide from Modena, Italy, which shows a carved image of the Orphic god Phanes (see fig. 25.5 on the next page).[29]

The relief was fully described at the beginning of the twentieth century by Belgian historical writer and archaeologist Franz Cumont (1868–1947), who wrote that:

> In an oval frame containing the 12 signs of the zodiac a naked youth [Phanes] is standing, holding a sceptre in his left hand and a thunderbolt in his right. His feet are hoof-shaped, like the goat-legs of the Greek god Pan. His body is encircled by the spirals of a snake whose head is seen above his head. Behind his shoulders with two wings the horns of a crescent are visible. On his breast the mask of a lion's head, while from his sides the heads of a ram and a buck are budding forth. The feet rest upon an upturned cone, which is without any doubt a half egg, from which flames are pouring forth. Above the curly head with five shining rays is the other half of the egg, also aflame.[30]

Fig. 25.5. Relief sculpture from the second century CE showing the Orphic god Phanes emerging from the cosmic egg and encircled by the 12 signs of the zodiac and the four winds (from Cumont 1903, fig 49). It can be found in the Modena Museum, Modena, Italy.

According to Orphic teachings, Phanes emerged from a cosmic egg created in the supercelestial realm by a serpent identified as the hero-god Herakles (Latin: Hercules), who was also Cronus or Kronos (Latin: Saturn), the god of time.[31] Friction produced by the four winds—represented on the Modena relief as four heads shown in each of the corners beyond the band containing the 12 signs of the zodiac—causes the egg to split into two pieces. The upper half becomes the vault of heaven while the lower part becomes the earth below. Between the two halves Phanes, or Aeon, who was seen to personify infinite time, manifests into being. As this happens the Great Serpent coils around him.

From the lower half of the egg flames emerge, signifying that Phanes is a physical manifestation of what is referred to as the Hypercosmic Sun, a kind of blazing ball of fire behind all creation existing at the center of the cosmos. Such ideas are first known to have been expounded by Pythagoreans such as the pre-Socratic philosopher Philolaus (470–circa 385 BCE) before being later adopted by Neoplatonists as well as by initiates of the cult of the Roman god Mithras.[32] It refers to a divine source of creation that shines forth its wreaths of fire or rays of light from the darkness of the supernal realm (see fig. 25.6a and b for two examples of how the Orphic concept of the Hypercosmic Sun would appear to have been interpreted by seventeenth-century English alchemist and Rosicrucian Robert Fludd).

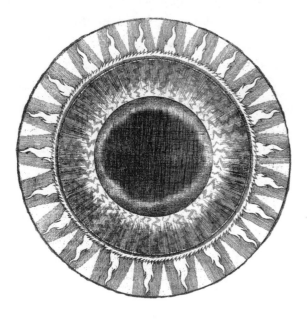

Figs. 25.6 a & b. Two illustrations by the British polymath and philosopher Robert Fludd (1574–1637) from his work *Utriusque Cosmi* (Fludd 1617, tractatus 1. book II, pages 55 and 58 respectively). They show, he says, "*lucis creatae primariae apparitio* ('the primary appearance of created light')." (See Fludd 1617, 55.) In each case, wreaths of fire emanate from a supernal sun existing in the unmanifested primordial darkness—a concept paralleling the Platonic, Mithraic, Orphic, and later, Ophite Gnostic idea of the Hypercosmic Sun.

In this manner, Phanes, whose name means "to bring light" or "to shine," comes to be identified with the sun god Helios, who in one Greek magical papyri is described as, "Thou who risest from the four winds, thou friendly good daemon, glittering Helios, shining over the whole earth, *thou art the great serpent who leadest these gods.*"[33] (Current author's emphasis.) Thus Phanes, as the personification of the Great Serpent, was seen to control not only the regular sun's passage through the 12 houses of the zodiac, but also, as we see next, when and where eclipses occur.

THE HEAD AND TAIL OF THE DRAGON

There are two places where the moon crosses the ecliptic causing solar eclipses. These were anciently known as *Caput Draconis*, the "Dragon's Head," and *Cauda Draconis*, the "Dragon's Tail." Astrologers and astronomers refer to them as the lunar nodes, with the "head" as the ascending node and the "tail" as the descending node. Their naming affirms the fact that the ecliptic was seen as symbolic of a great serpent or dragon, its head and tail marking the two regions of the ecliptic where eclipses can take place. Aside from being identified with the tail-biting Ouroboros of Greco-Egyptian art and literature, the eclipse dragon was known to Chaldean astrologers as Athalia (Greek: ἀθαλία, cognate with the Syrian-Arabic *āṯālyā*, meaning "veil" and "eclipse" as well as "dragon").[34]

Franz Cumont referred to Athalia as the *dracone caelesti*, the "celestial dragon," pointing out that, "An old opinion widespread in almost all the regions of the world states that a huge draco (snake) lived in the sky, and devouring and hiding the Sun and Moon, was the cause of their eclipses."[35] He wrote these words by way of an introduction to a Greek astrological textual fragment of medieval date published for the first time in 1929. It reveals not only the nature of this great serpent, but also where on the ecliptic its *two* heads and *two* tails could be found. According to Cumont:

> The Babylonians, i.e. the Chaldeans, call Athalia this *pneuma* (spirit) which has the shape of a snake with two heads and two tails and one of two heads [is] . . . in Libra and the other in Scorpio, and in the same way the tails too, one is in Aries in opposition to Libra, the other in Taurus, and they dominate the third part of the zodiacal circle."[36]

One of Athalia's heads was thus deemed to be in the zodiacal sign of Scorpio, while the other was seen to be in the neighboring constellation of Libra, the scales, which originally formed the claws of the celestial scorpion. Together these helped synchronize the movements of the eclipse dragon, dracone caelesti, with one at least of the two places on the ecliptic where the sun crosses the Milky Way, this being in the vicinity of Sagittarius and Scorpius. The position of the tails of Athalia seem a little confused, although Aries at least is next to Taurus, which, along with Gemini, marks the place where the ecliptic crosses the Milky Way on the opposite side of the sky.

A better understanding of where the heads and tails of the eclipse dragon were thought to be can be found in the Bundahišn, a Middle Persian work of the ninth century C.E. providing a Zoroastrian account of creation, cosmology, and eschatology. The book states that the Dragon's Tail was in the signs of "the Scorpion and the Sick Centaur"—in other words, Scorpio and Sagittarius—while the Dragon's head was in "Bad Fortune the Two Images," a reference to the sign of Gemini in the opposite half of the sky.[37] The text afterward states:

> The Dragon [the name used is Gōčihr] stood in the middle of the sky like a serpent (mār), its head in the Two Images [Gemini] and its Tail in the Centaur [Sagittarius], so that at all times there are six constellations between its Head and Tail; and its running is retrograde (so that) every 10 years the Tail reverts to where the Head (was) and the Head to where the Tail (was).[38]

Although the position of the head and tail of the eclipse dragon are here reversed, with the tail in Scorpius and Sagittarius and the head in Gemini, their relationship to the two locations where the sun's path crosses the Milky Way is undeniable. What is more, we are even given an explanation why this transposition can occur, as twice in every 19-year lunar cycle the head and tail of Gōčihr—in other words, the dragon controlling the ascending and descending nodes—switch places in a retrograde manner, going from Gemini to Sagittarius/Scorpio, and then back again. That these signs in particular are emphasized as the alternating locations of the head and tail of the Dragon, and the fact that at all times six constellations remain between the creature's Head and Tail, makes it clear that Gōčihr (a word that can mean "moon" or "nodes")[39] is one and the same as the Chaldean concept of Athalia, the envisaged intelligence behind the concept of the dracone caelesti.

Fig. 25.7. Double Ouroboros from the *Clavis Artis*, an alchemical manuscript published in Germany during the late seventeenth or early eighteenth century CE.

That the Bundahišn dragon is said to be "in the middle of the sky like a serpent" is probably a slightly confusing reference to the constellation of Draco in its role as the celestial serpent, either that or it could be a reference to the unerring presence of the eclipse dragon, its head and tail (in other words, the lunar nodes) reaching their apogee at the two places where the sun crosses the Milky Way. This allows us to picture the Bundahišn dragon as a kind of double Ouroboros: two serpents in a circle, each biting the other's tail, a symbol familiar from medieval works on the subject of alchemy (see fig. 25.7).

What also seems apparent is that the little winged dragon coiled around the umbo at the center of the alabaster bowl is itself simply a manifestation of the celestial serpent controlling the cycles of heaven and regulating the passage of time. The four winds identified as erotes on the bowl are one and the same as the four winds on the Phanes relief. In each case they create the friction allowing the cosmic egg to split apart to bring forth the physical universe. The double wreath of rays radiating tongues of fire from beneath the umbo is the visible light of the Hypercosmic Sun, which in the Modena relief is represented by Phanes emerging from the cosmic egg. Bathing in its divine light would have brought about Gnosis, the goal of the Gnostic or mystai, which can be seen in terms of total illumination attained through mystical communion with the Great Serpent,[40] something the shamans at Karahan Tepe would also appear to have wanted to achieve through their own ritual practices.

THE COMING OF THE CHRISTIANS

Although it might easily be argued that the alabaster bowl was produced by members of an Orphic mystery school existing either in inner Asia Minor or Syria, there is every reason to conclude that its true manufacturer was an Ophite Gnostic sect. In the early centuries of the Christian era, Gnostic sects absorbed all manner of strange religious notions from both the Greek and Oriental worlds, for, as Leisegang points out:

> In this period we find a renaissance of Orphism [that is, serpent worship], which is attested by the writings of the philosophers and the entire Christian literature down to the magic papyri. It was an age characterized by the revival of mystery cults, particularly Mithraism, but it was also the epoch of Christian gnosticism.[41]

The concept of Christ as the incarnate son of the divine Father and the mystery of the Great Serpent developed among many of the earliest Gnostic sects. By the third century CE, heresiologists—churchmen who actively campaigned against heretical Christian sects—had grouped under a single banner all Gnostic sects, whom they saw as devotees of God in the form of a snake. To them the sect members were all Ophites, from the Greek word *ophis*, meaning "serpent." This was despite the fact that each sect would have had its own idiosyncratic beliefs on the nature of the Great Serpent and how it related to a divine trinity of the Father, the Son (or Logos, that is, the Word), and what they termed Matter—in other words, physical existence.[42]

The bowl offers no emblems of Christianity, and Leisegang felt the need to point out "these Ophites, who were described by the early Christian Apologists as Christian heretics, were not real Christians at all, but pagans who invested their mystery god with the traits of the new Christ along with those of various Greek and oriental gods. The question can be settled only when we discover the meaning of the nude figures and their gestures."[43]

The worship of the serpent represented on the alabaster bowl, Leisegang suspected, showed the 16 naked figures having reached the "supercelestial space" *beyond the starry heavens.*[44] He proposed they were able to achieve this state of bliss and ecstasy through the experience of their communion rite. They were as souls that had departed this world to connect with the Nous, the mind or intelligence of the Great Serpent,[45] the same as would appear to have been happening thousands of years earlier at Taş Tepeler sites like Karhan Tepe.

THE BRILLIANCE OF THE DRAGON

We have seen how this same serpent appears to have been analogous with the dracone caelesti, the celestial dragon of the Chaldean astrologers, as well as the Gōčihr dragon of the Zoroastrians. Even though this particular dragon was identified with the ecliptic and was seen to cause eclipses, the fixed positions of its head and tail, coincident to where the sun crosses the Milky Way on either side of the sky, show it to be simply a variation of the world-encircling serpent.

This was something recognized by David Neil MacKenzie (1926–2001), a British scholar of Iranian languages, who made an important study of the astrological writings contained in the Bundahišn. He pointed out that the book's author describes the Milky Way as the "brilliance of the Dragon,"[46] adding that:

> According to Muslim astrologers, the Milky Way crosses the ecliptic in the signs Gemini and Sagittarius, i.e. where the Dragon's Head and Tail have their 'exaltations' ["their positions of greatest power"]. . . . Is it possible that the author of the statement concerning the Milky Way [being the "brilliance of the Dragon"] thought of the galaxy as in some way a permanent mark of the Dragon's most 'exalted' position, to which it returned approximately every score of years? . . . It is equally possible that the position of the Dragon . . . was the result of its identification with the observed galaxy.[47]

This, then, appears to confirm that the eclipse dragon, named as Athalia by the Chaldeans and Gōčihr by the Zoroastrians, is in fact the Milky Way serpent, which, if true, is a quite extraordinary realization. I say this for it would mean that the *dracone caelesti*, the "celestial dragon," is none other than the world-encircling serpent the Karahan community would seem to have recognized as controlling the motions of the heavens as much as 11,000 years ago. What is more, it is this same creature we see coiled around the umbo at the center of the Gnostic alabaster bowl, its presence signifying the unerring influence of the Hypercosmic Sun on material existence, something the mystai saw as the manifestation of God himself in his role as creator of the universe. It was this same cosmic force the Ophites strove to connect with through mystical communion services and their adoption of the snake as a symbol of godhead.

The fact also that one of the two "exaltations" of the eclipse Dragon, in other words its place of greatest potency, was thought to be in Sagittarius, and in some accounts in Scorpio, now confirms that the Great Serpent's head (and at other times its tail) was indeed thought to exist in the vicinity of the Galactic Bulge, which, as we know, marks the center of our own Milky Way galaxy.

Is it possible therefore that cosmological beliefs surrounding the Milky Way's role as the world-encircling serpent managed to survive from the age of Taş Tepeler across the millennia until they were developed more fully by the Chaldeans of Harran, the Zoroastrians of Persia, the Orphic mystery schools of Greece, and, of course, the Ophite Gnostic sects of Anatolia and the Near East?

It is a wild claim to make, although in a world where cosmological ideas and valuable astrological information might have remained intact across several millennia, I don't think we should dismiss the possibility out of hand. What is more, I have one more piece of evidence regarding the alabaster bowl that places its manufacture—and, by virtue of this, its apparent employment in Ophite mystical rites—fairly close to the Harran Plain, the original homeland of both Taş Tepeler and the Chaldean astrologers of Harran.

26

The Road to Rusafa

During their close examination of the Orphic alabaster bowl in the early 1930s, German classical archaeologist Richard Delbrueck and Dutch archaeologist Carl Wilhelm Vollgraff made what I consider to be an important statement concerning its possible place of manufacture. In their words:

> The alabaster of the bowl is snow-white and slightly crystalline at fresh breaks. Grey veins run through the mass. There are many cracks, sometimes so fine as to be visible only with strong magnification. The source of this alabaster cannot be determined. A stone which to the lay eye appears externally to be entirely identical is found in early Byzantine capitals in the Louvre from Rusafa in Syria; nothing so close seems to occur in Egyptian or Mesopotamian alabasters.[1]

If this is correct and the Orphic bowl was indeed made from alabaster of a type used in the construction of the former Byzantine-era city of Sergiopolis at Rusafa (also spelled Resafa), situated to the south of the Euphrates River close to Raqqa in northern Syria, then this brings us within striking distance of the Harran Plain. Indeed, Rusafa is just 105 miles (170 kilometers) south of Şanlıurfa and 87 miles (140 kilometers) south-southwest of Harran. To get to Rusafa from Şanlıurfa, all you need to do is journey south on the western edge of the Harran Plain, pass the turning to Harran, cross the border into Syria at Akçakale, and then follow the course of the Balikh River all the way to the Euphrates, immediately beyond which is Rusafa (see fig. 26.1 for a map showing the proximity of the various cities cited here).

Is it possible that the Ophite Gnostic sect responsible for the creation of the alabaster bowl came from somewhere close to Rusafa? Sergiopolis in early

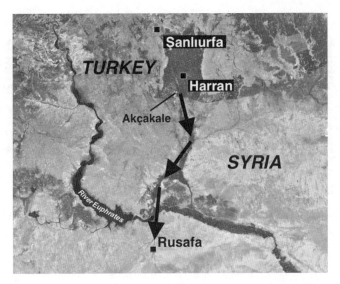

Fig. 26.1. Map showing the geographical relationship between
Rusafa, Harran, and Şanlıurfa (ancient Edessa).
Image by Google Earth and Andrew Collins.

Byzantine times was a major Christian center on a busy pilgrim route that included the Christian city of Edessa (modern-day Şanlıurfa). Even today there are traces of Gnosticism present at Rusafa. Its population consists mainly of Nusayris (or, more correctly, Alawites), an age-old Shia Muslim sect that practices a form of Sufi mysticism. This has been described as embracing a mixture of Islam, Gnosticism, and Christianity,[2] along with a strong belief in metempsychosis (the transmigration of souls)[3] and an acceptance of snake healers.[4] They have a series of holy books only revealed to members of the community, and they practice secret rites and ceremonies, some apparently of a sexual nature.[5]

Nusayris also celebrate the feasts of certain Christian saints, including Mary Magdalene,[6] who was said to have been the founder of an Ophite Gnostic sect called the Naassenes.*

---

*The *Philosophumena*, also known as *The Refutation of All Heresies*, by Hippolytus (third century CE) states that the Naassenes claim that their doctrine came to them from "James the Brother of the Lord [in other words, Jesus]" after it had been handed by him to "Mariamne" (see *Philosophumena*, bk. x, 480–481, in Hippolytus of Rome 1921, vol. ii, 153). Mariamne is none other than Mary Magdalene, who in the Gnostic texts was said to have become the leader of the Christians in Jerusalem following the departure of Jesus (see Collins 2004, chs. 15–16). The fact that Origen of Alexandria wrote that there are Gnostic Christians who follow "Mariamme," or "Mariamne" (Origen Against Celsus, bk. v, ch. 62) only seems to confirm what Hippolytus says.

Nusayri doctrine contains a series of metaphysical beliefs, the roots of which are said to have come from "the astral cult of Harran, to which he [the French Orientalist and archaeologist René Dussaud] traced the origin of the name Shamalis," this being a branch of the Nusayris called the Shemsi, meaning people or worshippers of the sun.[7] It has been proposed that the term Shamalis derives from veneration of the god Shamal as the greatest of gods and Primal Cause by the inhabitants of Harran (see chapter 24).[8] Dussaud, in an essential work on the Nusayris published in 1900, recorded that to the Shemsi the Harranian god Shamal "represented the sun in its nocturnal course."[9] In other words, for the Nusayris Shamal is not the regular sun but an expression of the sun in darkness, the Hypercosmic Sun, that casts forth its rays from the supernal realm existing in the primordial darkness.

All of this, or indeed none of this, might be of relevance to this debate. The connection, however, between the alabaster bowl and the ancient Byzantine city of Sergiopolis (modern Rusafa), the presence there of the Nusayris, their connections with the astral beliefs of the Harranians, and the fact that this Shia Muslim population appears to have recognized the existence of the Hypercosmic Sun are tantalizing at the very least. It does bring hope that the beliefs and practices that originated at Pre-Pottery Neolithic sites like Karahan Tepe could have survived across the millennia, slowly being filtered through important religious centers like Harran, Sogmatar, and Edessa (Şanlıurfa), as well as at places like Rusafa and Aleppo in Syria and Baghdad in Iraq. If so, then the question becomes: What more can we learn about the true nature of the Great Serpent or Perfect Serpent as it was known to the Ophite Gnostics? One sect in particular appears to have preserved more information on this subject than any other. This is the Peratae, and as we see next, they, too, will be found to have had strong links with the Chaldean astrologers of Harran.

27

Followers of the Serpent

One of the most interesting Ophite Gnostic sects that flourished during the first three centuries of the Christian era was the Peratae. The principal ancient source preserving knowledge of their profound metaphysical doctrine is the *Philosophumena*, also known as *The Refutation of All Heresies*. Dating to the early third century CE, it is attributed to the theologian Hippolytus of Rome (died 236 CE).[1] What the *Philosophumena* reveals about the Peratae's cosmological views will become crucial in better understanding what the peoples of Karahan Tepe might have been attempting to achieve during their own age. It will show also how astral beliefs in the Great Serpent gradually shifted away from the area of the Galactic Bulge, and the Milky Way as a whole, to a new location in the vicinity of the northern celestial pole.

THE ORIGINS OF THE PERATAE

The doctrine of the Peratae is said to have come from two individuals, Celbes (or Acembes) the Carystian and Euphrates the Peratic.[2] The term Peratic, the singular form of Peratae, is thought to derive from the Greek word περατής (*peratis*), meaning "passerby," a term taken from the book of Genesis 14:13, which reads "and the one who had fled told the news to Abram the passerby."[3] It refers to the fact that Abraham, the great patriarch of the Hebrew Bible and prophet of the Holy Koran, came originally from the other side of the Euphrates, that is, beyond its northern bank as seen from the perspective of a person in the Roman province of Syria.[4]

As we saw from the suggestion that the Orphic alabaster bowl might have had links with the ancient Syrian city of Rusafa, after crossing the Euphrates

River it is a relatively straight road northward to Edessa (modern Şanlıurfa). This is where Abraham is traditionally thought to have been born and raised at a time when the city was known as *Ur Kaśdim*, "Ur of the Chaldees" or "Ur of the Chaldeans," a name found in the book of Genesis.[5]

Where Ur of the Chaldees might have been located has been the subject of debate among theologians and biblical scholars for over 150 years. The British archaeologist Sir C. Leonard Woolley (1880–1960) laid claim to its discovery following extensive excavations he carried out between 1922 and 1934 at Tell el-Muqayyar, a royal cemetery of Sumerian age in Lower Iraq. This conclusion, although widely accepted today by the scholarly community, ignores age-old Muslim, Kurdish, Jewish, and Christian traditions identifying the birthplace of Abraham, and thus the location of Ur of the Chaldees, as Şanlıurfa, which until 1923 was called Urfa (a name still used today by local residents).[6] It lies just 28 miles (45 kilometers) north of Harran (or Haran, as it is called in the Hebrew Bible), where Abraham travels to after departing Ur of the Chaldees. It is there that he tarries a while, staying with his family, before making his epic journey south to Canaan, the land promised to him and his descendants by the god of the Israelites.

Knowing that Christian theologian and scholar Clement of Alexandria (150–211/215 CE) records in his *Stromata* (circa 203 CE) that some heresies "take their designation *from a place, as [do] the Peratici*,"[7] (current author's emphasis), tells us that Euphrates the Peratic, and perhaps even the Peratae as a whole, probably came from the northern part of the Roman province of Mesopotamia, corresponding to what is today southeastern Anatolia. If correct, then this takes us not only into the territory of the Chaldean astrologers of Harran, but also into the heartland of the Taş Tepeler culture. (By the way, Celbes the Carystian, the other founder of the Peratae, probably came from Karystos or Carystus, a small coastal town on the Greek island of Euboea, although beyond that nothing more is known about him.)

WHAT THE PERATAE BELIEVED

The Peratae, we are told, recognized a trinity of forces referred to as the Father, the Son (or Logos, meaning the Word), and Matter. The Father was ineffable and beyond the material universe. Matter constituted the physical world, and everything in it, while the Son was seen as the intermediary between the

Father and Matter. He, as we shall see, was identified with the Great Serpent, the same one shown as a curled up dragon on the Orphic alabaster bowl.

Snakes in the Bible

The Peratae identified the Serpent with stories from the Hebrew Bible where snakes had played what were considered positive roles, this being presumably to help convince members of their community that the creature has always been beneficial to those who follow the true path of God. For instance, the Son, they said, manifested to Moses when the rod belonging to his brother Aaron turned into a snake in the presence of Pharaoh, the king of Egypt, and gobbled up the staffs of the Egyptian magicians. These had likewise turned into snakes after being placed on the ground during a battle of magical supremacy.[8] It is the story told in the book of Exodus (see fig. 27.1).[9]

Hippolytus tells us also that the Peratic equates the Son with the "universal serpent . . . [who provided] the wise discourse of Eve, as well as the mystery of Edem."[10] This, of course, was a reference to the Serpent encountered by Adam and Eden in the Garden of Eden. Thus it becomes clear that the Peratae

Fig. 27.1. Aaron's rod changes into a serpent (shown on the right) that eats up the rods of Pharaoh's magicians, which have also turned into snakes. From the story told in the book of Exodus 7:8–13. (Illustration from Foster [1873] 1897.)

identified the Great Serpent with the creature that tempts Eve in the book of Genesis, convincing her and afterward Adam to eat of the forbidden fruit from the Tree of the Knowledge of Good and Evil (a matter explored in chapter 35).[11]

THE PATH OF THE PERFECT SERPENT

The Peratae additionally believed that the Son had manifested as the brazen (brass) serpent Moses erected on a pole when in the wilderness of Sinai (see fig. 27.2). This was so that anyone who looked upon this device who had been bitten by a snake would instantly recover, God having earlier sent a plague of snakes to torment the Israelites after they kept complaining about their predicament, the story told in the book of Numbers.[12]

Fig. 27.2. Memorial mural depicting the story of Moses and the Brazen Serpent (see the book of Numbers 21:4–9) located in the Anglo-Catholic All Saints Church in Margaret Street, London, built between 1850 and 1859.

Because Moses had erected the brazen serpent, the *Philosophumena* says: "Of this [act] alone, he [the Peratic] says, the image [of the Serpent] is in heaven, always conspicuous in light."[13] This becomes our first clue that the Serpent of the Peratae has a celestial form. The text continues:

> And if the eyes of any, he [the Peratic] says, are blessed, this one, looking upward on the firmament, will behold at the mighty summit of heaven the beauteous image of the serpent, turning itself, and becoming an originating principle of every (species of) motion to all things that are being produced.[14]

It thus becomes clear that the Great Serpent was seen by the Peratae as an all-powerful cosmic force without which all existence would cease, making him, as the Son, what the Platonic and Neoplatonic schools, as well the Christian Gnostics, called the Demiurge, the creator and animator of all things in the physical universe.

Next we find out from the *Philosophumena* where this serpent is placed in the sky:

> *Draco revolves, marvel mighty of monster dread. And on both sides of him have been placed Corona* [*Borealis*; in English, the "Northern Crown"] *and Lyra* [the constellation of the celestial lyre]; *and above, near the top itself of the head, is visible the piteous man "Engonasis"* [the constellation known to the Greeks as Herakles and to the Romans as Hercules].[15] (Original emphasis.)

Here we learn that the Serpent of the Peratae is personified in the heavens as the constellation of Draco, the great snake of ancient Greek astronomy that guards the ecliptic pole and during the fourth millennium BCE provided the heavens with a Pole Star in the form of Thuban (α Draconis). It was a role Thuban retained until around 2800 BCE, by which time it had drifted too far from the celestial pole to be classed as Pole Star. Immediately after this we read that, "And at the back of Engonasis is an imperfect serpent [a reference to the stars of Serpens], with both hands tightly secured by Anguitenens [the constellation of Ophiuchus], and being hindered from touching Corona that lies beside the perfect serpent."[16]

We are being told here about a star myth involving six constellations— Draco, Lyra, Hercules, Corona Borealis, Serpens, and, finally, Ophiuchus—all of which are not only in the same area of sky, but are stretched out between the northern celestial pole and the Galactic Bulge marking the center of the Milky Way galaxy. This, as we shall see, is an important observation.

THE SON OF THE SERPENT

The text of the *Philosophumena* tells us that the Peratae considered the constellation of Draco to be the "perfect serpent," while the asterism made up of the stars forming the upper body and head of Serpens, the snake held back by Ophiuchus, was the "imperfect serpent."[17] It bore this title because it reached out toward Corona Borealis as if about to strike it. Thus, in wrestling with the stars of Serpens, referred to in the text as "the Beast," Ophiuchus preserves the sanctity and perfection of the Northern Crown,[18] which would appear to have held a special place among the Ophite Gnostics. The implications of this star myth indicate that the Gnostics saw Corona Borealis as a symbol of *Gnosis*—in other words, the achievement of great insight or transformation through participation in their mystical rite.

Because of the crucial role Ophiuchus plays in protecting the Northern Crown from Serpens as the "imperfect serpent," he would appear to have been celebrated by some Gnostics—although not, it would seem, by the Peratae—as a personification of the Logos (Greek: Λόγος), which means "word, discourse, or reason."[19]

In Gnostic terms Ophiuchus thus became, quite literally, an astral manifestation of the Son of God, the intermediary between the Father and Matter, the same role the Peratae identified with the stars of Draco, the celestial serpent or dragon. As we saw in chapter 16, among the Taş Tepeler peoples of Karahan Tepe Ophiuchus, the serpent bearer or snake charmer, as well as the thirteenth sign of the zodiac, would appear to have become the celestial form of the shamans and initiates who were not only able to communicate directly with the cosmic serpent, but also handle and charm snakes, like the Psylli of Libya, the Marsi of Italy and, of course, the Yezidi of Anatolia and the Near East.

THE BRIDGE OF STARS EXPLAINED

It was perhaps inevitable that by the early Christian era the celestial location of the cosmic serpent had migrated from the area of the Milky Way to the constellation of Draco. This was no doubt due to the crucial role Draco had played as the perceived controller of cosmic time when Thuban (α Draconis) was Pole Star, an importance placed upon it as late as 3000 BCE, several thousand years after the age of Taş Tepeler.

Among the Ophite Gnostics, the only apparent memory of the Great Serpent's former associations with the Galactic Bulge appears to have been the role played by Ophiuchus in holding back Serpens, the Beast or "imperfect serpent," from striking Corona Borealis, the sparkling circlet of stars symbolizing the achievement of Gnosis or ultimate perfection.[20]

The fact that all six constellations important to the Gnostics were stretched out between the center of the Milky Way galaxy and the northern celestial pole is, in my mind, not without meaning. It preserves by way of a star myth the shift in the Great Serpent's identity from the area of the Galactic Bulge—marked by the constellations of Sagittarius, Ophiuchus, Scorpius, and, of course, Serpens—to its new role as guardian of the celestial pole in the form of the stars of Draco.

Such a realization makes us recall the Ouroboros, the serpent that bites its own tail from Greco-Egyptian art and literature. Not only was this a symbol of the world-encircling serpent and eclipse dragon—its head or heads in the vicinity of Scorpius and Libra and its body marked by the ecliptic path—but it had now come to be identified with the constellation of Draco. Its winding band of stars were seen to encircle—turn even—the cosmic axis around which the celestial bodies revolved each night.

ACHIEVING TRUE GNOSIS

The *Philosophumena* next tells its reader exactly what the Peratae believed about the cosmic nature of the "perfect serpent," for, according to Hippolytus:

> Intermediate, then, between the Matter and the Father sits the Son, the Word [Logos], the Serpent, always being in motion towards the unmoved Father, and (towards) Matter itself in motion. And at one time he [the Serpent] is turned towards the Father, and receives the powers into his own person; but at another time [he] takes up these powers, and is turned towards Matter. And Matter, (though) devoid of attribute, and being unfashioned, moulds (into itself) forms from the Son which the Son moulded from the Father.[21]

These are profound statements implying that the Serpent intercedes in the world of matter by using the "powers" gained from the Father. Sometimes the Son faces toward the Father to take in this cosmic energy, while at other times he turns around to face Matter in order to effect creation in the material universe. Almost certainly we have here a rather vague understanding of the manner in which the eclipse dragon periodically switches its head and tail between the signs of Scorpius/Sagittarius and Gemini, where the lunar nodes were deemed to be at their most exalted, or in other words, at their most powerful.

Who Is the Father?

If the Logos or Son in the doctrine of the Peratae is the Perfect Serpent, now switched from the area of the Galactic Bulge to the constellation of Draco, and Matter is the material universe, then who or what is the Father? A clue comes from the fact that for the Peratae "the Son derives shape from the Father after a mode ineffable, and unspeakable, and unchangeable."[22] What this implies is that the Son's own "shape" as a snake or serpent is determined by the Father, who is perceived as an unknowable, sentient being existing in the primordial darkness of the supercelestial realm, and only through the intervention of the Serpent can his divine force be experienced in the physical world. Beyond this we learn that for the Peratae, "No one . . . can be saved or return (into heaven) without the Son, and the Son is the Serpent. For as he brought down from above the paternal marks" of the Father he will proclaim "'I am the door.'"[23]

The Serpent was thus seen as a "door," gateway, or portal allowing access to a supercelestial energy and intelligence that could only be made manifest through the Father, and could only be reached through interaction with the Son. It was in this manner the Peratae believed that Gnosis was attainable, for as the *Philosophumena* next informs us:

In this manner, he [the Peratic] says, is the portrayed, perfect, and consubstantial genus drawn again from the world by the Serpent; nor does he (attract) anything else, as it has been sent down by him. For a proof of this, they adduce the anatomy of the brain, assimilating, from the fact of its immobility, the brain itself to the Father, and the cerebellum to the Son, because of its being moved and being of the form of (the head of) a serpent. And they allege that this (cerebellum), by an ineffable and inscrutable process, attracts through the pineal gland the spiritual and life-giving substance emanating from the vaulted chamber (in which the brain is embedded). And on receiving this, the cerebellum in an ineffable manner imparts the ideas, just as the Son [that is, the Serpent] does, to matter; or, in other words, the seeds and the genera of the things produced according to the flesh flow along into the spinal marrow.[24]

What Hippolytus seems to be describing here is how, through ritual communion with the *head* of the Serpent, a psychic connection with the divine energy and intelligence known as the Father is achieved. This is done, we are told, through a utilization of the "pineal gland" and "spinal marrow," whereby the "paternal marks," the divine message of the Father, is downloaded into the cerebellum, which is located in the rear part of the brain where it controls emotions. (In parapsychological studies the cerebellum has been linked with dreaming and psychic phenomena.)[25]

Quite incredibly, this is what Hippolytus tells us the Peratae believed was achievable during their mystical rite, a full-on, one-to-one communion with a supercelestial source via the head of the Perfect Serpent. The greater implications of this spiritual process adopted by the Peratae are that once this communion is in progress, participants would either be unable or would not want to "(attract) anything else." For them, this connection with the divine exemplified the ultimate mystical experience, the ultimate attainment of Gnosis, brought about through the acceptance into their bodies of the "powers" conveyed to them by the spirit of the Great Serpent in its role as the Son or Logos.

No wonder, then, that the Gnostics were condemned as heretics by the Church of Rome, which deemed that the only way humanity could communicate with God was through the intervention of an officially sanctioned bishop of the apostolic line of succession, which originates with the apostles of Jesus Christ. There was no way that any *direct* communion with God could be allowed, explaining the Church's relentless crusade to expose and eradicate Gnostic Christians wherever they might be found. Their profound beliefs and practices could not be allowed to prosper. But what was it they were doing, and how did they achieve communion with what they saw as a supercelestial intelligence that could manifest within the material universe in the form of a great snake? How might these processes be linked with the Karahan community's attempts to communicate with the more primeval form of this cosmic serpent, which they would seem to have identified with the Milky Way, its head coincident with the Galactic Bulge? As we see next, answers to these questions can be found not in Anatolia and the Near East, or indeed anywhere in southwestern Asia, but far away in the yogic and tantric practices of the East.

28

Raising of the Kundalini

In the modern age anyone with even a basic knowledge of mysticism can see that certain elements of the Ophite Gnostic doctrine are strikingly similar to yogic and tantric practices of the Indian subcontinent. This was noted, for instance, at the beginning of the twentieth century by English historian, writer, and translator G. R. S. Mead (1863–1933), an expert in the Gnostic religion. In his pioneering work *Fragments of a Faith Forgotten*, published in 1900, he noted that the serpent, so important to the Ophites, is "the Kuṇḍalinī, or serpentine force in man, which when following animal impulse is the force of generation, but when applied to spiritual things makes of a man a god."[1]

In this statement Mead was referring to the creative force known in Vedic tradition as kundalini, imagined as a coiled snake located inside the human body. Through a combination of ritual and meditational techniques the spirit of the kundalini is expected to uncoil itself and rise up the spinal cord from a position at the base of the spine known as the Muladhara or Root chakra. As this happens the kundalini, experienced as an immensely powerful energy, then rises up, activating other chakra centers until finally it reaches an area of the brain known as the pineal gland. Here is the sixth chakra, named Ajna, which many mystics believe awakens the "third eye" situated on the forehead.

Through this activation we are mentally able to connect with a perceived inner reality. Thereafter the yogic or tantric practitioner can expect the manifestation of a 1,000-petaled lotus, violet in color, which sits above the cranium. This forms the seventh and final chakra or energy center known as the Sahasrara or Crown chakra. Its opening is thought to coincide with the attainment of a state of bliss whereby the mind enters a kind of quantum realm in which communication with a supercelestial source of reality is achievable.

The kundalini spirit itself is thought of as a female deity or *devi*, this being a feminization of the Sanskrit word *deva*, meaning a male deity.[2] The actual name of the kundalini devi is Shakti, seen as a dynamic power associated with divine creation. In this way, Shakti can be seen as a female embodiment of the creative energy associated with fertility. In Sanskrit the term "Kundalini Shakti" actually translates as "serpent power,"[3] although it has been described also as the "serpent fire,"[4] a reference to how, when the kundalini ascends the spine, it can feel like an "intense heat."[5]

Many of these ideas regarding the chakra system admittedly go back no more than a century or so, and derive from Western interpretations of Eastern meditational practices.[6] That said, the yogic and tantric traditions expounded both within Hinduism and within certain forms of Buddhism do have very ancient roots. If this can be accepted, then it becomes possible that some Ophite Gnostic sects were utilizing mystical disciplines that, as Mead suspected, bore a striking resemblance to those found in places like India, Nepal, and Tibet.

From what Hippolytus tells us, meditational practices involving a kundalini-like spirit featured as part of the mystical rites of the Peratae, with the force of the Son or Great Serpent rising up the spinal cord to the pineal gland to enable the attainment of Gnosis, divine illumination and enlightenment. How these rites might have played out we can only guess at today, although the author of the *Philosophumena* did seem aware of certain rumors or indeed confessions from converts to the Church of Rome when he wrote:

> Employing this exemplar, (the heretics) seem to adroitly introduce their secret mysteries, which are delivered in silence. Now it would be impious for us to declare these; yet it is easy to form an idea of them, by reason of the many statements that have been made.[7]

Hippolytus is no doubt referring to the generalized view adopted during his day that Ophite Gnostic rites involved nudity and arguably even sexual activity, a conclusion that can be deduced from the carved imagery on the alabaster bowl. Although this is almost certainly correct, sexuality would probably have formed only a small part of the overall beliefs and practices of the Ophite Gnostics; the rest would have involved deep meditational practices involving communion with a cosmic power in the form of a serpent. To achieve this state of Gnosis there are clear indications from the Peratae doctrine that a perceived serpentine energy had to be allowed to overtake the body. This is suggested also in a Greco-Roman magical prayer in which "the Aeon of Aeons"—in other words, Phanes or Aeon, the god of infinite time—is invoked:

> Hail, temple of the air spirit! Hail, spirit who reachest from heaven to earth and from the earth, which lies in the center of the cosmos, to the borders of the abyss! Hail, spirit who enterest into me and takest hold of me, and departest from me in lovingkindness as God wills![8]

In addition to this, as Leisegang observed in his own study of the alabaster bowl, "We would seem to be dealing with a mystery [where] the mystai drew a snake between their thighs in order to consummate a mystical union with the god."[9] He is alluding here to the use of actual snakes, which unquestionably featured in such rites. One example of this is recorded in the *Panarion*, a work by Epiphanius of Salamis (died 403 CE), a heresiologist and bishop from Salamis in Cyprus, who staunchly upheld Christian orthodoxy and actively denounced Gnostic heresies. In his words:

> They have a snake, which they keep in a certain chest—the cista mystica— and which at the hour of their mysteries they bring forth from its cave. They heap loaves upon the table and summon the serpent. Since the cave is open it comes out. It is a cunning beast and, knowing their foolish ways, it crawls up on the table and rolls in the loaves; this they say is the perfect sacrifice. Wherefore, as I have been told, they not only break the bread in which the snake has rolled and administer it to those present, but each one kisses the snake on the mouth, for the snake has been tamed by a spell, or has been made gentle for their fraud by some other diabolical method. And they fall down before it and call this the Eucharist, consummated by the beast rolling in the loaves. And through it, as they say, they send forth a hymn to the Father on high, thus concluding their mysteries.[10]

Such rites were clearly undertaken in closely guarded shrines or, as is the case here, at remote cave sites far away from prying eyes. This said, the mystical rite used by the Peratae clearly involved an internal process whereby the force or energy represented by the snake was allowed to enter inside the body and rise up through the "spinal marrow" to the pineal gland, similar to the manner that the kundalini spirit ascends the spinal cord in yogic and tantric practices. If correct, then might there be some link between the carved imagery on the alabaster bowl and Eastern disciplines of the type imagined here?

THE CROWN OF 32 PETALS

As we have seen, the alabaster bowl shows 16 naked figures radially positioned around a winged dragon coiled up on an umbo or omphalos signifying the egg of creation. Below this umbo is a "double wreath of rays,"[11] which radiate out to go beneath the naked figures. This is very likely a representation of the Hypercosmic Sun along with the way that its tongues of fire penetrate the primordial darkness and bring into being its manifested form as the Perfect Serpent, which is what is experienced by the mystai in the supercelestial realm at the height of their mystical rite.

Almost certainly something similar was going on at Karahan Tepe with the snake genius being allowed to enter the bodies of celebrants, who would have been not only shamans and initiates, but also snake charmers and snake handlers like the Psylli of Libya, the Marsi of Italy, and the Yezidi of Anatolia and the Near East. In other words, they would have been earthly representatives of the Ophiuchus sky figure who is shown controlling Serpens, the active spirit of the Milky Way serpent, which was demonized by the Ophite Gnostics and switched in favor of the stars making up the constellation of Draco, the celestial dragon.

Leisegang drew attention to the number of mystai shown on the alabaster bowl, which is 16, pointing out that a 16-rayed sun symbol features in Greek and medieval art. In his opinion, the number chosen probably had a symbolic meaning.[12] The number 16 also crops up in Greco-Roman magical papyri with, in one instance, the Orphic god Phanes-Helios-Aeon being invoked as "the mighty one of heaven, the airy one, who derives his power from himself, to whom all nature is subordinated, who inhabits the whole inhabited earth, [whose] spear-bearers are the sixteen giants."[13]

As a number representing wholeness and completion, 16 and, of course, 32, the number of rays or tongues of fire radiating from the double wreath beneath the alabaster bowl's umbo, are the product of perfect numerical symmetry, since $1 + 1 = 2, 2 + 2 = 4, 4 + 4 = 8, 8 + 8 = 16$, bringing us to 32, which, of course, is $16 + 16$. So does the artistic representation of suns with either 16 or 32 rays simply reflect an artist's wish to create perfect symmetry, or did the carvers of the alabaster bowl see a special importance in the numbers 16 and 32?

Although the Sahasrara or Crown chakra is usually visualized as a lotus flower of 1,000 petals—indeed, Sahasrara means "thousand petaled"—some forms of the Crown chakra only have 32 petals. This is the case, for instance, in the Anuttarayoga Tantra tradition of Buddhist Vajrayana. Here, the Crown chakra is shown as a triangular device with 32 petals or channels radiating from it. In Tibetan Buddhism, this same *khor-lo* or chakra also has 32 petals and is described as "the plane of intellectual experience and of discriminating thought and is characterized as the focus of the great bliss of the *svabhavikakaya* [Tibetan: *bDe-chen-gyi 'khor-lo*]," the achievement of an enlightened form.[14]

Thus, to find that on the alabaster bowl the "double wreath of rays" emerging from the umbo and winged dragon consists of 32 petals is indicative of a strong interest in this particular number. The fact that Leisegang interpreted the double-rayed wreath as representing the "flaming light of the [supercelestial] sun"[15] seems to affirm that the number 32, as well as the number 16, reflects the importance of a hidden cosmological value, a matter we explore in chapter 33. (It should be pointed out that the Vishuddhi or Throat chakra has 16 petals. These apparently symbolize the 16 vowels of the Sanskrit language, along with the 16 *kalas* or stages of life development, known also as the 16 *siddhis* or gifts of Krishna.)

THE SECRET OF THE SEVEN POWERS

How then did the hemispherical circlet of stars known as Corona Borealis, the Northern Crown, come to symbolize the goal of the Gnostic—the achievement of Gnosis, that is, complete illumination and enlightenment through communication with the mind or intelligence (Nous) of the Great Serpent? The answer lies in the fact that there are seven stars making up its tiara-like crescent, with the brightest being Alphecca (α Coronae Borealis). Seven is, of course, a universally important number in mystical traditions. It also just happens to be the number of chakras or energy centers recognized as existing in the human body, the seventh and final one being the Sahasrara or Crown chakra. Although Anatolia and the Near East might seem a long way from the Indian subcontinent, there is evidence that some of the region's most ancient mystical doctrines recognized the same number of "powers" present within the human body.

This is seen, for instance, in a Sethian (and thus Ophite) Gnostic text of the second century CE titled *The Apocryphon of John* or *The Secret Book of John*. In this it is written that Yaldabaoth, the Demiurge or creator of the world in the form of a lion-headed serpent, on creating the First Man, Adam, endowed him with the seven powers of the seven rulers or archons. This is how the text puts it:

> Yaldabaoth said to the [seven] rulers or archons [Greek: ἄρχων], "Come, let us make a man after this heavenly image, but also in our own image, so that this man may bring us light." [So they] created with their own powers, in accordance with their own characters. Each of the [seven] powers contributed something to the man that corresponded to a part of the image they had seen, the image of the perfect first human. And they said, "Let us name him Adam, so that his name will be a shining power for us."[16]

The seven Gnostic rulers are, of course, synonymous with the Seven Stars, or seven planets, of the Chaldean astrologers, which, through their influence on the 12 signs of the zodiac, were seen to rule over human destiny.[17] In this manner Adam, the First Man, was considered a physical embodiment of all seven of these planetary influences, with each one thought to occupy some part of the body.

In a Gnostic text titled the *Poimandres*, which forms part of the *Corpus Hermeticum*,[18] or books of Hermes, we find further allusions to the endowment of Adam with the seven powers. Here the Demiurge, we are told, is opposed to the First Man, who in his Greek form is referred to as Anthropos. The Demiurge then creates the seven spirits of the planets, in response to which the Nous (here spelled Νοῦς)—in other words, God in heaven—is said to have given birth to his favorite son, the First Man, who was created in his own image. "According to one tradition," wrote Alexander Altman, an Orthodox Jewish scholar and rabbi in 1945, "the Νοῦς gives him [the First Man] the dominion over everything which has been created. The seven planetary powers take to him and endow him each with part of their own nature. Thus the *Demiurge* becomes his enemy, full of envy and hatred. He assumes more and more the role of a demonic power against God and the First Man."[19] (Original emphasis.)

Despite the variations on who actually bestowed this "anthropogonic sevenfold pattern" on Adam,[20] it is clear that as the First Man, the seven powers were necessary not only for his creation, but also for his continued connection with the seven archons or rulers that determine the destiny of human beings.

Although these seven powers are not linked specifically with energy centers of the body, and are instead associated more simply with body parts, it is easy to equate these ideas with the sevenfold chakra system of Vedic tradition and the achievement of Gnosis through an understanding of the sevenfold importance of Corona Borealis, the Northern Crown.*

A COMMON ORIGIN

Is it possible that all these sources gained their philosophies on the sevenfold nature of enlightenment from a common ancestral origin? Attempts have been made to link the carved art, architectural style, and religious symbolism found at sites like Nevalı Çori and Göbekli Tepe with Vedic traditions going back at least 4,000 years.[21] This is a valid subject of discussion, even though at this time it simply cannot be proven that southeastern Anatolia's Taş Tepeler culture had any direct contact with the Indian subcontinent.

Having stated this fact, it *is* conceivable that long-distance trading existed at this time between Anatolia and other parts of the ancient world. This surmise is strengthened in the knowledge that what we know today as the Silk Road, which stretches between China in the east and Europe in the west, passes through various old cities in Iran, Iraq, and Turkey. Branches of this ancient trade route even connect it with the Indian subcontinent.

Although we have no idea how long the Silk Road has been in use, the likelihood is that it has provided a means of communication between Anatolia and both Central Asia and the Indian subcontinent since the age of Taş Tepeler. If so, then trade in material goods, most obviously exotic stone materials, would have been accompanied by exchanges in religious and cultural ideas, despite the vast distances involved. Is it possible that all these mystical concepts involving a serpent power traveling through power centers of the body to create mystical illumination originated at places like Karahan Tepe during the Pre-Pottery

---

*The system of the *lataif,* the subtle energy centers of the human body found in Islamic Sufi tradition, might also be of interest here. Although there are variations in the number of lataif, with five or six being the usual number, in some Sufi systems there are seven. Indeed, their possible connection with the sevenfold chakra system of yogic and tantric tradition has been noted (see, for instance, New Age Islam 2021).

Neolithic Age? As we see in coming chapters, the sevenfold pattern once thought to exist within humankind and considered to be linked with seven celestial forces is something that appears to reflect a recurring pattern in nature that science is only now beginning to recognize for the first time.

PERATAE ORIGINS REVEALED

Some support for the involvement of the Chaldeans, the ancient inhabitants of Harran and Şanlıurfa, in this process comes from their concept of the Primal Cause of the cosmos being identified as Shamal, god of the north. As we saw in chapter 26, one class of the Nusayris—the strict Shia Muslim population that occupies large parts of Syria—known as the Shemsi, alleged worshippers of the sun, were thought by French Orientalist and archaeologist René Dussaud to have derived their name from the Harranian god Shamal.[22] Indeed, for them it would appear to have represented "the sun in its nocturnal course,"[23] an apparent allusion to the Hypercosmic Sun in its role as the dynamic force behind the manifestation and motion of the seven planets and 12 signs of the zodiac. If so, then their ideas regarding the existence of this supercelestial entity would appear to have originated among the Chaldean inhabitants of places like Harran.

The Peratae also would appear to have received their mystical doctrine either directly or indirectly from the Harranians, for according to Hippolytus, "The heresy of the Peratae, it has been made easily apparent to all, has been adapted from the (art) of the [Chaldean] astrologers with a change of names alone."[24] If this is the case, can we determine whether or not the Chaldean astrologers at places like Harran, Sogmatar, and Şanlıurfa really did gain their cosmological knowledge from lineal descendants of Taş Tepeler sites such as Karahan Tepe? It is this question we look at next.

29

Cities of the Serpent

The most obvious pagan mystery cult that might have preserved and passed on arcane knowledge at places like Şanlıurfa, ancient Edessa, during Roman times was that of Orpheus, the divine poet, musician, and prophet of Thracian descent.[1] In 1956, for instance, Syriac and Aramaic language scholar J. B. Segal (1912–2003) uncovered an impressive mosaic floor showing Orpheus seated amid various animals and birds that are being charmed by the music of his lyre. It was discovered inside a rock-hewn cave in the city's Eyup Mahallesi district (see fig. 29.1, p. 234).[2]

The mosaic has been dated to circa 228 CE, which coincides with the Roman takeover of the region in 214–217 CE, Edessa having formerly been part of the kingdom of Osroene ruled by the Abgarid dynasty of kings. It was around the time of the Roman conquest of the region that the Orphic mystery schools had started to assume an important role in the still pagan Roman Empire, explaining their appearance in a city already steeped in Christian tradition.[3] (A second example found in the city in 1980 is on display in its mosaic museum.)

As we have seen, one of the principal places that the Orphic hymns resurfaced during the second century CE is in Asia Minor, or Anatolia.[4] This almost certainly included the Roman province of northern Mesopotamia, the central hub of which was Edessa.

NABU THE ANNOUNCER

The Orphic mystery schools would have been important for the dissemination of underground beliefs and practices, which in Edessa would have been both Greek and Syrian-Aramaic in origin. It would be these disciplines that would

Fig. 29.1. Damaged Orpheus mosaic found in the city of Şanlıurfa by J. B. Segal in 1956 (from Bacon 1963, 209).

go on to inspire the doctrine of the Ophite Gnostics. It is a fact, however, that Edessa's Orphic mystery schools were heavily influenced by a preexisting oracular cult that had thrived in the city for many hundreds of years. This centered around the god Nabu, "the announcer,"[5] a Mesopotamian god who was seen as the inventor of writing and the transmitter of decrees from the gods. He also held the Tablets of Destiny that determined the length of a human life. Crucially, he was the "giver of oracles" revealing "the cosmic order of existence" as well as "a link between the divine and human worlds."[6]

From the late Assyrio-Babylonian period until Roman times, Nabu and his father Marduk were greatly celebrated and worshipped in Edessa. As, respectively, creator of the universe and keeper of the divine wisdom, Marduk and Nabu became the city's two most important deities.[7] (The chief female deity venerated at Edessa was the Syrian goddess Atargatis, known also as 'Athar'atha, Tar'atha, and Semiramis.)[8]

Nabu, who apparently held "primacy of place at Edessa,"[9] was also a major god at Harran.[10] There he was equated with the planetary influence of Mercury and through this the Roman god of the same name.[11] His Greek equivalent was Hermes, who would himself come to be identified with Nabu.[12] Hermes, or Hermes Trismegistus, the "thrice-great Hermes" as he became known, was celebrated as the author of the *Corpus Hermeticum*, the books of hermetic philosophy, which emerged out of Egypt between the first century BCE and the fourth century CE.[13]

The Arab chronicler Mas'ūdī (died circa 956 CE), known as the "Herodotus of the Arabs," wrote in his work *The Meadows of Gold and Mines of Gems* that the two great prophets of the Harranians were both called Orpheus.[14] Tamara Green, in her important study of Harranian religion titled *The City of the Moon God* (1992), believes that Mas'ūdī had in fact been referring to Hermes and Agathodaimon, the latter being one of the names used for the Demiurge in the form of a serpent.[15]

The thirteenth-century Arab geographer Al-Dimashqi (1256–1327) wrote that there were two types of Sabians (that is, Chaldeans), those who venerated the "celestial mansions"—in other words, the influence of the Seven Stars or seven planets and the 12 signs of the zodiac—and those who worshipped idols. The former group were said to have gained their knowledge from Agathodaimon, called also Seth, the son of Adam.[16]

So much did the Harranians venerate Seth or Agathodaimon as the founder of their doctrine that each year members of their community would go on pilgrimages to the Pyramids in Egypt to pay their respects to both his tomb and that of Hermes, which they obviously believed was located there.[17]

The fact that Agathodaimon was universally seen as a serpent tells us there must have been a belief among the Harranians that their knowledge of the seven planets and the 12 signs of the zodiac had come originally from a supernatural being in the form of a serpent. Why they might have come to believe that this snake deity was buried beneath the Pyramids of Giza is unclear. That said, a prevailing belief among the elder members of the local Arab Egyptian community living next to the Pyramids is that beneath the plateau at Giza, hidden within a secret chamber, is a great serpent named el-Hanash (Arabic for "the Snake"). He guards a great treasure (a "huge diamond" is mentioned) and will blind anyone who attempts to approach it. This is until the final days when there will come a person who, being pure of heart, will be blinded only in one eye. They will be the one to discover the great treasure el-Hanash protects.

I was told this story by someone from Nazlet el-Samman, the town situated by the Great Sphinx, when researching the book *Beneath the Pyramids*, published in 2009. This details the rediscovery in 2008 of a previously unrecorded cave complex beneath the northern part of the plateau, which one local tomb guardian, in all seriousness, firmly believed was haunted by el-Hanash, so much so that he flatly refused to enter it.[18] There seems little question that el-Hanash is a memory of the belief locally that the tomb of Seth-Agathodaimon lies beneath the plateau.

In Tamara Green's opinion the Harranians' insistence that their doctrine came originally from Seth-Agathodaimon speaks of the existence at Harran (and, we must presume, at Edessa) of a secret Orphic mystery cult where these ideas flourished.[19] If correct, this would support Mas'ūdī's claim that the Sabians or Chaldeans gained their teachings from two prophets both named Orpheus. Thus, we have confirmation that the pagans of Harran, Edessa, and, presumably, nearby Sogmatar, the supposed site of the seven planetary temples, gained their knowledge of the influence of the planets and the "celestial mansions," as Al-Dimashqi put it, from a cosmic deity in the guise of a serpent.

THE CULTS OF NABU AND MARDUK

As we have seen, a cult in the name of Orpheus existed at Edessa by the third century CE. Before, however, he became patron of the region's age-old wisdom teachings, they would appear to have formed part of the cult of his predecessor, Nabu, "the announcer." Evidence of this comes from a Syriac Christian text known as the *Oration*, incorrectly ascribed to Melito, a second-century CE bishop of Sardis near Smyrna in western Anatolia. The book lists the pagan gods worshipped at places like Edessa and Harran and also Mabbog, the Syriac name for Hierapolis, the famous city of antiquity located some 50 miles (80 kilometers) northeast of Aleppo in northern Syria. In connection with Mabbog, the author states, "Concerning Nabu that is in Mabbog what shall I write? That it is the image of Orpheus the Thracian magus all the priests in Mabbog know."[20]

These lines have perplexed commentators since Nabu and Orpheus are very clearly two different deities, the former of Mesopotamian origin and the other of Greek pedigree, although what the *Oration* makes clear is that those priests and worshippers who belonged to the cult of Nabu identified the deity with

"Orpheus the Thracian," suggesting that he was in the process of becoming their new patron. If this is correct, then in so doing the communities that now entered the Orphic mystery schools would have been able to preserve at least some of the arcane knowledge and wisdom that had previously formed part of the cult of Nabu. This is important to remember as we now look more closely at Nabu and why his religion might well have contained archaic beliefs and practices that almost certainly originated among the region's Taş Tepeler communities.

In Mesopotamian art, Nabu is generally shown alongside a large, wedge-shaped writing stylus, which was his principal symbol as patron of scribes and god of writing. He is also depicted standing on a dragon-like creature with horns named Mušḫuššu, this being an Akkadian word taken from the Sumerian MUŠ. ḪUŠ, meaning "the snake (MUŠ) that is red (or reddish) in color (ḪUŠ)." (See fig. 29.2.) Occasionally, texts allude to this red-colored serpent as being associated with the evil eye, with one reading, "The eye (is in the shape of) a red snake [MUŠ. ḪUŠ], the eye of the man (is) a red snake, the eye of the evil man is a red snake."[21]

Fig. 29.2. Late Assyrian seal from the eighth century BCE showing a worshipper between Nabu (left) and his father Marduk (right). Both gods stand on the Mušḫuššu serpent-dragon showing their authority over its influence and power (from Martin 1940, 39). The concept can be equated with the Christian symbolism surrounding the relationship between Saint George and the dragon or Saint Michael and the devil.

Snakes and Scorpions

Modern-day scholars writing on the subject of Babylonian astronomy identify Mušḫuššu with the Greek constellation of Hydra, the seven-headed serpent of the southern skies.[22] Whether or not this is correct remains unclear. More important is the fact that in some Babylonian astronomical texts Nabu is identified with the bright star Antares (α Scorpii), which was seen as the "heart" of ᵐᵘˡGIR.TAB, the Scorpion, our Scorpius constellation.[23] Thus Nabu, in this role, can quite literally be seen as an anthropomorphic personification of the influence either of this star alone or, more likely, of the stars of Scorpius as a whole.

The symbolism behind Nabu's association with the Scorpius constellation appears to have been preserved in an ancient text from the city of Babylon in southern Iraq recording a ritual to be performed in the lead-up to the Babylonian new year festival. Marduk is to be invoked at this festival, after which offerings should be made to his son Nabu. Two idols are to be fashioned by artisans and covered with "a shekel's weight of gold" and adorned with precious stones.[24] One idol, we are told, "holds in his left hand a serpent made of cedar-wood, and raises his right hand to Nebo," this being the Hebrew form of the name of the god, while the other "holds in his left hand a scorpion, and raises his right hand to Nebo."[25] Each should be "clothed with red garments," and their "loins . . . girded with a palm-branch." There are more instructions as to what is to be done, but then, on the sixth day, "when Nebo arrives at Ehursagtila [this being the temple of the god Ninurta], the executioner shall cut off their [that is, the idols'] heads; then a fire shall be kindled before Nebo, and they [the idols] shall be thrown into the fire."[26]

Both the snake and the scorpion are the two basic totems associated with Scorpius, and here they are together as the primary totems of Nabu, offering confirmation of his identification as a personification of the constellation of Scorpius. One is reminded of the carved relief of Nergal, the Babylonian god of the underworld, found at Hatra, Iraq, which shows the god in the company of snakes and scorpions, along with a three-headed Cerberus-like dog (see fig. 24.4, p. 193). Since Nergal ruled Scorpius, it seems clear that the snakes and scorpions are zoomorphic personifications of this constellation; the dog no doubt being the guardian of the Scorpionic gateway that, when open, permitted souls of the dead to access the Milky Way (see chapter 15).

Since Nabu was seen as a personification of Antares, and perhaps even of the Scorpius constellation as a whole, he must surely have played the same role as that attributed to Ophiuchus—the serpent holder or snake charmer of Greek and Arabic star lore—which lies directly next to Scorpius. As previously noted, the sun moves from Scorpius into Ophiuchus before entering Sagittarius on December 18 in the modern calendar. Arguably, in the past, both Ophiuchus *and* Scorpius were seen not only as representations of the active spirit of the Milky Way serpent, but also as expressions of the snake shamans who were able to wield, control, and channel this serpentine force.

PROPHETS AND PROPHETESSES

That Nabu is shown standing on the Mušḫuššu snake tells us he was seen to have full control over the creature's serpentine power, arguably for the purposes of oracular communication. If so, then such pronouncements would have been written down once voiced, which is no doubt why Nabu's symbol was the writing stylus and why he became the patron of scribes and the god of writing. So did the cult of Nabu preserve within it, no matter how abstract, the collective memory of the snake shamans suspected to have operated at Taş Tepeler sites like Karahan Tepe?

Some confirmation of this comes from the knowledge that in the West Semitic cities of Mari in eastern Syria and Emar in northern Syria during the Late Bronze Age (circa 1550–1200 BCE), Nābû (from Hebrew *nabi'*) was the name given to a specific group of divine prophets. The verb *nābû* is, in fact, Akkadian and has been generally thought by scholars to mean "to name, call, lament."[27] However, American Assyriologist and biblical scholar Daniel Fleming, a professor of Hebrew Bible and Ancient Near Eastern studies in the Skirball Department of Hebrew and Judaic Studies at New York University, has made a careful study of this topic and is convinced from his own research into the Nābû priests of Mari and Emar that the verb actually means "to call on, to invoke."[28] It cannot, in this context at least, mean simply "to lament," as the role of the Nābû at these cult centers was associated directly with divinatory and oracular practices.[29]

Fleming believes that the Nābû, and their female counterparts the Munabbiātu,[30] a name that includes the root nābû and can be interpreted as meaning "prophetesses,"[31] should be seen as male and female "invokers" or "invocation-specialists."[32] In his words, "Omens are taken and a spoken inquiry is made, and perhaps the divine response is given by oracle . . . or by some combination of methods."[33] In conclusion, Fleming sees the Nābû and Munabbiātu as "divinely 'called' prophets,"[34] interveners between the gods and humanity.

Crucially, the Nābû and Munabbiātu of Mari and Emar would appear to have come under the patronage of the goddess Išhara and may well have been linked to her temples.[35] As Fleming points out in connection with the function of these male and female prophets under the command of this female deity:

> Mesopotamian Išhara is known as a goddess of divination via her title *bêlet biri*, "mistress of divination," though this special role is not apparent at Emar. Altogether, the new terms *nābû* and *munabbiātu* give further definition to the picture of prophecy in ancient Syria, and offer the first direct evidence for religious personnel etymologically related to the biblical Hebrew *nabi'*.[36]

The Aromatic of Išhara

One interesting fact that might be of relevance to the function of the Nābû and Munabbiātu prophets and prophetesses is that the use of cannabis, a psychoactive plant, appears to have been associated directly with the cult of Išhara. Babylonian texts speak of *šim.ᵈIšhara*, the "aromatic of the goddess Išhara," which equates with the Akkadian *qunnabu*, meaning "cannabis."[37] American Assyriologist Erica Reiner points out that this term "may indeed conjure up an aphrodisiac through the association with Išhara, goddess of love."[38] This might be so, although one wonders whether the "aromatic of the goddess Išhara" was, in fact, employed by the Nābû and Munabbiātu to aid them in oracular communications and divination.

Perhaps burned as part of an incense mixed with other aromatic substances, cannabis would have been a perfect drug in this role—and to know that it was associated with the cult of Išhara is, I suspect, very important indeed.*

Išhara, as we have seen, was an anthropomorphic personification of ᵐᵘˡGIR.TAB, the celestial scorpion of Sumerian and, later, Babylonian sky lore, cognate with our own constellation of Scorpius. Thus it seems clear that the Nābû and Munabbiātu acted as oracular channels for the stellar influence of Scorpius, seen in terms of a cosmic snake and, presumably, at times as a celestial

---

*I also could not help but notice the word element *nabu* in the Akkadian *qunnabu*, meaning "cannabis," although whether this is cognate with the Akkadian *nābû*, interpreted as meaning "to name, call, lament," is unclear.

scorpion. The fact that the god Nabu was also a personification of the star Antares in Scorpius associates him directly with this tradition. It also tells us that Nabu himself is derived from a memory of the Taş Tepeler snake shamans who attained oracular communication with the active spirit of the Milky Way serpent synonymous with the stars of Scorpius. This association would appear to have been preserved in the god's control over the Mušḫuššu snake in the same manner that the sky figure Ophiuchus controls the celestial snake made up of the stars of Serpens.

Remember too that the "star of Išhara," mentioned in chapter 15, can itself be identified with Antares. This tells us that Išhara could well reflect a memory of the *female* shamans who operated at Taş Tepeler sites like Karahan Tepe, with their descendants going on to become the Munabbiātu prophetesses of Bronze Age Mari and Emar.

THE DEATH OF NABU AND THE RISE OF ORPHEUS

Nabu, as we have seen, would eventually emerge in southeastern Anatolia, as well as over the border in Syria, as one of the most influential gods worshipped in this region during Greek and Roman times. When the first Christians arrived in Edessa during the first century CE they publicly denounced the rites, rituals, and ceremonies being carried out there in the names of Nabu and Marduk. In his *Doctrina Addai* (the earliest extant version of which is from the end of the fourth century CE) the apostle Addai (or Thaddeus)—who was asked by King Abgar of Edessa to preach the word of God in Edessa—offers a useful picture of the pagan beliefs and practices taking place there at this time:

> For I saw in this city that it abounded greatly in paganism, which is against God. Who is this Nebo, an idol made which ye worship, and Bel [that is, Marduk], which ye honour?[39]

Later, after Addai has performed a series of healings in the city, he describes the scene once news of these miracles had begun to circulate among the local population:

> Shavida and Abednebo, chiefs of the priests of this city, with Piroz and Danqu, their companions, when they saw the signs which he [God] did, ran

and threw down the altars upon which they sacrificed before Nebo and Bel, their gods.[40]

THE SECRET SERPENT WORSHIPPERS OF EDESSA

It was at this time that Edessa's cult of the serpent, arguably under the patronage of Nabu, went underground, quite literally, only to reemerge with the introduction of the cult of Orpheus following the Romans' takeover of the region in the third century CE. Orpheus, of course, was seen as a musician, poet, and prophet. He was also a son of Apollo, the god of prophecy, who was himself associated with the symbol of the snake at oracular sites like Delphi in Greece. Indeed, due to Nabu's associations with oracular communication and divine prophecy, the Greeks identified him with Apollo.[41*]

AN ORACLE TO ORPHEUS

In 1956, as mentioned earlier, Syriac and Aramaic language scholar J. B. Segal uncovered a remarkable mosaic showing the god Orpheus with his lyre, this being found within a rock-hewn cave in Şanlıurfa's Eyup Mahallesi district. This cave shrine clearly functioned as a place where the Orphic mysteries were performed. Thus there seems little doubt that even after it became a major site of Christian pilgrimage a deep connection existed between the

---

*Interestingly enough, as the cults of Marduk and Nabu gradually disappeared from Edessa, some memory of their presence appears to have contributed to the popularity in the city of a folklore character named Nimrod (Drijvers 1980, 74), who was based on the legendary founder of the Tower of Babel in the book of Genesis (see Genesis 10:8–12). Nimrod's imagined castle in Edessa is identified with the city's 2,000-year-old citadel, which is located on a hill overlooking Balıklıgöl, the sacred area containing the Pools of Abraham as well as various important mosques. As a pagan king, Nimrod came up against the prophet Abraham, a worshipper of the true God who was born in Edessa, and attempted to burn him on a huge funeral pyre. God intervened, causing water to put out the flames and the firewood to become the thousands of carp that swim to this day in the Pools of Abraham. For the oldest mention of this story, see the Samaritan work *The Asatir*, ch. V, verses. 27–28 from the second to third century CE. (See "Pitron or Commentary to *The Asatir* ch. V, verses 27–28, Gaster [1927] 2015, 225.) Nimrod's wife or his daughter was said to have been in love with Abraham, and she, too, submitted to the flames to end her life. God, however, intervened, transforming her into a white carp that is said to be seen on rare occasions even to this day in the Pools of Abraham. One of the names given to Nimrod's wife is Semiramis, the name also applied to a Syrian goddess, half-human, half-fish in form, who was venerated in the city under the names Tar'atha, 'Athar'atha, and Atargatis (see Mackenzie 1915, 418, 423, 426).

ancient city and the Orphic mysteries. Venetian travelers of the Middle Ages mentioned Edessa under the name "Orphi," apparently through contact with the Persian world.[42]

It would be easy to suggest that "Orphi" is simply a mispronunciation of Urfa, the name of the city before it was granted the title Şanlıurfa, meaning "glorious [şanlı] Urfa," given to it in honor of the way that its inhabitants had resisted French occupation in the years following the First World War. There is, however, tentative evidence that the city was in fact the site of a prominent oracle called the Orphi. According to Philostratus the Athenian, a Greek Sophist of the second century CE, this oracle was venerated by the Babylonians and also by the Persian king Cyrus (who ruled 559–530 BCE). Philostratus called it "the head of Orpheus,"[43] a term that should not be confused with a similar oracle site on the island of Lesbos in Greece where the actual head of Orpheus was reportedly venerated.

English scholar and mythographer Jacob Bryant (1715–1804), in his pioneering work *A New System, or, An Analysis of Ancient Mythology*, published in 1776, wrote that, in his opinion, this Orphi "was Ur, in Chaldea, the seat of the ancient Magi, which was stiled Urphi, and Orphi, on account of its being the seat of an oracle. That there was such a temple is plain from Stephanus Byzantinus, who tells us . . . *The Chaldeans had an oracle as famous among the people of those parts, as Delphi was among the Grecians.*"[44] (Current author's emphasis.)

THE OPHITE CULTS OF EDESSA

All this is tentative evidence that Orphic mystery schools thrived at places like Edessa, Harran, and Hierapolis in northern Syria. As we have seen, these teachings would go on to inspire the doctrine of the Ophite Gnostics, who, although nominally Christian, embraced much older Chaldean astrological teachings revolving around Seth-Agathodaimon, whose form was that of a serpent, and also the dracone caelesti, the "celestial serpent," as Belgian scholar Franz Cumont called Athalia, the eclipse dragon. Both Seth-Agathodaimon and the dracone caelesti derived their existence, I suspect, from a much earlier belief that lingered in the same region to the effect that the Milky Way could be seen as a world-encircling snake associated both with cosmic creation and with the destiny of humankind.

Segal himself wrote that there remain clues to the former presence in Edessa of what he referred to as "a serpent cult."[45] In his important work *Edessa: The Blessed City* (1970), he cites an early Syriac chronicler who wrote that the founder of Urfa was one "Orhay, son of Hewya," with *hewya* or *hawwa* being an Aramaic word meaning "serpent."[46] Segal also cites a prominent Christian theologian and writer named Ephraim of Edessa (died circa 373 CE) who referred to the presence in the city of the "sons of the serpent," who "enchant the serpent and charm the scorpion."[47] The mention here of the serpent and scorpion immediately brings to mind the cult of Nabu along with the god's identification with the star Antares in the constellation of Scorpius.

Bar Hebraeus (1226–1286), a noted traveler and Maphrian (regional primate) of the Syriac Orthodox Church, also alludes to what appears to be this same underground cult of the snake at Edessa when he refers to the presence there of "the heresy of Gnostics, that is, those who worship the serpent."[48] Since we know that one of the founders of the Peratae, named as Euphrates the Peratic, probably came from northern Mesopotamia, it is decidedly possible that he obtained his Gnostic teachings from one or other of the Orphic mystery schools in Edessa.

So when we gaze upon the giant stone with its long serpentine neck emerging out of the western wall of Karahan Tepe's Pillars Shrine, are we looking upon a primordial form of Nabu, "the announcer," whose mysteries would go on to be preserved by the Orphic mystery schools and Ophite Gnostics who would come to thrive across the region in late antiquity? The strange head's open mouth suggests it is delivering an oracular communication in the same manner in which the snake shamans of Karahan Tepe would have made similar pronouncements within its rock-hewn enclosures. The question then becomes: How were these communications able to take place, and what connection, if any, did this process have with the yogic and tantric practices of Hindu and Buddhist tradition?

30

The Serpent Within

It appears possible that the Great Serpent, identified as the Milky Way with its head as the Galactic Bulge, was thought by the shamans at Karahan Tepe to be able to speak to them directly. What they were doing appears to constitute a more archaic, rawer form of what the Nābû and Munabbiātu prophets and prophetesses were doing in Bronze Age Syria and what the Pythia priestesses were achieving at the Oracle of Delphi in Greece.

The one thing all these groups appear to have in common is that their function was to act as mediums between a perceived intelligence existing within or beyond the celestial realms and waiting attendants in the physical world. What is more, all these groups would appear to have imagined this higher intelligence as being able to overshadow an individual so that they might act as a mouthpiece for the supposed cosmic entity. We can perhaps best see this process in operation by examining more closely how the Pythia (or Pythoness) at Delphi became a divine channel for the god Apollo, whose influence was understood to be serpentine in nature:

There (at Delphi) the Pythoness, a virgin priestess, prophesied under the intoxicating excitement of the vapours issuing from a cleft in the rocks above which she sat on a tripod; she was filled with the god himself and his spirit. The god, as was believed, entered into the earthly body, or else the priestess' soul, "loosed" from her body, apprehended the divine revelations with the spiritual mind. What she then "with frenzied mouth" foretold, was spoken through her by the god. When she said "I" it was Apollo who spoke to whomsoever it concerned. That which lived, thought and spoke in her so long as she was in frenzy, was the god himself.[1]

This tells us clearly that it was necessary for Apollo, in his guise as the serpent, to take over the body of the Pythia for her to make oracular pronouncements. Similar trance states where possession was involved were, I suspect, occurring at Karahan Tepe during the Pre-Pottery Neolithic Age. (See fig. 30.1 for an artist's impression of what this ritual might have looked like. See also the book's preface on page xix for an imaginative description of this ritual.) If so, then did these individuals simply invoke the spirit of the cosmic serpent, most obviously at the time of the summer and winter solstices, and hope for the best? Alternately, did they employ some more methodical process with comparisons to the yogic and tantric practices of the Indian subcontinent? These, as we have seen, feature an internal force seen in terms of a coiled snake located at the base of the spine and known as the kundalini spirit, which was activated through ritual and meditational processes.

It seems unlikely that the shamans of Karahan Tepe engaged in similar practices, although they might well have created their own ways of generating

Fig. 30.1. Artist's impression of shamans, both male and female, within Karahan Tepe's Great Ellipse (Structure AD) engaged in oracular communication with the cosmic serpent.
Illustration by Russell M. Hossain.

the kundalini spirit within their bodies in a manner similar to how the Peratae and presumably other Ophite Gnostic sects appear to have allowed the spirit of the Great Serpent to enter inside them.

PSYCHOACTIVE SUBSTANCES

We can only guess today how the shamans of Karahan Tepe were able to attain the necessary state of mind for possession to take place, although I am sure that it involved snakes as well as hallucinogens of some kind. What these could have been we cannot say, as no soil analysis studies have so far been published that might reveal what plants or fungi were being utilized by the Karahan community.

That said, and as I proposed in the book *The Cygnus Mystery*, published in 2006, a large number of the snakes shown in relief on T-pillars at Göbekli Tepe and on a damaged statue of a human head found at Nevalı Çori have stylized heads shaped like a cross section of the cap of a psilocybin mushroom, which is highly psychoactive.[2] In time, this stylized snake head appears to have become more and more abstract until eventually it was little more than an upturned letter *U* associated with a series of peck marks presumably representing the body of the snake. (For an example of this form of abstract serpentine art, see fig. 30.3, p. 252.)

It should also be mentioned that a species of giant reed found extensively on the Harran Plain and known as *Arundo donax* contains a series of psychoactive chemicals including DMT, bufotenin, and 5-MeO-DMT.[3] It is not known whether this might have been cultivated for use as a drug by the region's Taş Tepeler community, although the fact that it grows with such profusion in many parts of the Şanlıurfa province means this possibility cannot be ruled out.

SNAKES AND SEXUALITY

Snakes are universal symbols of magic and medicine, as well as fertility, cyclical renewal, and, of course, sexuality. As Hans Leisegang commented in connection with the Ophite Gnostic group who manufactured the alabaster bowl, "We would seem to be dealing with a mystery [where] the mystai drew a snake between their thighs in order to consummate a mystical union with the god."[4]

At Karahan Tepe the snake is the symbol most frequently seen carved on T-pillars, on statues, on walls, and on stone bowls; this much we have already established. It also cannot be without meaning that the rock-carved columns in the Pillars Shrine (Structure AB) have been deliberately fashioned to appear phallic in nature. This conclusion is emphasized in the knowledge that the heads of the four larger pillars seen in a line close to the room's western wall, along with maybe three or four of the smaller examples seen in the eastern part of the shrine, are much fatter than their stems.

It seems possible that these columns served a dual function, acting both as erect phalli and also as the teeth of the snake whose mouth and head is signified by the hollowed-out shape of the shrine. If, however, the columns do signify phalli, then we must ask ourselves why this might have been important in achieving communion with the Milky Way serpent in its role as the source of cosmic creation.

In a traditional binary sense, the act of penile erection in a male was something brought about by the actions and presence of a female, emphasizing the idea that women had the power to initiate the process of fertilization. It was therefore possibly the women of the community, the female shamans, who were responsible for ensuring that the Pillars Shrine remained a potent powerhouse of virile energy to mimic that required to connect with the perceived source of cosmic creation in the direction of the Galactic Bulge.

One might draw comparisons here with similar magical processes found in connection with the cult of Osiris in ancient Egypt. Osiris, the god of death and resurrection, was associated with fertility, cyclic renewal, and the fecundity of the land. In the story of Osiris, it is his sister-wife Isis and her sister Nephthys who use *heka*-magic to resurrect the god after he is murdered by his twin brother Set (Nephthys's own brother and husband).

The resurrection of Osiris, in his role as the mummiform god of the dead, was symbolized by the erection of the *djed*-pillar, a visual device signifying the backbone of Osiris. In this manner, Isis was able to mate with her husband and bring forth a son named Horus. Clearly, Osiris's return from the dead through the intervention of the two goddesses was itself a euphemism for penile erection, which in turn was seen as an act of divine creation brought about through the use of heka-magic. This magical power was symbolized in pictographic form as twin snakes, which also form the hieroglyph for the word *djed,* meaning "stable" or "stability." When personified in anthropomorphic form, heka is shown as a male deity holding a live snake in each hand.

Thus we can see that the force behind penile erection, in ancient Egypt at least, was deemed to be magical in nature, and connected with the symbol of the snake. Is it possible therefore to see the penile erection suggested by the carved columns within Karahan Tepe's Pillars Shrine as symbolic of a magical force that was associated not only with cosmic creation, but also with the act of human creation?

A large number of statues and relief carvings showing ithyphallic figures have been found at Göbekli Tepe and Karahan Tepe, as well as at other Taş Tepeler sites, many of which can be seen today in the Şanlıurfa Archaeological Museum. Indeed, other than a few very small, full-bodied female figurines carved out of limestone, along with an incised stone panel from Göbekli Tepe showing a woman dubbed the "Göbekli Goddess" with her legs spread apart to display her enlarged labia, almost all the statuary found at Taş Tepeler sites so far has been male, and often it is overtly sexual in nature.*

THE FIRST BULL LEAPER?

The latest example of this trend is the relief carving found at a Pre-Pottery Neolithic site some 9 miles (14 kilometers) west-southwest of Şanlıurfa in the village of Sayburç. As reported in chapter 6, in 2021 a local resident came forward and said that beneath his farmhouse was a storage area with a bedrock floor into which had been carved a large elliptical enclosure, only half of which is presently visible since the rest remains hidden beneath the building's foundations.

Seen on the enclosure's north wall are various carved figures in high relief. They include a man holding what appears to be a live snake (see plate 23). The legs of the figure are bent, indicating that he is jumping into the air. Could it be possible that this relief is the earliest known representation of bull leaping?

---

*The first recorded artifact to be found at Göbekli Tepe was a small ithyphallic statue. The owner of the land took the piece to the archaeological museum at Şanlıurfa and showed it to the staff there, hoping they might compensate him. They concluded it was probably made by a local shepherd and was of no monetary value. It was, however, kept in storage and eventually recognized as belonging to the Pre-Pottery Neolithic Age by Professor Klaus Schmidt, who at the time was working alongside Professor Harald Hauptmann at the site of Nevalı Çori in the northern part of Şanlıurfa province. It was the discovery of this statue that prompted Schmidt and his colleagues to personally inspect Göbekli Tepe, leading to the first excavations there in the fall of 1995.

Fig. 30.2 a and b. On the top (fig. 30.2a), an example of contemporary bull leaping from southern France, and on the bottom (fig. 30.2b) the relief panel from Sayburç arguably showing bull leaping taking place in southeastern Anatolia during the tenth millennium BCE. Fig. 30.2a by MLL and fig. 30.2b by Andrew Collins.

This practice was known to have featured prominently in Minoan Crete (circa 3000–1100 BCE). Bull leaping is also thought to have been practiced by early Hittite societies in Bronze Age Anatolia as early as 1650 BCE.* (See figs. 30.2 a and b for comparisons between the Sayburç relief possibly showing bull leaping and a photo of modern-day bull leaping in southern France, where this highly dangerous activity is known as *course landaise*. Only experienced cows aged between 2 and 14 years old are today used for this purpose.)

The male figure holds either a snake or an instrument like a rattle to bait the bull, showing his authority over the forces of the Earth, which in Anatolian tradition is likened to the body of a giant bull. When the animal shook, earthquakes and thunderstorms occurred, while its immense horns were imagined as holding up the starry heavens.[5] The bull is also quite obviously a symbol of male virility, whereas the snake is more generally associated with sexual desire, especially in the Abrahamic religions.

To the right of the advancing bull and apparent bull leaper is another male figure, this one surrounded on either side by advancing felines, most probably panther-leopards. This second figure faces outward and is three-dimensional in form. He holds his penis in a manner suggestive either of exhibitionism and/or the act of masturbation (see plate 24). Further evidence of sexual symbolism can be found immediately to the southeast of the aforementioned structure. A design carved onto the level bedrock gives the distinct impression of an abstract snake composed of an inverted U-shaped head with a series of peck marks signifying its body. The device is contained within what appears to be a vulva-shaped frame (see fig. 30.3). This rather abstract carved art is almost certainly contemporary with the bedrock enclosure.

The style of the extraordinary art preserved at Sayburç is identical to the Layer III activity at Göbekli Tepe, meaning that its rock-cut enclosure dates to somewhere between 9600 and 8800 BCE. This would then make it contemporary with the earliest phases of Karahan Tepe, which is located on the other side of the Harran Plain around 36.5 miles (59 kilometers) to the east of Sayburç. New excavations taking place at Sayburç have revealed a series of smaller enclosures, each one containing T-pillars up to 6 feet (1.8 meters) in

---

*Two bull-leaping scenes have been identified on a Hüseyindede vase from the early Hittite site of Hüseyindede Tepe (circa 1650 BCE), located near Yörüklü in the Turkish province of Çorum (see Taracha 2002). I want to acknowledge Debbie Cartwright for first suggesting that the Sayburç relief could show a person bull leaping.

Fig. 30.3. Pecked carving in the leveled bedrock at the site of the Pre-Pottery Neolithic sanctuary at Sayburç, near Şanlıurfa, southeastern Turkey. It shows a typical mushroom-shaped serpentine head and a body made up of pecked holes, all of which is contained in a vulva-like border. Photo by Andrew Collins.

height. Although these structures are 200–300 yards (180–275 meters) away from the aforementioned bedrock enclosure, it is anticipated that the complex stretches between the two locations, meaning that Sayburç is a huge occupational site that could rival both Göbekli Tepe and Karahan Tepe when fully exposed.

So whatever was going on at sites like Sayburç, Göbekli Tepe and Karahan Tepe, as well as the various other Taş Tepeler sites during the tenth millennium BCE, the carved art produced by this culture clearly demonstrates a complete openness when it comes to sexual prowess and human reproduction. We can only assume that this would have been reflected in whatever rites and rituals were taking place inside the shrines and installations and that these involved trance states, possession, snakes, and sexuality—practices that would eventually come to be associated with the mystical rites of the Orphic mystery schools and Ophite Gnostics that would thrive in the exact same region thousands of years later.

In this knowledge, the predominant use of snake imagery at Karahan Tepe perhaps symbolizes a creative force associated not simply with human reproduction, but also with cosmic creation. Should this prove correct, then the alignment both of the Pit Shrine (Structure AA) and of the Great Ellipse (Structure AD) toward the Galactic Bulge suggests that the process of creation was indeed associated with this region of the night sky. It is even possible that the Galactic Bulge's elliptical appearance caused it to be seen both as the head of the Milky Way serpent and as an egg of creation guarded by the mouth of a snake. If correct, this symbolism would parallel that of the oval mound being held in the mouth of Serpent Mound in Adams County, Ohio, which, as we have seen, archeoastronomer William E. Romain has identified as a representation of the Scorpius constellation (see chapter 21).

If we can imagine all these ideas being played out at Karahan Tepe at the height of its occupation, then how might these beliefs in cosmic creation be reflected in the act of *human* creation? Was this creative force imagined as a snake, similar to the concept of the kundalini spirit that was so important to the yogic and tantric practices of Hinduism and Buddhism? Did its presence help initiate shamanic experiences that would result in the supplicant connecting with the serpent's celestial counterpart? As we see next, the key to answering these questions is the manner in which the Western world has perceived the astrological influence of Scorpio on the human body.

31

Lord of the Signs

Have you ever wondered why people born under the sign of Scorpio are considered to be the most sexually active of all the signs of the zodiac? With online astrological blogs bearing titles such as "The Real Reason Why Scorpio Makes Us Think 'Sex'"[1] it's hard to get away from a belief that the influence of the constellation of Scorpius is somehow connected with eroticism and sexual prowess. How and why did this belief come about, and does it have any basis in truth? More important, what has any of this to do with frenzied shamanic rites taking place at Karahan Tepe in the tenth millennium BCE?

Most modern-day astrologers believe that the origin of Scorpio's apparent association with sexual activity goes back to the seventeenth century, when a school of physicians in Italy known as the Iatromathematicians applied the sciences of mathematics, mechanics, and astrology to figure out the nature of human anatomy. They allotted each of the 12 signs of the zodiac to a specific area of the human body, with Scorpio ruling over the "reproductive system, sexual organs, bowels, [and the] excretory system."[2]

Although the Iatromathematicians' attribution of the 12 zodiacal signs to different areas of the human anatomy certainly influenced how we view those born under the sign of Scorpio, the concept of what in medieval times would come to be known as Zodiac Man existed as far back as the first century CE.[3]

THE ORIGINS OF ZODIAC MAN

The concept of Zodiac Man, known also as Man of Signs (*Homo signorum*), Lord of the Signs (*Dominus signorum*), and Microcosmic Man, was born

out of the belief that every part of the human body was ruled over by a
different sign of the zodiac, with Aries at the head and Pisces at the feet.

Illustrations of Zodiac Man date from the eleventh century onward, with
none earlier. They are European in style and design (in other words, they

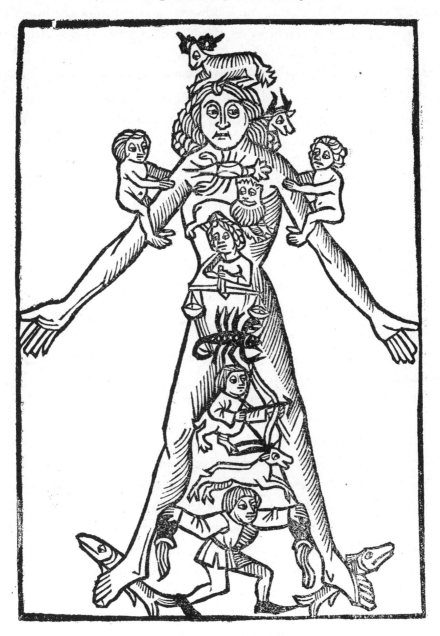

Fig. 31.1. Woodcut showing Zodiac Man from
The German Almanac (1484) by Hans (Johann) Schönsperger
(active Augsburg, Germany, 1481–1520).

display no obvious Arabic influence) and show a naked male figure, his arms and legs slightly apart, with either the signs of the zodiac or their pictorial representations placed on or around the body (see fig. 31.1, on the previous page). These illustrations were used by physicians, barber-surgeons, quack doctors, and, of course, astrologers and soothsayers, to determine whether or not it was the right time to conduct everything from surgery to bloodletting, the administration of medication, and even the cutting of hair and nails.[4]

Everything depended on the nativity of a person—in other words, the sign under which they were born and which house the moon, seen as a baleful influence, was in at the time of the intended bodily procedure. This determined which parts of the body were *not* to be touched using iron instruments or prescribed medicine of any kind.

The name given to this highly intimate form of astrological biology was zodiacal melothesia, the science of charting zodiac influences on the human body.[5] It formed part of a belief system whereby the planetary and zodiacal influences inherent to the physical body were viewed simply as a microcosm of a much greater macrocosmic existence governed by the seven planets and their influence on the 12 houses of the zodiac. By acknowledging the potency of this astrological process, human beings were able to harmonize with these celestial intelligences and in doing so, understand their impact on the physical body at any given time of the year based not so much on the position of the sun, but on the whereabouts of the moon.

This greater importance given to the moon, as opposed to the sun, is thought to be derived from an Akkadian source,[6] one perhaps associated with the moon god Sin, whose main temple in northern Mesopotamia called the Ekhulkhul ("Temple of Rejoicing") had existed in Harran since around 2000 BCE. As we shall see, there is every reason to suspect that a principal source behind the creation of Zodiac Man were the Chaldean astrologers of Harran.

Arguably, the earliest reference to the concept of Zodiac Man is an astrological text titled the *Astronomica* (circa 14 CE) written by Roman poet and astrologer Marcus Manilius, who flourished in the early part of the first century CE.[7] Without using illustration, he accredited the influence of the zodiacal signs to different parts of the human anatomy, saying of Libra and Scorpio: "*Libra regit clunes, et Scorpios inguine gaudet*" ["Libra rules the hips, and Scorpius rejoices in the groin"].[8] It is clear that even at this stage, the influence of Scorpius was associated with the reproductive organs.

An Egyptian papyrus text of the third century CE that is part of the John Rylands Library in Manchester, England, also alludes to Zodiac Man when its narrator, a priest named Peteésis, answers a question posed by the philosopher Plato in the following manner:

PLATO :—"What is the case with these phenomena?"

PETEÉSIS :—"Listen: the Sun is the right eye, the Moon the left, the tongue, smell, and hearing belong to Mercury, the viscera to Jupiter, the chest to Mars, the spleen to Venus, the kidneys to Saturn, the head to Aries, the neck to Cancer, the belly to Leo, the cheek and loins to Virgo, the buttocks to Libra, *the seat to Scorpio*."[9] (Current author's emphasis.)

Once again Scorpio is associated with the "seat" (Latin: *cathedra*) of the body, showing that this was clearly its fixed position and its most potent area of influence.

ZODIAC MAN—THE HARRAN CONNECTION

Evidence of a Chaldean involvement in the creation of Zodiac Man comes from Sextus Empiricus, a Greek Pyrrhonist philosopher and Empiric school physician who flourished circa CE 150. He speaks of the Chaldean notion that the various parts of the body "sympathize" with their corresponding zodiacal signs in order that "if any of the stars [that is, the planets] which are malificent at the time of nativity is in any of these signs it produces an imperfection in the part which bears the same name."[10] This clearly indicates that the principal point of origin of this concept was indeed Harran, the original home of the astrological teachings attributed to the Chaldeans.

Having made this statement, it should be pointed out that it has now been established that almost all of the attributions of zodiacal influences on the human body existed in Assyrio-Babylonian astrological and medical texts dating from the first millennium BCE. In these, the influence of Scorpius is always the same, ruling over the female genitalia and, in some cases, the womb and male member,[11] the same general area of the body as the Muladhara or Root chakra of Hindu and Buddhic tradition (fig. 31.2 on the next page).

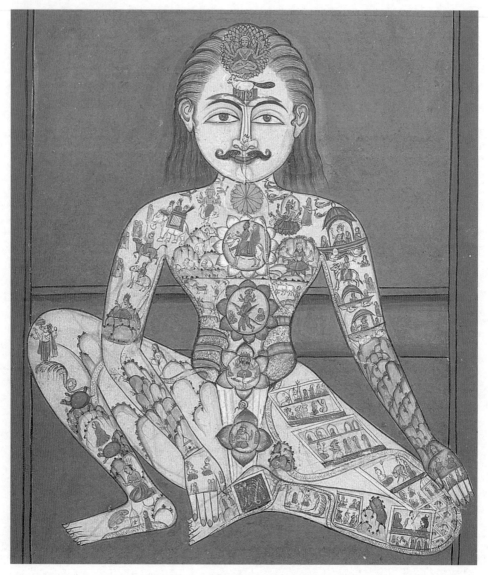

Fig. 31.2. Illustration showing the sevenfold chakra system of the body as portrayed in a Tantric text from the early nineteenth century CE. Note the small kundalini serpent immediately above the base chakra. From the *Sapta Chakra, Asanas and Mudras (Hata yoga)* manuscript (British Library, MS 24099).

ANSWERS FROM VEDIC ASTRONOMY

Are there links between the Babylonian or Chaldean idea that the zodiac sign of Scorpio rules the "seat" or cathedra of the human body and the Eastern concept of the kundalini spirit? The answer would appear to be yes. In Vedic astronomy, parts of the Scorpius constellation bear the name Mula, a Sanskrit term meaning "root," "base," or "foundation," due to the fact that it resonates with the human body's Muladhara or Root chakra.[12]

What is more, the Mula nakshatra, which constitutes the nineteenth lunar mansion of Vedic astrology, reflects the influence of the center of the Milky Way galaxy, something emphasized by the term Mula, which implies the foundation point of all creation.[13] Of the nine stars of Scorpius marking out this nakshatra, the star Shaula (λ Scorpii) most embodies this spirit, being the closest to Galactic Center (a matter we return to in chapter 32).[14]

This seems to further emphasize the ancient and seemingly universal belief that some kind of sympathetic resonance existed between the human act of creation associated with the body's reproductive organs and the area of sky seen in terms of the place of *cosmic* creation. This, as we have seen, would appear to be marked by the Galactic Bulge and nearby Scorpius constellation, both of which point us in the direction of Galactic Center.

The concept of Zodiac Man thus brings into focus a very ancient belief that the human body represents a microcosmic form of a powerful macrocosmic force reflected in the influence of the seven planets (the moon being the most important of the seven in Vedic astronomy) and 12 signs of the zodiac, with Scorpio always being associated with the act of human reproduction and sexuality. From this we can see that since earliest times there has been a strong belief that the area of sky corresponding with cosmic creation, marked by the stars of Scorpius, not only resonates with the human act of creation, but additionally helps stimulate or bring alive those areas of the body associated with sexual reproduction, the two seen as being intrinsically bound together in an almost quantum manner. From this has come the long-held belief, arguably conceived originally by the Chaldeans of Harran, that a direct connection exists between the astrological influence of Scorpio and human sexuality.

Is it possible that these powerful ideas were first developed in full among Anatolia's Taş Tepeler culture? If so, then this can help us to better understand not only the blatant phallic symbolism inside Karahan Tepe's Pillars Shrine, but also why the site has been found to contain such striking snake imagery, and why key enclosures were aligned toward the Galactic Bulge. Snakes are quite literally a visual expression of how the Milky Way serpent's active spirit, symbolized by the stars of Scorpius, could not only affect the human body, but also take control of it during rites of possession and oracular communication.

The question then becomes: did the Great Serpent really exist as a supercelestial intelligence out in the cosmos, or was it simply the creation of Karahan Tepe's Taş Tepeler community? That the Galactic Bulge, as the head of the cosmic serpent, corresponds with the center of our own Milky Way galaxy is something that our most ancient ancestors should never have known about. This, however, would appear to be contrary to the evidence, for as we see in the final part of this book, there are clear indications that the Karahan community's choice of the Galactic Bulge as the sky portal leading to the cosmic source of creation might well have been based on some knowledge of the Galactic Center, and in particular its dynamic impact on the rise and fall of life on Earth.

PART 8

THE ETERNAL RETURN

32

At the Center of it All

The Galactic Bulge, a bright, elliptical widening of the Milky Way located next to the constellation of Scorpius, marks the center of our own local galaxy. It consists of a vast region of tightly packed stars that include stellar nurseries, where stars are quite literally born into existence.[1] Somewhere in this intense activity, at an estimated 25,800 light years from the Earth and invisible to the naked eye, is the galaxy's true center (see fig. 32.1).[2] It is an enormous stellar object first detected by radio telescopes in 1954[3] and known today as Sagittarius A* (abbreviated to Sgr A* and pronounced "Sagittarius A star").[4]

Originally detected as a powerful source of radio signals coming from the heart of the galaxy, the object in question was first thought to be a standard black hole. At 4.2 million times more massive than our sun, with an

Fig. 32.1. Artist's impression of the Milky Way galaxy. At its center is the Galactic Bulge from which a series of spiral arms emerges. Photo by ESO/NASA/JPL-Caltech/M. Kornmesser/R. Hurt.

Fig. 32.2. Photo image showing the galaxy M81 (Messier 81), which, like the Milky Way galaxy, has a bright bulge at its center from which emerges a series of spiral arms. Photo by NASA, ESA, and the Hubble Heritage Team (STScI/AURA).

enormous gravitational field governing the orbits of stars at the center of the Milky Way, this unimaginable stellar object is today considered to be a supermassive black hole of the type suspected to exist at the center of most galaxies (see fig. 32.2). It was not, however, until 2022 that the world got its first glimpse of Sagittarius A* following the publication that year of a composite image of the supermassive black hole taken back in 2017 by the Event Horizon Telescope.[5]

THE CLUE IN THE STINGER

Sagittarius A* is situated between the stars of Sagittarius, Ophiuchus, and Scorpius, although, as its name suggests, from the perspective of Earth it is located just inside the officially established boundaries defining the constellation of Sagittarius. It lies some 5.6 degrees south of the ecliptic, close to a nebula called the Butterfly Cluster, known also as M6 (Messier 6) or NGC 6405. Nearby is the star Lambda Scorpii (λ Sco), which goes by the name of Shaula, from the Arabic al-Shaulah, meaning "the sting,"[6] since it forms the tip of Scorpius's hook-like stinger (see fig. 32.3). According to Iranian scholar and polymath Al Bīrūnī (circa 973–1050 CE), the star was also known as Mushālah, meaning "raised," a reference to the scorpion's sting, since it is always ready to strike.[7] If the Galactic Bulge can be seen as the head of the Milky Way serpent and the stars of Scorpius as its forked tongue, then Shaula would connect the snake's tongue with its open mouth.

Richard Hinckley Allen (1838–1908) in his invaluable work *Star Names: Their Lore and Meaning*, first published in 1899, wrote that a bright open star cluster named Ptolemy's Cluster—today known as M7 (Messier 7) or NGC 6475—looks as if it should be the natural extension of Scorpius's stinger. This, he pointed out, would have directed the viewer's eye toward "the nucleus of the Milky Way Galaxy."[8] Thus M7 and the nearby star cluster M6 would appear to have formed the original termination of the stinger. Together, these two stars were known by the Arabic name *Tāli' al Shaulah*, meaning something like "next to the stinger."[9]

As noted in chapter 31, in Vedic astronomy Shaula is the standout star in the cluster of nine Scorpius stars making up the Mula nakshatra, the nineteenth nakshatra or lunar mansion of Vedic astrology. It is considered to mark Galactic Center, something emphasized in the fact that its name, Mula, means "root" or "foundation." Mula, or Muladhara, is also, as we have seen, the name of the Root chakra in Eastern yogic and tantric practices, which reflects the cosmic influence of its celestial counterpart, a concept similar to the Western idea of zodiacal melothesia where the influence of Scorpio rules the reproductive organs, sexuality, and the human act of creation.

As the point of cosmic activation in our own local galaxy, the fact that Galactic Center coincides with Scorpius's stinger should be noted. Was this association some kind of warning or sign to humankind established at places like Göbekli Tepe where the stars of Scorpius appear for the first time as a scorpion? That the sting of a scorpion can be fatal could imply a very ominous portent indeed.

EARTH UNDER FIRE

Science writer Paul LaViolette (1947–2022), in an important work titled *Earth Under Fire: Humanity's Survival of the Apocalypse* (1997), wrote that

Sagittarius A* might not always have been as quiet as it is thought to be today. He proposed that as recently as 13,865 BCE this supermassive black hole sent forth bursts of high-energy cosmic rays that triggered changes in Earth's climate as well as a major cataclysm, something he referred to as the Galactic Superwave Theory.[10] LaViolette provided compelling evidence for this and other similar cosmic events that might have affected Earth, based on a scientific examination of ice core samples from Antarctica and Greenland.[11]

Paleoclimatologists who have made detailed studies not only of these same ice core samples, but also of lake and land sediment deposits from various parts of the world, are now in agreement that a major cosmic event affecting large parts of the northern hemisphere did indeed occur during the time frame offered by LaViolette.

Their findings, however, indicate that the impact occurred slightly later, probably around 10,800 BCE. This event, known as the Younger Dryas impact hypothesis, is today considered to have been triggered by the appearance in our skies of hundreds if not thousands of fragments of a disintegrating comet that peppered the northern hemisphere from North America in the west to Europe and southwestern Asia in the east. These impacts took the form of a series of terrifying airbursts that initiated mass wildfires—which consumed vast swatches of Earth's biomass—as well as unimaginable supertsunamis, volcanism, and unprecedented flooding across the globe. The impacts also triggered changes in the temperature and flow of ocean currents due to the rapid melting of the North American ice sheets, along with a nuclear winter (a period of complete darkness) that blocked out the sun for some considerable amount of time. What followed was the sudden onset of a mini ice age that lasted approximately 1,200 years, bringing us to a date in the region of 9600 BCE.[12]

The sudden drop in temperature would have forced the Epipaleolithic forerunners of the Taş Tepeler culture to journey southward from the Russian steppe north of the Black Sea, across the Caucasus Mountains into eastern Anatolia, where they would settle eventually in the vicinity of Lake Van circa 10,500–10,000 BCE. From there they would have spread westward into what is today the Şanlıurfa province, where, together with the Indigenous Anatolians, they initiated the construction of the earliest Taş Tepeler sites somewhere between 10,000 BCE and 9600 BCE.

As I make clear in *Göbekli Tepe: Genesis of the Gods* (2014),[13] there is compelling evidence that carved imagery found inside Göbekli Tepe's Enclosure D suggests a strong interest in the appearance of comets, due, it appears, to the constant fear that further major cataclysms could destroy the world.[14] This could well indicate that one of the installation's chief functions was to provide quick and easy access to the sky world so that shamans might be able to appease, battle, and even outwit the supernatural tricksters seen as responsible for bringing about the appearance in our skies of potentially hazardous comets.

Were these catastrophic events, which had occurred so recently in human history, linked to why the sting of Scorpius, marked by the star Shaula, was located so close to Galactic Center? Was there a connection between the Younger Dryas impact event and the painful burning sensation, and even the possibility of death, that can result from being stung by a scorpion? Were the stars of Scorpius, Shaula in particular, blamed for triggering this cataclysmic event that devastated the northern hemisphere?

LaViolette pointed out that the ice core samples that provided him with evidence of major cataclysms in Earth's recent history also indicated recurring patterns of activity, perhaps further cataclysms, across a period of tens of thousands of years. This led him to propose that the galaxy's supermassive black hole could affect Earth in a cyclical manner.[15] Moreover, in his opinion Scorpius's stinger is the key, for, as he made clear, "Since the Galactic center can at times release lethal outbursts of cosmic ray particles, such deadly symbolism is quite appropriate."[16]

So the supermassive black hole that might well have been responsible for cosmic creation in our own Milky Way galaxy might also be a destroyer of worlds. It is a far reaching proposal that might just explain why there is such a dichotomy of belief when it comes to the influence of the Scorpius constellation. On the one hand, in its role as a celestial snake and as the active spirit of the world-encircling serpent, it is seen as a beneficial influence, inspiring the creation and development of life on Earth. On the other hand, and in its role as a deadly scorpion, it would appear to have been blamed for one of the most terrifying events in human history. To understand how exactly this situation came about, and what its impact might have been on the emergence of Taş Tepeler during the tenth millennium BCE, we need to look more closely at the manner Galactic Center affects the world in which we live.

33

The Galactic Merry-Go-Round

It is a fact that our solar system constantly participates in a grand galactic merry-go-round many millions of years in duration. Let me explain. Imagine, if you can, a carousel horse as the gears of its mechanical roundabout persistently move it up and down while at the same time propelling it in a never-ending circular motion. This is exactly what happens to our sun, which is constantly circling around Galactic Center. Each time it moves upward it passes through the much denser midplane section of the galactic disk, and every time it goes back down it again passes through this same dense section of the galaxy.

Eventually this circular motion will bring the solar system back to where it began its journey. One complete revolution on the galactic merry-go-round takes around 224 million years, a time period defined as a cosmic year.*

Calculations relating to the big bang theory suggest that the universe came into existence approximately 13.7 to 13.8 billion years ago. It was not, however, until somewhere between 13.44 and 13.45 billion years ago, around 250 to 360 million years after the big bang, that matter was born and space-time initiated.[1] From then on through to the present day there have been exactly 60 cycles of 224 million years.

In astronomical terms our solar system is now emerging from another

---

*It should be noted that there have been various estimates on the length of the cosmic year, ranging from 200 to 250 million years, with 220 million years being quoted most often (see, for instance, Firsoff 1974, 185; Ridpath 2012, s.v. "cosmic year," 195; etc.). I have chosen the more specific value of 224 million years (after Choudhary 2022).

passage through the densely populated midplane section of the galactic disk, having just passed through it while coming up from below.[2]

More important to life on Earth, however, is the fact that geoscientists studying Earth changes across the past 545 million years—including convection patterns in the Earth's core and mantle, along with global tectonics, volcanism, geomagnetic field reversals, shifts in the seabed, and extinction cycles in the fossil record—have come to realize the presence of cyclic oscillations in the range of 30 million years.

THE EXTINCTION CLOCK

As far back as the 1920s, British geologist Arthur Holmes (1890–1965) determined a periodicity in Earth's formation using basic radiometric data relating to tectonic activity.[3] American geologist and paleontologist Amadeus William Grabau (1870–1946) noted the same periodicity in the 1930s. He recognized a cyclic oscillation in the emergence and decay of marine fossils, which, like Holmes, he saw as recurring every 30 million years.[4] These oscillations formed part of what he called the "pulsation theory."[5]

Then, in 1977, paleontologists Alfred G. Fischer and Michael A. Arthur of Princeton University, examining marine biological diversity and oceanic climate, were able to fine-tune this oscillation to 32 million years, proposing that it was the result of periodic tectonic activity.[6]* It was not, however, until 2020 that Fischer and Arthur's proposal that these cyclical oscillations lasted for approximately 32 million years was finally confirmed.

In a paper helpfully titled "A 32-Million Year Cycle Detected in Sea-Level Fluctuations over the Last 545 Myr"[7] that appeared in *Geoscience Frontiers* in 2020, Michael R. Rampino, a professor of biology and environmental studies at New York University, and his colleague, American atmospheric scientist Ken Caldeira, outlined their own discovery of a clear 32-million-year oscillation in the rise and fall of Earth's biodiversity. What they go on to say is quite remarkable, for, in their opinion, "the pacing" of these cyclic pulses "could be the result of some external astrophysical forcing," suggesting "a correlation with the oscillation of the solar system through the Galactic plane, which might

---

*A number of geoscientists have also noted cyclic oscillations in Earth's geologic record. See Rohde and Muller 2005, Lieberman and Melott [2009] 2012, and Rampino 2017 for summaries of these proposals, which all feature different lengths of time.

affect terrestrial geophysics."[8] In other words, the solar system's participation in the grand galactic merry-go-round might well be responsible for the existence of the recurring 32-million-year extinction clock.[9]

The exact cause of this oscillation cycle remains a matter of speculation and debate, with Rampino and his colleagues concluding that it results from the solar system passing through the densely populated midplane section of the galactic disk.[10] As this happens, the solar system experiences powerful gravitational pulls from something present there. This could be vast gas clouds, dark matter, or maybe other more exotic phenomena. Whatever the answer, it is theorized that this inter-action between the solar system and the galactic midplane section triggers the release of comets held in suspension within the Oort Cloud, which is a thick layer of icy objects located just beyond the outer edge of the solar system.[11] The sun's gravitational pull then causes these comets to fall into the inner solar system, a journey that can take anywhere up to a couple of million years to complete.[12]

When, however, these comets *do* reach perihelion—that is, their closest pass of the sun—they can break up into much smaller fragments that will assume new orbits. Some of them will then assume a collision course with Earth. This, of course, can lead to the mass annihilation of life, as was the case with the KT Boundary event that resulted in the disappearance of the dino-saurs some 65 million years ago.[13] At least five major extinction events are pres-ent in Earth's geological record, all of which would probably have destroyed humanity if it had been around at the time.[14]

Rampino is certainly the most vocal of the geoscientists concerning the impact on life of these 32-million-year oscillation cycles, making it clear they relate to "the structure and dynamics of the Milky Way galaxy."[15] In his com-pelling book *Cataclysms: A New Geology for the Twenty-first Century*, published in 2017, he says that, "To understand our planet, one must study Earth in its cosmic context,"[16] a sentiment that will hopefully begin to resonate with other geoscientists working in this important field of study.

What I find intriguing about Earth's extinction clock is that 32 million years just happens to be 1/7th of 224 million years, the estimated length of a cosmic year. What this means is that the solar system passes through the midplane section of the galactic disk seven times in every one cosmic year (see fig. 33.1, p. 270). However, at the end of one cosmic cycle, the solar system will be at the opposite stage in the oscillation cycle to where it began, due to the sun's fairground-horse-like movement through the galactic midplane. In other

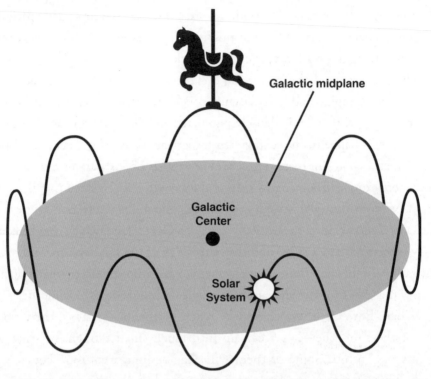

Fig. 33.1. The circular motion made by the solar system as it navigates the
galactic midplane. Each of its seven oscillations corresponds to one of Earth's
32-million-year extinction cycles, meaning that one complete revolution of
Galactic Center takes around 224 million years. Illustration by Nick Burton.

words, if it started the cycle above the galactic midplane then it would end it
beneath the midplane and, of course, vice versa.

In this manner, our solar system's next revolution of Galactic Center would
exactly mirror its position during its previous revolution (see fig. 33.2 for a full
visual explanation of how this oscillation cycle works). What this implies is
that the cosmic merry-go-round in fact takes *two* cosmic years to complete,
each revolution of Galactic Center being approximately 224 million years in
length. This means it would take the sun a staggering 448 millions years for it
to return to the starting position of its first cycle, showing that this inordinate
amount of time is necessary for the solar system to complete one full double
revolution of the Milky Way.

Since the beginning of space-time some 13.44 billion years ago, there have
been exactly 60 cycles of a cosmic year with a length of 224 million years,

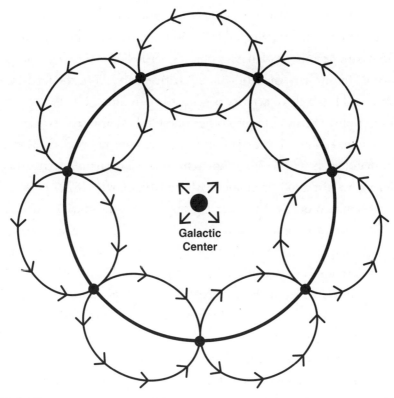

Fig. 33.2. The circular motion of the sun around Galactic Center. One revolution of seven oscillations, each 32 million years in duration, takes 224 million years to complete. This is shown as seven peaks and troughs with their direction of flow arrowed. The sun's next 224-million-year revolution is shown as seven more peaks and troughs that exactly mirror those of the previous 224 million years. These flow in the same direction. This makes it clear that the sun only returns to its starting position at the commencement of the first revolution after completing two full perambulations of Galactic Center, a time period amounting to approximately 448 million years. Illustration by Nick Burton.

even though our own solar system has only been around for an estimated 4.571 billion years (with the earliest examples of fossils on Earth being around 3.5 billion years old).

THE MILANKOVITCH CYCLES

There exists further evidence that gravitational effects associated in some manner with Galactic Center have had an impact on the rise and fall of life on

Earth. I say this as our planet experiences what is known as apsidal precession with a periodicity in the range of 112,000 years. Apsidal precession refers to the orbital path defining a planetary object's perihelion—the closest it comes to its host star (in our case the sun)—along with its aphelion, the farthest it gets away from it. This cycle of activity is generally determined by the gravitational effect of not only the sun but also other celestial bodies in the system.

Apsidal precession is just one of several interconnected periodicities referred to by climatologists as the Milankovitch cycles. The name derives from the Serbian geophysicist and astronomer Milutin Milanković (1879–1958). He was the first person to properly determine the impact that the gravitational effects of celestial bodies have on Earth's long-term climate, most obviously the onset and cessation of ice ages.[17] Once again, although this process might seem unrelated to galactic astronomy, geoscientists like Rampino see the Milankovitch cycles as perhaps not unrelated to the Earth's extinction cycle of 32 million years.[18]

If this is correct then it is an interesting supposition, for if you multiply 112,000 years (the duration of one cycle of apsidal precession) by 2,000, you get 224 million years, the length of a cosmic year. What this means is that approximately 2,000 cycles of apsidal precession will occur during the time it takes for the sun to complete one revolution of Galactic Center.

If these idealized values of cyclical division and time durations of what might be called "cosmic fractalization" stand up to scrutiny, it means that the celestial time clock defining Earth's climatic history is but a microcosmic expression of cosmic mechanisms determined by dynamic forces associated with Galactic Center.

That peoples of the past might have had some knowledge of the galaxy's impact on the rise and fall of life on Earth would be ridiculous to suggest. What they did perhaps become aware of, however, was the rhythmic nature of the cosmos and its cyclical influence on the physical world, something that would certainly appear to have been the case during the pioneering years of geological exploration.

In 1795, for instance, in his book *Theory of the Earth*, Scottish geoscientist James Hutton (1726–1797) concluded that within the geological record was evidence of great cycles of destruction and renewal, adding that "these regular events, show us the operation of perfect intelligence forming a design."[19] This deistic approach to geology, popular in the early nineteenth century, largely fell out of favor following the publication in 1830 of a highly influential book titled *Principles of Geology* by Scottish geologist Sir Charles Lyell (1797–1875). He spoke out against rising theories suggesting that nature contained evidence of repeating cycles, comparing such foolish notions with, in his words:

> The philosophical reveries of some Egyptian and Greek sects, who represented all the changes both of the moral and material world as repeated at distant intervals, so as to follow each other in their former connexion of place and time. For they compared the course of events on our globe to astronomical cycles, and not only did they consider all sublunary affairs to be under the influence of the celestial bodies, but they taught that on the earth, as well as in the heavens, the same identical phenomena recurred again and again in a perpetual vicissitude.[20]

In demonstrating that known natural causes could adequately explain Earth's history, Lyell suitably silenced those proposing that sudden and seemingly cyclical changes in the geological record were caused by catastrophic events in Earth's history. His proposed form of gradualism, which is the theory that everything happens very gradually, in slow increments and never through sudden, unexpected episodes, made adherents of catastrophism seem little better than the superstitious astrologers of the past. As we have seen, however, the new geology being posited today by the likes of Michael Rampino and his colleagues shows that Earth really is subject to recurring cycles of growth and decay associated with the solar system's movement around Galactic Center.

IS GOD A SUPERMASSIVE BLACK HOLE?

God does not need to have been involved directly in these actions, although we cannot get away from the fact that the rise and fall of life on Earth might be heavily determined by the presence of a supermassive black hole at the center of the Milky Way galaxy. If so, then are its cyclical actions related to the presence of a sentient being, a living entity, existing in its own right? In other words, is Sagittarius A* sentient?

Such far-reaching ideas are voiced by those who adhere to the concept of panpsychism, the view that individual consciousness is everywhere, even within stars.[21] In a paper titled "Is the Sun Conscious?" published in the *Journal of Consciousness Studies* in 2020, biologist Rupert Sheldrake proposed not only that our sun could be conscious, but also that the supermassive black hole at the center of our galaxy might itself be a sentient being. In his words:

> The sun is influenced by the electro-magnetic patterns of activity within the galaxy as a whole, which could in turn be closely connected with a galactic mind, perhaps centred in or around the supermassive black hole at the galactic centre. The galactic mind could influence what happens here on earth through its effects on the sun and the solar mind.[22]

If the galaxy's supermassive black hole is indeed the source of Sheldrake's proposed "galactic mind," then it can be seen as tied in with the dynamic forces controlling the different oscillation cycles that star systems such as our own experience during the course of a cosmic year. This might force us to reconsider the views of pioneering geologists like James Hutton, who wrote that "these regular events [in the geologic record], show us the operation of perfect intelligence forming a design."[23]

BLACK HOLES BUILD HOST GALAXIES

Although Hutton was quite clearly thinking of the Christian God when he wrote these words, if we substitute "supermassive black hole" for "God" we might be closer to the truth than we realize. Maybe our own localized form of God *is* the supermassive black hole at the center of our Milky Way galaxy. Consider this thought in the knowledge that astrophysicists now believe it possible that supermassive black holes (known officially as active galactic nuclei or AGNs) very probably "build" their own host galaxies through the periodic ejection of highly energetic particles. These are cast out into the interstellar medium by what are known as "relativistic" jets of plasma, which are produced in line with the object's axis of spin. It is proposed that these highly energetic plasma jets, which eject electromagnetic radiation on multiple frequencies, interact with clouds of gas, which leads to the formation of fledgling galaxies.

The blazar HE0450-2958—an active galactic nucleus with a recorded relativistic jet—has been observed forming stars at a rate of around 350 suns per year.[24] Returning to Sagittarius A*, our own galactic nucleus, we know that it produces enormous amounts of plasma and light and is considered the most prolific breeding ground for the formation of new stars anywhere in the galaxy.

This means it was almost certainly responsible for the initial spark that set in motion the creation of the Milky Way galaxy.

With these thoughts in mind, it might indeed be appropriate to see our own supermassive black hole as the creator of our localized region of the material universe. This is not to say we think of this being as God the Father sitting on an interstellar cloud. Far from it; any sentience it might possess could well act in a manner similar to an artificial intelligence programmed to oversee the expansion, maintenance, and cyclical motion of every star system it contains, as each one pirouettes its way around Galactic Center during the course of a cosmic year.

In a more abstract way, this is the story of creation adhered to by members of the Orphic mystery schools and later Ophite Gnostic sects. They appear to have believed in a supernal deity comparable with the Hypercosmic Sun of Neo-Platonic and Mithraic tradition, or the Central Fire of Pythagoreans such as Philolaus, which was thought to occupy the center of the cosmos. The sun behind the sun was said to cast forth its tongues of fire to affect creation in the material universe. So were these tongues of fire simply an intuitive expression of the plasma jets that the supermassive black hole Sagittarius A* projects into the interstellar medium to create the stuff of stars? Did this creation process lead to the gravitational inertia that started the galactic merry-go-round we recognize today as the cosmic year? If so, then there seems no reason why our forebears might not have intuitively interpreted this creative process as the carefully measured act of an all-powerful, all-knowing, omnipotent architect of the universe.

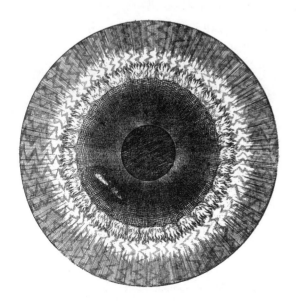

Fig. 33.3. A further illustration by the British polymath and philosopher Robert Fludd (1574–1637) from his work *Utriusque Cosmi* (Fludd 1617, tractatus 1. book II, page 63). It once again shows the manifestation of the material universe from "the primary appearance of created light." It is hard not to see this illustration as a representation of the supermassive black hole at the center of the Milky Way galaxy.

Fig. 33.3 shows how seventeenth-century alchemist and Rosicrucian Robert Fludd envisioned the emergence of "created light" from a supernal sun existing in the primordial darkness. The illustration's likeness to a black hole seems inescapable.

THE POWER OF SEVEN

It should be emphasized once again that the ancients could not have been consciously aware of the cyclical influence of Galactic Center on this world. It is, however, possible that our ancestors were intuitively aware of the cosmological forces that determine our fundamental relationship with Galactic Center, in particular the seven-fold nature of the cosmic year and its fractalization down into more easily recognizable cycles of time. This, I believe, is evidenced in the manner that creation myths repeatedly feature sevenfold symbolism. The Hebrew Bible, for instance, tells us that God created the universe and everything within it in six days, and then rested on the seventh day.[25]

Theologians assume that the biblical concept of the seven days of creation is purely reflective of the fact we have a seven-day week. This, however, is almost certainly not the case, since a sevenfold division of time appears in Sumerian literature, including the recurring importance of "seven days."[26]* Other examples of sevenfold symbolism in creation myths can be cited. In Vedic tradition the universe in its role as the cosmic egg is said to have been surrounded by seven layers.[27] This same sevenfold symbolism appears in the doctrine of the Ophite Gnostics. In his tract *Against the Valentinians*, the Church heresiologist Tertullian (born 160 CE) informs his reader that the Valentinians—the followers of the theologian Valentinus (100–180 CE)—say that on creating the world, the Demiurge, who is a serpent,[28] "completes the sevenfold stages of heaven itself, with his own throne above all."[29] Through this act of creation,

---

*The number seven was considered a mystical number in Sumerian tradition even though there are no explanations for why this should have been. It has been suggested that the number is important because in the Mesopotamian sexagesimal system, seven is the first number that fails to divide the number 60 into a whole number fraction (see Muroi 2014), although whether this is the case remains unclear. There are many examples of the importance of seven as a mystical number in Sumerian, Sumero-Akkadian, and Babylonian texts, including "seven gods," "seven evil gods," "seven planets," "seven censors," "seven (divine) standards," "seven children," "seven days," "seven wisdoms," "seven winds," "the snake with seven tongues," and "festival of the seventh day," as well as the "seventh trial" and "seventh mountain" in the *Epic of Gilgamesh* (see Muroi 2014 for the sources of all these uses of the mystical number seven in Mesopotamian literature.)

Tertullian says, "he [the Demiurge] had the additional name of Sabbatum from the hebdomadal [or sevenfold] nature of his abode. . . . These heavens . . . they consider to be intelligent, and sometimes they make angels [in other words, the seven powers or archons] of them, as indeed they do of the Demiurge himself."[30]

The name of the Demiurge being given as Sabbatum is derived from the Greek word *sabbaton* and the Hebrew *shabbāth* meaning "rest," as in the day on which God rests after creating the world in six days. In Yezidi tradition, after bringing into manifestation the physical universe and all it contains God (Yezidi: Xwadē, Xwadī, or Xudā) creates seven luminous divine emanations, or divine beings, to preside over it, the most important of whom is 'Azazîl. God appoints over them Malak Tâwûs (Yezidi: Tâwûsê Melek), the Peacock Angel. The seven divine emanations are able to incarnate in physical form, with one becoming Sheikh 'Adi (also known as Sheikh 'Adi bin Musafir and in Yezidi Šeyx 'Ādī), the great reformer of the Yezidi religion.

Within the Yezidi open-air sanctuary attached to the abandoned village of Mağaraköy (Kurdish: Kiweh or Kiwex) in the İdil district of Şırnak province, southeastern Turkey, there is an impressive stone shrine topped with seven fluted conical towers, each honoring one of the faith's seven divine beings (see plate 39). On the right side of the sanctuary's walled entrance is a carved representation of the Yezidi black snake, which could well represent the active spirit of the world-encircling snake spoken about in the folklore attached to the Yezidis of Van in eastern Anatolia.

As we saw in chapter 28, the Sethian Gnostic tract titled *The Apocryphon of John* or *The Secret Book of John* informs its reader that Yaldabaoth, the Demiurge, on creating Adam, the First Man, endowed him with the seven powers of the seven rulers so that they might have control over human destiny.[31] The seven rulers are themselves expressions of the seven planets, which through their influence on the 12 signs of the zodiac were seen to rule over every part of the human body.[32]

Among the Harranians it was the Primal Cause, Shamal, who brought into manifestation the Seven Stars (or seven planets) and the 12 signs of the zodiac. Among the sun-worshipping Shemsi, the branch of the Nusayris of Syria whose point of origin was almost certainly Harran, Shamal was "the sun in its nocturnal course,"[33] a reference seemingly to the concept of a supernal sun existing in the primordial darkness from where it casts forth its tongues of fire to create the physical universe.

OPHION AND THE PELASGIAN CREATION MYTH

By far the best-preserved association between sevenfold symbolism, cosmic creation, and the Great Serpent is the foundation myth of the Pelasgians, the extremely ancient, pre-Hellenic inhabitants of Greece. It features the "great serpent" Ophion (a name simply meaning "serpent"), who is said to have ruled the world with his mother Eurinome during an epoch before even the coming of the god Cronus, the supercelestial creator god of Orphic tradition.

Eurinome (or Eurynome) was said to have been the Goddess of All Things. She emerged naked out of the primary chaos but having done so found nothing solid on which she could place her feet. So she divided the sky from the sea and "wove a single dance on the waves" and began the "work of creation."[34] The Pelasgian creation myth then continues by saying that Eurinome "grabbed coldest North Wind and rubbed her hands, and behold, the great serpent Ophion [appeared]." Thereafter, we are told:

> Eurinome danced to keep warm, dancing with the rhythm more and more wild until Ophion, on desire, wrapped her in its coils the limbs of the goddess and they mated. . . . And so Eurinome became pregnant. Now she, flying over the sea, took the form of a dove and, time debit [or time passed], laid the Universal Egg. By order of the goddess, Ophion rolled *seven times around the egg*, until it hatched and brought forth all things that exist, daughters of Eurinome: the Sun, the Moon, the Planets, the Stars, the Earth with its mountains, with its rivers, with its trees and herbs and living creatures. . . . The goddess then created the seven planetary powers and placed at the head of each of them a Titan and a Titaness.[35]* (Current author's emphasis.)

This quite remarkable creation myth bears some similarities to Orphic cosmogony, which also involves the creation of an egg through the intervention of a cosmic serpent. In the Pelasgian account, however, Ophion rolls around this "Universal Egg" seven times in order to hatch it (see fig. 33.4). This action

---

*The Titans were the pre-Olympian gods of Greece, with their female counterparts being the Titanides or Titanesses. There were six male Titans, including Cronus, and six female Titanesses, making 12 in all. In Greek myth the Titans were considered the offspring of Ouranos and Gaia, hence their title, the Uranides.

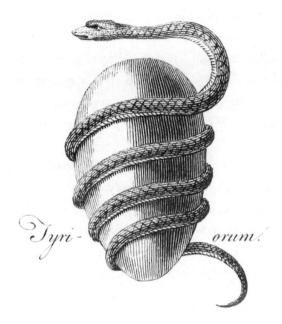

Fig. 33.4. The "Universal Egg" of Pelasgian tradition with the serpent Ophion wrapped around it. Illustration from *A New System, or, An Analysis of Ancient Mythology* (vol. II, plate iv) written by Jacob Bryant (1715–1804) and published in 1774. Engraving by James Basire (1730–1802).

brings forth everything within the material universe including the "seven planetary powers," paralleling the Ophite Gnostic concept of the emergence of the seven powers or archons and the Harranian (and thus Chaldean) belief in Shamal bringing forth the influence of the seven planets and 12 zodiacal constellations. Can Ophion's rolling motion thus be seen as a reflection of the sevenfold cyclical nature of Earth's participation in cosmic cycles governed by Galactic Center? It seems indeed possible.

CLUE TO THE LUWIAN SCRIPT

The important point about the Pelasgian creation myth is that it could be the oldest and thus the least tainted of all the accounts of the manifestation of the physical universe in a sevenfold manner as well as the involvement of the Great Serpent in this process. We can say this for there seems every chance that the Pelasgians, although considered the pre-Hellenic inhabitants of Greece, came originally from Anatolia, something hinted at in the knowledge that their language appears to have been a form of Luwian (pronounced *loo-we-an*). This is an archaic language (linked with modern-day Albanian) used extensively by the Bronze Age and later Iron Age inhabitants of Anatolia and northern Syria, circa 2000–600 BCE.[36]

A connection between the Luwian language and the Pelasgians (whose name, by the way, means "followers of the stork" due to their various peregrinations) is important for one vitally important reason. Historical researcher Manu Seyfzadeh and Boston geologist Robert Schoch have drawn a number of comparisons between the Luwian hieroglyphic script and carved glyphs seen on T-pillars at Göbekli Tepe (particularly one that matches the Luwian sign for "god").[37*]

Despite the enormous difference in time periods between Anatolia's Taş Tepeler civilization and the Bronze Age peoples of Greece and Anatolia, I firmly believe that the findings of Seyfzadeh and Schoch are indeed valid. The Luwian language and the peoples associated with it, the Pelasgians in particular, might well hold important clues regarding the emergence of what could constitute the world's first hieroglyphic script seen today at sites like Göbekli Tepe and Karahan Tepe.

LUWIAN CLUES AT DELPHI

Important to this current debate is the fact that along with the Luwian language's conveyance from Anatolia into Greece by the time of the Bronze Age, there might also have been a transmission of cosmological beliefs regarding the cyclic nature of the universe, along with its sevenfold symbolism, and the intervention of a cosmic serpent in this creation process.

A number of place names in Greece hint at the preexistence of an extremely important culture that might well have established key cult centers, including Delphi, where traces of human occupation go back to the Neolithic Age.[38] This culture has been identified as Pelasgian in nature.[39] In addition to this, there are clear indications that the pre-Hellenic Greeks of the region spoke a form of Luwian,[40] forcing us to consider the possibility that the Oracle as a sanctuary long predated the arrival of the Hellenic Greeks.

Was Delphi's oracular shrine originally established by a Luwian-speaking community whose ancestors had begun their journey as far east as Anatolia? Had that community acknowledged the importance of female priestesses as vessels for a supernatural entity in the form of a serpent, one that would even-

---

*Prior to the work of Seyfzadeh and Schoch (2019) researcher JJ Ainsworth posted on social media (November 19, 2015) tentative links between the glyphs seen on Göbekli Tepe T-pillars and matching Luwian logograms (including the sign for "god").

tually be symbolically "slain" by the incoming, more male-dominated, cult of the god Apollo? If this really is what happened in the lead-up to the role played by the Pythia at Delphi, then was it possible that the site's Luwian-speaking Pelasgian community had their roots in the Taş Tepeler world of southeastern Anatolia? The fact that both locations probably saw individuals being possessed by a spirit in the form of a snake to make oracular pronouncements tends to suggest the answer could be yes.

SEVENFOLD SYMBOLISM AND GÖBEKLI TEPE

Confirmation of the Taş Tepeler culture's apparent interest in recognizable sevenfold symbolism comes from Göbekli Tepe. On the front edge of the rock-cut, rectangular plinth that supports Pillar 18 in Enclosure D, seven strange-looking birds are shown in high relief (see fig. 33.5). They stand in line facing westward toward the direction of sunset.

Accounts of cosmic creation and cosmic time cycles often feature seven birds. There are the seven swans that draw the creator god Brahma in Vedic myth and the seven geese of Chumash tradition that fly into the night sky and

Fig. 33.5. The seven seemingly flightless birds on the front edge of the rock-cut plinth supporting Enclosure D's Pillar 18 at Göbekli Tepe. Photo by Andrew Collins.

become the seven stars of the Big Dipper, an asterism seen by many ancient cultures as a kind of cosmic crank handle responsible for turning the nearby celestial pole. By far the most enigmatic association between seven birds and cosmic time is found in Great Britain, where folktales speak of the Seven Whistlers, occasionally described as the "seven geese."

It is said that if the call of the Seven Whistlers is heard at night, it portends a coming disaster. Their myth, however, finds its fullest form in the English county of Shropshire in association with an ominous hill composed almost entirely of black quartzite and known as Stiperstones.[41] According to the story, one of the whistlers became detached from the main group, and since then the remaining six birds have flown around the slopes of the hill looking for their lost companion. It is said that should they ever catch up with it, the end of the world will surely follow.[42]

The Seven Whistlers story is a prime example of what might be described as a universal expression of sevenfold creation (the appearance of the Seven Whistlers), involving cyclical time (the seven birds flying around the hill) and eventual entropy (the loss of one of the birds, its six companions trying without success to find it, and the belief that should ever this occur the end of the world will follow).

Similar ideas are, I believe, behind the appearance of the seven birds seen on the plinth supporting Enclosure D's Pillar 18 at Göbekli Tepe. This seems especially so in the knowledge that this blatantly anthropomorphic pillar has a carved belt buckle showing what appears to be a three-pronged comet, immediately beneath which is the relief of a fox pelt loincloth.

As I demonstrate in *Göbekli Tepe: Genesis of the Gods* (2014), the fox is a universal symbol of the cosmic trickster, with its tail representative of cataclysms brought about by the appearance of comets in our skies.[43] Therefore, we can imagine the seven birds seen on the plinth supporting Pillar 18 as emblematic of cosmic creation, sevenfold cyclical time, and eventual entropy and destruction, which in the case of Göbekli Tepe would be an allusion to the Younger Dryas impact event.

IŠHARA AND SEVENFOLD SYMBOLISM

Bringing the concept of sevenfold symbolism in the act of cosmic creation even closer to Anatolia is the fact that the goddess Išhara was said to have brought

Fig. 33.6. Kudurru boundary stone showing an arched serpent, perhaps representing the Milky Way, beneath which is the scorpion ᵐᵘˡGIR.TAB, identified with the goddess Išhara and the star Antares in Scorpius. Next to the scorpion are seven stars signifying the Sebitti, "the seven" or "group of seven." These have been identified with the star cluster known as the Pleiades. Photo by Andrew Collins.

forth the Sebitti or Sebittu, meaning "the seven" or the "group of seven."[44] Even though Babylonian mythology imagines the Sebitti as seven gods of war, their sevenfold nature suggests they originally formed part of a much older myth associating Išhara with sevenfold creation.

On kudurru boundary stones from the Kassite period of Babylonian rule (see chapter 20), the scorpion representing both Išhara and the stars of Scorpius is invariably shown directly beneath an arched serpent, signifying, in my opinion, the Milky Way (see fig. 33.6). Next to the scorpion, seven dots are grouped together in a manner suggesting they are representative of the Sebitti. In astronomical terms, these seven dots are usually identified with the cluster of seven stars in the constellation of Taurus known as the Pleiades.[45]

If Išhara can be associated with cosmic creation, then it shows that her existence is not only extremely ancient, but also that she can be seen as a perfect expression of Galactic Center's sevenfold influence on the world through her association with the nearby Scorpius constellation. Interestingly, the inhabitants of Išhara's Bronze Age cult center at Kizzuwatna in southern-central Anatolia spoke a form of Luwian,[46] perhaps showing their own descendance from the region's highly advanced Taş Tepeler culture.

If Išhara does signify the creative forces of Galactic Center, then we must also now reconsider the role played by the Shahmaran, the Snake Mother of Anatolian folklore. She is said to have had seven snake heads, six at the end of her six legs and a seventh at the end of her serpentine tail. Her sevenfold nature connects her not only with the goddess Išhara, but also with the creatrix Eurinome featured in the Pelasgian creation myth. In this manner the Shahmaran can herself be seen as a reflection of the Milky Way serpent's sevenfold influence on the world.

THE NUMBER 32 AS A MEASURE OF TIME

The connection with the Anatolian Snake Mother brings us back to the Karahan community's own apparent interest in the Galactic Bulge, which its astronomer shamans appear to have recognized as the head and thus the mind and intelligence of the Milky Way serpent. Did they also become aware that the Milky Way galaxy's impact on the solar system could be recognized not just in terms of sevenfold cycles of activity, but also how the number 32, as a measure of time, is reflective of the periods of oscillation involved in the solar system's passage around Galactic Center during a cosmic year? Seven, as we have seen, defines the divisional relationship between Earth's biodiversity cycles of 32 million years and a cosmic year of 224 million years.

Were cycles of time featuring the number 32 intuitively understood by the ancients who incorporated these numbers into their myths of creation, just as they did the number seven? We have seen how the numbers 16 and 32 feature prominently in the symbolism of the alabaster bowl, where they relate, respectively, to the number of mystai involved with the Gnostic mystical rite and the number of tongues of fire emerging from the double wreath of rays symbolizing the supernal sun existing in the primordial darkness. We have seen, too, how, in the cosmological symbolism of both Hindu and Buddhist mysticism, the number 32 plays an important role (see chapter 28).

Did our ancestors become intuitively aware of how certain key numbers, most obviously 7 and 32, were important to the cosmic mechanisms governing the rhythmic cycles of life and how this was reflected in macrocosm out there in the cosmos?

The community at Karahan Tepe was, I suspect, able to intuitively grasp such profound cosmological ideas regarding the importance of the center of the Milky Way galaxy and the fractalization of its mechanical effects on the world. However, by the time Karahan Tepe was abandoned circa 8000 BCE, the midsummer sun no longer synchronized with Galactic Center. Indeed, the world would have to wait many thousands of years for the next time it would align with one of the solstices, and when this did finally happen, half a precessional cycle later, it occurred not at the time of the summer solstice but as the sun rose on the day of the *winter* solstice. This momentous occasion came on December 21, 2012, a date some of us will remember very well. Why that date sticks in the memory has, as we see next, *everything* to do with what might have been happening at Karahan Tepe and why this galactic alignment remains important today.

34

Maya Cosmogenesis

December 21, 2012, as many of us will recall, was the end date of the Mayan Long Count calendar. Consisting of 13 baktuns, each 144,000 days or 394.26 tropical years in length,[1] the Long Count was most probably created in the Mexican state of Chiapas in the first century BCE. It was then backdated to begin on August 11, 3114 BCE, so that it could end 5,125 years (13 baktuns) later on December 21, 2012.[2] It cannot be coincidence that five of these 13 baktun cycles equal 25,625 years. This is remarkably close to the length of one precessional cycle of Earth's axis of around 25,800 years, suggesting that the Maya were very much aware of the concept of precession.[3]

It was at Izapa—an extensive pre-Columbian archaeological site in Chiapas, founded during the culture's Formative Period (2000 BCE–250 CE) and existing as a thriving city during the Classic Period (250 CE–900 CE)—that the Long Count appears for the first time.[4] So it is interesting that at Izapa we find evidence of an interest in Galactic Center, along with alignments of key monuments toward sunrise on the winter solstice.[5]

At Izapa we see pictorial representations of a cosmic tree or celestial "crossroads"[6] identified as the point at which the sun crosses the Milky Way coincident to the southern termination of the Dark Rift.[7] Mayan cosmologist John Major Jenkins (1964–2017) came to realize that the relief carvings at Izapa indicated that winter solstice alignments there did not reflect the site's age of construction, but instead looked forward to the much-anticipated synchronization between the solstitial sun and the Galactic Bulge. This would take place at the culmination of the 13-baktun cycle on December 21, 2012, which was seen as a coming time of great transformation and rebirth.[8]

Relief carvings on standing stelae at the site depict scenes from the

Popol Vuh, the sacred text of the K'iche' (Spanish: Quiché) Maya of the Guatemalan highlands.[9] This records the journey of the Hero Twins Hunahpu and Xbalanque, who enter onto the Xibalba Be, or Road to Xibalba (or the "Black Road"), identified with the Milky Way's Dark Rift.[10] Their aim is to avenge the murder of their father One Hunahpu, which will signal the return of the sun at the time of the 2012 solstitial alignment with Galactic Center.[11]

Jenkins's quite astounding ideas with respect to the Mayan civilization's knowledge of astronomy feature in his 1998 book *Maya Cosmogenesis 2012*.[12] In this he provides compelling evidence that to the Maya the Galactic Bulge was a place of cosmic creation. It was also seen as a pregnant womb, a place of anchoring time, and a portal through which human beings either achieved incarnation or entered the afterlife.[13] In his later work titled *Galactic Alignment*, published in 2002, Jenkins provides much additional evidence to suggest that various ancient cultures around the world recognized the Galactic Bulge as a place of cosmic creation, and even as a cosmic serpent.[14]

The discovery, however, that Karahan Tepe's Pit Shrine was aligned to the last time the solstitial sun synchronized with Galactic Center implies that the site's Taş Tepeler inhabitants were thinking along the same lines as the Maya of Central America. In other words, the two civilizations must have shared common cosmological beliefs and spiritual aspirations.

For the Mayan shaman astronomers, the two arms of the Milky Way created by the Dark Rift were the massive jaws of a sky creature identified with the Milky Way itself. The creature in question was identified as a caiman or crocodile,[15] a great snake,[16] a jaguar,[17] and even as a great toad.[18] This echoes the Karahan community's suspected interpretation of the Galactic Bulge as the head of the world-encircling serpent with the stars of Scorpius as its active spirit.

That the astronomical traditions of the Maya of Central America and the Taş Tepeler people of southeastern Anatolia were aligned seems important. The connection, however, cannot have been direct. The two civilizations existed several thousand years apart and on different continents so there cannot have been any direct contact between them. Despite this, both cultures appear to have recognized the Galactic Bulge as a source of cosmic creation— the Karahan community probably by inheriting long-standing traditions that went back to 10,800 BCE, when the synchronization between the summer solstice and Galactic Center was probably first recognized. The Maya, on the

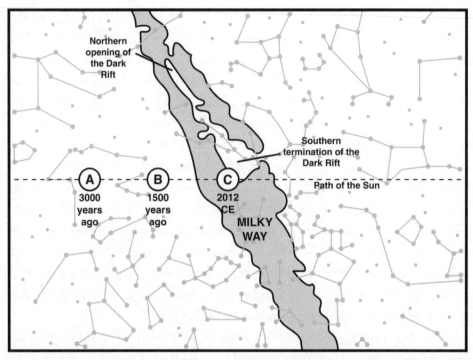

Fig. 34.1. The progress of the midwinter sun as it has gradually synchronized with Galactic Center across the past 5,000 years, this being the approximate length of one complete 13-baktun cycle of the Mayan Long Count calendar (after Jenkins 1998, fig. 51). Image by Nick Burton.

other hand, appear to have gained their interest in this area of the sky through careful astronomical observation across a considerable length of time. It is unfortunate that the kings and astronomer priests of the Maya, who had been looking toward this important moment in time for as much as 2,000 years, were not around to see the solstitial sun synchronized with Galactic Center on December 21, 2012 (see fig. 34.1 for a diagram of the midwinter sun's progress toward Galactic Center up until 2012).[19]

Even though it was widely publicized that the 2012 solstitial alignment with Galactic Center was a one-off event, this is not strictly true.

The sun will still be in the proximity of Galactic Center at the time of the winter solstice for many centuries to come, something we should be aware of as we strive to understand the extraordinarily advanced mindset of Anatolia's Taş Tepeler inhabitants. Right now, the sun comes closest to Galactic Center at the moment it exits the constellation of Ophiuchus and enters Sagittarius, an event that occurs on December 17/18 each year. This is, of course, 3 days prior to the winter solstice, although very clearly the combined influence of the Galactic Center—in its capacity as the Hypercosmic Sun of the supercelestial realm—and its synchronization with our own regular sun will, I am sure, remain strong at this time for many decades to come.

A few minutes after dawn on the winter solstice at Karahan Tepe, the sun begins to cast its rays through a porthole window into the Pillars Shrine, where the giant stone head with its extended serpentine neck is suddenly illuminated by a vertical dagger of golden light. The head appears to quite literally come alive, something observed for the first time in the modern era by Hugh Newman and JJ Ainsworth on December 20, 2021. It is as well to remember that as this solar spectacle begins to take place the sun is synchronized near perfectly with the supermassive black hole at the center of our galaxy, exactly as it was at the time of the summer solstice in the tenth and eleventh millennium BCE. It might thus be seen as strangely serendipitous that these rock-hewn structures should be exposed only when the solstitial sun once again aligns with this same area of the sky.

As JJ and Hugh openly admit, without my discovery of the Pit Shrine's summer solstice alignment two months before their first visit to Karahan Tepe, they might never have been drawn to make their own incredible discovery. Indeed, Karahan Tepe's winter solstice alignment might have gone unnoticed forever, especially with plans for the excavations to be housed beneath a roof even more elaborate than that seen today at Göbekli Tepe.

The casting of the first light of the sun on the giant head inside the Pillars Shrine on the winter solstice has, we can only but imagine, awakened the spirit of the Great Serpent identified with the Galactic Bulge and the stars of Scorpius. We don't know what the Karahan community might have called this supercelestial being whose head and active spirit would appear to have corresponded with the center of the Milky Way galaxy. What we do know, however, is that during much later ages this same cosmic force, in its guise as the Great Serpent, would come to be identified variously as Nabu the Announcer, the god Apollo, the goddess Išhara (and through her the Shahmaran of Anatolian folk tradition), and even, as we see next, the Serpent that tempted Adam and Eve in the Garden of Eden.

35

In the Realm of Adam

Does mental interaction with a supermassive black hole at the center of our own local galaxy really enable a connection with the divine? Did ancient peoples come to recognize the existence of a creative force existing in this area of the sky—one that they saw as having a powerful impact on the rise and fall of life on Earth?

For the inhabitants of Karahan Tepe, it was perhaps a strange amalgam of both these possibilities. By this I mean that the synchronized alignment between the sun at midsummer and the perceived head of the Milky Way serpent was seen as a divinely inspired point of synchronization with the mind or intelligence of this perceived cosmic entity.

Biologist Rupert Sheldrake has proposed that if Sagittarius A*—the name given by astronomers to the supermassive black hole at the center of the galaxy—is conscious, then it could be the source of a "galactic mind" that affects life on Earth. If this is truly the case, then perhaps we really should be considering the possibility that some peoples of the past came to recognize this dynamic force as evidence for the existence of a single omnipotent god behind all creation. What is suspected to have been going on at Karahan Tepe might thus have had some impact on the concept of a monotheistic god that was able to create the universe in just seven days, echoing the seven-fold, cyclic motion of the solar system as its revolves around Galactic Center. If this is correct then it begs the question of whether activities at Taş Tepeler sites in southeastern Anatolia could have influenced the mythical origins of the three main Abrahamic faiths—Judaism, Christianity, and Islam.

IN THE GARDEN OF EDEN

One thing that seems clear from the outset is that southeastern and eastern Anatolia, along with the Middle Euphrates Valley of northern Syria, can be considered the cradle of human civilization. So many firsts for humanity occurred in these regions that this seems undeniable. The earliest agriculture, the earliest animal husbandry, the earliest construction of rectilinear buildings, the earliest fermenting of beer and wine, the earliest appearance of metallurgy, the earliest manufacture of textiles, and the earliest use of a system of hieroglyphs all occurred there.[1] This tells us that the Taş Tepeler culture possessed the necessary sophistication and infrastructure to be truly classified as the world's first post–Ice Age civilization.

It cannot be coincidence then that all this was happening in a part of the world that the Hebrew Bible's book of Genesis tells us was the location of the terrestrial paradise where God placed Adam and Eve, the First Man and First Woman, following the creation of the world. This paradise was said to have been located where a "river . . . going out from Eden to water the garden" splits to become four "chief rivers"—the Pison, the Gibon [or Gihon], the Hiddekel (Tigris), and the Phrat (Euphrates).[2]

Since medieval times, theologians, historians, and, more recently, archaeologists have been happy to accept that the Garden of Eden was located in southern Iraq's Basra province, where the rivers Tigris and Euphrates converge to become the 120-mile (200-kilometer) waterway known as the Shatt al-Arab. That might be so; however, in books such as *From the Ashes of Ashes* (1996), *Gods of Eden* (1998), *Göbekli Tepe: Genesis of the Gods* (2014), and *The Cygnus Key* (2018), I provide ample historical and geographical evidence to ably demonstrate that the true site of the Garden of Eden was located not where these two great rivers empty into the Persian Gulf but *where they take their rise* in southeastern and eastern Anatolia.[3]

Two of the rivers of Paradise can be easily identified. They are, of course, the Tigris and the Euphrates, both of which rise in the mountains of eastern Turkey. The other two rivers, the Gihon and Pison,[4] are almost certainly, respectively, the Araxes, which rises close to the slopes of Bingöl Dağları (Bingöl Mountain) in the Armenian Highlands of eastern Turkey before flowing eastward into the Caspian Sea, and the Greater Zab. This rises in the east of the country before flowing through the Zagros Mountains and entering northern

Iraq, where it eventually joins the River Tigris. The ancient Nestorian Church has long recognized the Greater Zab as being the Pison of biblical tradition.[5]

This tells us that the place where human civilization emerged in monotheistic tradition can quite easily be equated with what is today southeastern and eastern Turkey. Indeed, there have long been historical and ethnographical indications that all the key events in the book of Genesis, from the age of Adam all the way down to the life of Abraham and his immediate family, occurred in southeastern and eastern Anatolia.[6] This surmise is supported by the existence of various legends that speak of the Garden of Eden as having once existed in this region. One story, for instance, says the terrestrial paradise was drowned beneath the rising waters of Lake Van following the Great Flood.[7] Another story speaks of an offshoot of the Tree of Life from the Garden of Eden being grown into a great tree by the monks of an Armenian monastery located in mountains beyond the city of Mush in eastern Turkey (the quest to find this lost monastery is outlined in *Göbekli Tepe: Genesis of the Gods*).[8]

The Place of Descent

It should also be pointed out that the best candidate by far for what is known in theological terms as the Place of Descent, the mountaintop on which the Ark of Noah came to rest after the waters had receded at the time of the Great Flood, is Mount Judi (Turkish: Cudi Dağı) in eastern Anatolia, which is approximately 170 miles (273.5 kilometers) east-northeast of Karahan Tepe. Since late antiquity, the mountain has been acknowledged in this role by Jews, Syrian Christians, Muslims, and Kurds alike. Claims that Mount Ararat (Turkish: Ağrı Dağı), situated in the extreme eastern part of Anatolia, close to the border with neighboring Armenia, is the Place of Descent go back only to the fifth century CE and appear to have come about due to the fierce rivalry that existed at this time between the Syrian Church and the Armenian Church.[9]

THE STORY OF ADAM AND EVE

Such legends tell us that the Indigenous peoples of the region, whether they be Jewish, Christian, Muslim, or Kurdish, have all firmly believed that the Garden of Eden, as the place of emergence of humanity, and the Place of Descent, in its role as the place of humanity's reemergence in the aftermath of the Great Flood, both existed in either southeastern or eastern Anatolia.

How then might stories of Adam and Eve and the Garden of Eden be important to the emergence of Taş Tepeler as much as 6,000 years *before* the Hebrew Bible tells us God created the world?

Condensing human history to fit the narrative of the book of Genesis is something that has long stilted our understanding of the first appearance of civilization in the Near East, since, according to biblical chronology, Adam, the First Man, was created in 4004 BCE, while the flood of Noah is said to have taken place in 2348 BCE (see fig. 35.1). Only by completely ignoring these conflated chronologies, which would never have been important

Fig. 35.1. Adam and Eve in the terrestrial paradise, from *Adams Synchronological Chart or Map of History* of 1871. Note the accompanying biblical chronology that gives 4004 BCE as the date of creation.

to the Indigenous peoples of southeastern and eastern Turkey anyway, can we start to make sense of the kernels of information contained in the stories surrounding Adam and Eve in local legend. Before exploring these, however, we need to understand what the Hebrew Bible tells us about the First Man and the First Woman.

The book of Genesis says that after creating the world God made the terrestrial paradise and placed within it a man named Adam and afterward a woman named Eve. They live together in harmony until one day a serpent convinces Eve and through her, Adam, that they should eat of the forbidden fruit of the Tree of the Knowledge of Good and Evil.[10] God has forbidden them to do this on pains that they will die if they do. But the Serpent tells them they will not die, so Adam and Eve eat of the fruit of the tree and immediately become aware that they are naked.[11]

Fig. 35.2. Engraving by French engraver Nicolas Chaperon (circa 1612–1656) depicting Adam and Eve's expulsion from the terrestrial paradise (from Chaperon 1649, plate 7).

God is naturally very angry at this disobedience and asks Adam and Eve who has told them it is okay to eat of the Tree of the Knowledge of Good and Evil. They say the Serpent, throwing all blame on the appearance of this creature. Due to their evil actions, and to ensure the couple do not eat of the other tree in the garden, the Tree of Life, and live forever, God casts them out (see fig. 35.2).[12] Adam and Eve then set up anew beyond the terrestrial paradise, where they must now "eat bread" and till the land until they "return to the ground."[13]

For most people, the biblical narrative regarding the transgressions of Adam and Eve is no more than an allegorical tale about the consequences of disobedience and how a woman can succumb to the temptations of evil. Such outdated views were created by a dominantly patriarchal society that long postdated the events being described in the book of Genesis. What if, however, some parts of the story of Adam and Eve in the Garden of Eden really do have a basis in historical reality? What can this tell us about what might have been going on in southeastern Anatolia as early as the tenth millennium BCE?

THE FIRST KAABA

During my first visit to Şanlıurfa in 2004, I began to hear stories regarding the prophet Abraham's early life in the city, and his encounters with the wicked tyrant Nimrod, the builder of the Tower of Babel in the book of Genesis. I also heard snippets of information regarding Adam being connected with Şanlıurfa. I had listened with interest to these accounts without coming to any real conclusions. This was until December 21, 2022, a year and a day after Hugh Newman and JJ Ainsworth had first witnessed Karahan Tepe's winter solstice alignment (see the appendix for a full account of Hugh and JJ's discoveries in their own words).

Just after midday, I was standing inside the Şanlıurfa Archaeological Museum within the incredible, full-sized reconstruction of Göbekli Tepe's Enclosure D. With me were my Turkish friends Ufuk Bölükbaşı and Neslihan Tokat, along with Hugh Newman, who had just returned from once again recording the illumination of the giant stone head inside Karahan Tepe's Pillars Shrine (I was able to witness this spectacle twice during my visit there in December 2022). It was then that a woman, a lifelong resident of Şanlıurfa, approached us and, speaking in Turkish, started to relay information to my friends that I quickly realized was of great importance to understanding how

Fig. 35.3. The full-size reproduction of Göbekli Tepe's Enclosure D inside the Şanlıurfa Archaeological Museum, showing the author between the two gigantic monoliths at its center. Photo by Andrew Collins.

the activities of the inhabitants of the Taş Tepeler sites locally might have been preserved in local folklore.

The woman, whose name was Naz, had been told when just a child that God had instructed the prophet Abraham to erect two pillars, which became the first Kaaba, the most important of all Islamic holy shrines. This is located in the Grand Mosque at Mecca in Saudi Arabia and is visited each year by as many as 2.5 million people taking part in the *hajj*, the holy pilgrimage that all Muslims are obliged to do as least once in their lifetime. The woman asked whether it was possible that the *original* Kaaba could have been Göbekli Tepe, which also has two almighty pillars, fiberglass reproductions of which we were standing beneath as this conversation was taking place (see fig. 35.3).

It was an intriguing and highly imaginative proposition, and, should it ever be considered that the Kaaba might have had a previous location, then looking toward an age-old site like Göbekli Tepe, located close to the traditional site of the Garden of Eden, makes perfect sense.

One of Şanlıurfa's ancient names is el-Ruha. It is Aramaic and means "the soul" or "the spirit." Local tradition says it refers to the manner in which God made the First Man, Adam, and then endowed him with a soul, after which he was placed in the terrestrial paradise, located somewhere in the vicinity of Şanlıurfa.

Adam's association with the area is further emphasized by the city's oldest attested name, which is Aramaic Adma', Syriac Adme, or Hebrew Adamah, all meaning "red," "red ground," or "red earth."[14] It refers to the severe red earth of the nearby Harran plain, which lies immediately to the east and south of the city. The term is cognate with to the Hebrew word Adam, which means "red," "reddy," or "to be red,"[15] implying that the earth on which the First Man was given life was blood red in color. Thus, Adamah as a place name refers to the location where God created Adam using the blood-red earth found to this day on the nearby Harran Plain.

ADAM AND EVE'S INVENTION OF AGRICULTURE

In a separate legend, God is said to have given Adam the Black Stone, which would afterward become the main focus of worship at the Kaaba. Adam was ordered to erect the First Altar to house this precious holy relic, which following his death was given into the custodianship of his third son, Seth. The Black Stone was then lost during the flood of Noah and only rediscovered when the location of the First Altar was revealed to Abraham by the angel Jibrā'īl (Gabriel).[16] Despite these stories surrounding the Black Stone and the establishment of the First Altar becoming attached with the Kaaba in Mecca, could they have originated in Şanlıurfa? Was the Black Stone, perhaps a meteorite of some kind, connected in some way with the city's role as both the place of Adam and the birthplace of Abraham?

The woman we met in the museum, however, had more to say on the subject of Adam's presence locally. She pointed out that after Adam departed the terrestrial paradise, he established the first farm at what is today Harran, inventing agriculture in the process. The connection here with Harran is highly significant and has long been known to the peoples of the region. Indeed, one version of the story relates how, after departing the Garden of Eden, Adam and Eve enter the Harran Plain, which at the time was "like a corner of Paradise."[17] There they settle and are soon struck by the beauty of the fragrant flowers, the tall plants, the chirping of birds, and the power of a wondrous tree set in the midst of it all.[18]

You see, Adam had brought with him out of Paradise a red pomegranate and a "white rose branch," which he and Eve plant on the plain. This causes the plants to grow to head height, flowers to bloom either with red or with white flowers—their colors honoring the heavenly nature of the red pomegranate and white rose—while the white rose branch grows into a mighty tree.

Encouraged by these miracles, Adam sets forth to plow the ground, but what were they to grow? The book *Şanlıurfa: The City of Civilizations Where Prophets Met*, edited by Alparslan Açıkgenç and Abdullah Ekinci and published in 2017, provides the answer:

> While thinking what to plant, Eve opened the palm of her hand to find a grain of wheat she had brought from Heaven. With delight, they got to work.[19]

Thereafter Adam fashions a plow from a branch of the white rose tree and with Eve's assistance they plow the land. The task they have given themselves, however, proves to be enormous (see fig. 35.4). The harvest the first year is small, and each year they have the same problem until one day, in the noontime heat, a "yellow ox directed its horns toward the plow,"[20] causing it to move with relative ease.

In delight Adam kisses the ox's eyes, after which we are told:

> Every start at plowing was preceded by a grateful kiss. According to popular belief, the Plain of Harran is the site where the first person stepped onto the earth, and the place where the earth was plowed and oxen worked the land for the first time. The sacredness of wheat, the white rose, and pomegranate stems from their being brought from Paradise. Even today, the ongoing tradition of the farmers' kissing of the oxen dates back to the time of Adam.[21]

So we find that not only did Adam and Eve invent agriculture, but they also grew the first wheat! This remarkable fact now becomes of paramount importance to our understanding of Taş Tepeler's participation in the birth of agriculture. Not only does the earliest evidence for the domestication of wild cattle come from the Pre-Pottery Neolithic sites of Çayönü in southeastern Anatolia,[22] and Dja'de in the Middle Euphrates Valley of north-

Fig. 35.4. Having left the terrestrial paradise Adam and Eve
now till the land, planting the first crops, including, according to tradition,
the first wheat (from Foster [1873] 1897).

ern Syria,[23] but genetic research has also now determined the true origins of domesticated wheat.

As many as 68 modern strains, used to make everything from bread to beer, pasta, and cakes, can be traced back to a type of wild wheat called einkorn that grows to this day on the slopes of a mountain named Karaca Dağ (pronounced *ka-ra-je-dah*),[24] meaning that this region has to be the place of emergence of domesticated wheat.

Karaca Dağ is an extinct volcano located some 68.5 miles (110 kilometers) northeast of the city of Harran and around 50 miles (80 kilometers) east-northeast of Göbekli Tepe. On a clear day you can see Karaca Dağ from Göbekli Tepe. It can also be seen from the top of Zakzuk Dağı, which lies immediately to the north of Karahan Tepe (see chapter 12).

Thus we can say that wheat was first domesticated and widely grown in the very same region that the Taş Tepeler culture established their own vast network of settlements and cult centers, this occurring at the same time that agriculture first appears in southeastern Anatolia. So there has to be a very real chance that folk traditions relating to how Adam and Eve grew the first wheat on the Harran Plain are in fact abstract memories not only of the earliest domestication of einkorn by the region's Taş Tepeler culture, but also perhaps of the first use of wild cattle to help plow the land.

That the Taş Tepeler culture was responsible for the earliest known widespread cultivation of wheat is not in doubt. At Göbekli Tepe, for instance, large stone vats used to brew beer have been found in structures dating from the Early to Middle Pre-Pottery Neolithic B period. Traces of chemicals known to form during the beer production process have been detected within their interiors.[25]

So if the local folk traditions regarding Adam cultivating the first wheat at Harran can be seen as a memory of the first widespread use of einkorn by the Taş Tepeler culture, then perhaps we should look again at the story regarding Abraham's rediscovery of the Black Stone and the First Altar, and his erection in front of the altar of twin pillars. Is it possible that these legendary twin pillars are not so much based on those that stand to this day at the center of Göbekli Tepe's Enclosure D, but are in fact the memory of twin sets of T-pillars of the type that might once have been present in or around Şanlıurfa itself?

What is more, the twin pillars raised by Abraham are surely the same as the twin pillars the antediluvian patriarch Enoch, an ancestor of Abraham, is said to have set up to preserve the arts and sciences prior to the Great Flood.[26] A similar set of twin pillars, one made of brick and the other made of stone (see fig. 35.5), are said to have been set up by Seth, the third son of Adam, to preserve the arts and sciences of heaven prior to a major cataclysm where the world "was to be destroyed at one time by the force of fire, and at another time by the violence and quantity of water."[27]

These are the words of the Jewish writer Flavius Josephus (37–100 CE) in his work *The Antiquities of the Jews*. He adds that the pillars of Seth were to be found in "Siriad,"[28] in other words, Syria or, more correctly, somewhere in the Syrian empire.*

During the second century BCE, Edessa (modern-day Şanlıurfa) became the capital as well as the royal residence of Osroene, which formed part of the

---

*Before William Whiston's celebrated translation of Josephus's works, which were first published in 1737, earlier translators identified Siriad with Syria. See, for instance, Josephus 1700.

Fig. 35.5. The twin pillars erected before the flood of Noah to preserve the arts and sciences of heaven (from the *Adams Synchronological Chart or Map of History* of 1871). Here they are credited to Methuselah, the son of Enoch, Noah, and his son Shem. Traditionally, however, they were attributed to either Enoch or Adam's third son Seth. Are such stories an abstract memory of the twin pillars erected at Taş Tepeler sites in the Şanlıurfa region?

Syrian Seleucid Empire. Even after Osroene declared its independence and became its own kingdom in circa 132 BCE, the kings of Edessa, most of whom were named either Abgar or Manu, continued their strong link with Syrian culture and tradition, while the Syrian-Aramaic language remained in use. There is thus every reason to suspect that the pillars of Seth were indeed thought to be in "Siriad," that is, somewhere in the Syrian empire. This tells us that they, too, perhaps form part of an ancestral memory regarding the presence of twin pillars at Taş Tepeler sites across the Şanlıurfa region.

Seth, as we have seen, was the legendary founder of the Chaldeans of Harran. He was identified with Agathodaimon, the Demiurge or creator of the world in the form of a serpent. Enoch, too, we should recall, is integrally linked with Harran. As we saw in chapter 24, the oldest occupational mound in the area is the 10,000-year-old Tell Idris, with Idris being the Arabic form of the name Enoch.

In addition to this, Bar Hebraeus, the thirteenth-century traveler and Maphrian (regional primate) of the Syriac Orthodox Church, wrote that the founder of Orhay, that is, Şanlıurfa, was Enoch, "whom the Greeks call Hermes Trismegistos."[29] Was this all simply an abstract memory of the establishment in and around Şanlıurfa of Taş Tepeler sites in the wake of the Younger Dryas mini ice age? This, as we shall recall, began in 10,800 BCE and continued to assault the northern hemisphere until its abrupt cessation around 9600 BCE, arguably due to another cataclysmic event that dramatically increased global temperatures almost overnight.

Could it be possible that the Serpent of Eden is in fact an abstract memory of Taş Tepeler inhabitants' very real veneration of the cosmic serpent at places like Karahan Tepe? Does Adam and Eve being told by the Serpent of Eden that it was okay to eat of the Tree of the Knowledge of Good and Evil recall how the shamans of Karahan Tepe were able to attain divine knowledge about the movement of the stars and its control of human destiny through interaction with the Galactic Bulge as the head of the Milky Way serpent? Was this then the true origin of the form of astrology taught by the Chaldeans of Harran involving the cyclic influence of the seven planets and 12 signs of the zodiac under the control of the Primal Cause, Shamal?

It is worth noting that an ancient Jewish religious work known as the book of Jubilees—the earliest examples of which were found among the Dead Sea Scrolls between 1947 and 1956 at Qumran in Israel—relates how Cainan, the legendary founder of Harran, uncovered an inscription carved on a stone stela. When translated it was found to contain the antediluvian science of astrology as taught by the Watchers,[30] the flesh and blood angels who, in the book of Enoch, are said to have provided mortal kind with the arts and sciences of heaven. The book of Jubilees tells us that the knowledge revealed by the stela became the basis of the beliefs of the Chaldeans, that is, the inhabitants of Harran, whose progenitor was Cainan's father, Arphaxad, the son of Shem and grandson of Noah.[31] The name Arphaxad simply means "Ur of the Chaldees,"[32] returning us to the site of Abraham's birthplace at nearby Şanlıurfa.

In the knowledge that stories of the Watchers, and their giant offspring the Nephilim, are perhaps the memory of the shamanic elite responsible for the emergence of Taş Tepeler, could the stone stela found by Cainan be based on an abstract memory of the profound knowledge and wisdom that had emerged from T-pillar-building Taş Tepeler sites as early as the mid-tenth millennium BCE? Was this the true source of the Harranians' starry wisdom, adopted from their forerunners who inhabited Tell Idris and other similar early Neolithic settlements on the Harran Plain as much as 10,000 years ago?

Were these forbidden arts and sciences of heaven, including astrology and agriculture, seen to be delivered to the snake shamans present at places like Karahan Tepe by the spirit of the Great Serpent, and if so, was this recalled in the story of how the Serpent beguiled Adam and Eve into eating of the forbidden fruit in the terrestrial paradise?

IDENTIFYING THE FORBIDDEN FRUIT

We normally assume that the forbidden fruit the Serpent of Eden encourages Eve to pluck from the Tree of the Knowledge of Good and Evil was a shiny red apple, or even a pomegranate, which is how it is most often represented in religious art. Some accounts, however, particularly in Islamic religious literature, identify the forbidden fruit not as a fruit at all, but as "an ear of wheat."[33] If correct, then it means Adam and Eve were tempted by the Serpent of Eden not into eating some delicious fruit, but into cultivating and consuming wheat. This, of course, brings to mind the story about Adam and Eve creating the first farm on the Harran Plain and with this inventing agriculture and growing the first wheat. So why might "an ear of wheat" have been seen as the forbidden fruit that, after being consumed, caused the first couple to lose their innocence?

The answer to this question lies in the impact that the agricultural revolution would have had on the preexisting Paleolithic population that had thrived unhindered in the region for tens of thousands of years prior to this time. With the introduction of animal husbandry and the cultivation of the land, the peoples of southeastern Anatolia underwent enormous changes in lifestyle.

Instead of being hunter-gatherers catering only for their immediate family and perhaps a slightly wider social group, they were compelled to inhabit urban centers where they would have been employed in specific jobs their entire lives. Indeed, they would probably have been born into specific trades, their fathers or mothers having done the same thing during their own lifetimes.

Everything from grain cultivation to beer fermentation, bread making, house building, stone carving, working in quarries, maintaining trading posts, digging irrigation ditches and house foundations, and even protecting settlements from attack would have been required for the day-to-day running of places like Jericho in the Palestinian West Bank and Aşıklı Höyük in central Turkey.

At this last site, founded circa 8200 BCE, people lived within a tight network of claustrophobic alleyways that included workshops where exquisite obsidian bracelets, mirrors, and necklaces were produced. This part of their lifestyle might sound fulfilling, although the effects of physical labor at Aşıklı Höyük were another thing altogether. Skeletal remains found there indicate that the men lived until they were 55 to 57 years of age, with most of the women living only until they were between 20 and 25 years of age.[34] As I noted in *Göbekli Tepe: Genesis of the Gods*:

> Severe trauma and injuries to the shoulders and spine indicate that these women carried heavy loads during their lives or were bending over or kneeling constantly, perhaps in front of a saddle quern used to make cereal grain. The skeletal remains of the men, on the other hand, show signs of joint disease and trauma of the type that might be expected from constant heavy labor, such as wood logging, construction work, and tilling the land.[35]

Clearly, living in what might be described as the world's first industrial age, where everyone had to have a home and be fed daily, would have taken its toll on the local population, and I am sure similar styles of living were emerging at Pre-Pottery Neolithic sites across Anatolia and the Near East. Is this what is meant in the book of Genesis when it speaks of Adam and Eve eating of the Tree of the Knowledge of Good and Evil and realizing that they are naked and losing their innocence—the innocence of the Paleolithic lifestyle being lost forever through the rapid spread of agriculture throughout Anatolia and the Near East?

Perhaps the book of Genesis really does preserve the memory of an extraordinary civilization of the ancients that, despite the ethics of its establishment, thrived across the Şanlıurfa region during the Pre-Pottery Neolithic Age. Not

only can we be certain that it was the first culture to successfully domesti-
cate and grow wheat, but it also domesticated wild cattle, as well as other farm
animals, and as a result of this new agrarian lifestyle it almost singlehandedly
kickstarted the Neolithic Revolution. Across the next several thousand years
this would spread into every part of the ancient world, carrying with it an
incredible understanding of megalithic architecture and the importance of synchronizing ceremonial and ritual monuments with the movement of the sun,
moon, and stars.

Anatolia's Taş Tepeler culture would eventually be replaced by the Ceramic
Neolithic world of the Halaf culture (circa 6500–5000 BCE), whose distinctive painted ware has been found extensively both in southeastern Anatolia
and in neighboring Syria. They in turn transitioned into the Ubaid culture
(circa 5000–3800 BCE), whose settlements underlie various Sumerian cities in Lower Mesopotamia (modern-day Iraq) including Ur, Uruk (or Erech),
Lagash, and Eridu.[36] What this suggests is that aspects of the culture, technology, and religion of the Halaf and the later Ubaid culture were passed on both
to the Sumerian civilization and to its successors, the Akkadian, Assyrian, and
Babylonian civilizations that thrived in both Upper and Lower Mesopotamia.

STANDING THE TEST OF TIME

Long after the initial emergence of the Taş Tepeler culture across the Şanlıurfa
region some 12,000 years ago, Karahan Tepe was constructed, with one of
its principal functions being to communicate with the creative force seen to
be behind the cyclic motion of the heavens, something its inhabitants came
to associate with a world-encircling serpent identified with the Milky Way.
Through the employment of shamanism, the Karahan community would
appear to have developed an intuitive awareness of the dynamic forces behind
the growth and decay of life on Earth. This, as we now know, seems governed
by the powerful actions of the supermassive black hole, Sagittarius A*, at the
center of our galaxy.

What these people appear to have achieved was quite profound in nature,
although, unfortunately, with the emergence of the earliest monotheistic religions in the Near East, the collective memory of the cosmic serpent's involvement in human affairs was, I suspect, either distorted into something it wasn't
or simply denounced as anathema. Only God could create the universe and,

within it, the world in which we live; this act could not have been the result of the intervention of some lowly serpent! In contrast with this belief was the Greek Orphic and later Ophite Gnostic concept of the Great Serpent being the Demiurge, the creator of this world, an action taken under the command of or, in some cases, in disobedience of, a much greater power imagined as a supernal sun casting forth its rays from the primordial darkness.

This attitude toward the Great Serpent in its role as the Demiurge is the true origin, I believe, behind the story of the Serpent of Eden said to have beguiled Eve and, through her, Adam into eating of the Tree of the Knowledge of Good and Evil. In the case of the Serpent of Eden, the book of Genesis tells us God passed judgment on it, saying, "Because thou hast done this, cursed [art] thou above all the cattle, and above every beast of the field: on thy belly dost thou go, and dust thou dost eat, all days of thy life."[37]

Through their adoption of the Orphic hymns, the Ophite Gnostics would appear to have come closest to understanding the true nature of communications with the mind (Nous) or intelligence of the Great Serpent in its role as an expression of the Milky Way galaxy's creative forces. This comes through in their doctrine and in the profound symbolism of the alabaster bowl. Because of their personal connection with the divine the Ophite Gnostics were persecuted until virtually all trace of their profound teachings and mystical rites had been expunged from the pages of history. Now we have the opportunity once again to understand the true nature of the Nous, in other words, the manner in which we too can connect with the dynamic forces behind all creation, not only out there in the cosmos, but also within ourselves. This would be true illumination and enlightenment. One matter remains to be discussed, however, and this is the true identity of Eve, Adam's companion, for her story must also now be told.

36

Identifying Eve

If the legends of Adam's presence in Şanlıurfa really do preserve an abstract memory of the Taş Tepeler culture's domestication and cultivation of wheat, while stories connecting Abraham with the foundation of the first Kaaba perhaps recall the construction of some of the more notable T-pillar sites in the region, then who exactly was Eve? Did she exist as a real person, or is she a metaphor for something else—something more profound? And, last, why was she and not Adam made to take the blame for being tempted by the Serpent of Eden? For her supposed sins, God angrily told her, "I multiply thy sorrow and thy conception, in sorrow dost thou bear children, and toward thy husband [is] thy desire, and he doth rule over thee."[1]

The name Eve comes from the Hebrew Ḥawwāh, meaning "to breathe," or "to live," or "to give life," since in Abrahamic tradition she is considered the "mother of life." The Arabic name for Eve is Ḥawwā, meaning "life," although *hawwa* can also mean "snake." Her name in Aramaic also translates as "snake," while the third-century Christian theologian and scholar Clement of Alexandria in his *Exhortation to the Heathen* noted that, "according to the strict interpretation of the Hebrew term, the name Hevia [that is, Eve], aspirated, signifies a female serpent."[2]

Many depictions of Eve in religious art show her in the company of the Serpent of Eden (see fig. 36.1, for instance). It is she, not Adam, who communicates with the Serpent, affirming that the alternative interpretation of her name as meaning "snake" tells us she was not only the mother of humankind, but also a "Snake Mother," a surmise strengthened in the knowledge that in Yezidi tradition Eve is associated not with a single serpent, but with multiple snakes and also scorpions.[3]

Fig. 36.1. *Adam and Eve* by Franz Stuck (1920),
showing Eve with the Serpent of Eden. She holds the forbidden fruit
as Adam succumbs to the temptation.

Almost certainly, the First Woman of Hebrew tradition is related to the snake and scorpion goddess Išhara and, through her, Anatolia's own Snake Mother, the Shahmaran. All three of these mythological women—Eve, Išhara, and the Shahmaran—are, I sense, derived from the abstract memory of female shamans communicating with the world-encircling serpent at Taş Tepeler sites such as Karahan Tepe. Any knowledge and wisdom they gained from this perceived celestial source was no doubt thought to derive from an intelligence in the form of a snake—a snake that would go on to be immortalized as the Serpent of Eden (see fig. 36.2). In addition to this, this same snake would also become an expression of Eve herself in her role as the primordial Snake Mother.

This is not to say that the cosmic snake was wholly female or that all the shamans at Karahan Tepe were women, only that the manner in which the communications were delivered, whether they be via male shamans or female shamans, would go on to determine the gender of this perceived cosmic intel-

Fig. 36.2. Eve and a female serpent from the Furtmeyr Bible,
Regensburg, Germany, dating to shortly after 1465. Even though the
Serpent of Eden is male in both the Hebrew Bible and the Holy Koran,
it is difficult not to associate this female form of the serpent with the
Shahmaran, Anatolia's own Snake Mother.

ligence in later mythological traditions. Whereas from a female perspective the
snake would become associated with goddesses such as Išhara, Tiamat, and
the Shahmaran, from a male perspective the cosmic serpent would come to
be identified with male deities such as Nabu—"the announcer"—the Gnostic
Demiurge, and, of course, the Serpent of Eden, which is generally considered male in Abrahamic tradition. In essence, the world-encircling serpent
was neither male nor female—*it was androgynous, without a fixed gender*—a
point to remember when we gaze upon the giant stone head in Karahan Tepe's
Pillars Shrine.

THE DEVOURER OF WORLDS

To other factions within the Taş Tepeler culture, however, there is evidence that the influence of Galactic Center and the stars of Scorpius on this world became emblematic of something quite different. This is suggested by the fact that the sting of the celestial scorpion might well have been seen as the cause of a global catastrophe that we can today identify as the Younger Dryas event. As we have seen, this would seem to have been triggered by a cometary impact that devastated large parts of the northern hemisphere and in North America alone might well have been responsible for the sudden demise of its thriving Clovis population.[4]

In Abrahamic lore, this same terrifying catastrophe was almost certainly remembered as the major cataclysm before which Seth, the third son of Adam, erected two pillars on which were inscribed the arts and sciences of heaven so that they might be preserved before the world "was to be destroyed at one time by the force of fire, and at another time by the violence and quantity of water."[5] These two pillars, as we have seen, are almost certainly an abstract memory of the twin sets of T-pillars once found at the center of all major enclosures at Taş Tepeler sites.

How the stars of Scorpius came to be associated with this world-changing event in human history has everything to do with the synchronization between the solstitial sun and Galactic Center, which, as we have determined, is an extremely rare astronomical event that occurs only twice in a precessional cycle of approximately 28,500 years. The precise moment of synchronization between the solstitial sun at the time of midsummer and Galactic Center can be shown to have last occurred around 10,800 BCE. Although this was 1,800 years *before* the foundation of Karahan Tepe, the synchronization would still have been close enough for it to have remained meaningful in the tenth millennium BCE.[6]

There is no obvious reason why a solstitial alignment toward Galactic Center might itself trigger a cosmic catastrophe down here on Earth—unless, of course, this synchronization between the two different celestial bodies was considered cyclical or astrological in nature. Such ideas have now to be seen in the knowledge that some geoscientists have today come to believe that dynamic forces associated with Galactic Center determine when major catastrophes and extinction events take place on Earth. So periodic synchronizations with Galactic Center and global cataclysms *are* related—in a cyclical sense at least.

THE GOOD SCORPIUS AND EVIL SCORPIUS

Having said this, the fact that Galactic Center synchronizing with the sun at the time of the summer solstice coincided with the onset of the Younger Dryas in circa 10,800 BCE could help explain why some Taş Tepeler factions might have come to see the stars of Scorpius as harbingers of global cataclysms. In Sumerian sky lore, Scorpius is the scorpion ^{mul}GIR.TAB, which means something like "sharp weapon" or "sharp sting," a clear reference to the scorpion's stinger.[7] Almost certainly, this name came down to the Sumerians from even earlier cultures, most obviously the region's Ubaid inhabitants. They, as we have seen, were the direct successors of northern Mesopotamia's Halaf culture, who probably benefitted from the cultural and religious legacy left behind by southeastern Anatolia's Taş Tepeler civilization. Remember, the Scorpius constellation, signified by the presence of the carved relief of a scorpion, appears on Göbekli Tepe's Pillar 43, which dates to circa 9600 BCE.

It seems likely that the stars of Scorpius were identified as a sky figure in the form of a scorpion in the aftermath of the Younger Dryas, this coming after the sun's solstitial alignment with Galactic Center at the same time that the cometary impact took place, in other words around the year 10,800 BCE. The terrifying impact of the air blasts caused by the disintegration of this comet fragment were perhaps likened to the heat and pain, as well as the potential death, caused by the sting of a scorpion. This rather dark interpretation of Scorpius's symbolism, however, was completely at odds with how the community at Karahan Tepe saw the function of its stars. For them, I suspect, the stars of Scorpius represented the active spirit of the Milky Way serpent, which was seen both as a source of cosmic creation and as the controller of cyclical time.

If all this is correct, it means that two opposing views could well have prevailed among the Taş Tepeler inhabitants of southeastern Anatolia regarding the true nature of the Scorpius constellation. One saw it as evil and as a symbol of the devourer of worlds, while the other saw it as the source of divine knowledge and wisdom. How can we reconcile this situation with what we know about the emergence of the Taş Tepeler world sometime around 10,000 BCE?

To begin with, we must assume there was more than one faction involved with the building activities of Taş Tepeler, each having its own distinctive ethnic background and cultural traditions. Some groups would have had links with the Epipaleolithic Natufian peoples of the Levant, especially at locations like Jericho in the Palestinian West Bank and even farther south at important settlements like Helwan in northern Egypt. As I demonstrate elsewhere, Helwan had firm links with Taş Tepeler sites in southeastern Anatolia as early as 9000 BCE and thousands of years later would become instrumental in the rise of the Egyptian Pyramid age.[8] Other groups would have migrated southward via the Russian steppe from as far east as the Urals, Siberia, and Mongolia, a journey that, as we saw in chapter 6, might well have begun as much as 30,000 years ago.

Further groups associated with Taş Tepeler would no doubt have been related to the Indigenous Zarzian mountain peoples of the Zagros and Taurus mountains, while still others would surely have originated in western and southern Anatolia, where they would have had links with maritime cultures able to navigate the Mediterranean Sea. These cultures would almost certainly have had connections with places such as Cyprus, Crete, and the Aegean archipelago, as well as the Greek mainland.

Thus there would have been a melting pot of cultural and religious ideas coming from peoples originating in different parts of the ancient world, all of them coming together under the Taş Tepeler banner. So it makes good sense that some factions would have regarded the Scorpius constellation as the destroyer of worlds, while others might have recognized it as the place of cosmic creation, an act reflected in microcosm with the creation of life within the human body.

All this leaves me inclined to believe that those responsible for founding the Karahan community were an offshoot of the Göbekli Tepe society. One of Karahan Tepe's primary functions was, I am convinced, to commune with the active spirit of the Milky Way serpent via the Galactic Bulge and stars of Scorpius, even though others of their culture had come to believe that this same set of stars was emblematic of how Earth was very nearly destroyed during the Younger Dryas impact event.

In popular astrology, the First Woman, Eve, is seen as an expression of the dark, serpentine, and also quite sexual elements of the Scorpius constellation.[9] It is even possible that Scorpius, as the devourer of worlds, was seen both in terms of the Serpent of Eden and as a woman who could take the form of a snake. Since we know that as the goddess Išhara, Scorpius was seen as female in gender, this could help explain why the figure of Eve became so maligned in Hebrew myth and legend, for as the perceived cause of the Younger Dryas she was seen as the root of all evil that befalls the world. This was despite the fact that she was also the First Woman, and thus the mother of humanity as well as the source of its wisdom. In this manner Eve, or at least her Neolithic forerunner, assumed two diametrically contrasting roles—one as the serpentine mother of life and the other as a scorpionic devourer of worlds.

In truth, however, Eve, like Išhara, Tiamat, and the Shahmaran, was, I feel sure, the memory of the powerful presence in our skies of the world-encircling serpent, coupled with the actions of the female shamans who at sites like Karahan Tepe were able to connect with what they saw as the celestial snake's mind or intelligence located in the direction of the Galactic Bulge and stars of Scorpius. It was this divinely inspired knowledge and wisdom, perceived as coming from a source coincident to the center of our own Milky Way galaxy, that I firmly believe helped inspire the rise of civilization.

When I think back to my own first visit to Karahan Tepe in 2004, it was not just the mysterious nature of the place that caught my imagination. It was the fact that if the blue scorpion I'd nearly touched beneath the fallen fragment of T-shaped pillar had actually stung me, I would have suffered severe pain, great discomfort, and maybe even death. That is a disconcerting thought for anyone to process as they try to understand the greater implications of an unexcavated archaeological site belonging to the same culture that constructed Göbekli Tepe.

Although I didn't know it at the time, the incident with the scorpion must have had a deeper impact on me than I had at first realized. I say this for, on my return to the United Kingdom, I found myself obsessing about the meaning of these incredible sites I had been able to inspect for the first time after nearly a decade of writing about the myths and legends surrounding those who had inspired the origins of civilization in southeastern and eastern Anatolia.

I thought about Göbekli Tepe, with its carved pillars and stone enclosures unlike anything else I had ever seen anywhere else in the world. I thought about Harran, the ancient city of the Chaldeans, and the symbolic meaning of its ominous Astronomical Tower. I thought about Sogmatar, the location of the fabled seven planetary temples of the Sabians. And I thought about Karahan Tepe, somewhere almost no one knew about, not even the inhabitants of the Tektek Mountains.

One night, late, all these thoughts exploded onto paper as I began to scribble down wild ideas on all these sites, ideas that would go on to inspire the writing of my book *The Cygnus Mystery*, published two years later in 2006.

What I wrote down about Karahan Tepe that fateful night in June 2004 seemed crazy at the time, so it was quickly forgotten. Some two decades later, however, those scribbled notes now take on a profoundly prophetic meaning, hinting perhaps that Karahan Tepe's Scorpionic influence might well have been trying to communicate something of importance to me during my initial visit there, just as it had inspired the site's snake shamans at the height of their power and influence. Here is what I wrote:

> *Karahan Tepe, the Place of the Devourer,*
> *Let her form be the Scorpion,*
> *Her higher forms being the serpent, and eagle,*
> *Her time Scorpio, the month of October.*
> *Encoding knowledge of life and death.*
> *The place of the scorpion and the snake.*
> *Karahan Tepe was aligned to Scorpio,*
> *Scorpio brought forth the Devourer,*
> *Out of the sky to bring forth the next age,*
> *The influence of Karahan*
> *Out of the world that had been,*
> *Symbolizing a time of contact,*
> *With the original source.*[10]

37

The Greatest Confirmation

In this final chapter we return to the incredible discoveries made at Karahan Tepe in 2023 and announced to the world during the fall of that year. These, of course, included the giant statue of a man exhibiting his penis and the caricature-like vulture found in a standing position next to it in the same enclosure. As stated at the end of chapter 1, this book was written and submitted to the publisher months before our visits to the site in September 2023. Nothing of that original text has been changed to accommodate the greater implications of these new discoveries. It is now time to more thoroughly examine what has been found and try to put this information into the context of the theories proposed not only in this book, but also in my previous volumes on the same topic.*

From the first moment I was able to line myself up with the suspected orientation of the new enclosure, I realized it was directed toward the summit of another hill called Ceylan Tepesi (meaning "Peak or Crest of the Gazelle"). Located around three-quarters of a mile (1.2 kilometers) north-northeast of Karahan Tepe, it is marked by a cluster of farm buildings (see fig. 37.1). The structure's directional orientation was unlikely to be toward the south-south-west, since the ground rose in this direction, making observation of the local horizon more or less impossible. What is more, the location of the circular porthole stone in the northern part of the enclosure, with twin pillars on either side and an altar-like area between them, surely defined the enclosure's most obvious direction of orientation.

---

*These include *From the Ashes of Angels* (1996), *The Cygnus Mystery* (2006), *Göbekli Tepe: Genesis of the Gods* (2014), and *The Cygnus Key* (2018), along with *The Path of Souls* (2014), *Denisovan Origins* (2020), and *Origins of the Gods* (2022), the last three co-authored with Gregory L. Little.

Fig. 37.1. The alignment of orientation between the new enclosure at Karahan Tepe and the summit of a hill marked by farm buildings three-quarters of a mile (1.2 kilometers) away to the north-northeast. Image by Andrew Collins.

This same orientation from south to north defined the suspected experiential journey of the supplicant between the Great Ellipse (Structure AD), the Pillars Shrine (Structure AB), and the Pit Shrine (Structure AA) down on Karahan Tepe's lower level, something made clear by Necmi Karul himself (see chapter 3). This south-to-north orientation is seen also in connection with cult buildings at various other Neolithic sites in Anatolia, including Çatal Höyük, Çayönü, Göbekli Tepe, Aşıklı Höyük, and Hallan Çemi, the north being associated with darkness, death, and the turning of the heavens about the celestial pole.

STELLAR TARGETS

So the pressing question, even after coming away from my initial viewing of the new enclosure in mid-September 2023 (we would observe it on two further occasions during our visit), was whether it might be aligned toward a celestial object rising from the local horizon. Without wishing to preempt any possible

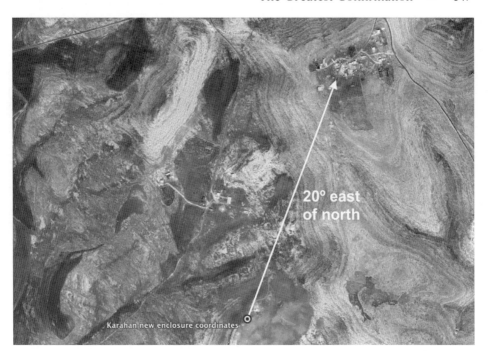

Fig. 37.2. View showing the angle of orientation between the new enclosure found at Karahan Tepe and the nearby hilltop farm on Ceylan Tepesi.
Image by Google Earth and Andrew Collins.

ground-sky matches, I first checked Google Earth and determined the angle of projection between the location of the enclosure and the summit of the nearby hill. This turned out to be 20 degrees east of north (see fig. 37.2).

I then moved on to the Stellarium open-source planetarium, which would show me the skies as seen from the latitude of Karahan Tepe during the epoch in question. Since, however, precession causes the stars and Milky Way to shift their positions very slowly with respect to the local horizon, it was essential that I entered the correct time frame to determine whether the enclosure did indeed target any notable stellar object. What year was I to choose? Exactly how old *was* the new enclosure?

From the outset, I had suspected from the size and appearance of its T-pillars that the structure dated to the Late Pre-Pottery Neolithic A period, suggesting a date of construction in the range of 9100–8800 BCE. What, then, was the official view of Necmi Karul and his colleagues at the University of Istanbul regarding the age of the enclosure? Some newspaper reports said it was 11,400 years old (the date generally given for the earliest stone enclosures down on the lower level), while other reports said it was 11,000 years old or as young as 10,500 years old. Pending the publication of radiocarbon dates relating to the new enclosure, I decided to stick with a potential construction date in the region of 9000 BCE. (see page 324 for the latest update on the age of the enclosure)

After entering the necessary coordinates into Stellarium, the computer screen displayed the night sky as it would have appeared to the inhabitants of Karahan Tepe 11,000 years ago. I scrolled around to view the north-northeastern horizon, and then clicked the time key forward hour by hour to show the entire sky across a 24-hour period. The day I used for this exercise was the winter solstice, which, as we have seen, appears to have marked the time of a major solar alignment in connection with the Pillars Shrine's giant stone head. It was also the shortest day of the year, making the long night beforehand ideal for observing the stars.

CYGNUS AGAIN

What I found seemed at first to be too good to be true. Yet there it was: the only notable star that made its first appearance at an azimuth of 20 degrees east of north during the epoch in question was the bright star Deneb in the constellation of Cygnus. Six hours after sunset on the night in question it would have reached an altitude of approximately 3 degrees, 48 minutes (down to 2 degrees, 52 minutes by a date of 8800 BCE and 2 degrees by 8600 BCE), meaning that by this time it would have been just about visible above the horizon, making it a good target to use for this purpose.

Deneb, as previously discussed, marks the northern opening of the Milky Way's Dark Rift, which on this night would have been seen arching across into the eastern sky. As noted earlier, Deneb was considered by some ancient cultures to mark the point of entry into the sky world. More important still is the fact that at this time Karahan Tepe's Great Ellipse down on the hill's lower level would have targeted the southern termination of the Dark Rift, which highlights the position of the Galactic Bulge and stars of Scorpius. This enclosure, as we have seen, is aligned by virtue of its long axis approximately 10 degrees south of east. At the point Deneb appeared in the sky the Great Ellipse would have targeted Galactic Center almost precisely (see fig. 37.3). This confirms what we had previously determined—that the people of Karahan Tepe held a particular interest not only in the star Deneb and

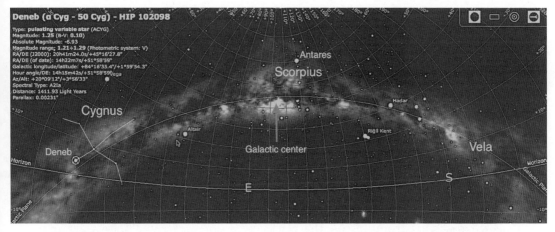

Fig. 37.3. View of the night sky as seen from Karahan Tepe in 9000 BCE, showing
Deneb rising in the north-northeast and the Milky Way arching across the sky
with the brightest area of the Galactic Bulge between 95 degrees and 115 degrees
azimuth. Image made using the Stellarium free open-source planetarium.

Dark Rift, but also in the area of sky marked by the Galactic Bulge and stars
of Scorpius.

GALACTIC PLANE

Thus, from the latitude of Karahan Tepe on the night of the winter solstice in
9000 BCE, the entire length of the Milky Way's Dark Rift would have been
visible in the northeastern and eastern night sky following the rising of Deneb.
This is an important realization, as it provides a realistic reason why this particular star, above any other, might have become important to the Taş Tepeler
culture of southeastern Anatolia. Its first appearance, particularly at the time
of the winter solstice, highlighted the availability of the Dark Rift as a celestial
path enabling the soul or spirit, either that of a deceased person or that of a
shaman, to access the Galactic Bulge in its role as the head of the Milky Way
serpent.

Personal Confirmation

What is most pleasing about these compelling findings regarding the placement and orientation of the new enclosure at Karahan Tepe is that they provide undeniable support for the theories proposed in this book. They include

the fact that the directional orientation of the experiential journey between the three, interconnected, subsurface enclosures on the hill's lower slopes—the Great Ellipse, Pillars Shine, and Pit Shrine—not only follow the same roughly south-to-north alignment, but also target the setting of the star Deneb circa 9000 BCE as it disappears down into Keçili Tepe. Even more incredible is the fact that, as I wrote in chapter 8, this alignment was found to be "approximately 20 degrees west of north," in other words, 340 degrees azimuth, this being an exact mirror reflection of the alignment found in association with Karahan Tepe's new enclosure, which is 20 degrees *east* of north.

So whereas the experiential journey played out within the three interconnected rock-cut structures on the hill's lower slopes targeted the *setting* of Deneb as it sank down into Keçili Tepe situated in the north-northwest, the directional orientation of the new enclosure targeted the *rising* of the same star as it became visible above another prominent hill located in the northnortheast. This type of directional symmetry simply cannot be coincidence, and it tells us very clearly that certain key enclosures at Karahan Tepe were without a doubt oriented toward Deneb in the constellation of Cygnus, which was seen not only as a point of entry to the sky world, but also as the brightest star in an important sky figure identified as a vulture (remember too that in Armenia, even to this day, the stars of Cygnus are identified as Angegh, the vulture).

IMPORTANT ANCESTOR

This now brings us back to the two extraordinary statues found inside the new enclosure at Karahan Tepe. If the presence of the vulture can be seen as signifying the incoming influence of Cygnus, then what about the giant human statue found next to it? It likewise faces into the enclosure, perhaps suggesting that it, too, once signified the arrival of a celestial influence. Since, however, its orientation is just a few degrees different from the enclosure's own northnortheasterly axis, the chances are the vulture and human statue are linked.

No less than four of the key installations at Göbekli Tepe (Enclosures B, C, D, and H) are directed north-northwestward via their porthole stones toward the setting of Deneb, while all their twin central pillars face southward into the enclosure.[1] Is it possible, therefore, that these anthropomorphized T-pillars were seen as representations of a celestial influence inbound from the

Milky Way's Dark Rift? If correct, then we have to consider the possibility that twin sets of T-pillars represented the return of great ancestors seen as responsible for the emergence of Taş Tepeler. Should this be so, then the enormous statue found in the new enclosure at Karahan Tepe might well have signified something similar—the return of a revered ancestor, its apparently erect penis symbolizing sexual prowess, male virility, and the foundation of an earthly lineage associated directly with the builders of the enclosure.

This has been the conclusion of Ted Banning, an anthropology professor at the University of Toronto, who proposes that the male statue probably represents "an important ancestor associated with the building in which it was found."

"The fact that the figure is clutching its penis," he says, "is also consistent with this interpretation by potentially symbolizing that this person was the progenitor of a social group, such as a lineage or clan, associated with the building."[2]

THE GOD-LIKE SKY PEOPLE

If the new statue really does represent "an important ancestor," as Banning suggests, then can this remarkable piece of prehistoric art be placed into a more familiar contextual background? As mentioned in chapter 17, the late Professor Klaus Schmidt, the discoverer of Göbekli Tepe in 1994, said that the T-pillars at the site probably represent Anunna, that is Anunnaki, who in Sumerian, Akkadian, and Babylonian mythology were seen as the divine founders behind the emergence of the first city-states on the Mesopotamian plain in what is today southern Iraq.[3] If so, then can we identity the giant statue found in the new enclosure at Karahan Tepe as a representation of this same divine lineage? Are we looking upon the first true likeness of an Anunnaki? (See figs. 37.4a and 37.4b, p. 322.)

Even if this is correct, the question then becomes: What is an Anunnaki? We know they are said to have gifted humanity with "sheep and grain," metaphors most assuredly for the invention of animal husbandry and agriculture. But who were they really?

The Babylonian word Anunnaki, generally interpreted as meaning "gods of heaven (*an* or *anu*) and earth (*ki*)," derives from a much older Sumerian source. This is Anna, Anuna, or Anunna (^{dingir}AN.NA, ^{dingir}AN.NUN.A, or ^{dingir}AN.UN.NA), meaning something like "those of princely seed," "gods of the sky,"[4] or even

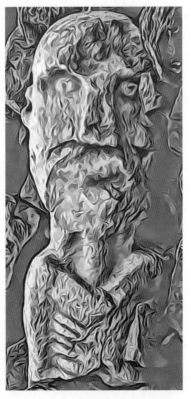 

Fig. 37.4a and 37.4b. Two views of the giant statue found inside the
new enclosure at Karahan Tepe. Images by Andrew Collins.

"divine [*dingir*] ones of the sky"—quite literally, the "sky people."* Whereas some
might use this interpretation to support the popular belief that the Anunnaki
were spacemen who came down from the sky in ancient times, a more obvious
explanation of the name refers to divine ancestors of an earlier epoch. If so, then
their association with the sky could imply they were holders of intimate knowledge regarding the celestial bodies and their effect upon life on Earth (the roots
of both astronomy and astrology). It was this knowledge and wisdom that I suspect that the Anunna, or Sky People, carried with them into Anatolia sometime
before the emergence of Taş Tepeler around 10,000 BCE.

So where exactly did the Anunna come from?

---

*The Sumero-Akkadian name [dingir]AN.UN.NA can be broken down as *dingir*, "divine," *an*, "sky,
heaven, the sky god An," *un*, "people," and *na*, a noun case used generally to show possession,
which when put together can thus be read as either "people (possessive of) the sky, heaven, or sky
god An," or, more simply, the "sky people."

THE TRUE ANCESTORS OF TAŞ TEPELER

As we saw in chapter 6, Turkish archaeologists are today proposing that the ancestors of Anatolia's Taş Tepeler culture came from as far east as Siberia and Mongolia, with their earliest migrations having begun as much as 30,000 years ago. This is something I have argued in my own books, proposing that the forebears of Taş Tepeler were hybrid descendants of a hominin population now known to have thrived in Siberia and seemingly also in Mongolia down to around 45,000 years ago.

Known today as the Denisovans (pronounced *dee-nis-o-vans*), they were closely related to the Neanderthal population of the western Eurasian continent and had the ability to create beautiful jewelry (look up the Denisovan bracelet) as well as the earliest bone needles, which were probably used to make tailored clothing. They made basic musical instruments in the form of whistles or flutes, meaning that they must have had at least a basic knowledge of musical notes, and designed the standard hunter-gathering tool kit used by our own ancestors throughout the Upper Paleolithic Age (circa 45,000–11,600 years ago).[5] What is more, they appear to have monitored the cycles of the sun and moon.[6]

The Siberian Denisovans (as opposed to their cousins, the Sunda Denisovans, who inhabited eastern and southeastern Asia, Island Southeast Asia, and Australia, down to around 30,000 years ago) are thought to have first come into contact with anatomically modern humans (*Homo sapiens sapiens*) at sites like Tolber-16 in northern Mongolia sometime between 45,000 and 30,000 years ago. There the two populations interbred, with the hybrid offspring of that meeting eventually carrying the Denisovans' ancestry, as well as its advanced knowledge of stone tool technologies, westward into southwestern Asia, something that would have occurred between 30,000 and 13,000 years ago.[7]

From the meager anatomical knowledge currently available to us, the Siberian Denisovans appear to have been enormous in size, comparable to the largest WWE wrestler or American football player. If their hybrid descendants really can be seen as the great ancestors of those who founded Taş Tepeler, then I strongly suspect that this is what the giant statue newly uncovered at Karahan Tepe actually represents—an abstract memory of one of its oversized founders, a Denisovan–anatomically modern human (*Homo sapiens sapiens*) hybrid whose origins date back to the age of the last Siberian Denisovans at places like the famous Denisova Cave in Siberia and the Tolbor-16 site in northern Mongolia.

These then, in my opinion, were the true founders of Taş Tepeler, the true Anunna, or Sky People, in other words those who provided the first knowledge of the stars and how they are able to affect life on Earth. These were the first astronomers, the first watchers of the skies, and the first astrologers. It was their descendants who would go on to inspire the emergence of Taş Tepeler and the foundation of great ceremonial centers like Karahan Tepe, Göbekli Tepe, and many more of the Neolithic ceremonial and ritual centers that are still waiting to be uncovered in every part of southeastern and eastern Turkey.

UPDATE—SPRING 2024

A return to Karahan Tepe in March 2024 brought fresh information about the site. Necmi Karul and his colleagues now believe that the new enclosure being exposed right now on the top of the hill dates to the lower end of circa 9000–8700 BCE. This means that estimates concerning its alignment toward the rising of Deneb are even more accurate than first thought. A survey of the site also now shows that it is far bigger than previously imagined with a suspected diameter of approximately 108 feet (33 meters), the largest stone enclosure discovered so far at any Taş Tepeler site.

On the eastern edge of the current excavations, at the base of the hill, a new enclosure has been uncovered. Dubbed "the Kitchen," it was found to contain large numbers of faunal remains, hinting at its function as a place of preparation for rituals and ceremonies taking place in the nearby Great Ellipse (Structure AD).

Among the faunal remains found in the Kitchen are those of the Anatolian meadow viper, which Karul and his colleagues now suspect formed part of the community's diet. These snakes, both alive and dead, probably also featured in shamanic practices including oracular communications with the Milky Way serpent. More significantly, it was the Anatolian meadow viper that in chapter 3 of this book was successfully compared with the snakelike appearance of the Pillars Shrine (Structure AB). Confirmation that this highly poisonous species was not only known to the Karahan community, but also probably featured in their rituals and ceremonies, now makes it even more likely that both this structure and the neighboring Pit Shrine (Structure AA) were sculpted to resemble the heads of snakes.

Secrets of Karahan Tepe

The Discovery of a Stunning Winter Solstice Alignment

HUGH NEWMAN AND JJ AINSWORTH

The city of Şanlıurfa, southeastern Turkey, December 20, 2021. The alarm woke us suddenly at 5:00 a.m. In our confused state, we remembered we were up against the clock. We simply had to be out at Karahan Tepe for sunrise, as the previous evening Hugh, who had briefly visited the site the previous afternoon, had received a message from site custodian Ismail Can. The message said that officials and the archaeologists were coming first thing in the morning to cover over the site for the winter. So we dressed, washed, grabbed our cameras, and ate our breakfast in the car. Clouds were in the sky, and as we climbed into the rental car, we prayed they would disperse in time for the sunrise.

As we drove at a speed probably on the edge of the legal limit, we discussed what we might see when we got there. Today was the winter solstice. It was cold and windy, but the forecast looked good. We felt we would witness something remarkable this morning, as our good friend the author Andrew Collins had already found an alignment featuring the summer solstice sunset in connection with Karahan Tepe's Pit Shrine (Structure AA). The winter solstice sunrise is on the same alignment but in the opposite direction, so was this also built into the site, we wondered?

The clock was ticking and we felt we'd be lucky to get a few minutes at the site before the officials arrived. We turned off the highway onto the newly paved road through the arid Tektek mountains with dozens of stone hills protruding out of a Martian-like landscape that seemed almost devoid of life. It felt like we were visiting another world. It was a few minutes after sunrise, yet some clouds were still blocking the light. Would we see anything worthy of this effort? Would the sun grace us with its presence?

We messaged Ismail, who agreed to be our official guide for the morning. We drank an obligatory glass of tea with him and his brothers before hurriedly climbing the hill to the area of excavation. The sun was starting to break through, and as the cold wind made its icy presence felt, the first light was hitting some of the enclosures. We had made it to Karahan Tepe, arguably the most important archaeological discovery of the twenty-first century, and we would not be disappointed.

EXPLORING THE SITE

Karahan Tepe (formerly called Keçili Tepe) lies approximately 23 miles (37 kilometers) southeast of its more famous sister site, Göbekli Tepe, which was built a few hundred years earlier. Karahan Tepe could be as much as 11,400 years old, and was in use for at least 1,000 years. Over 250 monoliths are recorded at the site, mostly T-pillars, as well as many unique stone carvings and statues recently unearthed. As at Göbekli Tepe, this site is covered with many strange depictions of humans, symbols, and animals. It also has a sunken pit containing phallic-shaped pillars as well as a three-dimensional portrayal of a giant human head with a serpentine neck. The artifacts from the excavation are now on display at the Şanlıurfa Archaeology Museum.

Karahan Tepe is a unique Pre-Pottery Neolithic complex built upon a large, natural limestone hill. When viewing the horizon from its peak, it feels like it is in the middle of nowhere. There are several sites of a similar age and style currently being excavated in a zone designated with the title "Taş Tepeler," meaning "Stone Hills/Mounds." This covers an area spanning approximately 120 miles (200 kilometers) in length. Karahan Tepe is one of 12 sites under investigation. They include Göbekli Tepe, which is the only one currently open to the public. At the time of writing, Karahan Tepe is yet to officially open, but visitors are welcome.

Hugh first explored the unexcavated site of Karahan Tepe in 2014 with Andrew Collins, with a further visit in 2015, and more recently with JJ in

2018. During these visits, all that was visible were the tops of T-pillars on the surface of the hill, an 18-foot (5.4-meter) unfinished T-shaped monolith on the hill's western slopes, and some relief carvings on a few stones.[1]

EXCAVATION BEGINS

In 2019, excavation finally began, led by archaeologist Necmi Karul, associate professor in the Prehistory Department of Istanbul University. By the time of our visit in 2021 less than 5 percent of the site had been excavated. Karul wrote a fascinating paper examining the techniques and implications of the burying process,[2] suggesting the Pillars Shrine (Structure AB), a sunken area of 23 feet (7 meters) by 19.5 feet (6 meters) with 10 bedrock pillars, a free-standing monolith, and a protruding carved head on the western wall, was a particularly important part of the complex. Its elongated neck has serpent scales etched into it and a V-shape under the chin. On the southeast edge of the pit is a 27.5-inch-wide (70-centimeter) porthole, which leads out to the main enclosure. As at Göbekli Tepe, numerous holed stones have been unearthed at Karahan Tepe, but why was this one, which is carved from the natural bedrock, in this exact position in relation to the Pillars Shrine?

The Pillars Shrine has a roughly egg-shaped plan and the eleventh pillar is the only one not carved directly out of the bedrock; rather, it is inserted into a carved socket at its base. Martin Sweatman suggests this could be one half of an oval-holed stone.[3] Standing 5.25–5.58 feet (1.6–1.7 meters) high, the four pillars lined up in front of the head were crafted more elaborately than those in the back row, which are 3.3–4.6 feet (1–1.4 meters) tall. All pillars are conical, perfectly upright, and all except one are shaped like an erect phallus. Below the porthole are worn steps, which may have been where people would climb down after entering through the hole from Structure AD.

OBSERVING THE WINTER SOLSTICE SUN EFFECT

The authors visited Karahan Tepe early in the morning of the winter solstice in 2021 (and more recently in December 2022) to see if any alignments would be revealed. Having a long-standing interest in archaeoastronomy, and with the existence of numerous alignments proposed at both Karahan Tepe and Göbekli Tepe, this was the first time the site had been excavated enough to witness such phenomena. Through a series of serendipitous events we arrived at the site in time to record something remarkable.

The sunrise took place at 7:37 a.m. Clouds temporarily blocked our view, but 10 minutes later we photographed a small blade of sunlight highlighting one side of the protruding head. The light continued to slowly light up the serpentine neck and one cheek, and then it moved toward the mouth and neck, taking nearly 45 minutes before disappearing from the face completely. The blade of light was coming directly through the porthole stone and rotating westward at an angle where it would become wider and illuminate more of the face during the process (see fig. A.1).

As the sun rose higher, more of the stone cranium was bathed in light, but the 11 pillars still remained mostly in the shade. JJ set up a camera to film the process, while Hugh got shots from as many angles as possible. From 8:30 a.m., the top part of the porthole blocked the light to the head, but at 8:50 a.m., the forehead and scalp were photographed in full sunlight.

We wondered if the structure was designed to illuminate the neck and face, pause for a moment of darkness, then finally reveal a "halo" of light around the top of the head. As the sun continued rising, darkness prevailed in the

Fig. A.1. The path of the sun shortly after its first appearance at the time of the winter solstice, as it penetrates the porthole window between Structure AD (the main enclosure) and Structure AB (the Pillars Shrine) and hits the giant head emerging from the west wall of the latter.
Photo by Hugh Newman.

Pillars Shrine. It took some time to sink in that we were the first observers of this phenomenon since this part of the site was deliberately covered over around 10,000 years ago. We felt as if we were witnessing one of the biblical gods, or a "Shining One," who had emerged from his or her slumber to gaze upon a very different world.

It also appears from the layout of the larger enclosure (Structure AD) that the sun would have shone between the two central pillars when they were upright, going through the porthole at a sharp angle, before hitting the stone head, to illuminate the chamber in the manner described. Necmi Karul has stated that the stone head "looks to the entrance"[4] toward the porthole stone, as though the eyes were carved to show it looking through the hole toward the winter solstice sunrise.

It is worth noting that natural features at the site may have been recognized by the original builders, who perhaps saw the stone protrusion (which later was carved into the shape of a head and neck) and then carved out a hole in the upright bedrock. We hypothesize that this area was chosen to be an early observation platform used by starwatchers, possibly from Göbekli Tepe, before it was built into what we see today.

ARCHAEOASTRONOMICAL ANALYSIS

"The two solstices were strongly emphasized. . . . Midwinter, moreover, was recorded almost twice as heavily as midsummer. . . . It is clear the turning points of the year, particularly the time of change from darkness and cold to light and warmth, were of very great importance to prehistoric people."[5] These are the words of the famous British archaeologist Aubrey Burl (1926–2020) on the importance of solstitial alignments at megalithic sites in Britain, Ireland, and Brittany in France. Was Karahan Tepe's own winter solstice alignment of a similar nature to those reported in connection with stone and earthen monuments in other parts of the world?

We sent our initial findings to Andrew Collins,[6] who, with veteran archaeo-astronomer and engineer Rodney Hale, checked to see whether Karahan Tepe's winter solstice alignment would have been valid when the site was constructed. They found that during this epoch the sun's rays would have passed through the porthole at a similar angle to what it does today, clearly illuminating the stone head.

We returned to Karahan Tepe in December 2022 with Andrew Collins to observe the sunrise over three consecutive mornings and get a more accurate assessment of the phenomenon. Before we give you our results, note that over the past 10,000 years the angle of the ecliptic has shifted by about 1 degree. The Earth was at its maximum tilt in 8700 BC, which is very close to the date of Karahan Tepe. This solstice angle would have also been very close to the extreme solstice angle at its most southerly position as part of the 41,000-year cycle at 24.5 degrees (it is now at 23.44 degrees). This change in Earth's tilt from the obliquity cycle slightly changes the position of the winter solstice sunrise over millennia. This means that when Karahan Tepe was being constructed, the angle was approximately one degree further south than today at the latitude of Karahan Tepe. The timing of the solstice has shifted considerably due to the precession of the equinoxes (a 25,800-year-cycle where a slight wobble of Earth's axis shifts by 1 degree every 72 years) from around mid-February in 9000 BCE to around December 21 in the current era. However, this does not affect the position of the sunrise at the time of the winter solstice. The winter solstice was then, and is now, the shortest day and longest night of the year. All this has been taken into account for our analysis of the alignment.

During our visit in December 2022, we took stills using the Theodolite app of the sunrise and noted its position on the horizon. We later compared this to where the sun would have risen in the tenth millennium BCE.

On December 20, 2021, the sunrise was at 7:37a.m.; this is an azimuth 119 degrees and 50 minutes. The sun started shining through the porthole at 7:47a.m. at azimuth 121 degrees and 28 minutes and 2 degrees altitude and continued until 8:30a.m. at 128 degrees and twelve minutes azimuth at an altitude of 8 degrees and 50 minutes. On the winter solstice in 9000 BCE, the sunrise was at 7:57a.m.; this is an azimuth of 121 degrees and 1 minute. Ten minutes later, at 8:07a.m. the sun reached 122 degrees and 44 minutes azimuth and altitude of 2 degrees when it started illuminating the stone head. This would continue, as it does in 2021, for about 45 minutes. This takes into account refraction for a temperature of 15 degrees Celsius.

To summarize, the sun would appear just over 1 degree to the right (south on the horizon) compared to where the sun is located in the current era. The sun's average diameter is 0.536 degrees in width. Basically, just over 1 sun-width would fit between the current sunrise and that of 9000 BCE (due to the change in the ecliptic). This is notable, and the stone head would have had a better illumination in the earlier era, because rather than the initial rays of light hitting the back of the neck of the stone head, they would begin closer to the face, and therefore illuminate it in a more complete way.

We also noted a 0.3 degree lower angle of sunrise 11,000 years ago, which would have also allowed for a slightly better illumination. These two differences combined prove that this alignment was not only valid, but may also have provided a better light effect on the head. We can now theorize that the alignment was deliberate and the precise location of the porthole window was essential for this purpose.[7]*

It is arguably the world's oldest known "solar clock" using the winter solstice to restart the annual cycle. The light coming through the porthole stone during the equinoxes and summer solstice sunrises (and all in-between) would be out of line with the stone head and would not touch any of the pillars in the Pillars Shrine. Therefore, the winter solstice alignment at Karahan Tepe works perfectly as an annual marker to begin the year and can still be witnessed today.

Archaeoastronomers are usually thought to look for the moment of sunrise as a specific time marker, but as we witnessed at Karahan Tepe, the alignment begins about 10 minutes later. Numerous other sites previously noted for their solar alignments also do not follow this rule. For example, the winter solstice at Newgrange (circa 3200 BCE) in Ireland's Boyne Valley is also "late" in astronomical terms as it begins 4 minutes after sunrise and lasts for a total of 17 minutes.

The sun's light passes through a very small porthole stone (or light box) above the main entrance at Newgrange, illuminating the passageway and roofed chamber and highlighting certain carvings and a stone bowl on its way through. A 9.5-inch (24-centimeter) polished sandstone phallus was found at Newgrange, with archaeologists commenting that fertility rites may have been carried out there.[8] The original Gaelic name of Newgrange, An Uanh Greine, means "Cave of the Sun." At nearby Loughcrew, the equinox sunrise (in March and September) illuminates numerous carvings moving slowly west to east across the inscribed stone. This takes 50 minutes to complete.

---

*During the initial excavation of the Pillars Shrine (Structure AB), it was revealed that the top part of the portal stone was fragile, and it was subsequently repaired by the excavation team to preserve its integrity. It does, however, occupy its original position (personal communication by the authors with Ismail Can, December 2022).

A winter solstice sunrise alignment is found at Karnak in Egypt (circa 2055 BCE), where for 25 minutes the sun's rays pierce the Sanctuary of Amun-Ra, finally reaching the "Holy of Holies" in the heart of the site. On Rapa Nui (Easter Island) in the Pacific, a system of holes bored in the rock at the Orongo ruins were found to indicate the December 21 solstice (summer solstice in the southern hemisphere).[9]

In Malta, the megalithic temple of Ħaġar Qim (circa 3600 BCE) has an entrance oriented to the winter solstice. Direct sunlight passes through the entrance doorway and falls onto the main altar. As the sun climbs higher, it shifts to the left side along the main corridor and reaches the full length of the passageway before it begins to retreat. A similar phenomenon occurs at Mnajdra (circa 3500 BCE), also in Malta, where a dagger of light illuminates a vertical slab in the first apse. On the summer solstice it appears on the other side of the apse.[10]

Many Maltese sites have porthole stones, like those found both at Göbekli Tepe and at Karahan Tepe. These were used to direct the light of sunrise into the interior of temples. According to Dutch author and independent researcher Lenie Reedijk, who has made a detailed study of the archaeoastronomical alignments at the Maltese temples, some of the structures could well be contemporary with Taş Tepeler sites in southeastern Anatolia.[11]

Two substantial summer solstice alignments have been found at Jericho (9000 BCE to circa 600 CE) and Atlit Yam (7400 BCE to 6000 BCE) in Israel. Jericho, famous for its walls and stone tower, is located in the Palestinian West Bank, east of Jerusalem, with continuous occupation since Pre-Pottery Neolithic times. The Jericho Tower dates to 8300 BCE and is 30 feet (9 meters) wide and 28 feet (8.5 meters) tall with an interior stepped passage oriented at an azimuth of 290 degrees (or 20 degrees north of west). Some 10,000 years ago the summer solstice sunset would have illuminated the passageway of the tower.[12]

Atlit Yam is a submerged Late Pre-Pottery Neolithic B complex, situated 30 feet (9 meters) underwater off the northern Carmel coast and covering around 10 acres (4 hectares). Its notable feature is a stone semicircle with cup marks on it. Next to the circle are parallel stone walls that align to the summer solstice.*

---

*Archaeoastronomer Clive Ruggles confirmed that the two corridors at Atlit Yam were "oriented in the direction of sunrise on the June solstice" (see Bergeron 2014 and Galili et al. 2011).

At Chaco Canyon, Arizona (circa 850) a small, yet remarkable petroglyph of a spiral or labyrinth records a blade of light entering from a thin gap in the rocks above, marking the solstices. On the winter solstice, two daggers of light appear on either side of the petroglyph for 49 minutes, during which they precisely frame the spiral.[13] On the summer solstice one "light dagger" illuminates the central axis of the spiral.

Stonehenge (circa 3000 BCE), famous for its summer solstice sunrise alignment, is also aligned to the winter solstice sunrise.[14] There is a direct sight line that runs through the monument, aligning along the "Altar Stone" through a deliberately carved notch (which frames it perfectly) and pointing directly at the rising of the sun over Coneybury Hill in the distance. Stonehenge also contains a perfect winter solstice sunset orientation matching the direction of the avenue (exactly opposite to the summer solstice sunrise).[15] Feasting and community gathering also took place over the winter solstice at nearby Durrington Walls. Furthermore, three huge Mesolithic postholes found at the site date back to 8000 BCE.

A beautifully decorated megalithic tomb on this island of Gavrinis in the Morbihan Gulf of Brittany hides a unique winter solstice phenomenon. Not only does it precisely align to the sunrise, it also incorporates the extreme southerly position of the moon every 18.6 years just as accurately. A laser-like beam runs along the floor of the chamber and hits the left side of two stones which form the back wall, and as the light slowly widens and sinks, it illuminates only the left stone before it hits the floor—whereas the stone at the top right receives moonlight every 18.6 years when the lunar orb rises at its most southerly point on the horizon.

Other sites in the Carnac area include the Crucuno Quadrilateral megalithic site (circa 4000 BCE) that incorporates the winter and summer solstices to its corners. It is laid out as a 3-4-5 Pythagorean triangle, measuring 30 by 40 by 50 megalithic yards in size (a megalithic yard is 2.72 feet or 0.83 meters and features frequently in the design of British stone circles). At the Dolmens de Rondossec, also in Brittany, two megalithic chambers are aligned to the winter solstice when its back stone gets illuminated. Furthermore, the angle of the solstice at this latitude is the diagonal of a perfect 3-4-5 Pythagorean triangle. This was not only incorporated into individual sites, but also determines the placement of monuments across vast distances. Strikingly similar landscape geometries have been found in the

Taş Tepeler region (details of this will be revealed in a forthcoming book by Hugh and JJ).

At Karahan Tepe, this particular discovery may have been the world's first sundial (or a negative sundial, as the light rather than the shadow is the marker), as it measures the solar year to within a few minutes. The light coming through the porthole stone during the equinoxes and summer solstice sunrises (and all dates in between) would be out of line with the stone head and would not touch any of the pillars in the Pillars Shrine, illuminating only part of a blank wall between the porthole and the head. Therefore, the winter solstice alignment at Karahan Tepe works perfectly as an annual time marker to begin the year, and it can still be witnessed today.

Did a roof at Karahan Tepe block the alignment?

Artistic representations of the site suggest the main enclosure at Karahan Tepe, Structure AD, once had a roof held up by T-pillars. No evidence of any roofs have, however, been found either at Karahan Tepe or at Göbekli Tepe. The only circumstantial evidence for this idea comes from proposals that these structures were in fact either domestic or communal "houses" (although incredibly rich in symbolic content, built with monoliths up to 18 feet [5.5 meters] tall).[16] In regard to Karahan Tepe, if a roof had once existed there, it would have been quite possibly the largest in the world at the time as the enclosure is 75 feet (23 meters) across. Even if one had been in place, it could easily have had an opening to the southeast to allow the low passing of the sun to illuminate the stone head on the winter solstice.

A temporary roof over the Pillars Shrine may have some basis in reality as it has clear ledges and flat surfaces that could have been used to support one. The winter solstice phenomenon, having been directly observed in real time, is hard to ignore. If a roof did once exist there it would only have enhanced the experience, illuminating the chamber in a quite profound way, much like we see at places like Newgrange in Ireland.

SUMMER SOLSTICE SUNSET
AND A LUNISOLAR CALENDAR

In addition to Karahan Tepe's winter solstice alignment, there are further indications that the site was used to observe and measure movements in the sky.

During the night, at the time of the winter solstice, the Milky Way slowly rises horizontally through the sky before the sunrise occurs. Furthermore, in October 2021, Andrew Collins found a summer solstice sunset alignment, oriented along the primary direction of the second unfinished hypogeum pit (Structure AA). This revealed that some 2.5 hours after sunset the Milky Way would have been vertical on the horizon, exactly where the sun had earlier set (see chapter 15).[17]

Collins also found an alignment from the southern recess of the main enclosure (Structure AD), through the porthole stone, and over the freestanding monoliths in the Pillars Shrine toward the peak of nearby Keçili Hill (where there are hypogeum-like caves and rock-cut structures). This would have targeted the setting of Cygnus and the Milky Way's Dark Rift during the epoch in question. Similar alignments toward Cygnus exist at Göbekli Tepe (see chapters 4 and 17). Also at Göbekli Tepe, Enclosure F (a smaller, later structure west of the main group) is oriented to within a degree of the rising of the sun at the time of the summer solstice and the setting of the sun at the winter solstice.[18]

Martin Sweatman suggests a lunisolar calendar was in use at Karahan Tepe (and is shown also on Pillar 43 at Göbekli Tepe).[19] The 11 pillars in the Pillars Shrine, he proposes, represent 11 lunar months and 11 epagomenal days (an intercalary month), which are used to complete a solar year. The freestanding eleventh pillar could represent the summer solstice, which Sweatman believes was established as a unique epagomenal day at Göbekli Tepe. The stone head may represent the final lunar month of the year.*

Although Sweatman's ideas do not take into account the newly discovered winter solstice alignment (which could give credence to his theory), they certainly contribute to the debate. This alignment is highly likely to have been the observable annual time marker that restarted the calendar year. The moon, as Sweatman emphasizes, may also have played a part in the calendrical and ceremonial cycle.

---

*To summarize Sweatman's findings: the stone head represents 1 lunar month or 29 or 30 days. The 11 pillars could signify 11 more lunar months, making 354 days, with the 11 pillars also signifying the 11 epagomenal days (of which one, the summer solstice, is special), making 365 days or 1 solar year in total.

THE MOON AND ECLIPSES

It is an astronomical fact that during the 18.61-year lunar standstill cycle there would have been certain full moons around the time of the summer solstice. These would have moved along the same path as the winter solstice sun. When this happened, the bright full moon would have lit up the stone head through the porthole, much like the sun does at the winter solstice. Skywatchers at this time are likely to have identified these moments, which occur when the full moon is located on or near one of the nodes in the "solstice" positions, as special in some way.

We asked Andrew Collins and Rodney Hale to investigate this matter, and they concluded that "in 9015 BCE according to Stellarium and Hale's calculations the full moon would indeed have cast its light into Structure AB to illuminate the stone head on the west wall, just as the sun would have done at the time of the winter solstice."[20] This synchronization between the moon and the Pillars Shrine would have occurred just before the summer solstice (which would have occurred during the month of August in 9015 BCE).*

A full moon in such a position has a high likelihood of being eclipsed, because it is always located directly opposite the sun. When the sun is at standstill during the summer solstice and the moon takes the position where the sun was at winter solstice, eclipses occasionally occur and could have been recorded at Karahan Tepe by direct observation. If one year it occurred on or close to the summer solstice, it may also have coincided with the Milky Way rising vertically in the sky 2.5 hours after sunset.

More research needs to be carried out to check this, but this rare alignment of the full moon, a possible eclipse, and the Milky Way would have been a spectacular sight during the summer solstice period. The solstices were clearly important time markers for the megalith builders in the Taş Tepeler region.

The Importance of Venus in Timekeeping

In addition, there is potential evidence for the use of longer cycles at Karahan Tepe during the time frame of its use. Every 8 years, Venus would rise 1 hour before sunrise with enough brightness to illuminate the giant stone head. This same Venus alignment has been reported in connection with Newgrange's own winter solstice phenomena, and so it might also have been used to mark time.

---

*A date of 9015 BCE was used for this exercise. A similar alignment would have occurred around this same time during every 18.61-year lunar standstill cycle (via Andrew Collins).

In the same years as Venus's heliacal rising at the time of the winter solstice, the planet rises close to the sun at the time of the equinoxes. Since Venus is the third-brightest object in the sky, it could well have been visible at this time, especially since on some occasions it can rise at any time up to 2 hours before the sun itself.

Across a period of 8 solar years, Venus completes 5 synoptic cycles, each one being 584 days in length. At the end of this time the planet roughly returns to the same position in which it started the cycle.

In the same years as Venus's heliacal rising at the time of the winter solstice, the planet rises 30 minutes *after* sunrise on the vernal equinox (around March 21 in today's calendar); this occurring once every 8 years (or 5 Venus years), and since Venus is the third brightest object in the sky, it could well have been visible even in daylight. However, on the equinoxes of 9004, 9006, and 9009 BCE, it would have risen between 1 and 2 hours before the sun, indicating it was being observed during the equinox periods, and was clearly visible in the night sky, again, following the same path as the sun.

The stone head in the Pillars Shrine faces east, toward the spring and autumn equinox sunrises (although its eyes are gazing toward the porthole window). Along with this, a channel is carved out of the bedrock from the Pillars Shrine in this direction (at the time of writing filled up with rubble). The eastern sky is also the direction of another phenomenon that occurs during the equinox sunrise: the rising of the constellation of Leo, which may have been seen as a leopard rather than a lion (there are a significant number of leopard carvings at Karahan Tepe). This appears in the night sky just before sunrise. Authors Robert Bauval and Graham Hancock controversially theorized that the Sphinx in Egypt faces eastward as a marker for the rising of Leo during the vernal equinox as far back as 10,500 BCE.[21] (In the current era, Pisces rises in the east.) We must ask now: Was it observed at sites such as Karahan Tepe first, but in the guise of a leopard?

Combined with the winter solstice marker in time, Karahan Tepe may have been the innovation center designed to bring the movements of the sky down to Earth and fix these calendars in place, no doubt counting the days to establish important times for celebration and also to know when to plant crops and breed livestock. Another Taş Tepeler site that has come to light, called Sayburç, contemporary with Karahan Tepe, has a tantalizing translation of its name: *say* means "counting," *burç* means "sign of the zodiac," and *birc* (in Kurdish) means "tower or watchtower." It seems that even place names still today hold keys to understanding the purpose of these sites.

THE END OF KARAHAN TEPE

At some point, perhaps close to 8000 BCE, it was decided to close down Karahan Tepe. After nearly 1,500 years of use, the final observation of the winter solstice alignment may have been chosen for this special day, before the Pillars Shrine was carefully filled in with stone, debris, and soil, with larger flagstones finally completing the process. Those who took part in this decommissioning of the site can be imagined foreseeing the future, envisioning who would be the first people to witness this unique winter solstice illumination once again. That day came on December 20, 2021, and will no doubt be witnessed by many more in the years to come.*

HUGH NEWMAN is the author of *Göbekli Tepe and Karahan Tepe: The World's First Megaliths* (2023), *Earth Grids* (2008), and *Stone Circles* (2017) and coauthor of *Giants On Record: America's Hidden History, Secrets in the Mounds and the Smithsonian Files* (2015), *The Giants of Stonehenge and Ancient Britain* (2021), *Megalith: Studies In Stone* (2018), and *Geomancy* (2021). He is an explorer, Megalithomania Conference organizer, and tour/expedition leader. He has appeared on the History Channel, Discovery, Gaia TV, Smithsonian Channel, and Science Channel, and has a BA Hons in Journalism and Film Production. **www.megalithomania.co.uk**

JJ AINSWORTH is a researcher and explorer from the United States, who is an expert on ancient symbolism and connections between sites worldwide. She has featured on *Forbidden History* (Discovery Channel), *Secrets of the Lost Ark* (Science Channel), numerous radio shows and podcasts, and has published articles on the Ancient Origins and Graham Hancock websites. She is a tour/expedition leader and has given lectures at Megalithomania and the Origins Conference in the UK. **www.youtube.com/c/megalithicmaiden**

---

*An earlier version of this article, which has since been updated, was published on the Graham Hancock website. See Newman and Ainsworth 2022.

Notes

FOREWORD

1. Collins 2014b.

CHAPTER 1.
THE GREAT DISCOVERY

1. Schmidt 2012, 131.
2. Mellaart 1967, 166–68.
3. Tarihi 2023.

CHAPTER 2. KARAHAN TEPE—
THE BEDROCK ENCLOSURES

1. Karul 2021, 23.
2. Karul 2021, 23.
3. Karul 2021, 23.
4. Karul 2021, 24.
5. Karul 2021, 24.

CHAPTER 3. STRUCTURE AA—THE PIT SHRINE

1. Karul 2021, 23–24.
2. Karul 2021, 24.
3. Karul 2021, 25.
4. Karul 2021, 25.
5. Karul 2021, 25.

6. Mellaart 1967, 104.

7. Hodder 2006, 123.

8. Karul 2021, 21.

CHAPTER 4.
IT BEGAN WITH GÖBEKLI TEPE

1. Schmidt and Dietrich 2010.

2. This was originally determined by the present author working with British engineer Rodney Hale. See Collins 2018, ch. 23.

3. For a full account of the alignments toward Deneb found at Göbekli Tepe, see Collins 2018, ch.2.

4. Tedlock 1996, 356; Jenkins 1998.

5. See Collins 2018, chs. 4–5.

6. See Little 2014 for a full exploration of this topic.

7. Collins 2018, 27.

8. See Collins 2014a, 4; Collins 2018, 27.

9. Deitrich et al. 2012; Dietrich 2016.

10. UNESCO 2018.

11. TGA 2021.

CHAPTER 5.
HILL OF THE DARK LORD

1. The book in question was *Harran: The Crossroad of Civilizations* by A. Cihat Kürkçüoğlu and Zuhal Karahan Kara, which had been published one year earlier in 2003. Section 3.17 features Karahan Tepe (pages 77–78). See Collins 2004a for a full account of this remarkable journey through southeastern Turkey.

2. Collins 2004a. See also Collins 2006, chs. 1–2.

3. Kürkçüoğlu and Karahan Kara 2003, 77–78.

4. Kürkçüoğlu and Karahan Kara 2003, 77–78.

5. Çelik 2010, 259, fig. 6.

6. Çelik 2017, 5, fig. 11.

7. Çelik 2000.

8. Çelik 2000.

9. Çelik 2011.

10. Çelik 2011, 247; Karul 2022.

11. Collins 2014b.

12. See, for instance, Spray 2021 and Thomas 2022.

CHAPTER 6.
THE BIRTH OF TAŞ TEPELER

1. TGA 2021.
2. TGA 2021.
3. TGA 2021.
4. TGA 2021.
5. TGA 2021.
6. Çelik 2014, 11, 19, 20–21; Çelik 2017.
7. Çelik 2014, 15, 21.
8. Çelik 2014, 20–21.
9. Özdoğan 2022.
10. Collins 2018, 330–31; Collins and Little 2020, ch. 15.
11. Kodaş 2019, Kodaş 2021.
12. Hurriyet 2022.
13. Hurriyet 2022.
14. Hurriyet 2022.
15. Hurriyet 2022.
16. Hurriyet 2022.
17. For more on this subject see Collins 2014a, chs. 19–23, and Collins 2018, chs. 9 and 34.
18. Formozov 1959, 59, 68, 71. For a good review of Formozov's hypothesis, see Stetsyuk 2012.
19. Collins 2018, chs. 8–10.
20. Collins 2018, ch. 10.
21. Burney 1977, 15.
22. Çelik 2014, 16.
23. See Karul 2021, 24, in connection with Str. AB and Karul 2021, 25, in the case of Str. AA.
24. Çelik 2011, 246.
25. Karul 2021, 23.
26. Karagöz 2021.
27. Karagöz 2021.

CHAPTER 7.
THE MYSTERIES OF THE GREAT ELLIPSE

1. Collins 2018, ch. 23.
2. Collins 2018, 192–93.
3. Marshall 2016.
4. Collins 2018, 203–4.
5. Srinivasan 1996, 26.

6. McBride 2014, 357–358.

7. Lienhard 2000. See also Bagley 2005, 55, 65, 68, 83, for further information on the use of the minor third in ancient Chinese instruments.

CHAPTER 9.
THE PLACE OF EMERGENCE

1. Collins 2006.

2. Collins 2014a, ch. 7; Collins 2018, ch. 2.

3. Schoch 2012, 53–57.

4. Magli 2019.

5. Lorenzis and Orofino 2015, particularly page 42.

6. For a full study of this subject see Little 2014.

7. Lankford 2007b, 186, 208.

8. See Little (2014) 2016, Little 2015, Little 2016a, Little 2016b, Little 2016c, Little 2016d, Little 2016e, Little 2016f, Little 2016g, Little 2016h, Little 2016i, 2016j.

9. Tedlock 1996, 356; Jenkins 1998, 10–11, 13, 61, 106, 117; Milbrath 1999, 41, 271.

10. Freidel, Schele, and Parker 1993, 55, 73, 76.

11. Milbrath 1999, 271; Starr 2008, D-64.

12. Milbrath 1999, 41.

13. See Collins 2014a, chs. 12–15.

14. O'Brien, 2012.

15. Wenger [1980] 1991, 34, 61.

16. Collins 2014a, 86–88; Collins 2018, 12–14.

17. Uyanik 1974, 12.

18. VAMzzz 2021. For a perfect photo showing a man slithering along the ground in the belief that he is a snake during the 2009 Wai khru festival, see the photo on the Getty Images website page titled "Living with Spirits."

19. See, for example, Herskovits 1937, 172.

CHAPTER 10.
MAD ENGLISHMEN

1. See Collins 2009 for a full account of the rediscovery of Giza's lost cave world.

2. Glosbe, s.v. "girl in northern Kurdish—keç" 2015.

3. Wikipedia 2022. "Breast-shaped hill."

4. Personal communication with Sabahattin Alkan.

5. Blasweiler 2014, 7.

CHAPTER 12. HALF MOONS AND ROCK TEMPLES

1. Güler, Çelik, and Güler 2012, 166 and fig. 4.
2. AWOL 2015–2021.
3. See Çelik 2016 for a full record of the site.
4. Sagona and Zimansky 2015, 74.

CHAPTER 13. REALM OF THE SNAKE MOTHER

1. Yıldıran 2001.
2. Wiggerman 2011.
3. Rahmouni 2007, xxiii; Murat 2009, 160.
4. Blasweiler 2014, 18.
5. White [2007] 2008, 179.
6. Blasweiler 2014, 15.
7. Murat 2009, 161–62, 164, 175–76, 183, 187.
8. Murat 2009, 163, 175.
9. Murat 2009, 161, 163.
10. Murat 2009, 176.
11. Murat 2009, 176, 188.
12. Murat 2009, 167.
13. Glosbe, s.v. "girl in northern Kurdish—keç" 2015.
14. Murat 2009, 160, 175 n.17.
15. See Frahm and Carolus 2021.
16. AWOL 2015–2021.
17. White [2007] 2008, 179.
18. Papazian 2015.
19. Yıldıran 2001.
20 Papazian 2015.

CHAPTER 14. CELESTIAL SYNCHRONIZATION

1. Data obtained using the Stellarium 0.12.4 open-source planetarium software.
2. See Collins 2014a, 4; Collins 2018, 27.

CHAPTER 15. THE SCORPIONIC GATEWAY

1. Santillana and von Dechend 1969, 243–44.
2. Santillana and von Dechend 1969, 243.

3. Alexander 1920, 185.

4. Santillana and von Dechend 1969, 244.

5. White [2007] 2008, 178.

6. Blasweiler 2014, 16.

7. WLW 2021.

8. Rahmouni 2007, xxiv; Allen [1899] 1963, s.v. "Scorpio, or Scorpius, the Scorpion," 360–72.

9. Genesis 49:17 (all Bible references are from *Young's Literal Translation* unless otherwise stated). See also Allen [1899] 1963, s.v. "Scorpio, or Scorpius, the Scorpion," 360–72.

10. Allen, 1899, s.v. "Scorpio, or Scorpius, the Scorpion," 360–72.

11. Co-Operation in Mesopotamia 2023.

12. Murat 2009, 160, 175 n.17.

13. Vogh 1977.

CHAPTER 16. THE COSMIC SNAKE CHARMER

1. See Allen [1899] 1963, s.v. "Serpens," 374–76.

2. Allen [1899] 1963, s.v. "Ophiuchus vel Serpentarius, the Serpent-holder," 299–303.

3. Allen 1963 [1899], s.v. "Ophiuchus vel Serpentarius, the Serpent-holder," 299–303.

4. Savage-Smith [1984] 1985, 153, 155.

5. Thanks for Neslihan Tokat for this information.

6. White [2007] 2008, 190–91.

7. White [2007] 2008, 190–91.

8. Black et al. 1998, lls. 26–36.

9. Schmidt 2012, 206–7.

10. Allen [1899] 1963, s.v. "Ophiuchus vel Serpentarius, the Serpent-holder," 299–303.

11. McClintock and Strong 1880, s.v. "Serpent-charming," 586–87.

12. Schjellerup 1874, 95, 98, fig. 13.

13. Bochart 1796, vol. 3, 164.

14. Drower 1941, 27, 183.

15. Drower 1941, 27.

16. Collins 1996, ch. 13.

17. Drower 1941, 146, 153.

CHAPTER 17. PILLAR 43—PART ONE: THE VULTURE AND THE SCORPION

1. Collins 2014a, ch. 7.

2. Collins 2018, ch. 2.

3. Vahradyan and Vahradyan 2013.

4. Teryan 2017.

5. Belmonte 2010.

6. Rahmouni 2007, xxiv.

7. Blasweiler 2014, 16.

8. Uyanik 1974, 12.

9. Burley 2013.

10. Sweatman and Tsikritsis 2017; Hancock 2015, 318–27.

11. Collins 2014a, 50–52.

12. Avalon Marshes 2016.

13. Driscoll 2006, 69.

14. Jones 2019.

CHAPTER 18. PILLAR 43—PART TWO:
THE HOLE IN THE SKY

1. Eliade 1964, 262.

2. Allen [1899] 1963, s.v. "Lyra, the Lyre or Harp," 280–88.

CHAPTER 19. PILLAR 43—PART THREE:
THE FOX AND THE SNAKE

1. Allen [1899] 1963, s.v. "Scorpio, or Scorpius, the Scorpion," 360–72.

2. Cooley 2008, 184.

3. Gore 1909, 222.

4. Gore 1909, 222.

5. Gore 1909, 222. See also Allen [1899] 1963, s.v. "Ophiuchus vel Serpentarius," 297–302.

6. Miller 1997, 202–3.

7. Miller 1997, 203.

8. Miller 1997, 202–4.

CHAPTER 20. THE MILKY WAY SERPENT

1. Allen [1899] 1963, s.v. "The Galaxy, or Milky Way," 474–85.

2. Personal communication with Khanna Omarkhali in December 2022.

3. Personal communication with Sabahattin Alkan.

4. Allen [1899] 1963, s.v. "The Galaxy, or Milky Way," 474–85. The reference in the Hebrew Bible to the Milky Way as the Crooked Serpent is Job 26:13.

5. Theoi, s.v. "Okeanos" 2005.

6. For the full text of the *Enūma Eliš*, see Mark 2018.

7. Brown 1900, vol. ii, 29; Rogers 1998, 14.

8. Encyclopedia.com, s.v. "Mixcoatl," accessed 2024.

9. Jenkins 1998, 52.

10. Allen [1899] 1963, s.v. "The Galaxy, or Milky Way," 474–85.

11. Wisdom Library 2022.

12. Bender 2022.

13. Bender 2022.

14. Bender 2022.

15. Bender 2022.

CHAPTER 21.
RIDING THE SNAKE

1. Jenkins 1998, 9, 52, 56, 103.

2. Milbrath 1999, 38.

3. Crystalinks 2005.

4. Bender 2022.

5. Gresky, Haelm, and Clare 2017.

6. Harner 1973, 160–64.

7. The White Arrow 2022.

8. Herskovits 1937, 172.

9. Ward 2021, 10.

10. Ward 2021, 10.

11. Ward 2021, 10.

12. Ward 2021, 10.

13. O'Conner and Kellerman 2018.

14. Bender 2022.

15. Romain 2022.

16. Personal communication with William F. Romain, February 14, 2023.

CHAPTER 22.
THE SHINING SERPENT

1. Collins 2021.

2. Barkai and Liran 2008.

3. Collins and Hale 2022.

CHAPTER 23.
ORACULAR COMMUNICATION

1. "Hymn 3 to Apollo," 370. See Anonymous 1914, *Hesiod, the Homeric Hymns and Homerica.*
2. For more on this topic see Chappell 2006.
3. Mathisen 2020.
4. Kingsley 1999, 133–34.
5. Kingsley 1999, 134.
6. Kingsley 1999, 134.
7. Kingsley 1999, 134.

CHAPTER 24.
THE STAR WORSHIPPERS OF HARRAN

1. Dodge 1967, 62.
2. Dodge 1967, 84.
3. Yardimci 2008, 362–64.
4. See Lloyd and Brice 1951, 77–111. They report on surface finds at Harran, including distinctive ceramic ware belonging to the Halaf culture.
5. Dodge 1967, 64–65, 70.
6. Dodge 1967, 69.
7. Dodge 1967, 69; Green 1992, 194.
8. Dodge 1967, 60.
9. Dodge 1967, 63.
10. Dodge 1967, 70.
11. Dodge 1967, 74–75.
12. Green 1992, 195.
13. Richter 2004, 264.
14. Rogers 1998, 12; Black, George, and Postgate [1999] 2000, s.v. "Ukaduhha, Kadduhha," 419.
15. Rogers 1998, 13
16. Dodge 1967, 60.
17. Leisegang [1955] 1978, 207.
18. Jáuregui 2010, 35–36, 46–47, 81 after the work of Otto Kern (1910). See also Jáuregui 2015.
19. Collins 2018, ch. 6.
20. White, 2007, 194, 254.
21. Halloran [1996] 1999.
22. Weiss 2020, 40.

CHAPTER 25. THE MYSTERY OF THE ALABASTER BOWL

1. See, for instance, Delbrueck and Vollgraff 1934, Leisegang [1955] 1978, and Lozanova-Stantcheva 2016, all of which advocate for an Orphic origin of the bowl's symbolism.
2. Delbrueck and Vollgraff 1934, 129.
3. Lozanova-Stantcheva 2016, 84.
4. Delbrueck and Vollgraff 1934.
5. Leisegang 1939.
6. Leisegang [1955] 1978.
7. Delbrueck and Vollgraff 1934, 136.
8. Leisegang [1955] 1978, 196.
9. Delbrueck and Vollgraff 1934, 134; Leisegang [1955] 1978, 197.
10. As quoted in Leisegang [1955] 1978, 194.
11. Delbrueck and Vollgraff 1934, 139.
12. Delbrueck and Vollgraff 1934, 129.
13. Lozanova-Stantcheva 2016, 84, 86.
14. Delbrueck and Vollgraff 1934, 130, 135; Leisegang [1955] 1978, 195, 211; Lozanova-Stantcheva 2016, 85.
15. Lozanova-Stantcheva 2016, 85.
16. Delbrueck and Vollgraff 1934, 132.
17. Leisegang [1955] 1978, 196.
18. Leisegang [1955] 1978, 196.
19. Delbrueck and Vollgraff 1934, 132.
20. Leisegang [1955] 1978, 209, 215.
21. Delbrueck and Vollgraff 1934, 132.
22. Leisegang [1955] 1978, 201–2.
23. Leisegang [1955] 1978, 196.
24. Leisegang [1955] 1978, 233.
25. Delbrueck and Vollgraff 1934, 132; Leisegang [1955] 1978, 236–39.
26. Leisegang [1955] 1978, 236, and particularly 236 n.10 where he provides references to Aristophanes's parodying an Orphic initiation.
27. Leisegang [1955] 1978, 240.
28. Leisegang [1955] 1978, 245.
29. Leisegang [1955] 1978, 208–11.
30. Cumont 1902, 2.
31. Leisegang [1955] 1978, 210.
32. Ulansey 1994.
33. Leisegang [1955] 1978, 220.
34. See Pirtea 2017 for a full study in the origins and use of the name āṭālyā.

35. Cumont 1929, 194. Translation from original French as quoted in Bellizia 2010, 4.

36. Cumont 1929, 195–96. Translation from original Greek as quoted in Bellizia 2010, 4.

37. MacKenzie 1964, 515.

38. MacKenzie 1964, 515–16.

39. MacKenzie 1964, 515 n. 26.

40. Edwards 1996, 74.

41. Leisegang [1955] 1978, 218.

42. Leisegang [1955] 1978, 230.

43. Leisegang [1955] 1978, 232.

44. Leisegang [1955] 1978, 233.

45. Leisegang [1955] 1978, 233.

46. MacKenzie 1964, 523.

47. Mackenzie 1964, 525.

CHAPTER 26. THE ROAD TO RUSAFA

1. Delbrueck and Vollgraff 1934, 137.

2. Moosa 1987, 255–56.

3. Mahajjah Institute 2016.

4. Moosa 1987, 367.

5. Springett 1922, 140ff.

6. Moosa 1987, 393, 406.

7. Moosa 1987, 339.

8. Moosa 1987, 340–41.

9. Quotation from Green 1992, 203, but see also Dussaud 1900, 82–86, 201–2.

CHAPTER 27. FOLLOWERS OF THE SERPENT

1. Hippolytus of Rome 1921, vols. I and II.

2. Hippolytus of Rome 1921, bk. v, p. 190, in Legge's translation vol. i, 149; Hippolytus of Rome 1921, bk. x, ch. 10, in Legge's translation vol. ii, 154.

3. See Patristic Bible Commentary, "Catena [Genesis] Chapter 14."

4. Hippolytus of Rome 1921, vol. 1, 146 n. 1.

5. See Genesis 11:28, 11:31, 15:7.

6. Rendsburg 2019.

7. Clement of Alexandria 2004, bk. vii, ch. 17.

8. Hippolytus of Rome 1921, bk. v, p. 201, in Legge's translation vol. i, 155.

9. Exodus 7, 9–15.

10. Hippolytus of Rome 1921, bk. v, p. 201, in Legge's translation vol. i, 155.

11. Genesis 3:7.

12. Numbers 21:6, 8–9.

13. Hippolytus of Rome 1886, bk. v, ch. 11.

14. Hippolytus of Rome 1886, bk. v, ch. 11.

15. Hippolytus of Rome 1886, bk. v, ch. 11.

16. Hippolytus of Rome 1886, bk. v, ch. 11.

17. Hippolytus of Rome 1886, bk. v, ch. 11.

18. Hippolytus of Rome 1921, bk. x, p. 125, in Legge's translation, vol. i, 110–11.

19. Hippolytus of Rome 1886, bk. iv, ch. 48.

20. Hippolytus of Rome 1886, bk. v, ch. 11.

21. Hippolytus of Rome 1886, bk. v, ch. 12.

22. Hippolytus of Rome 1886, bk. v, ch. 12.

23. Hippolytus of Rome 1886, bk. v, ch. 12.

24. Hippolytus of Rome 1886, bk. v, ch. 12.

25. See Gooch 2007 for a full study of the cerebellum's function in the attainment of dreams and psychic phenomena.

CHAPTER 28.
THE RAISING OF THE KUNDALINI

1. Mead 1900, 203–4.

2. Avalon [1919] 1924, 1.

3. Avalon [1919] 1924, 1.

4. Avalon [1919] 1924, 4.

5. Avalon [1919] 1924, 4.

6. See Avalon [1919] 1924, for a good review of this topic and its adoption into Western mysticism at the beginning of the twentieth century.

7. Hippolytus of Rome 1886, bk. v, ch. 12.

8. Leisegang [1955] 1978, 224, 224 n. 34.

9. Leisegang [1955] 1978, 245.

10. Epiphanius bk. I, ch. 37 as quoted in Leisegang [1955] 1978, 231.

11. Leisegang [1955] 1978, 196.

12. Leisegang [1955] 1978, 235.

13. Leisegang [1955] 1978, 236.

14. Lauf 1989, 24.

15. Leisegang [1955] 1978, 196.

16. Gnosticism Explained 2021.

17. McCoy 2020.

18. See Reitzenstein 1904.

19. Altmann 1945, 377–78.

20. Orlov 2013.

21. See, for instance, Raina 2012, and Reddy 2020.

22. Moosa 1987, 340–41.

23. Quotation from Green 1992, 203, but see also Dussaud 1900, 82–86, 201–2.

24. Hippolytus of Rome 1921, bk. v, p. 198, in Legge's translation vol. i, 153.

CHAPTER 29. CITIES OF THE SERPENT

1. Segal 1970, 51–52; Drijvers 1980, 191–92.

2. Segal 1970, 3 n. 1, 52.

3. Segal 1963, 202, 214–15.

4. Jáuregui 2010, 35–36, 46–47, 81 after the work of Otto Kern (1910). See also Jáuregui 2015.

5. Richter 2006.

6. Green 1992, 34.

7. Segal 1970, 45–46, 51–53.

8. Segal 1970, 45–46.

9. Green 1992, 70.

10. Green 1992, 33–34, 70–72.

11. Green 1992, 70.

12. Segal 1970, 46; Green 1992, 71.

13. Van Bladel 2009, 78, 80.

14. Green 1992, 173.

15. Green 1992, 173.

16. Green 1992, 173.

17. Green 1992, 110, 139, 174, 212

18. Collins 2009, ch. 20.

19. Green 1992, 173.

20. As quoted in Segal 1970, 34.

21. Kotzé 2017, 104.

22. White [2007] 2008.

23. Hunger 1987–1990. s.v. "Lisin." 32; Black and Green 1992, 122; Thompson 2011–2020, 18. Wee 2016, 143.

24. Hooke 1962, 101–3.

25. Hooke 1962, 103.

26. Hooke 1962, 103.

27. Fleming 1993, 175.

28. Fleming 1993, 178.

29. Fleming 1993, 179–80.

30. Fleming 1993, 177.

31. Stokl 2010, 48.

32. Fleming 1993, 182.

33. Fleming 1993, 181.

34. Fleming 1993, 181.

35. Fleming 1993, 176–77, 182.

36. Fleming 1993, 182.

37. Reiner 1995, 35.

38. Reiner 1995, 35.

39. As quoted in Drijvers 1980, 34.

40. As quoted in Drijvers 1980, 34.

41. Drijvers 1980, 70–73.

42. Browne 1928, 389.

43. Bryant 1776, 134.

44. Bryant 1776, 134–35.

45. Segal 1970, 106.

46. Segal 1970, 2 n.4, 106.

47. Segal 1970, 106.

48. Segal 1970, 106.

CHAPTER 30.
THE SERPENT WITHIN

1. Oesterreich 1930, 314, translation of the original German from Rohde [1894] 1898, "vol. ii, pp. 60 sq."

2. Collins 2006, 209–14.

3. Trout 2004.

4. Leisegang [1955] 1978, 245.

5. Personal communication between the author and Sabahattin Alkan in May 2023.

CHAPTER 31.
LORD OF THE SIGNS

1. Nadège 2020.

2. Nadège 2020.

3. Clark 1982, 14.

4. Clark 1982, 13.

5. Clark 1982, 13.

6. Clark 1982, 17.

7. Clark 1982, 16.

8. Breiter 1908, II, 462.

9. Johnson, Martin, and Hunt 1915, 2–3, no. 63, ll. 2–12; Clark 1982, 18 n. 20.

10. Charles 1982, 19.

11. See Wee 2015, 231, Tables 1A, 1B, 1C, 2.

12. Wisdom Library 2016.

13. Nandakumar 2021.

14. Nandakumar 2021.

CHAPTER 32.
AT THE CENTER OF IT ALL

1. NASA 2017.

2. NAOJ 2020.

3. Kraus, Ko, and Matt 1954.

4. Brown 1982.

5. Event Horizon Telescope Collaboration 2022.

6. Allen, [1899] 1963, s.v. "Scorpio, or Scorpius, the Scorpion," 360–72.

7. Allen, [1899] 1963, s.v. "Scorpio, or Scorpius, the Scorpion," 360–72.

8. Allen, [1899] 1963, s.v. "Scorpio, or Scorpius, the Scorpion," 360–72.

9. Allen, [1899] 1963, s.v. "Scorpio, or Scorpius, the Scorpion," 360–72.

10. LaViolette 1997, 56.

11. LaViolette 1997, 89–93, 112–20, 178–81.

12. See, for instance, Legrand and De Angelis 1995; Firestone, West, and Warwick-Smith 2006; Firestone et al. 2007; Bunch et al. 2012; Wolbach et al. 2018a; Wolbach et al. 2018b. See also Hancock 2015 and Hancock 2019 for in-depth accounts of the evidence for and against the Younger Dryas impact event.

13. See Collins 2014a, chs. 12–15.

14. See Collins 2014a, chs. 12–15.

15. LaViolette 1997, 299, 301–3.

16. LaViolette 1997, 35.

CHAPTER 33.
THE GALACTIC MERRY-GO-ROUND

1. World Today News 2021.

2. Rampino 2017, 145.

3. Lewis 2002, 173–74; Rampino 2017, 151.

4. Grabau 1936; Grabau 1940, 15.

5. Grabau 1936; Grabau 1940. For a summary of Grabau's pulsation theory see Lieberman and Melott [2009] 2012.

6. Fischer and Arthur 1977. See also Fischer 1982.

7. Rampino and Caldeira 2020. See also Rampino and Stothers 1984a and Rampino and Stothers 1984b for their initial work on this subject.

8. Rampino and Caldeira 2020, 2064.

9. See Rampino 2017, chs. 11 and 12, for a full history of this theory and the academic community's negative reception to it.

10. Rampino 2017, ch. 11.

11. Rampino 2017, 141.

12. Rampino 2017, 145.

13. Rampino 2017, 149.

14. See Raup and Sepkoski 1982 for a review of the proposed "big five" extinction events in Earth's geological history.

15. Rampino 2017, 157.

16. Rampino 2017, 158.

17. See Buis 2020 for an introduction to the Milankovitch Cycles.

18. Rampino 2017, 152–53.

19. Hutton 1795, ch. III, n.p.n.

20. Lyell 1830, 156–57.

21. *Mind Matters* 2022.

22. Sheldrake 2021, 25.

23. Hutton 1795, ch. III, n.p.n.

24. Kazan 2009.

25. Genesis 1:1–21, 2:1–2.

26. Muroi 2014.

27. Dasa 2019.

28. Valentinus, [1885] 2000, chs. 2–4.

29. Valentinus, [1885] 2000, ch. 20.

30. Valentinus, [1885] 2000, ch. 20.

31. Gnosticism Explained 2021.

32. McCoy 2020.

33. Quotation from Green 1992, 203, but see also Dussaud 1900, 82–86, 201–2.

34. Chulev 2013. See also the version in Graves [1951] 1971, vol. 1, 27–28.

35. Chulev 2013.

36. On the subject of the Luwian language see Peza and Peza 2014; Woudhuizen 2019, 1189–1213; Papakitsos 2020, 330–31.

37. Seyfzadeh and Schoch 2019.

38. Teffeteller 2011.

39. Teffeteller 2011.

40. Teffeteller 2011.

41. Burne 1883, vol. i, 231–32; Harrison 1950. See also Wordshore 2017 for a good review of old and more modern accounts of the Seven Whistlers.

42. Burne 1883, i, 231–32.

43. Collins 2014a, chs. 12–14.

44. Wiggerman 2011.

45. Rogers 1998, 118–19, table. 3.

46. Yakubovich 2011, 536-37.

CHAPTER 34. MAYA COSMOGENESIS

1. Jenkins 1998, 23.

2. Jenkins 1998, xxxiv–xxxvi, 21–23, 105, 110–11, 121.

3. Jenkins 1998, 122.

4. Jenkins 1998, 11, 105.

5. Jenkins 1998, 11.

6. Jenkins 1998, 24, 56, 106.

7. Jenkins 1998, 9–11, 107.

8. Jenkins 1998, 42, 105.

9. Jenkins 1998, 11.

10. Tedlock 1996, 356; also Jenkins 1998, 10–11, 13, 61, 106, 117.

11. Jenkins 1998, 59, 116.

12. Jenkins 1998.

13. Jenkins 1998, 25, 28–31, 38–39, 107, 112.

14. Jenkins 2002.

15. Jenkins 1998, 122.

16. Jenkins 1998, 9, 52, 56, 103.

17. Jenkins 1998, 56, 61, 122.

18. Jenkins 1998, 112, 118.

19. Jenkins 1998, 44, 121.

CHAPTER 35. IN THE REALM OF ADAM

1. See Collins 1996 and Collins 2014a for a full account of all these firsts for humanity occurring in southeastern Anatolia and the Near East as a whole. See Seyfzadeh and Schoch 2019 for their findings regarding comparisons between the Anatolian Luwian script and glyphs seen on T-pillars at Göbekli Tepe.

2. Genesis 2:10–14.

3. Genesis 2:10–14.

4. Genesis 2:11, 13.

5. Wigram and Wigram 1914, 264; Nichols [1992] 2010, 59.

6. Albright [1940] 1941, 179–81.

7. Massey 1883, II, 231.

8. Collins 2014a, ch. 28.

9. For a full discussion with primary references regarding the historical whereabouts of the Place of Descent, see Collins 2014a, ch. 30.

10. Genesis 2:7, 21–23, 3:1–7.

11. Genesis 3: 8–13.

12. Genesis 3: 22–24.

13. Genesis 3:19, 23.

14. See Harrak 1992 for a full study of Edessa's ancient place names. See also Guénon [1970] 2003, 29.

15. Guénon [1970] 2003, 29.

16. Glasse 2001, s.v. "Ka'bah," 245–47.

17. Açıkgenç and Ekinci 2017, 189.

18. Açıkgenç and Ekinci 2017, 189.

19. Açıkgenç and Ekinci 2017, 190.

20. Açıkgenç and Ekinci 2017, 190.

21. Açıkgenç and Ekinci 2017, 190.

22. Hongo et al. 2009.

23. Helmer et al. 2005. See also Bollongino et al. 2012 and UCL 2012.

24. Heun 1997.

25. Mann 2011, 57; Ghose 2012; Dietrich 2016; Curry 2021.

26. Mackenzie 1872, s.v. "Enoch," 200–2.

27. Josephus [1737] 1873, "The Antiquities of the Jews," bk. 1, ch. 2, v. 3. See also Williams 1940.

28. Josephus [1737] 1873, "The Antiquities of the Jews," bk. 1, ch. 2, v. 3.

29. Segal 1970, 2.

30. Wintermute 1985, Book of Jubilees 8:1–4.

31. Josephus, [1737] 1873, "The Antiquities of the Jews," bk. 1, ch. 6, v. 4.

32. Hommel 1897, 292–97.

33. Sale 1877, "Al Koran" 5, note d.

34. Esin and Harmankaya 1999, s.v. "Aşıklı," 115–32.

35. Collins 2014a, 369.

36. Albright [1940] 1941, 99.

37. Genesis 3:14.

CHAPTER 36.
IDENTIFYING EVE

1. Genesis 3:16.
2. Clement of Alexandria 1867, 27.
3. Personal communications with Khanna Omarkhali and Sabahattin Alkan.
4. Firestone, West, and Warwick-Smith 2006.
5. Josephus [1737] 1873, "The Antiquities of the Jews," bk. 1, ch. 2, v. 3.
6. Jenkins 1998, 109, and checked using free sky program Stellarium, version 0.12.4.
7. White [2007] 2008, 178.
8. Collins 2018, chs. 8–10.
9. See, for example, Blankley 2017.
10. Collins 2004b.

CHAPTER 37.
THE GREATEST CONFIRMATION

1. Collins 2018, ch. 3.
2. Jarus 2023.
3. Schmidt 2012, 206–7.
4. Falkenstein 1965.
5. Collins 2018, ch. 40.
6. Collins and Little 2022, ch. 190–91.
7. Holder 2019.

APPENDIX. SECRETS OF KARAHAN TEPE:
THE DISCOVERY OF A STUNNING
WINTER SOLSTICE ALIGNMENT

1. Newman 2014.
2. Necmi 2021.
3. Sweatman 2023.
4. Graham Hancock interviewing Necmi Karul inside the Pillars Shrine on "Legacy of the Sages," episode 5, *Ancient Apocalypse*, 2022.
5. Burl 2000, 62.
6. For a full account of our initial discoveries at the site in December 2021, see Newman and Ainsworth 2021.
7. Personal communication by email with Andrew Collins and Rodney Hale in December 2021.

8. Murphy and Moore 2006, 173.

9. Ramirez and Huber 2000, 53, 110, and ancient-wisdom 2015.

10. Vassallo 1999.

11. Reedijk 2018, 126.

12. Barkai and Liran 2008.

13. ancient-wisdom 2015.

14. Banton 2022.

15. Daw 2012.

16. Banning 2011.

17. Collins 2021.

18. Collins 2014b.

19. Sweatman 2023.

20. Collins and Hale 2022.

21. Hancock and Bauval 1996, 76.

Bibliography

Abbreviations: n.d. = no date; n.n. = no name given;
n.p. = no publisher known; n.p.d. = no publication details;
n.p.n. = no page number(s) given; n.p.p. = no place of publication given.

Açıkgenç, Alparslan and Abdullah Ekinci (eds.). 2017. *Şanlıurfa: The City of Civilizations Where the Prophets Met.* Istanbul, Turkey: Albukhary Foundation/ KUM Publishing.

al-Sufi, 'Abd al-Rahman ibn 'Umar. [964] 1417. *Suwar al-kawākib.* n.p.d. (Library of Congress, Arabic manuscript, SM16, Fol. 1b–173a.)

Albright, William Foxwell, [1940] 1941. *From the Stone Age to Christianity: Monotheism and the Historical Process.* Baltimore, MD.: Johns Hopkins Press.

Alexander, H. B. 1920. *The Mythology Of All Races.* Vol. XI, *Latin American.* Boston: Marshall Jones.

Allen, Richard Hinckley. [1899] 1963. *Star Names: Their Lore and Meaning.* New York: Dover Publications.

Altmann, Alexander. 1945. "The Gnostic Background of the Rabbinic Adam Legends." *The Jewish Quarterly Review* 35, no. 4 (April 1945): 371–91.

ancient-wisdom. 2015. "Chaco Canyon: (The 'Sun Dagger')." ancient-wisdom website.

ancient-wisdom. 2015. "Easter Island." ancient-wisdom website.

Ancient World Online, The (AWOL). 2020. "The Max von Oppenheim Photo Collection Online," 2015–2021. *AWOL* blog, November 27.

Anonymous. Early 19th century CE. *Sapta Chakra, Asanas and Mudras (Hata yoga).* British Library, MS 24099. n.p.d.

Anonymous. 1914. *Hesiod, the Homeric Hymns and Homerica.* English translated by Hugh G. Evelyn-White. Accessed at the Perseus Digital Library website. London: William Heinemann Ltd.; New York: Macmillan.

Antonello, Elio. 2013. "The Myths of the Bear." ArXiv website, submitted 2 May.

Archi, Alfonso. 2007. "The Soul Has to Leave the Land of the Living." *Journal of Ancient Near Eastern Religions* 7 (2): 169–95.

Avalon, Arthur [John George Woodroffe]. (1919) 1924. *The Serpent Power.* Madras, India: Ganesh & Co.

Avalon Marshes. 2016. "The Sweet Track & Other Wooden Trackways." Avalon Marshes website.

Bacon, Edward, ed. 1963. *Vanished Civilizations of the Ancient World.* New York, London, Toronto: McGraw-Hill Book Company.

Bagley, Robert. 2005. "The Prehistory of Chinese Music Theory." *Proceedings of the British Academy* 131: 41–90.

Banning, E. B. 2011. "So Fair a House: Göbekli Tepe and the Identification of Temples in the Pre-Pottery Neolithic of the Near East." *Current Anthropology* 52, no. 5 (October 2011): 619–60.

Banton, Simon. 2022. "The Secondary Solstice Axis." Stonehenge Monument website (May 9).

Barkai, Ran, and Roy Liran. 2008. "Midsummer Sunset at Neolithic Jericho." *Time and Mind: The Journal of Archaeology, Consciousness and Culture* 1, no. 3 (November): 273–84.

Bayer, Johann. 1603. *Uranometria: omnium asterismorum continens schemata, nova methodo delineata, aereis laminis expressa.* Augsburg, Germany: Christoph Mang.

Bellizia, Lucia. 2010. "Of the Judgements on the Lunar Nodes." Translated by Margherita Fiorello. Skyscript website.

Belmonte, Juan Antonio. 2010. "Finding Our Place in the Cosmos: The Role of Astronomy in Ancient Cultures." *Journal of Cosmology* 9: 2052–62.

Bender, Herman, 2022. "A Serpent's Tale: The Milky Way." Researchgate website.

Bergeron, Jean, dir. 2014. *The Mystery of Atlit Yam* documentary.

Black, Jeremy, and Anthony Green. 1992. *Gods, Demons and Symbols of Ancient Mesopotamia: An Illustrated Dictionary.* Austin, TX: University of Austin Press; London: British Museum Press.

Black, Jeremy, Andrew George, and Nicholas Postgate, eds. [1999] 2000. *A Concise Dictionary of Akkadian.* Wiesbaden, Germany: Harrassowitz Verlag.

Blankley, Bethany. 2017. "Scorpio's Sting: No Match for the Suffering Servant." *Hedgerow* blog. Patheos website, November 5.

Blasweiler, Joost. 2014. "The Ancestors Cult in Kanesh and the Goddess Išhara: Part II of The Stepgate and the Gate of God: The Royal Clan of Kanesh and the Power of the Cult." Academia.edu website.

Bochart, Samuel. 1796. *Hierozoicon Sive De Animalibus S. Scripturae: Cum Indicibus Locupletissimis*, Volume 3. Leipzig: Libraria Weidmannia.

Bollongino, Ruth, et al. 2012. "Modern Taurine Cattle Descended from Small Number of Near-Eastern Founders." *Molecular Biology and Evolution* 29, no. 9 (September 2012): 2101–104.

Breiter, Theodor, ed. 1908. *M. Manilius Astronomica: I. Text—II. Kommentar.* Leipzig, Germany: Dieterich'sche Verlagsbuchhandlung Theodor Weicher.

Brown Jr., Robert. 1900. *Researches into the Origin of the Primitive Constellations of the Greeks, Phoenicians and Babylonians.* 2 vols. London: Williams and Norgate.

Brown, Robert L. 1982. "Precessing Jets in Sagittarius A: Gas Dynamics in the Central Parsec of the Galaxy." *The Astrophysical Journal* 262 (November 1): 110–19.

Browne, Edward G. 1928. *A Literary History of Persia, Vol III: The Tartar Dominion (1265–1502).* Cambridge: Cambridge University Press.

Buis, Alan. 2020. "Milankovitch (Orbital) Cycles and Their Role in Earth's Climate." *News*, NASA website, February 27.

Bunch, Ted E., et al. 2012. "Very High-Temperature Impact Melt Products as Evidence for Cosmic Airbursts and Impacts 12,900 Years Ago." *PNAS* website, June 18.

Burl, Aubrey. 2000. *The Stone Circles of Britain, Ireland and Brittany.* New Haven: Yale University Press.

Burley, Paul. 2013. "Göbekli Tepe—Temples Communicating Ancient Cosmic Geography." Graham Hancock website.

Burne, Charlotte Sophia, ed. 1883. *Shropshire Folk-Lore: A Sheaf of Gleanings, Volume 1.* London: Trubner & Co; Shrewsbury: Adnitt & Naunton; Chester: Minshull & Hughes.

Burney, Charles. 1977. *From Village to Empire: An Introduction to Near Eastern Archaeology.* Oxford: Phaidon Press.

Bryant, Jacob. 1776. *A New System, or, An Analysis of Ancient Mythology. . . .* 3 vols. London: Printed for T. Payne, P. Elmsley, R. White, and J. Walter.

Campbell, Joseph, ed. [1955] 1978. *The Mysteries: Papers from the Eranos Yearbooks.* Bollingen Series XXX, vol. 2. Princeton, NJ: Princeton University Press.

Çelik, Bahattin. 2000. "A New Early-Neolithic Settlement: Karahan Tepe." *Neo-Lithics* 2–3/00: 6–8.

———. 2010. "Hamzan Tepe in the Light of New Finds." *Documenta Praehistorica* 37 (December): 257–68.

———. 2011. "Karahan Tepe: A New Cultural Centre in the Urfa Area in Turkey." *Documenta Praehistorica* 38 (December): 241–54.

———. 2014. "Differences and Similarities between the Settlements In Şanlıurfa Region Where 'T' Shaped Pillars Are Discovered." *Turkish Academy of Sciences Journal of Archaeology* 17: 9–24.

———. 2016. "Şanlıurfa İli Merkez İlçesi Neolitik Dönem ve Öncesi Yüzey Araştırması, 2014." In Keskin 2016: 409–26.

———. 2018. "A New Pre-Pottery Neolithic Site in Southeastern Turkey: Ayanlar Höyük (Gre Hut)." *Documenta Praehistorica* 44 (December): 360–67.

Chaperon, Nicolas. 1649. *Sacrae historiae: Acta a Raphaele Vrbin. in Vaticanis xystis ad pictvrae miracvlvm expressa Nicolavs Chapron Gallvs a se delineata et incisa D.D.D* [*Gravures du Vatican*]. Rome: Petrus Mariette.

Chappell, M. 2006. "Delphi and the Homeric Hymn to Apollo." *Classical Quarterly* 56 no. 2 (December): 331–48.

Charlesworth, J. H., ed. 1985. *The Old Testament Pseudepigrapha*, vol. 2. London: Darton, Longman and Todd.

Choudhary, Arpita. 2022. "Universe: Solar System, the Sun, Planets, the Moon." The Education King website, February 3.

Chulev, Basil. 2013. "Pelasgi/Balasgi, Belasgians (Pelasgians/Pelasgi/Pelasti/Pelišti)— the Archaic Mythical Pelasgo/Stork-people from Macedonia." Privately published; available at the Internet Archive website.

Clark, Charles. 1982. "The Zodiac Man in Medieval Medical Astrology." *Quidditas* 3: Article 3.

Clement of Alexandria. 1867. *Exhortation to the Heathen.* In *The Writings of Clement of Alexandria, Vol. 1.* Translated by the Rev. William Wilson. Vol. 4 of the *Ante-Nicene Christian Library: Translations of the Writings of the Fathers Down to A.D. 325*, edited by Alexander Roberts and James Donaldson. Edinburgh: T&T Clark.

Clement of Alexandria. 2004. *The Stromata (Book VII)*, chap. 17. New Advent website. Revised and edited for New Advent by Kevin Knight. From Clement of Alexandria. 1885. *The Stromata*, translated by the Rev. William Wilson. In *Ante-Nicene Fathers, Vol. 2: Fathers of the Second Century*, edited by Alexander Roberts and James Donaldson. American ed. Buffalo, NY: Christian Literature Publishing Co.

Collins, Andrew. 1996. *From the Ashes of Angels: The Forbidden Legacy of a Fallen Race.* London: Penguin.

———. 1998. *Gods of Eden: Egypt's Lost Legacy and the Genesis of Civilization.* London: Headline.

———. 2004a. "One Week in Southeastern Turkey—The Cradle Of Civilization." Andrew Collins website.

———. 2004b. "The Circle of Cygnus." Unpublished manuscript.

———. 2006. *The Cygnus Mystery: Unlocking the Ancient Secret of Life's Origins in the Cosmos.* London: Watkins Books.

———. 2009. *Beneath the Pyramids.* Virginia Beach: 4th Dimension Press.

———. 2012. *Kuğu Takımyıldızı'nın Gizemi: Yaşamın Kozmostaki Kökenlerinin Kadim Sırrı Çözülüyor.* Istanbul: Avesta.

———. 2014a. *Göbekli Tepe: Genesis of the Gods.* Rochester, VT: Bear & Company.

———. 2014b. "Karahan Tepe: Göbekli Tepe's Sister Site—Another Temple of the Stars?" Academia.edu website.

———. 2018. *The Cygnus Key.* Rochester, VT: Bear & Company.

———. 2020. "Scrutiny of Göbekli Tepe's Construction Reveals Celestial Secrets." Ancient Origins website, May 1.

———. 2021. "Andrew Collins Karahan Tepe Update #2 Prof. Necmi Karul's paper on the new discoveries explained." Andrew Collins YouTube channel, October 25.

Collins, Andrew and Rodney Hale. 2014. "Göbekli Tepe and the Rebirth of Sirius." Academia.edu website.

———. 2015. "Göbekli Tepe and the Rising of Sirius." Academia.edu website.

———. 2022. "A Brief Look at Full Moon Risings at Karahan Tepe for the Epoch 9000–9015 BCE and Some Thoughts on Lunar Synchronizations with the Interior of the Site's Structure AB (Pillars Shrine)." Unpublished manuscript.

Collins, Andrew and Gregory L. Little. 2020. *Denisovan Origins.* Rochester, VT: Bear & Company.

———. 2022. *Origins of the Gods.* Rochester, VT: Bear & Company.

Cooley, Jeffrey L. 2008. "'I Want to Dim the Brilliance of Šulpae!' Mesopotamian Celestial Divination and the Poem of 'Erra and Išum.'" *Iraq* 70: 179–88.

Coombs, Alistair. 2017. "Denisovan Star Trails: Archaic Memory of the Pleiades in the World's First Story." Graham Hancock website, December 13.

Co-operation in Mesopotamia. 2023. "Women of NE Syria Maintain Cultural Heritage Through Handicrafts." 2023. Co-operation in Mesopotamia website, January 21.

Crystalinks. 2005. "Cherokee Prophecies: Prophecy of the Rattlesnake." Crystalinks website.

Cumont, Franz. 1902. "Notice sur deux bas-reliefs mithriaques." *Revue Archéologique* 40: 1–13.

———. 1903. *The Mysteries of Mithra.* Translated by Thomas J. McCormack. London: Kegan Paul, Trench and Trübner; Chicago: Open Court Publishing & Co.

———. 1929. "De dracone caelesti (excerptum e cod. Paris. gr. 2423, fol. 9). In Cumont 1929: 194–99.

———. ed. 1929. *Catalogus Codicum Astrologorum Graecorum: Codicum Parisinorum,* vol. 8, pt. 1. Brussels: Henrici Lamertin.

Curry, Andrew. 2021. "How Ancient People Fell in Love with Bread, Beer and Other Carbs." *Nature* website, June 22.

Daily Sabah. 2020. "New Karahantepe Settlement May Be Older than Göbeklitepe." *Daily Sabah* website, November 27.

Dasa, Mayesvara. 2019. "Water is the First Covering of the Universal Shell, Not Earth." Harekrsna website, August 8.

Daw, Tim. 2012. "Stonehenge—The Resurrection Alignment." Sarsen.org website, July 24.

Day, John, ed. 2010. *Prophecy and Prophets in Ancient Israel: Proceedings of the Oxford Old Testament Seminar.* London: T&T Clark.

DeConick, April D. and Grant Adamson, eds. 2013. *Histories of the Hidden God: Concealment and Revelation in Western Gnostic, Esoteric, and Mystical Traditions.* Durham, County Durham, UK: Acumen Publishing.

Delbrueck, R. and W. Vollgraff. 1934. "An Orphic Bowl." *The Journal of Hellenic Studies* 54 no. 2: 129–39.

Dietrich, Oliver. 2016. "Out for a Beer at the Dawn of Agriculture." *Tepe Telegrams* blog, DAI newsblog website, April 24. Accessed January 25, 2018.

Dietrich, Oliver, et al. 2012. "The Role of Cult and Feasting in the Emergence of Neolithic Communities: New Evidence from Göbekli Tepe, South-Eastern Turkey." *Antiquity* 86 no. 333: 674–95.

Dodge, Bayard. 1967. "The Sabians of Harran." In *American University of Beirut Festival Book (Festschrift)*, edited by Fûad Sarrûf and Suha Tamim, 59–85. Beirut: American University of Beirut.

Driscoll, K. 2006 "The Early Prehistory in the West of Ireland: Investigations into the Social Archaeology of the Mesolithic, West of the Shannon, Ireland [Unpublished MLitt thesis]." Galway, Ireland: Department of Archaeology, National University of Ireland.

Drijvers, H. J. W. 1980. *Cults and Beliefs at Edessa.* Leiden: E.J. Brill.

Drower, E. S. 1941. *Peacock Angel.* London: John Murray.

Dussaud, René E. 1900. *Histoire et religion des Noṣairîs.* Paris: Émile Bouillon.

National Astronomical Observatory of Japan (NAOJ). 2020. "Earth Faster, Closer to Black Hole in New Map of Galaxy." NAOJ website, November 26.

Edwards, Mark J. 1996. "The Naming of the Naassenes: Hippolytus, Refutatio V.6–10 as Hieros Logos." *Zeitschrift für Papyrologie und Epigraphik* 112: 74–80.

Eliade, Mircea. 1964. *Shamanism: Archaic Techniques of Ecstacy.* Princeton, NJ: Princeton University Press.

Encyclopedia.com, s.v. "Mixcoatl." Accessed February 13, 2024.

Esin, U. M., and S. Harmankaya. 1999. "Aşıklı." In *Neolithic in Turkey, The Cradle of Civilization: New Discoveries*, edited by Mehmet Özdoğan and Nezih Başgelen, 115–32. Istanbul: Arkeoloji ve Sanat Yayinlari.

Etgu, Muslum. 2023. "Göbeklitepe ancient site in Türkiye breaks visitor record by hosting 850,000 people last year." Anadolu Agency (AA) website, January 9.

Event Horizon Telescope Collaboration. 2022. "First Sagittarius A* Event Horizon Telescope Results. I. The Shadow of the Supermassive Black Hole in the Center of the Milky Way." *The Astrophysical Journal Letters* 930, no. 2 (May 1): L12.

Falkenstein, A. 1965. "Die Anunna in der sumerischen Überlieferung." In Güterbock and Jacobsen: 127–40.

Firestone, R. B., et al. 2007. "Evidence for an Extraterrestrial Impact 12,900 Years Ago That Contributed to the Megafaunal Extinctions and the Younger Dryas Cooling." *Proceedings of the National Academy of Sciences* 104 (41): 16016–21.

Firestone, Richard, Allen West, and Simon Warwick-Smith. 2006. *The Cycle of Cosmic Catastrophes.* Rochester, VT: Bear & Company.

Firsoff, V. A. 1974. *Life Among the Stars.* London: Allan Wingate.

Fischer, Alfred G. 1982. "Long-Term Climatic Oscillations Recorded in Stratigraphy." In National Research Council 1982: 97–105.

Fischer, Alfred and Michael A. Arthur. 1977. "Secular Variations in the Pelagic Realm." In *Deep-Water Carbonate Environments*, edited by Harry E. Cook and Paul Enos, 19–50, SEPM Special Publication No. 25 from the Society of Economic Paleontologists and Mineralogists.

Flamsteed, John. 1729. *Atlas Coelestis.* London: Margaret Flamsteed/James Hodgson.

Fleming, Daniel. 1993. "Nābû and Munabbiātu: two new Syrian religious personnel." *The Journal of the American Oriental Society* 113, no. 2 (April–June 1993): 175–83.

Fludd, Robert. 1617. *Utriusque Cosmi Maioris Scilicet et Minoris Metaphysica, Physica atque Technica Historia.* 2 vols. Oppenheim, Germany: Hieronymus Gallerus for Johann Theodorus de Bry.

Formozov, A. 1959. *Etnokulturniie oblasti na territorii evropeiskoi ciasti SSSR v kamen-nom veke (Ethnokulturgebiete der Steinzeit im europäischen Teil de Sowjetunion).* Moscow: n.p.

Foster, Charles. [1873] 1897. *Bible Pictures and What They Teach Us: Containing 400 Illustrations from the Old and New Testaments.* Philadelphia: Charles Foster Publishing.

Frahm, Ellery, and Christina M. Carolus. 2021. "End of the Line? Obsidian at Umm Qseir, a Halafian Farmstead in the Syrian Steppe." *Journal of Archaeological Science: Reports* 38, no. 1 (August).

Furtmeyr Bible. Circa 1465. Regensburg, Germany (Staatsbibliothek, Munich, Cgm 8010a, fol. 10r).

Freidel, David, Linda Schele, and Joy Parker. 1993. *Maya Cosmos: Three Thousand Years on the Shaman's Path.* New York: Perennial.

Galili, E., et al. (2017b). "Atlit-Yam: A Unique 9000 Year Old Village Submerged Off the Carmel Coast, Israel–the SPLASHCOS Field School (2011)." In: Bailey, G. N. et al, eds. *Under the Sea: Archaeology and Palaeolandscapes of the Continental Shelf.* Springer, Cham, pp. 85–102.

Galili, Ehud, et al. 2020. "Israel: Submerged Prehistoric Sites and Settlements on the Mediterranean Coastline—the Current State of the Art." In *The Archaeology of Europe's Drowned Landscapes*, edited by Geoff Bailey et al., 443–81. New York: Springer.

Gaster, Moses, ed. [1927] 2015. *The Asatir: The Samaritan Book of the Secrets of Moses.* Eugene, OR: Wipf & Stock.

Ghose, Tia. 2012. "Alcohol: Social Lubricant for 10,000 Years." LiveScience website, December 31.

Glasse, Cyril. 2001. *New Encyclopedia of Islam.* Walnut Creek, CA: AltaMira Press.

Glosbe online dictionary (English to Kurdish Kurmanji), s.v. "girl."

Gnosticism Explained. 2021. "The Secret Book of John." Gnosticism Explained website.

Gooch, Stan. 2007. *The Origins of Psychic Phenomena: Poltergeists, Incubi, Succubi, and the Unconscious Mind.* Rochester, VT: Inner Traditions.

Gore, J. Ellard. 1909. *Astronomical Curiosities: Facts and Fallacies.* London: Chatto & Windus.

Grabau, Amadeus W. 1936. *Palaeozoic Formations in the Light of the Pulsation Theory, Vol. 1: Taconian and Cambrian Pulsation Systems.* 2nd ed. Peking [Beijing]: National University of Peking Press.

———. 1940. *The Rhythm of the Ages.* Huntington, NY: R.E. Krieger.

Graves, Robert. [1951] 1971. *The Greek Myths*, 2 vol. Harmondsworth, UK: Penguin Books.

Green, Tamara. 1992. *The City of the Moon God: Religious Traditions of Harran.* Leiden: E. J. Brill.

Gresky, Julia, Juliane Haelm, and Lee Clare. 2017. "Modified Human Crania from Göbekli Tepe Provide Evidence for a New Form of Neolithic Skull Cult." *Science Advances* 3, no. 6.

Guénon, René. [1970] 2003. *Traditional Forms and Cosmic Cycles.* Hillsdale, NY: Sophia Perennis.

Güler, Mustafa, Bahattin Çelik, and Gül Güler. 2012. "New Pre-Pottery Neolithic Settlements from Viranşehir District." *Anadolu/Anatolia* 38: 164–80.

Güneri, Semih, Ayça Avcı, and Ahmet Z. Bayburt. 2022. "Upper Paleolithic Siberian Migrations to the Near East via Silk Road." *BRIQ Belt & Road Initiative Quarterly* 3, no. 4 (August 2022): 62–74.

Güterbock, Hans G. and Thorkild Jacobsen, eds. 1965. *Studies in Honor of Benno Landsberger on his Seventy-fifth Birthday, April 21, 1963.* Chicago: University of Chicago Press.

Haklay, Gil and Avi Gopher. 2020. "Geometry and Architectural Planning at Göbekli Tepe, Turkey." *Cambridge Archaeological Journal* 30, no. 2 (May): 343–57.

Halloran, John Alan. [1996] 1999. [Sumerian Lexicon. No official title]. Sumerian.org website.

Hancock, Graham. 2015. *Magicians of the Gods: The Forgotten Wisdom of Earth's Lost Civilisation.* New York: Coronet.

———. 2019. *America Before: The Key to Earth's Lost Civilization*. New York, NY: Coronet.

———. 2022. "Legacy of the Sages." *Ancient Apocalypse*, episode 5. Los Gatos, CA: Netflix.

Hancock, Graham and Robert Bauval. 1996. *Keeper of Genesis: The Quest for the Hidden Legacy of Mankind*. Heineman.

Harner, Michael J. 1973. "Common Themes in South American Indian Yagé Experiences." In *Hallucinogens and Shamanism*, edited by Michael Harner, 155–175. London/New York: Oxford University Press

Harrak, Amir. 1992. "The Ancient Name of Edessa." *Journal of Near Eastern Studies* 51, no. 3: 209–14.

Harrison Jr., Thomas P. 1950. "The Whistler, Bird of Omen." *Modern Language Notes* 65, no. 8 (December 1950): 539–41.

Helmer, D., et al. 2005. "Identifying Early Domestic Cattle from the Pre-Pottery Neolithic Sites on the Middle Euphrates Using Sexual Dimorphism." In *The First Steps of Animal Domestication: New Archaeological Approaches*, edited by J. D. Vigne, J. Peters, and D. Helmer, 86–94. Proceedings of the 9th International Council for Archaeozoology, Durham, 23–28 August 2002. Oxford, UK: Oxbow Books.

Herskovits, Melville J. 1937. *Life in a Haitian Valley*. New York: Alfred Knopf.

Heun, Manfred, et al. 1997. "Site of Einkorn Wheat Domestication Identified by DNA Fingerprinting." *Science* 278, no. 5341 (November 14, 1997): 1312–14.

Hippolytus of Rome. 1886. "Refutation of All Heresies, Book 5." New Advent website. Revised and edited for New Advent by Kevin Knight. From Hippolytus. 1886. *Refutation of All Heresies*, translated by J. H. MacMahon. In *Ante-Nicene Fathers, Vol. 5*, edited by Alexander Roberts, James Donaldson, and A. Cleveland Cox. Buffalo, NY: Christian Literature Publishing Co.

Hippolytus of Rome. 1921. *Philosophumena or the Refutation of All Heresies*, 2 vols. Translated by F. Legge. London: Society for Promoting Christian Knowledge; New York: The Macmillan Company.

Hodder, Ian. 2006. *The Leopard's Tale: Revealing the Mysteries of Çatalhöyük*. London: Thames and Hudson.

Holder, Kathleen. 2019. "Humans Migrated to Mongolia Much Earlier Than Previously Believed." UC Davis website, August 16.

Hommel, Dr. Fritz. 1897. *The Ancient Hebrew Tradition*. Translated by Edmund McClure and Leonard Crossle. New York: E. & J. B. Young; London: Soc. for Promoting Christian Knowledge.

Hongo, H. J., et al. 2009. "The Process of Ungulate Domestication at Cayönü, Southeastern Turkey: A Multidisciplinary Approach Focusing on *Bos* sp. and *Cervus elaphus*. *Anthropozoologica* 44 (1): 63–73.

Hooke, S.H. 1962. *Babylonian and Assyrian Religion.* Oxford: Basil Blackwell.

Hunger, H. 1987–1990. s.v. "Lisi(n)." In *Reallexikon der Assyriologie und Vorderasiatischen Archäologie. Vol. 7: Libanukšabaš—Medizin*, edited by Erich Ebeling and Bruno Meissner, 7, 32. Berlin, New York: Walter de Gruyter.

Hurriyet. 2022. "Migration from Siberia behind formation of Göbeklitepe." *Hurriyet Daily News* website, June 28.

Hutton, James. 1795. "Of Physical Systems, and Geological Theories, In General." In *Theory of the Earth*, chap. 3. Edinburgh: Creech. Reproduced at Sacred Texts website.

Jarus, Owen. 2023. "11,000-year-old Statue of Giant Man Clutching Penis Unearthed in Turkey." LiveScience website, October 16.

Jáuregui, Miguel Herrero de. 2010. *Orphism and Christianity in Late Antiquity.* New York: De Gruyter.

Jáuregui, M. Herrero de. 2015. "The Poet and His Addressees in Orphic Hymns." In *Hymnic Narrative and the Narratology of Greek Hymns*, edited by Andrew Faulkner and Owen Hodkinson, 224–43. Mnemosyne, Supplements series, vol. 384, editor in chief Jacqueline Klooster. Leiden: E.J. Brill.

Jenkins, John Major. 1998. *Maya Cosmogenesis 2012.* Rochester, VT: Bear & Company.

———. 2002. *Galactic Alignment: The Transformation of Consciousness According to Mayan, Egyptian, and Vedic Traditions.* Rochester, VT: Bear & Company.

Johnson, J. de M., Victor Martin, and Arthur S. Hunt. 1915. *Catalogue of the Greek Papyri in the John Rylands Library, Manchester, Volume II: Documents of the Ptolemaic and Roman Periods (nos. 62–456).* London: Longmans Green & Company.

Jones, Trevor. 2019. "Cygnus Constellation." AstroBackyard website. July 25.

Josephus, Flavius. 1700. *Flavii Josephi, Antiquitates Judaicarum, libri quatuor priores, et pars magna quinti.* Edited by Edward Bernard. Oxford: The Sheldonian Theatre.

———. [1737] 1873. *Antiquities of the Jews—Book I.* In *The Genuine Works of Flavius Josephus The Jewish Historian, etc.*, translated by William Whiston: 26–51. London/ New York, Melbourne: Ward, Lock & Co.

Karagöz, Büşra. 2021. "Karahantepe'nin gönüllü nöbetçileri: 24 yıldır bugünü bekledik." Yeni Şafak website, September 26.

Karul, Necmi. 2021. "Buried Buildings at Pre-Pottery Neolithic Karahantepe." *Türk Arkeoloji ve Etnografya Dergisi* 82: 21–31.

———. 2022. "Şanlıurfa Neolitik Çağ Araştırmaları Projesi: Taş Tepeler/2022." *Journal of Archaeology & Art (Arkeoloji ve Sanat)* 169 (January–April): 7–8.

Kazan, Casey. 2009. "New Discovery: Supermassive Black Holes Create Galaxies." The Daily Galaxy website, December 1. Accessed via the Wayback Machine.

Keskin, Candaş ed. 2016. 33: Araştırma Sonuçları Toplantısı, May 11–15, 2015 Erzurum (vol. 2). Ankara: Turkey: T.C. Kültür ve Turizm Bakanlığı/Kültür Varlıkları ve Müzeler Genel Müdürlüğü.

Kingsley, Peter. 1999. *In the Dark Place of Wisdom*. Point Reyes, CA: The Golden Sufi Center.

Kodaş Ergül. 2019. "Un Nouveau Site du Néolithique Précéramique dans la Vallée du Haut Tigre: Résultats Préliminaires de Boncuklu Tarla." *Neo-Lithics: Ex Oriente* 19: 3–15.

Kodaş, Ergül. 2021. "Communal Architecture at Boncuklu Tarla, Mardin Province, Turkey." *Near Eastern Archaeology* 82, no. 2 (May 2021): 159–65.

Kotzé, Zacharias. 2017. "The Evil Eye of Sumerian Deities." *Asian and African Studies* 26, no. 1: 102–15.

Kraus, J. D., H. C. Ko, and S. Matt. 1954. "Galactic and Localized Source Observations at 250 Megacycles per Second." *The Astronomical Journal* 59. December: 439–43.

Kürkçüoğlu, A. Cihat and Zuhal Karahan Kara. 2003. *Harran: The Crossroad of Civilizations*. Şanlıurfa, Turkey: Harran District Governorship Cultural Publications.

Lamer, Hans. 1931. "Eine spatgr. schale mit orphischer" *Philologische Wochenschrift* 51, 653–56.

Lankford, George E. 2007a. "The Great Serpent in Eastern North America." In *Ancient Objects and Sacred Realms: Interpretations of Mississippian Iconography*, edited by F. Kent Reilly III and James F. Garber, 107–135. Austin: University of Texas Press.

Lankford, George E. 2007b. "The 'Path of Souls': Some Death Imagery in the Southeastern Ceremonial Complex." In *Ancient Objects and Sacred Realms: Interpretations of Mississippian Iconography*, edited by F. Kent Reilly III and James F. Garber, 174–212. Austin: University of Texas Press.

Lauf, Detlef Ingo. 1989. *Secret Doctrines of the Tibetan Books of the Dead*, translated by Graham Parkes. Boston; Shaftesbury, UK: Shambhala Publications.

LaViolette, Paul A. 1997. *Earth Under Fire: Humanity's Survival of the Apocalypse*. Schenectady, NY: Starburst Publications.

Layton, B., ed. 1980. *The Rediscovery of Gnosticism, Volume 1: The School of Valentinus*. Proceedings of the International Conference on Gnosticism at Yale, March 28–31, 1978. Leiden: E. J. Brill.

Legrand, M. R. and M. De Angelis. 1995. "Origins and Variations of Light Carboxylic Acids in Polar Precipitation." *Journal of Geophysical Research* 100, no. D1: 1445–62.

Leisegang, Hans. 1939. "Das Mysterium der Schlange. Ein Beitrag zur Erforschung des griechischen Mysterienkultes und seines Fortlebens in der christlichen Welt." In *Eranos-Jahrbuch 7*, edited by Olga Fröbe-Kaptcyn, 151 250. Switzerland: Eranos Foundation.

Leisegang, Hans. [1955] 1978. "The Mystery of the Serpent." In *The Mysteries: Papers from the Eranos Yearbooks*, edited by Joseph Campbell, 194–260. Bollingen Series XXX, vol. 2. Princeton, NJ: Princeton University Press.

Lewis, Cherry L. E. 2002. "Arthur Holmes' Unifying Theory: From Radioactivity to Continental Drift." In *The Earth Inside and Out: Some Major Contributinos to Geology in the Twentieth Century*, edited by David R. Oldroyd, 167–183. Geological Society of London, Special Publication 192.

Lieberman, Bruce S. and Adrian L. Melott. [2009] 2012. "Whilst this Planet Has Gone Cycling On: What Role for Periodic Astronomical Phenomena in Large Scale Patterns in the History of Life?" arXiv website.

Lienhard, John H. H. 2000. "Ancient Chinese Bells." *Engines of Our Ingenuity* no. 175. Produced and hosted by Houston Public Media.

Little, Greg. 2014. *Path of Souls: The Native American Death Journey*. With preface and afterword by Andrew Collins. Memphis, TN: Eagle Wing Books.

Little, Greg. (2014) 2016. *The Illustrated Encyclopedia of Native American Indian Mounds and Earthworks*. Memphis, TN: Eagle Wing Books, Inc.

———. 2015. Path of Souls. Video documentary. Memphis, TN: ATA Memphis Productions.

———. 2016a. "America's Ancient Indian Mounds Yield Secrets." Newswire.com, March 7.

———. 2016b. "America's Ancient Mound Alignments to Stars Reveal Widely-Shared Rituals and Beliefs." *AP Magazine*, June.

———. 2016c. "Ancient Earthwork at Winchester, Indiana Shows Stellar Alignments to Cygnus & Orion." *AP Magazine*, August.

———. 2016d. "Indiana's Angel Mounds Complex Shows Stellar Alignments to the Path of Souls." Newswire.com, May 5.

———. 2016e. "Marietta, Ohio's Ancient Earthworks: Star Alignments as a Portal to the Path of Souls." *AP Magazine*, February.

———. 2016f. "Ohio's Ancient Liberty Earthworks Show Stellar Alignments to the Path of Souls Death Ritual." *AP Magazine*, September.

———. 2016g. "Sending Souls to the Stars: Magic Machines of Earth in Butler County, Ohio." *AP Magazine*, October.

———. 2016h. "Star Portal Alignments at the Moundville, Alabama Native American Indian Mound Complex." *AP Magazine*, April.

———. 2016i. "Was the Path of Souls Ritual a Worldwide Phenomenon?" *AP Magazine*, July.

———. 2016j. "Were the Portsmouth Earthworks a Portal to the Path of Souls?" *AP Magazine*, January.

Lloyd, Seton and William Brice. 1951. "Harran." *Anatolian Studies* 1, 77–111.

Lorenzis, Alessandro de and Vincenzo Orofino. 2015. "New Possible Astronomic Alignments at the Megalithic Site of Göbekli Tepe, Turkey." *Archaeological Discovery* 3: 40–50.

Lozanova-Stantcheva, Vanya. 2016. "Mystery of Creation: On the Interpretation of an Orphic Cup." In *Megalithic Monuments and Cult Practices*, compiled by Dimitriya Kostadinova Spasova: 84–97. Proceedings of the Second International Symposium, Blagoevgrad, 12–15 October. Blagoevgrad, Bulgaria: Neofit Rilski University Press.

Lyell, Charles. 1830. *Principles of Geology, Being an Attempt to Explain the Former Changes of the Earth's Surface, by Reference to Causes Now in Operation, vol 1.* London: John Murray.

MacKenzie, D. N. 1964. "Zoroastrian Astrology in the Bundahišn." *Bulletin of the School of Oriental and African Studies* 27, 511–29.

Mackenzie, Kenneth R.H. (ed.) 1872. *The Royal Masonic Cyclopædia of History, Rites, Symbolism, and Biography.* London: Bro. John Hogg.

Macrobius. [1483] 1513. *En tibi lector candidissime.* Venice, Italy: Joannes Rivius.

Magli, Giulio. 2019. "Possible Astronomical References in the Project of the Megalithic Enclosures of Göbekli Tepe." *Archaeological Discovery* 7, no.2 (February 1), n.p.n.

Mahajjah Institute. 2016. "The Nusayri Religious System: Metempsychosis." Mahajjah Institute website.

Manilius, Marcus. *Astronomica.* See Breiter, 1908.

Mann, Charles C. 2011. "The Birth of Religion: The World's First Temple." *National Geographic Magazine* 219, no. 6 (June): 34–59.

Mark, Joshua J. 2018. "Enuma Elish: The Babylonian Epic of Creation–Full Text." *World History Encyclopedia* website, May 4.

Marshall, Steve. 2016. "Acoustics of the West Kennet Long Barrow, Avebury, Wiltshire." *Time and Mind* 9, no. 1: 43–56.

Martin, Richard A. 1940. *Ancient Seals of the Near East.* Chicago: Field Museum Press.

Massey, Gerald. 1883. *The Natural Genesis*, 2 vols. London: Williams and Norgate.

Mathisen, David Warner. 2020. "Heracles and Apollo and the Tripod of the Delphic Oracle." Star Myths of the World website, July 6.

McBride, Alexis. 2014. "The Acoustics of Archaeological Architecture in the Near Eastern Neolithic." *World Archaeology* 46, no. 3, 349–61.

McClintock, Rev. John and James Strong. 1880. *Cyclopaedia of Biblical, Theological, and Ecclesiastical Literature, Vol. 9: RH–ST.* New York: Harker & Brothers.

McCoy, Daniel. n.d. "Archons." Gnosticism Explained website.

Mead, G. R. S. 1900. *Fragments of a Faith Forgotten: Some Short Sketches Among the Gnostics Mainly of the First Two Centuries.* London and Benares: Theosophical Publishing Society.

Mellaart, James. 1967. *Çatal Hüyük: A Neolithic Town in Anatolia.* London: Thames and Hudson.

Milbrath, Susan. 1999. *Star Gods of the Maya: Astronomy in Art, Folklore, and Calendars.* Austin: University of Texas Press.

Miller, Dorcas S. 1997. *Stars of the First People: Native American Star Myths and Constellations.* Boulder, CO: Pruett Publishing Company.

Mind Matters. 2022. "Panpsychism: If Computers Can Have Minds, Why Can't the Sun?" *Mind Matters* website, August.

Moosa, Matti. 1987. *Extremst Shiites: The Ghulat Sects.* Syracuse, NY: Syracuse University Press.

Murat, Leyla. 2009. "Goddess İšhara." *Tarih Araştırmaları Dergisi* 28, no. 45 (May): 159–90.

Muroi, Kazuo. 2014. "The Origin of the Mystical Number Seven in Mesopotamian Culture; Division by Seven in the Sexagesimal Number System." arXiv website, July 19.

Murphy, Anthony, and Richard Moore. 2006. *Island of the Setting Sun: In Search of Ireland's Ancient Astronomers.* Dublin: Liffey Press.

Nadège. 2020. "The Real Reason Why Scorpio Makes Us Think 'Sex.'" *Medium* website, June 20.

Nandakumar, Anu. 2021. "Mula Nakshatra Captured as Part of Scorpio Constellation with Mobile Astrophotography." *Medium* website, October 28.

National Research Council. 1982. *Climate in Earth History: Studies in Geophysics.* Washington, DC: The National Academies Press.

New Age Islam. 2021. "Buddhist Mysticism Influenced Islamic Sufism in a Big Way." New Age Islam website, November 24.

Newman, Hugh. 2023. *Göbekli Tepe and Karahan Tepe: The World's First Megaliths.* Glastonbury, Somerset: Wooden Books.

Newman, Hugh. 2014. "The Forgotten Stones of Karahan Tepe, Turkey." Ancient Origins website, updated July 29.

Newman, Hugh and JJ Ainsworth. 2021. "Karahan Tepe: Stunning New Discovery of Winter Solstice Sunrise Alignment." Ancient Origins website, updated December 22.

———. 2022. "Secrets of Karahan Tepe: The Discovery of a Stunning Winter Solstice Alignment (Part 1)." Graham Hancock website, first published December 2, 2022, updated October 2023.

Nichols, Aidan. [1992] 2010. *Rome and the Eastern Churches: A Study in Schism.* Edinburgh: T&T Clark.

O'Brien, Christopher. 2012. "May 2012 Expedition to Sipapu 'The Place of Emergence' Part One." Our Strange Planet website, July 21.

O'Conner, Patricia T. and Stewart Kellerman. 2018. "Speaking with a Forked Tongue." Grammarphobia website, August 10.

Oesterreich, T.K. 1930. *Possession: Demoniacal and Other among Primitive Races among Primitive Races, in Antiquity, the Middle Ages, and Modern Times.* London: Kegan Paul, Trench, Trubner & Co.

Oppenheim, Janet. 1985. *The Other World: Spiritualism and Psychical Research in England, 1850–1914.* Cambridge: Cambridge University Press.

Origen. n.d. *Contra Celsum, Book V.* New Advent website. Revised and edited for New Advent by Kevin Knight. From Origen. n.d. *Contra Celsum*, translated by Frederick Crombie. In *Ante-Nicene Fathers, Vol. 4*, edited by Alexander Roberts, James Donaldson, and A. Cleveland Cox. Buffalo, NY: Christian Literature Publishing Co.

Orlov, Andrei. 2013. "Adoil Outside the Cosmos: God Before and After Creation in the Enochic Tradition." In DeConick and Adamson 2013: 30–57.

Orr, R. B. 1920. *Thirty-second Annual Archaeological Report, Being Part of the Appendix to the Report of the Minister of Education, Ontario.* Toronto: Clarkson W. James.

Özdoğan, Eylem. 2022. "The Sayburç Reliefs: A Narrative Scene from the Neolithic." *Antiquity* 96, no. 390 (December): 1599–1605.

Özdoğan, M. and N. Başgelen, eds. 1999. *Neolithic in Turkey—The Cradle of Civilization: New Discoveries*, 2 vols. Istanbul: Arkeoloji ve Sanat Yayınları.

Papakitsos, Evangelos C. 2020. "Enquiring the Nature of Pelasgic Language(s) via Information Systems Modelling." *EPRA International Journal of Multidisciplinary Research* 6, no. 8 (August): 325–35.

Papazian, Sjur. 2015. "The Origin of the Dragon Cult." Cradle of Civilization website, April 17.

Patristic Bible Commentary. n.d. "Catena [Genesis] Chapter 14." Patristic Bible.

Percy, Bishop, trans. 1847. *Northern antiquities; or, An historical account of the manners, customs, religion and laws, maritime expeditions and discoveries, language and literature of the ancient Scandinavians . . .* London: H.G. Bohn.

Peza, Luftulla and Liljana Peza. 2014. "Hitite [sic] Language is a Dialect of Pelasgian/Albanian Language." *Dodona* 1, 40–43.

Pidgeon, William. 1858. *Traditions of the De-Coo-Dah and Antiquarian Researches: Comprising Extensive Explorations, Surveys, and Excavations of the Wonderful and Mysterious Earthen Remains of the Mound-Builders in America, etc.* New York: Horace Thayer.

Pirtea, Adrian. 2017. "Is There an Eclipse Dragon in Manichaeism? Some Problems Concerning the Origin and Function of āṯalyā in Manichaean Sources." In *Zur lichten Heimat: Studien zu Manichäismus, Iranistik und Zentralasienkunde im Gedenken an Werner Sundermann*, edited by Turfanforschung, 535–54. Wiesbaden, Germany: Harrassowitz.

Putnam, F. W. 1890. "The Serpent Mound of Ohio." *Century Magazine* 39: 871–88.

Rahmouni, Aicha. 2007. *Divine Epiphets in the Ugaritic Alphabetic Texts.* Translated by J. N. Ford. Leiden: E. J. Brill.

Raina, Neeta. 2012. "The Sanskrit–Vedic Analysis of the Göbekli Tepe Site in Turkey." *Vedic Cafe* blog, July 27.

Ramirez, Jose Miguel and Carlos Huber. 2000. *Easter Island: Rapa Nui, a Land of Rocky Dreams.* n.p.p., Chile: Carlos Huber Alvimpress Impresores.

Rampino, Michael R. C. 2017. *Cataclysms: A New Geology for the Twenty-First Century.* New York: Columbia University Press.

Rampino, Michael and Ken Caldeira. 2020. "A 32-Million Year Cycle Detected in Sea-Level Fluctuations over the Last 545 Myr." *Geoscience Frontiers* 11, no. 6: 2061–65.

Rampino, Michael and R. B. Stothers. 1984a. "Geological Rhythms and Cometary Impacts." *Science* 226, no. 4681 (December): 1427–31.

———. 1984b. "Terrestrial Mass Extinctions, Cometary Impacts and the Sun's Motion Perpendicular to the Galactic Plane." *Nature* 308: 709–12.

Raup, D. M. and J. J. Sepkoski. 1982. "Mass Extinctions in the Marine Fossil Record." *Science* 215, no. 4539 (March): 1501–3.

Reddy, Gautham V. 2020. "Göbekli Tepe and Its Potential Connection to the Vedic Culture." *Medium* website, Jan 12.

Reedijk, Lenie. 2018. *Sirius, the Star of the Maltese Temples.* n.p.p.: MaletBooks.

Reilly III, F. Kent, and James F. Garber, eds. 2007. *Ancient Objects and Sacred Realms: Interpretations of Mississippian Iconography.* Austin: University of Texas Press

Reiner, Erica. 1995. "Astral Magic in Babylonia." *Transactions of the American Philosophical Society* 85, no. 4: i–xiii and 1–150. Philadelphia: The American Philosophical Society.

Reitzenstein, Richard. 1904. *Poimandres: Studien zur Griechisch-Ägyptischen und Frühchristlichen Literatur.* Leipzig: Teubner.

Rendsburg, Gary. 2019. "Ur Kasdim: Where Is Abraham's Birthplace?" The Torah website.

Richter, Christina. 2018. "The Magic of Astro-Medicine." Christina Richter website, July 16.

Richter, Thomas. 2004. *Untersuchungen zu den lokalen Panthea Süd- und Mittelbabyloniens in altbabylonischer Zeit.* 2nd ed. Vol. 257 of *Alter Orient und Altes Testament.* Münster, Germany: Ugarit-Verlag.

———. 2006. "Nabû." In *New Pauly Online*, English translation edited by Christine F. Salazar (Antiquity) and Francis G. Gentry (Classical Tradition). Netherlands: Brill.

Ridpath, Ian. 2012. *A Dictionary of Astronomy.* Oxford: Oxford University Press.

Rintoul, M. C. 2014. *Dictionary of Real People and Places in Fiction*. London/New York: Routledge.

Roberts, Rev. Alexander and James Donaldson, eds. 1867. *Ante-Nicene Christian Library; Translations of the Writings of the Fathers Down to A.D. 325, Volume 4: The Writings Of Clement Of Alexandria, Volume 1*. Edinburgh: T. and T. Clark.

Rogers, John H. 1998. "Origins of the Ancient Constellations: I. The Mesopotamian Traditions." *Journal of the British Astronomical Association* 108, no. 1: 9–28.

Rohde, Erwin. [1894] 1898. *Psyche: Seelencult und Unsterblichkeitsglaube der Griechen* (2 vols). Tübingen & Leipzig, Germany: J. C. B. Mohr.

Rohde R. A. and R. A. Muller. 2005. "Cycles in fossil diversity." *Nature* 434: 208–10.

Romain, William F. 2022. "Observations Concerning the Milky Way, Serpent Mound, Newark and Mound City Earthworks." *Journal of Skyscape Archaeology* 8, no. 1: 120–30.

Royal Astronomical Society of Canada. 1926. "Notes and Queries: Precession of the Equinoxes Discovered by the Babylonians." *Journal of the Royal Astronomical Society of Canada* 21: 215–16.

Sagona, Antonio and Paul Zimansky. 2015. *Ancient Turkey*. London: Routledge.

Sale, George. 1877. *The Koran: Al Coran of Mohammed; With Explanatory Notes; Various Readings From Savary's Version of The Koran; Preliminary Discourse on the Religious and Political Condition of the Arabs before the Days of Mohammed*. London: William Tegg & Co.

Santillana, Giorgio de and Hertha von Dechend. 1969. *Hamlet's Mill: An Essay on Myth and the Frame of Time*. Boston: Gambit.

Sarrûf, Fûad and Suha Tamim, eds. 1967. *American University of Beirut Festival Book (Festschrift)*. Beirut: American University of Beirut.

Savage-Smith, Emilie. [1984] 1985. *Islamicate Celestial Globes: Their History, Construction and Use*. With a chapter on iconography by Andrea P. A. Belloli. *Smithsonian Studies in History and Technology* 46: 1–354. Washington, D.C.: Smithsonian Institution Press.

Schjellerup, H. C. F. C. 1874. *Description des étoiles fixes/composée au milieu du dixième siècle de notre ère par l'astronome persan Abd-al-Rahman al-Sûfi. Trad. littérale de deux ms. arabes de la Bibliothèque Royale de Copenhague et de la Biliothèque Impériale de St. Pétersbourg avec des notes*. Saint Petersburg, Russia: Eggers.

Schmidt, Klaus. 2012. *Göbekli Tepe: A Stone Age Sanctuary in South-Eastern Anatolia*, Berlin: Ex Oriente e.V.

Schmidt, Klaus and Oliver Dietrich. 2010. "A Radiocarbon Date from the Wall Plaster of Enclosure D of Göbekli Tepe." *Neo-Lithics* 2/10: 82–83.

Schoch, Robert. 2012. *Forgotten Civilization: The Role of Solar Outbursts in Our Past and Future*. Rochester, VT: Inner Traditions.

Schönsperger the Elder, Hans [Johann]. 1484. *German Almanac*. Augsburg, Germany: Hans Schönsperger the Elder.

Segal, J. B. 1963. "The Sabian Mysteries." In *Vanished Civilizations of the Ancient World*, edited by Edward Bacon, 201–20. New York, London, Toronto: McGraw-Hill Book Company.

Seyfzadeh, Manu and Robert Schoch. 2019. "World's First Known Written Word at Göbekli Tepe on T-Shaped Pillar 18 Means God." *Archaeological Discovery* 7, no. 2: 31–53.

Sheldrake, Rupert. 2021. "Is the Sun Conscious." *Journal of Consciousness Studies* 28, no. 3–4: 8–28.

Spasova, Dimitriya Kostadinova, compiler. 2016. *Megalithic Monuments and Cult Practices*. Proceedings of the Second International Symposium, Blagoevgrad, 12–15 October. Blagoevgrad, Bulgaria: Neofit Rilski University Press.

Spray, Aaron. 2021. "Karahan Tepe is Called the 'Sister Site' of Gobekli Tepe in Turkey (and Is Just as Old)." The Travel website, October 31.

Springett, Bernard H. 1922. *Secret Sects of Syria and the Lebanon, Consideration of Their Origin, Creeds and Religious Ceremonies, and Their Connection with and Influence upon Modern Freemasonry*. London: George Allen & Unwin.

Srinivasan, M. R. 1996. *Physics for Engineers*. New Delhi, India: New Age International.

Starr, Eileen M. 2008. *A Collection of Curricula for the STARLAB Maya Skies Cylinder, The World of the Maya*. Yulee, FL: Science First/STARLAB.

Steadman, Sharon R. and Gregory McMahon, eds. 2011. *The Oxford Handbook of Ancient Anatolia 10,000–323 BCE*. Oxford: Oxford University Press.

Stetsyuk, Valentyn. 2012. "Primary Settling of Eastern Europe and Asia by Homo sapiens." Valentyn Stetsyuk website.

Stöffler, Johannes. [1512] 1524. *Elucidatio fabricae usuque astrolabii*. Oppenheim, Germany: Jakob Köbel.

Stokl, Jonathan. 2010. "Female Prophets in the Ancient Near East." In *Prophecy and Prophets in Ancient Israel: Proceedings of the Oxford Old Testament Seminar*, edited by John Day, 47–61. London: T&T Clark.

Süel, Aygül, ed. 2019. *Acts of the IXth International Congress of Hittitology, Çorum, September 08–14, 2014: Volume II*. Ankara, Turkey: Baski.

Sweatman, Martin B. 2022. "Representations of Calendars and Time at Göbekli Tepe and Karahan Tepe Support an Astronomical Interpretation of Their Symbolism." *Prehistory Decoded* blog, posted March 17, 2023.

Sweatman, Martin B. and Dimitrios Tsikritsis. 2017. "Decoding Göbekli Tepe with Archaeoastronomy: What Does The Fox Say?" *Mediterranean Archaeology and Archaeometry* 17, no. 1: 233–50.

Taracha, Piotr. 2002. "Bull-Leaping on a Hittite Vase. New Light on Anatolian and Minoan Religion." *Archeologia (Warszawa)* 53: 7–20.

Tarihi, Güncelleme. 2023. "Göbeklitepe ve Karahantepe'deki kazı çalışmaları: İnsan ve hayvan heykeli bulundu." Hurriyet website, September 29.

Tedlock, Dennis, trans. 1996. *Popol Vuh: The Definitive Edition of the Mayan Book of the Dawn of Life and the Glories of Gods and Kings.* New York: Touchstone. Translation originally published in 1985 under the title *Popol Vuh: The Mayan Book of the Dawn of Life* by Simon & Schuster in New York.

Teffeteller, Annette. 2011. "67.3 Teffeteller [Annual Meeting]." Society for Classical Studies website.

———. 2012. "The E at Delphi: The Problem with Privileging Plutarch." Paper presented at the 143rd Annual Meeting of the American Philological Association, Philadelphia, PA, January 5–8, Society for Classical Studies website.

NASA. 2017. "Stars at the Galactic Center." Photograph. NASA website.

Teryan, Angela. 2017. "Armenia and Britain [Excerpt from "Ancient written sources of European peoples about their ancestral homeland–Armenia and Armenians"]." Art-A-Tsolum website.

TGA: Türkiye Tourism (TGA). 2021. "Türkiye Illuminates its Neolithic Heritage with TAŞ TEPELER." Türkiye Tourism Promotion and Development Agency website.

Theoi. 2005. "Okeanos." Theoi Greek Mythology website.

Thissen, Laurens. 2002. "Appendix I: The CANeW 14C Databases, Anatolia 10,000–5000 cal. BC." In *The Neolithic of Central Anatolia. Internal Developments and External Relations During the 9th–6th Millennia CAL BC*, edited by Gérard and L. Thissen, 299–337. Proceedings of the International CANeW Round Table, Istanbul, 23–24 November. Istanbul: Ege Yayınları.

Thomas, Sean. 2022. "Is an Unknown, Extraordinarily Ancient Civilisation Buried under Eastern Turkey?" *The Spectator* website, May 8.

Thompson, Gary D. 2011–2020. "Ancient Zodiacs, Star Names, and Constellations: Essays and Critiques: Chronological Development of Mesopotamian Star-Lists in the Second Millennium BCE." Westnet webpage.

———. [2003] 2018. "Episodic Survey of the History of the Constellations, E: Late Mesopotamian Constellations. Part 6: Kassite *kudurru* iconography as constellations." Westnet webpage.

Trout, K. 2004. "Tryptamine Content of Arundo donax." The Vaults of Erowid website (March 22).

Trouvelot, E. L. *The Trouvelot Astronomical Drawings Manual*. New York: Charles Scribner's Sons.

University College London (UCL). 2012. "DNA Traces Cattle Back to a Small Herd Domesticated around 10,500 Years Ago." UCL News website, March 27.

Ulansey, David. 1994. "Mithras and the Hypercosmic Sun." In *Studies in Mithraism*, edited by John R. Hinnells, 257–64. Rome: "L'Erma" di Brettschneider.

UNESCO. 2018. "Göbekli Tepe." World Heritage List. UNESCO World Heritage website.

Ussher, John. 1865. *A Journey from London to Persepolis, Including Wanderings in Daghestan, Georgia, Armenia, Kurdistan, Mesopotamia, and Persia*. London: Hurst and Blackett.

Uyanik, Muvaffak. 1974. *Petroglyphs of South-Eastern Anatolia*. Graz, Austria: Akademishe Druck-u. Verlagsanstalt.

Vahradyan, Vachagan and Marine Vahradyan. 2013. "About the Astronomical Role of 'Qarahunge' Monument." Annunner website.

Valentinus. [1885] 2000. *Against the Valentinians*. New Advent website. Revised and edited for New Advent by Kevin Knight. From Ante-Nicene Fathers, Vol. 3. 1885. Edited by Alexander Roberts, James Donaldson, and A. Cleveland Coxe. Buffalo, NY: Christian Literature Publishing Co.

VAMzzz. 2021. "Sak Yant Tattoos or Magic Tattoos." VAMzzz Occult Blog webpage. March 19.

Van Bladel, Kevin. 2009. *The Arabic Hermes: From Pagan Sage to Prophet of Science*. Oxford: Oxford University Press.

Vassallo, Mario. 1999. "Sun Worship and the Magnificent Megalithic Temples of the Maltese Islands." Academia.edu website.

Vigne J. D., J. Peters, and D. Helmer (eds.). 2005. *First Steps of Mammal Domestication: New Archaeozoological Approaches*. Oxford, UK: Oxbow Books.

Vogh, James. 1977 *Arachne Rising: The Thirteenth Sign*. London, Toronto, Sydney. and New York: Hart Davis, MacGibbon/Granada Publishing.

Ward, Richard. 2021. *Born of Blood and Fire: On the Origins, Evolution, History and Practices of the Haitian Petwo Rite*. London: Scarlet Imprint.

Wee, John Z. 2015. "Discovery of the Zodiac Man in Cuneiform." *Journal of Cuneiform Studies* 67: 217–33.

Wee, John Z. 2016. "A Late Babylonian Astral Commentary on *Marduk's Address to the Demons*." *Journal of Near Eastern Studies* 75, no. 1: 127–67.

Weiss, Daniel. 2020. "Temple of the White Thunderbird." *Archaeology* (January/February), 38–45.

Wenger, Gilbert R. [1980] 1991. *The Story of Mesa Verde National Park*. Mesa Verde National Park, CO: Mesa Verde Museum Association.

Whiston, William (trans.). [1737] 1873. *The Works of Flavius Josephus.* London, UK: Nelson and Sons.

White Arrow, The. 2022. "Icaro." The White Arrow website.

White, Gavin. [2007] 2008. *Babylonian Star-Lore: An Illustrated Guide to the Star-Lore and Constellations of Ancient Babylonia.* London: Solaria Publications.

Wiggermann, Frans A. M. 2011. "Siebengötter A. Mesopotamien." In *Reallexikon der Assyriologie und Vorderasiatischen Archäologie,* edited by Erich Ebeling, 459–66. Berlin, New York: Walter de Gruyter.

Wigram, Rev. W. A. and Edgar T. A. Wigram. 1914. *The Cradle of Mankind: Life in Eastern Kurdistan.* London: Adam and Charles Black.

Wikipedia. 2022. "Breast-shaped hill."

Williams, Bro. W. J. 1940. "The Antediluvian Pillars in Prose and Verse." *Transactions of the Quatuor Coronati Lodge* 51: 100–125.

Wisdom Library. 2016. "Mula, Mūlā, Mūla, Muḷa, Muḷā: 61 Definitions." Wisdom Library website.

———. 2022. "Sheshanaga, Shesha-naga, Śeṣanāga: 5 Definitions." Wisdom Library website, updated July 25.

WLW. 2021. "Arahsamnum 2021: Ishara." *Do haniwa dream of ceramic sheep?* (blog), Tumblr website.

Wintermute, Orval S., trans. 1985. "Jubilees: A New Translation and Introduction." In *Old Testament Pseudepigrapha,* vol. 2, edited by James H. Charlesworth. Garden City, NY: Doubleday.

Wolbach, Wendy S., et al. 2018a. "Extraordinary Biomass-Burning Episode and Impact Winter Triggered by the Younger Dryas Cosmic Impact 12,800 Years Ago. 1. Ice Cores and Glaciers." *Journal of Geology* 126, no. 2 (March): 165–84.

———. 2018b. "Extraordinary Biomass-Burning Episode and Impact Winter Triggered by the Younger Dryas Cosmic Impact 12,800 Years Ago. 2. Lake, Marine, and Terrestrial Sediments." *Journal of Geology* 126, no. 2 (March): 185–205.

Wordshore. 2017. "The Seven Whistlers." MetaFilter website, October 30.

World Today News. 2021. "Let There Be Light! Scientists Have Discovered When the Universe Ended in Darkness and the Stars Lit Up." World Today News website, June 28.

Woudhuizen, Fred C. 2019. "Origin of the Luwian Hieroglyphic Script." In *Acts of the IXth International Congress of Hittitology, Çorum, September 08–14, 2014: Volume II,* edited by Süel, 1189-1213. Ankara, Turkey: Baski.

Yakubovich, Ilya. 2011. "Luwian and the Luwians." In *The Oxford Handbook of Ancient Anatolia 10,000–323 BCE,* edited by Sharon R. Steadman and Gregory McMahon, 534–47. Oxford: Oxford University Press.

Yardimci, Nurettin. 2008. *Mezopotamya'ya açilan kapi Harran.* Istanbul: Ege Yayın.

Yıldıran, Neşe. 2001. "Yakın Doğu Sembolizminde Akrep, Yılan: Akrep-Adam ve Şahmeran." *Folklor/Edebiyat* 7, no. 27: 5–22.

Young, Robert. 1898. *Young's Literal Translation of the Holy Bible.* Heraldmag.org. PDF available.

Zick, Michael. 2000. "Der älteste Tempel der Welt." *Bild der Wissenschaft* 8 (August): 60–66.

Zoroaster (pseudo). Late 17th/early 18th century CE. *Clavis Artis* (3 volumes). Germany: privately published.

Index

BOOKS OF RELATED INTEREST

Göbekli Tepe: Genesis of the Gods
The Temple of the Watchers and the Discovery of Eden
by Andrew Collins

Origins of the Gods
Qesem Cave, Skinwalkers, and Contact with
Transdimensional Intelligences
by Andrew Collins and Gregory L. Little, Ed.D.
Foreword by Erich von Däniken

Denisovan Origins
Hybrid Humans, Göbekli Tepe, and the Genesis of the
Giants of Ancient America
by Andrew Collins and Gregory L. Little, Ed.D.

The Cygnus Key
The Denisovan Legacy, Göbekli Tepe, and the Birth of Egypt
by Andrew Collins

Slave Species of the Gods
The Secret History of the Anunnaki and
Their Mission on Earth
by Michael Tellinger

The Mystery of Doggerland
Atlantis in the North Sea
by Graham Phillips

There Were Giants Upon the Earth
Gods, Demigods, and Human Ancestry:
The Evidence of Alien DNA
by Zecharia Sitchin

Forgotten Civilization
The Role of Solar Outbursts in Our Past and Future
by Robert M. Schoch, Ph.D.

INNER TRADITIONS • BEAR & COMPANY
P.O. Box 388 • Rochester, VT 05767
1-800-246-8648 • www.InnerTraditions.com

Or contact your local bookseller